THE PENGUIN

MARK SHIELD c̲c̲ ... .y Life and contribute to several other magazines. He has finished the first draft of his great Australian novel, *Betty Boop – The Pistol Packin' Mamma*, expanded his radio show on the National Evening Show with Angela Catterns, and shared a stretch limmo with Jackie Collins (but that's another story). He has a television program on the Foxtel lifestyle channel, and there are plans to make another series. He remains a committed wine larrikin and iconoclast, but suspends such antics to work for charities like the Smith Family, the Fred Hollows Foundation, the Brotherhood of St Laurence and the Starlight Foundation. His parallel career as an aviation writer seems to have developed the gliding capacity of a house brick but, undaunted, he continues to collect rejection slips. He still manages to avoid having a cellar ('Wines are like buses should be: there's another good one along any minute, so why drink the same wine twice?'). He gets great joy from a good bottle and believes that good company is essential when drinking great wine.

HUON HOOKE discovered wine while working as a raw and slightly astringent cadet reporter on *The Murrumbidgee Irrigator* in the NSW Riverina. He followed the flow south to Albury where he matured somewhat (with the help of local Rutherglen tokay) and then across to the Barossa where he further ripened, studying wine marketing in the warm climate of Roseworthy College. He spent a while mellowing in the cellars of Best's and Yellowglen where he worked vintage, finally reaching marketability when he arrived in Sydney in 1982 to work in wine retailing. A fiercely independent freelancer, he has supported himself solely from writing, lecturing, judging and educating for 14 years. Currently, he writes a weekly column in the *Sydney Morning Herald* and *Good Weekend*, and monthly in *Gourmet Traveller*, and contributes to various publications, including *Decanter* and two overseas wine guides apart from this one. He judges in about 10 shows a year and runs wine courses in Sydney where he lives. He chairs the judging of Australia's Wine List of the Year Awards (see inside) and occasionally finds time to relax and enjoy a glass of the product while watching the cricket. He published a biography, *Max Schubert Winemaker*, in 1994, and his latest book, *Words on Wine*, hit the shelves in 1997.

THE PENGUIN
GOOD
AUSTRALIAN
WINE
GUIDE

98|99
EDITION

MARK SHIELD & HUON HOOKE

PENGUIN BOOKS

Penguin Books Australia Ltd
487 Maroondah Highway, PO Box 257
Ringwood, Victoria 3134, Australia
Penguin Books Ltd
Harmondsworth, Middlesex, England
Penguin Putnam Inc.
375 Hudson Street, New York, New York 10014, USA
Penguin Books Canada Limited
10 Alcorn Avenue, Toronto, Ontario, Canada M4V 3B2
Penguin Books (NZ) Ltd
Cnr Rosedale and Airborne Roads, Albany, Auckland, New
Zealand
Penguin Books (South Africa) (Pty) Ltd
4 Pallinghurst Road, Parktown 2193, South Africa

First published by Penguin Books Australia Ltd 1998

10 9 8 7 6 5 4 3 2 1

Copyright © Penguin Books Australia Ltd, 1998
Copyright © ⟨ℝ⟩ 1998

Photograph of Mark Shield courtesy of the author
Photograph of Huon Hooke by Geoff Lung
Typeset in Adobe Garamond by Midland Typesetters
Maryborough, Victoria
Printed in Australia by Australian Print Group
Maryborough, Victoria

ISBN 0 14 027725 0
ISSN 1038-6467

Contents

ACKNOWLEDGEMENTS
The authors wish to thank all those people in the wine industry who helped make this book possible. Instead of listing them and risking omissions, thanks to all – including the dedicated folk at Penguin Books who worked on this book.

Introduction

There's no escaping the fact that the year following the publication of last year's *Good Australian Wine Guide* was dominated by the release and fanfare surrounding the so-called 'white Grange'. One jaundiced journalist dubbed it the 'white Bin 389', because while the wine was not that significant, the hype surrounding its release was a public relations triumph.

Penfolds Yattarna made quite a splash in the general electronic and print media, and most of the dedicated wine press were caught up in the hype. Punters went into a buying frenzy, and retailers set the price at $150 – double the recommended retail price of $75. No-one seemed to want to know what the wine tasted like; they all wanted to know how much would it be worth this time next year. Sadly, most of the bottles will never be opened. It seemed to sum up a year in which wine prices went well beyond the means of the average consumer. A good bottle of red now costs more than a bottle of top-shelf single-malt whisky.

Grange also got into the act when some fraudulent bottles were discovered. This loss of innocence proved Australian wine has finally come of age: we now have something worth forging! It also showed the dark side that emerges when wine becomes a collector's item and not a joyous part of life.

The wine industry remains buoyant and exports are strong. Again there is a dark side: financial institutions are warning of the risks of investing in vineyards. The scramble to put vines in the ground has seen speculators throwing both caution and science to the winds and planting unsuitable varieties on unsuitable sites.

Informed planting, then, is in the hands of the big companies. They are developing new areas and divesting themselves of unwanted vineyards that are planted with non-premium fruit. Typical of the thinking is BRL Hardy, which wants to become self-sufficient in premium varieties and buy only non-premium (wine cask) grapes on the open market. This will give them an ability to control prices, and may forecast bleak times for independent growers in less glamorous regions.

There have been more than 20 000 hectares of new vines planted, amounting to an investment of around $630 million. Shiraz was the most planted variety, followed by cabernet sauvignon and chardonnay. Red varieties accounted for 78 per cent of new plantings.

In large-company terms Southcorp Wines Pty Ltd remains the biggest, followed by Orlando-Wyndham, BRL Hardy, Mildara Blass and Rosemount. Also in the top ten are McWilliams, S Smith and Son (Yalumba), Cranswick Smith & Sons, De Bortoli and Brown Brothers. The companies listed on the stock exchange did very well and the average market valuation of wine companies kept parity with the market average benchmark.

There were a few dramatic company takeovers. Petaluma acquired a large slice of Stonier's, and Pipers Brook acquired practically most of Tasmania when it took control of Heemskerk, Rochecombe and Buchanan's. The Jansz label went to S Smith & Sons. Miranda opened a large winery in the King Valley, Victoria, and BRL Hardy announced a large vineyard and winery development in the Canberra region.

In terms of exports, the total for 1996–97 was 154 975 032 litres compared with 10 829 000 litres in 1985–86, which is a great success story for all but local consumers who, to a certain extent, are footing the bill. Forty-three per cent of exports went to the UK; the US accounted for 21 per cent. A total of 22.8 per cent of Australian production was exported. (Wine tourism is another side industry that seems destined to expand. Its current estimated worth is $400 million annually, and the plan is to grow it to $1100 million by 2025.)

As for production, Australia accounted for 2 per cent. Australians drank 18.2 litres per capita. Compare this with France, which leads the consumption race, at 63 litres per capita. In terms of local consumption, 55 per cent was white wine; 24 per cent red wine; 11 per cent sparkling wine; 8 per cent fortified wine; and rosé and other wine products accounted for the rest. About 60 per cent of wine sales were in soft pack (wine casks).

In the vineyards, Clare Valley has been expanded almost to the limits of growth, 'limits' being the availability of underground water. The same restrictions are starting to apply to the Barossa Valley. However, not all regions are expanding; the Hunter Valley seems to be shrinking under the weight of resort development. Other vineyards may also begin to feel some shrinking effects, with 50 per cent of Australian vineyards vulnerable to phylloxera. Most vignerons believe its spread to South Australia is inevitable, and some are already replanting on American rootstock. If the spread does occur it will be through carelessness with unsterilised equipment or ignorance on the part of consumers visiting cellar doors.

As far as industry moves go, Peter Douglas ended his tenure at Wynns Coonawarra to take up a position in the US. He follows the former head of the Australian Wine Research Institute, Dr Terry Lee, who moved to Gallo last year. The Douglas departure caused much scrabbling in the ranks at Southcorp because it's a glamorous position.

The flying winemakers (young Australian winemakers who fly around the world making wine) continue to ply their trade. So much so that if you're a winemaker and you can't list overseas experience on your CV, you're made to feel inadequate. Most ambitious winemakers make sure they have two vintages per year, and northern-hemisphere experience seems vital for those who wish to rise through the ranks.

The big promotional event for 1998 will be the Wine Australia '98 exhibition held in Melbourne. The first event was held at Darling Harbour in 1996 and was trumpeted as a great success. It was a typically Sydney affair with lots of hoopla. The consumers enjoyed the event and were very well behaved. (As one observer put it: 'The only drunks were on the winemakers' side of the counter'.) It will be interesting to compare the Sydney event with that in Melbourne. Already politics is getting into the act. If you read that Jeff Kennett stole the event from the Emerald City, don't believe it; it was always in the plot that Wine Australia would alternate between the two capitals.

The line-up for this year's *Guide* was impressive and the debate as protracted as ever. There were very few faulty wines (apart from corked wines), but remember that there are over 1000 wineries in

Australia which, on average, produce at least 10 labels each, so the wines rated in any book smaller than *Webster's Dictionary* will be only a small sample of what's available.

We've opted for a balanced selection with a view to national distribution. As ever, the prices quoted are only a guide. Prices are very volatile at the moment and subject to change (upwards, sadly) at any time. We calculate the prices on a 40-per-cent mark-up on top of the LUC (into-store cost), which includes all taxes. Some retailers work on a lower mark-up, so it pays to shop around.

By-the-glass Wine in Restaurants and Wine Bars

You're eating out at a smart restaurant with a group of four. The waiter asks for the entrée orders: one person wants a young riesling with her fish, one wants a rich chardonnay with his chicken, another wants pinot noir with her beef carpaccio, and you? Well, you'd prefer to keep sipping that fine Tassie bubbly with your oysters.

What to do? Well, until someone invents a *quattro gusti* bottle of wine, your best bet is wine by the glass. That way, everyone gets a wine to match their dish. No fights.

Wine by the glass is no longer a novelty in restaurants; indeed, it's an essential part of any good wine list. An average restaurant or brasserie will have at least a couple of reds, a brace of whites and a bubbly by the glass, rotated often enough to keep regular patrons interested. Of course, Cognac and tawny port by the glass have been with us much longer, but in the late nineties wine by the glass has become quite specialised. Some restaurateurs extend it to specialty or super-expensive wines, and more than a few now offer wine by the 'taste' in a smaller glass as well as a regular glass. Typical portions are 150 ml for a glass, and 60 or 70 ml for a 'taste'. Wines by the 'taste' take the by-the-glass concept a step further. At anywhere between $3 and $5 a taste for most Aussie wines, depending on the restaurant, you can afford to have a small sample of the goods to see if you really want to order a full bottle.

A good by-the-glass restaurant will have a range of choice, with diverse regions, styles, price-levels and makers, and perhaps an import or two. Top Sydney restaurant Forty One has six chardonnays ranging from a $7.50 Preece to a $30 Leeuwin Estate.

The sorts of wines that people usually drink only a glass at a time, such as bubbly and botrytised sticky whites, are prime candidates for by-the-glass listings. So are the really expensive wines:

several restaurants in Sydney and Melbourne have offered 1990 Chateau d'Yquem by the taste at $45 to $50. This is the only way most people will ever get to taste such pricey nectar. (It's on Wine Banc's list in Sydney for $485 a bottle.)

Perhaps the most impressive use of wine by the glass is at Forty One's Krug Room. Here, the entire list of 35 to 40 wines is available by the glass, including a bevy of ultra-expensive Krug Champagnes. Of course, they don't keep one of each open all the time: far from it. Whatever bottles are open at any given time are promoted to make sure they move.

Advantages

Wine by the glass is very much a phenomenon of the times. It's booze-bus friendly, which encourages moderate drinking, and it allows an increasingly food-and-wine-conscious restaurant-going public to experiment to their hearts' content. The great diversity of wine is therefore better appreciated. It's also a great convenience and overcomes the problem of one wine not meeting the needs of everyone at the table. Different people have different wine preferences: even if everyone's eating the same dish, they might choose to vary their drinks. But people eating out as a group don't usually order the same course, and one wine is unlikely to go well with all the dishes. That's the time to call for the by-the-glass list.

Sometimes, say the restaurateurs, customers will finish a bottle or two but, finding it's not quite enough, they'll order a glass each to finish off with. In the past you had no option but to order another bottle, and if it was too much, you had to walk away from it, leaving it half-finished.

The wine industry also benefits because the system promotes the sensible use of wine as well as the enjoyment of diversity. Dietmar Sawyere of Forty One says about 25 per cent of his lunch customers have wine by the glass because they don't want to drink too much, especially if they have to go back to work; however, at dinner it's almost all by the bottle. At Armstrong's, sommelier Guy Vaillant finds less difference, with 40 to 45 per cent of customers ordering wine by the glass at lunch and about 30 per cent at dinner, when 'people can relax and enjoy their wine'.

Vaillant uses the by-the-glass system to introduce new and lesser known wines to his clients. He cites David Traeger Merlot and new wines from Andrew Thomas in the Hunter. Sawyere agrees: 'In chardonnay, we have the popular wines like Petaluma and Mountadam, but Kumeu River is a special favourite of mine and we recommend it, and we often find they'll take a glass, then like it so much they buy a bottle'. Forty One also uses by-the-glass for expensive rarities, such as 1987 Grange for $55. 'It's our biggest selling wine by the glass in the evenings, apart from Champagne.'

Drawbacks

The drawbacks are largely to do with the execution, not with the idea itself. The main problem is the risk of getting a glass of stale wine, poured from a bottle that wasn't opened the same day. This is a hazard when a restaurant has too many wines by the glass. They simply may not have enough demand to turn over enough bottles to ensure all the wines are fresh all of the time.

How can you tell if the wine is likely to be stale? Nobody is going to admit it if a bottle's been open for a week, so your only guide is your nose. If you think the wine is stale, say so and the waiter may open a fresh bottle.

Can you tell which wines are least likely to be stale? There's no simple answer, because as a diner you can't always predict which wines will be turning over regularly at a given establishment. Very busy brasseries might sell many bottles of each 'pouring' wine every day, and can afford to throw out the remnants of the last one or use it for cooking. An unfortunate by-product of the craze for wines by the glass is the tendency for some restaurants – that don't have sufficient demand – to offer too many wines by the glass, simply to be seen to be giving a superior service.

Finally, it's rare for the diner to be shown the bottle. This is a drawback for the winemaker because the identity of the wine is not on view, or if it is, it's usually at the bar some distance away. An opportunity to promote the label is missed. Some do make a point of showing the label by pouring the glass at the table.

Wine list consultant Peter Bourne is critical. 'Wine by the glass is poorly presented in most places. Often, wine companies pay a pouring allowance, but the label is never seen.' As a frequent diner-out, Bourne's main criticism is that restaurants play it too safe, often having nothing out of the ordinary available for pouring. 'You've finished a bottle and you want just one more glass of something different to round off the meal, but there's nothing of interest on the by-the-glass list.'

Freshness

Freshness is more important than range. A restaurant with a small selection of good wines by the glass that are always fresh is preferable to one with a big range of wines that are sometimes stale. There are exceptions: Logue's Eating House in Balmain offers every wine on the list by the glass. But it's a small list and the high turnover means the wines are always fresh.

The attitude of the restaurateur has a lot to do with freshness. If a restaurateur tries to stretch things, quality suffers. The price of pouring wines usually incorporates a margin to account for wastage, but many restaurateurs try to have it both ways. They should discard any wine that's been open too long or has lost its freshness. Writing the opening date on the label is a good habit for staff to get into. Ideally, there should be a competent taster on hand at the start of service to taste each open bottle and decide if it's fresh enough to serve. Failing this, there should be a policy of throwing them out after a certain number of days.

Most reds and whites can stand being open for two or three days, as long as they're looked after. They should be stoppered tightly and put in a fridge to reduce oxidation. Some varieties keep longer than others. A delicate riesling, for instance, may fade faster than a robust, oaky chardonnay. Most reds last longer than whites, but even that's not a certainty. An oxidatively made red such as a Penfolds will usually last longer than many other makers' reds. Also, the less a wine's been handled, the better it will keep. One that's only been accessed once will usually stay fresher longer than one that's been accessed several times.

According to the sommeliers and restaurateurs, wastage is not a significant problem. 'I have had to throw wine away only about three times in the last year,' says Guy Vaillant. Others say that when an expensive wine is open, they tell all the waiters to recommend it and that minimises the chance of its being left to go stale. At Forty One, two days is the maximum and then any wine left over is sent to the kitchen. Some restaurants use leftover wine for staff education.

Storage

There are many gadgets and systems purporting to preserve opened bottles. They include gas blanketing systems, air-evacuating pumps and, for sparkling wines, pumps that do the reverse, forcing air into the bottle to maintain pressure and keep the bubbles in the wine.

In fact, simply refrigerating an opened sparkling wine (with an appropriate clamp-type seal) will keep it for several days. The colder the wine, the more slowly it will lose gas because carbon dioxide is more soluble at lower temperatures. And no, Agnes, hanging a silver teaspoon in the neck is no help at all!

Sparkling wine has an advantage over still because the dissolved CO_2 guards it against oxidation. But opened bottles of still wine can keep several days, especially if the ullage is minimal. After years of research, HH has found no advantage in air pumps, and little value in gas blanketing systems, although some people – including experienced restaurateurs – find the latter useful. Sydney's newest wine bar, Wine Banc, is one of many using the latest thing in inert gas systems called The Wine Guardian. The gas is an argon blend, with no taste or smell, and users report that it works better than nitrogen or CO_2.

How Much Should You Get?

There's no agreed standard for the quantity of wine restaurants should serve by the glass. Some will give you a thimble and fill it to the brim; others will give you a fishbowl, which makes the same quantity of wine look disappointingly small.

Few menus state the quantity poured. The question is: should they? People seldom query the quantity of wine bought by the glass, which suggests either that Australians are still novices at dealing with wine by the glass or that they're happy in the belief that they're getting a convenient service.

Some top-flight restaurants nominate the quantity per serve, and it's usually 150 ml per glass. This works out at a nice round five glasses per bottle. A 'taste' is usually 70 ml. Wine Banc offers these quantities, and they come in a Riedel glass with plimsoll lines clearly marked on the bowl.

Is It Good Value?

Yes, in our experience almost always. Mostly, you can divide the price of a full bottle by the price of a glass and it comes to about five, the number of serves per bottle. Often, there's a small premium on the price of a glass, but most people are happy to pay it for the convenience. You're more likely to walk out sober, and there's less chance you'll leave an unfinished bottle (that you've paid for) on the table.

Two past winners of the Tucker Seabrook Australia's Wine List of the Year Award, Melbourne's France-Soir and Walter's Wine Bar, price their pouring wines at one-fifth or a little more than a fifth of what they charge for a full bottle. However, it isn't always easy to fathom the methods used in pricing wines. Often, champagne prices are much more attractive by the glass than by the bottle. One Sydney restaurant was selling Veuve Clicquot La Grande Dame 1989 at $220 a bottle but only $29 by the glass. If you had a party of five and you each ordered a glass, theoretically accounting for one entire bottle, you'd pay $145 instead of $220! A hell of a saving. The distributor was probably giving them an incentive to pour it by the glass, a well-known method of stimulating sales.

It seems fair that, all other things being equal, there should be a small premium on the price of a wine by the glass to allow for the extra work in serving (and conserving) it. And reasonable customers will probably be prepared to pay a little extra for the convenience of a single glass of fine wine in good condition. In other words, it's a great service, so enjoy it. Bottoms up!

Mark Shield's Favourite Things

'What's the best wine you've ever drunk?' That's the inevitable party question for a long-distance wine writer, and there's a glib stock answer: 'It hasn't happened yet'.

Hopefully there's truth in that. I'm an optimist at heart, and I hope to steal the words of Oscar Wilde (who was supposed to be sipping champagne on his deathbed): 'I'm dying beyond my means'. I'd like to exit with a flute of Krug, but in reality I'll probably say aaaarrrgggghhhh!

If the question were reframed to ask: 'Name some of your most memorable wines', that would be different – and answerable. I'm sure we all remember special wines and usually there's a sense of occasion that kindles the memory.

For example, I remember the 1963 Lindemans Rouge Homme Cabernet Sauvignon. I can't go into the details for fear of incriminating the guilty party; however, the said guilty party was at a tasting at Coonawarra, and the wine was trotted out at a retrospective tasting. Thrusting a glass into her hand I said, 'Remember this?'

'Nope.'

'Two Faces, pepper steak?'

'Nope.'

'What do you think of the wine?'

'Pretty fagged out. I want to go to the craft shop.'

Well *I* remember the 1963 Rouge Homme and admittedly these days it's pretty fagged out. Never mind, time marches on. I also remember the 1965 Tulloch Private Bin Dry Red and there was no hanky-panky involved. The wine just spoke for itself. For the same reason I also remember the 1959 Tatachilla Burgundy, and a revisit last year confirmed it is alive and well. Most of that vintage went to Buckingham Palace, and it's probably still sitting there gathering dust.

For me, the memorable wines are part of an event. I can usually remember the circumstances and great wines become a very personal thing. For example, I first tried the 1959 Tatachilla at a Greek BBQ with the then proprietors of High Y Cellars in Ashburton. The second occasion was on d'Arry's Veranda after we had concluded judging the McLaren Vale Wine Show. That was 20 years later, and in both cases I was blown away – what a wine!

When it comes to white wines, the 1963 Lindemans White Burgundy Bin 2250 was pretty special at its peak. I had that at a bridge game, and I was so distracted I was soundly thrashed. The 1946 Seppelt Sparkling Burgundy still looks good and makes a beaut birthday drink. I had a 1920 Lafite with the proprietors of Gatehouse Cellars who had a lot less wrinkles than I do. But what's the point if the best is yet to come?

If truth be told the legends of yore might have been magnificent in their time, but they were also very few in number. They stood out in a cesspool. In the last 50 years Australian wine has come of age, and the good wines are many rather than few. Happily, the great wines can be multiplied by 10 and many of these come from areas that weren't even planted 50 years ago. For example, 30-plus years ago Margaret River was a feasibility study and The Pyrenees was an earthmoving contractor's pipedream. There's no reason the discoveries should stop here. Who knows, in 10 years we could be tasting wine from new vineyards in Mount Gambier or the Dargo High Plains.

So any question about favourites has to be answered with the stock reply: 'It hasn't happened yet!' That's not really a fib – it's a certainty.

The Rating System

The rating system used in this guide is designed to give you an immediate assessment of a wine's attributes, as they will affect your purchasing decision. The symbols provide at-a-glance information, and the written descriptions go into greater depth. Other wine guides are full of numbers, but this one places importance on the written word.

The authors assess quality and value; provide an estimate of cellaring potential and optimum drinking age; and give notes on source, grape variety, organic cultivation where applicable, decanting, and alcohol content. We list previous outstanding vintages where we think they're relevant.

We assess quality using a cut-down show-judging system, marking out of a possible 10. Wine show judges score out of 20 points . . . three for nose, seven for colour, 10 for palate . . . but any wine scoring less than 10 is obviously faulty, so our five-glass range (with half-glass increments) indicates only the top 10 points. When equated to the show system, two and a half to three glasses is roughly equivalent to a bronze medal, and five glasses, our highest award, equals a high gold medal or trophy-standard wine.

Value is arrived at primarily by balancing absolute quality against price. But we do take some account of those intangible attributes that make a wine more desirable, such as rarity, great reputation, glamour, outstanding cellarability, and so on. We take such things into account because they are part of the value equation for most consumers.

If a wine scores more for quality than for value, it does not mean the wine is overpriced. As explained below, any wine scoring three stars for value is fairly priced. Hence, a wine scoring five glasses and five stars is extraordinary value for money. Very few wines manage this feat. And, of course, good and bad value for money can be found at $50 just as it can at $5.

If there are more stars than glasses, you are looking at unusually good value. We urge readers not to become star-struck: a three-glass three-star wine is still a good drink.

Where we had any doubt about the soundness of a wine, a second bottle was always sampled.

Quality

♟♟♟♟♟	The acme of style, a fabulous, faultless wine that Australia should be proud of.
♟♟♟♟?	A marvellous wine that is so close to the top it almost doesn't matter.
♟♟♟♟	An exciting wine that has plenty of style and dash. You should be proud to serve this.
♟♟♟?	Solid quality with a modicum of style; very good drinking.
♟♟♟	Decent, drinkable wine that is a cut above everyday quaffing. You can happily serve this to family and friends.
♟♟?	Sound, respectable wines, but the earth won't move.
♟♟	Just okay, but in quality terms, starting to look a little wobbly.

(Lower scores have not been included.)

Value

★★★★★	You should feel guilty for paying so little: this is great value for money.
★★★★ʳ	Don't tell too many people because the wine will start selling and the maker will put the price up.
★★★★	If you complain about paying this much for a wine, you've got a death adder in your pocket.

★★★ʳ   Still excellent value, but the maker is also making money.

★★★   Fair is fair, this is a win–win exchange for buyer and maker.

★★ʳ   They are starting to see you coming, but it's not a total rip-off.

★★   This wine will appeal to label drinkers and those who want to impress the bank manager.

★ʳ   You know what they say about fools and their money . . .

★   Makes the used-car industry look saintly.

Grapes

Grape varieties are listed in dominant order; percentages are cited when available.

Cellar

Any wine can of course be drunk immediately, but for maximum pleasure we recommend an optimum drinking time, assuming correct cellaring conditions. We have been deliberately conservative, believing it's better to drink a wine when it's a little too young than to risk waiting until it's too old.

An upright bottle ▮ indicates that the wine is ready for drinking now. It may also be possible to cellar it for the period shown. Where the bottle is lying on its side ➥ the wine is not ready for drinking now and should be cellared for the period shown.

▮   Drink now: there will be no improvement achieved by cellaring.

▮ 3   Drink now or during the next three years.

➥ 3–7   Cellar for three years at least before drinking; can be cellared for up to seven years.

➡ 10+   Cellar for 10 years or more; it will be at its best in 10 years from this book's publication date.

Alcohol by Volume

Australian labelling laws require that alcohol content be shown on all wine labels. It's expressed as a percentage of alcohol by volume, e.g. 12.0% A/V means that 12 per cent of the wine is pure alcohol.

Recommended Retail Price

Prices were arrived at either by calculating from the trade wholesale using a standard full bottle shop mark-up, or by using a maker-nominated recommended retail price. In essence, however, there is no such thing as RRP because retailers use different margins. The prices in this book are indicative of those in Sydney and Melbourne, but they will still vary from shop to shop and city to city. They should only be used as a guide. Cellar-door prices have been quoted when the wines are not available in the retail trade.

ⓥ Organic

The wine has passed the tests required to label it as 'organically grown and made'.

▌ Decant

The wine will be improved by decanting.

ⓢ Special

The wine is likely to be 'on special', so it will be possible to pay less than the recommended retail price. Shop around.

Best Wines

Every year it's the same embarrassment of riches when we come to deciding the award winners. Too many worthy wines, and, it's unfortunate to report, the issues of price and availability are every year more important considerations. There are some wines that cannot be ignored, regardless of price. Others that cannot seriously be considered because the 'Sold Out' sign goes up a few days after they're released. So this year's Penguin Award for the Wine of the Year goes to a people's wine – not necessarily the greatest chardonnay that came on sale in 1998 but a wine of irreproachable quality, unbelievable value . . . and a wine that just about everybody can buy at their local bottle shop.

On the other hand, the award for the Best White Wine went to an altogether different wine: very expensive, but a great Aussie wine of truly world class. This one also won the award for Best Chardonnay, and we'd love to be able to afford to stash a case of it away in our cellars. In our dreams . . .

On a negative note, the red wines from 1995 have not been as exciting as we would have liked – especially the cabernets, and especially in South Australia. Likewise pinot noir from both '95 and '96 in the cool areas left a lot to be desired. The weather was generally just a bit too cool. The good news is that '97 was a top year in those same cool areas, so watch out for the pinots and fuller-bodied varieties from 1997. On the other hand, shiraz from the warmer parts of South Australia didn't suffer the same setbacks as cabernet in '95, and there are many lovely rich wines.

So, without further ado, drum roll please . . . And the winners are . . .

**Penguin Wine of the Year
& Best Bargain White**

(any grape variety or blend)

Lindemans Bin 65 Chardonnay 1998

'Flavour with softness' is the motto of Phillip John, chief winemaker at Lindemans, and this wine really delivers. It's taken the international markets by storm over the past decade, and continues to get even better with succeeding vintages. Its success is well-deserved because, in our view, there's nothing anywhere in the world to touch it for flavour and quality at the price. At well under a tenner, it's a veritable vinous Volksie: a people's wine! (See page 259).

Best White Wine & Best Chardonnay

Leeuwin Estate Art Series Chardonnay 1995

A truly mind-bending Aussie chardonnay that tastes great now, will age superbly, and need doff its lid to no other chardonnay – and that includes Burgundy. (See page 257).

Best Red Wine

Cullen Cabernet Sauvignon Merlot 1996

A fabulous cabernet from a model WA boutique winery, where the quality is as high as the yields are low. (See page 56).

Best Sparkling Wine

Scarpantoni Black Tempest

A fabulous, wild 'n' stormy new brew from a lesser known family winery in McLaren Vale. Get a bottle for the Christmas turkey. (See page 346).

Best Fortified Wine

Seppelt DP 117 Show Fino
This famous dry sherry has a new lease of life due to a change in the law. The new version is less alcoholic and a delight to sip with pre-prandial snacks. (See page 376).

Picks of the Bunch

BEST CABERNET SAUVIGNON
Katnook Estate 1996
The price is getting high but what a wine! The '96 Coonawarra cabs are well worth a detour, and this is the best we've seen from Katnook to date. It's a very rich, strongly oaked, cellarworthy red. (See page 94).

BEST SHIRAZ
Waterwheel 1996
Peter Cumming makes delicious wine and believes in affordable prices. As the rest of the wine industry loses the plot on prices, his value for money is more and more remarkable. (See page 174).

BEST PINOT NOIR
Seppelt Sunday Creek 1997
Seppelt's Ian 'Macca' McKenzie is making a statement here: big companies *can* make decent pinot. A delicious pinot at our kind of price. (See page 155).

BEST RED BLEND/OTHER VARIETY
d'Arenberg The Custodian Grenache 1996
A monumental effort from a stalwart winery which is truly the custodian of some of the oldest and best grenache vines in the country. In this case old vines and low yields *do* add up to concentrated wines of great quality. (See page 57).

BEST RIESLING
Crabtree Watervale 1997
The '97 vintage produced a welter of terrific rieslings from Clare, but Robert Crabtree's came rocketing out of left-field and bowled us over. (See page 213).

BEST SEMILLON
McWilliams Mount Pleasant Elizabeth 1993
A peak vintage for this great stayer. A mature Hunter semillon in full glory, to drink or cellar further. Discover the delights of aged white wine at a user-friendly price! (See page 264).

BEST WHITE BLEND/OTHER VARIETY
Chapel Hill Verdelho 1997
Pam Dunsford's debut effort with this grape is a triumph. Could this be the start of a new trend in the Vale? (See page 211).

BEST SWEET WINE
Miranda Golden Botrytis 1995
This is a new award, and the Miranda wins for both quality and charity – it's a great sticky and the price is very drinkable, too. (See page 266).

Bargains

BEST BARGAIN RED
Ingoldby Cabernet Sauvignon 1996
Great value. When Mildara moves in the prices stay competitive and in this case the quality hasn't been compromised. A cuddly bottle of McLaren Vale sunshine. (See page 91).

BEST BARGAIN BUBBLY
Hardys Omni NV
If there is a better sub-$10 fizz about, it's news to us. Now you *can* have champagne tastes on a beer budget. (See page 341).

BEST BARGAIN FORTIFIED
Morris Liqueur Muscat
This is a $15 wine which tastes like $25. Morris's are the muscat masters: say that ten times over, quickly. Then reward yourself with a glass of it. (See page 371).

Best New Producer

Nepenthe Vineyards, of Lenswood, Adelaide Hills
This ambitious and highly professional venture includes the first new winery in the Hills since Petaluma, and the winemaker is one of the best tech heads in the biz – Peter Leske, ex-Wine Research Institute. Every one of Leske's first crop of white wines is a beaut, and we predict a distinguished future for Nepenthe.

Australia's Wine List of the Year Awards, 1998

It's something of a shock to look at restaurant wine lists and then at retail liquor stores: the difference in the wines they sell is amazing, and the gap is widening. Does this mean there's a difference between the sorts of people who dine out and those who imbibe at home? Not really. The main reason for the gap is the price differential between bottle shops and restaurants. While bottle shops add roughly a 40-per-cent mark-up to the cost of a bottle of wine, restaurants typically add at least 100 per cent. The price difference is very obvious to customers, and restaurateurs are sensitive about this. They avoid the sorts of wines that tend to be in every bottle shop, especially those that are discounted and heavily promoted. These wines make restaurants look expensive. Hence the situation where wine lists are heavily weighted towards rarer boutique wines, which are seldom found in the average bottle shop.

The syndrome is encouraged by the boutique wine producers, who don't really need liquor stores and who figure they get wider exposure for each bottle if they thinly spread their allocation around a number of high-profile restaurants. The unhappy outcome is that unless you're a wine-head, you can find yourself staring blankly at a wine list, not recognising a single name on it.

Such anomalies aside, restaurant wine lists in this country are getting better all the time. There's still a vast backdrop of lower- to mid-priced eateries where wine is either ignored or treated very off-handedly, but more and more are becoming wine-aware. Restaurateurs are working harder to cater for an increasingly wine-interested public.

Australia's Wine List of the Year Awards, organised by wholesale wine merchant Tucker Seabrook & Co, is an attempt to encourage higher standards in restaurant wine lists. It's judged by a panel of wine writers and other experts headed by co-author of this book, Huon Hooke. It's voluntary to enter, and about 400 restaurants are judged each year, with more than 100 earning a rating. Criteria include the quality and range of wines, pricing, balance, depth of older vintages, number of wines by the glass, suitability to the type of restaurant and cooking, and – very importantly – appearance, design and general 'user-friendliness'. You can be sure of a decent bottle at a fair price if you go to any of these restaurants.

National Winner

Forty One Restaurant, NSW ♟♟♟

Hall of Fame National Winners
(previous national winners maintaining three glass ratings)

France-Soir, Vic. (1997 winner) ♟♟♟

Walter's Wine Bar, Vic. (1996 winner) ♟♟♟

Dear Friends Garden Restaurant, WA (1995 winner) ♟♟♟

Cicada, NSW (1994 winner) ♟♟♟

Hall of Fame Category & State Winners
(winners of their state or category more than three times)

The Grape Food & Wine Bar (Qld winner) ♟♟♟

University House, Vic. (Best Club Restaurant) ♟♟♟

Universal Wine Bar (SA winner) ♟♟♟

Fee & Me (Tas. winner) ♟♟

Fringe Benefits (ACT winner) ♟♟

State & Territory Winners

ACT	Caffe Della Piazza ♟♟♟
NSW	Forty One Restaurant ♟♟♟
NT	Boardroom Restaurant ♟

Qld	Walter's Wine Bar & Restaurant ♟♟♟
SA	Chloe's Restaurant ♟♟♟
Tas.	Alexanders Restaurant ♟♟
Vic.	Syracuse Restaurant & Wine Bar ♟♟♟
WA	Stephenies ♟♟♟

Category Winners

BEST
RESTAURANT   Forty One Restaurant, NSW ♟♟♟

BEST SMALL
WINE LIST   The European, Vic. ♟♟

BEST CLUB
RESTAURANT   Sorrento Golf Club, Vic. ♟

BEST PUB
RESTAURANT   The Dolphin Hotel, NSW ♟♟♟

BEST CAFÉ /
BRASSERIE /
TRATTORIA   Wine Bar II, Vic. ♟♟♟

VERY HIGHLY RECOMMENDED ♟♟♟
Adams of North Riding Restaurant & Guest House, Vic.; Armstrong's Brasserie, NSW; Banc & Wine Banc, NSW; Belmondo, NSW; Blake's Restaurant, SA; Buon Ricordo, NSW; Caffe Della Piazza, ACT; Charcoal Grill on the Hill, Vic.; Chloe's Restaurant, SA; Cicada, NSW; Circa, The Prince, Vic.; Claudine's French Restaurant, NSW; Darling Mills, NSW; Dear Friends Restaurant, WA; Dogs Bar, Vic.; Est Est Est, Vic.; Forty One Restaurant, NSW; France-Soir, Vic.; Friends, WA; Hotel Australia – Shepparton, Vic.; Jacques Reymond Restaurant; Vic.; Jardines Restaurant, NSW; La Grillade Restaurant, NSW; Le Restaurant, Vic.; Marchetti's Latin

Restaurant, Vic.; Mask of China, Vic.; Merrony's, NSW; Morans Restaurant & Café, NSW; One Fitzroy Street, Vic.; Ozone Hotel, Vic.; Pier, NSW; Ristorante Roberto, Vic.; Stefano's Restaurant, Vic.; Stephenies, WA; Syracuse Restaurant & Wine Bar; Vic.; The Bathers Pavilion, NSW; The Dolphin Hotel, NSW; The Duck Restaurant & Wine Bar, Vic.; The Grape Food & Wine Bar; Qld; The Melbourne Wine Room, Vic.; Universal Wine Bar, SA; University House, Vic.; Walter's Wine Bar & Restaurant, Qld; Walter's Wine Bar, Vic.; Watermark Restaurant, NSW; Wine Bar II, Vic.

HIGHLY RECOMMENDED ♟♟

Alexanders Restaurant, Tas.; Barry's Country Guest House & Restaurant, NSW; B-Coz Restaurant, Vic.; Becco, Vic.; Bilson's Restaurant, NSW; Bistro Deux, NSW; Bistro E, Vic.; Bistro Moncur, NSW; Bistro Pave, NSW; Café Latte, Vic.; Caterina's Cucina E Bar, Vic.; Chinois, Vic.; Cicciolina, Vic.; Cottage Point Inn Restaurant, NSW; Courtney's Brasserie, NSW; Darley's Restaurant, NSW; Durham's Restaurant, SA; Eleonores Restaurant, Vic.; Enzo Restaurant, Vic.; Finches of Beechworth Country Guest House, Vic.; Fortuna Village Restaurant, Vic.; Fringe Benefits, ACT; Gekko Restaurant, NSW; George's Restaurant, NSW; Grand Mercure Hotel Bowral Heritage Park, NSW; Grange Restaurant, SA; Grossi Ristorante Italiano, Vic.; Il Bacaro, Vic.; Isthmus of Kra, Vic.; Juniperberry, ACT; Kables, NSW; L'Avventura, NSW; La Mensa, NSW; Lake House Restaurant, Vic.; Lindenderry at Red Hill, Vic.; Logues Eating House, NSW; Lynch's Restaurant Wintergarden, Vic.; Marco Polo East West Cuisine, Qld; No. 44 King Street, WA; One One Seven Restaurant, NSW; Paramount, NSW; Pavilion on the Park, NSW; Pieroni, Vic.; Raphael's Restaurant, NSW; Ritz Carlton Dining Room; NSW; Sails on the Bay Restaurant, Vic.; San Francisco Grill, NSW; Sweetwater Café; Vic.; Tables of Toowong, Qld; The Centennial, NSW; The Chesser Cellar, SA; The Clubhouse Restaurant, Qld; The European, Vic.; The Lion Hotel, SA; The Lobby Restaurant, ACT; The Melbourne Supper Club, Vic.; The Old George & Dragon Restaurant, NSW; The Point, Vic.; The Stag Restaurant, Vic.; The Stokehouse, Vic.; The Victory Hotel, SA; Witch's Cauldron Restaurant, WA.

RECOMMENDED ♥

Abacus, Vic.; Acqua Blu, Tas.; Adams at La Trobe, Vic.; Aix Bistro Café, Qld; Alex's Italian Restaurant, NSW; Alley Blue Kitchen & Bar, Vic.; Archie's on the Park, NSW; Artis Restaurant, Qld; Atlantic Restaurant, ACT; Avondale Golf Club, NSW; Baguette Restaurant, Qld; bar corvina, Vic.; Bluewater Bistro, NSW; Boardroom Restaurant, NT; Breezes Restaurant, Qld; Café Chagall, Qld; Café Provincial, Vic.; Caffe Bizzarri, Vic.; Caffé E Cucina, Vic.; Cannibals, NSW; Canterbury-Hurlstone Park RSL Club, NSW; Champagne Brasserie, Qld; Charters Towers, Qld; Chifley's at the Kurrajong, ACT; China Tea Club, ACT; Chine on Paramount, Vic.; Churchers on Richmond Hill, Vic.; Cibo Ristorante Pasticciera, SA; Cin Cin, WA; Colonnade Café Restaurant, NT; Continental Hotel Sorrento, Vic.; Corn Exchange Brasserie, NSW; Court Wine Bar, WA; Credo Restaurant, NSW; Daniel's Restaurant, Qld; Downtown Motel, NSW; East Empress Restaurant, Vic.; Edward's Waterfront, Vic.; Encore Restaurant, NSW; Fishy Affair, WA; Flouch's, Vic.; Fresh Ketch, NSW; Halcyon Restaurant, Vic.; Half Moon, Vic.; Hanuman Thai and Nonya Restaurant, NT; Hardy's Restaurant, SA; Jaspers Restaurant, NSW; Jonah's, NSW; Jordon's Seafood Restaurant, NSW; Kingston Hotel Restaurant, Vic.; Marchetti's Tuscan Grill, Vic.; Marine Café, Vic.; Mercers Restaurant, Vic.; Merretts Restaurant at Pepper's Anchorage, NSW; Mezzaluna, NSW; Mietta's Queenscliff Hotel, Vic.; Milsons Restaurant, NSW; Neptune Palace, NSW; O'Connell's Centenary Hotel, Vic.; Oscar W's Wharfside Redgum Grill & Deckbar, Vic.; Plume Chinese Restaurant, Vic.; Poff's Restaurant, Vic.; Potters Cottage Restaurant, Vic.; Punch Lane Wine Bar & Restaurant, Vic.; RACV Club, Vic.; Rawson Restaurant, NSW; Richmond Hill Café and Larder, Vic.; Ristorante Fellini, Qld; Royal Motor Yacht Club, NSW; Sails Beach Café, Qld; Sails on the Bay, Qld; Sails Restaurant Williamstown, Vic.; Schouten House, Tas.; Scusa Mi, Vic.; Shakahari Vegetarian Restaurant, Vic.; Shark Fin House, Vic.; Siggi's at the Heritage on the Botanic Gardens, Qld; Sorrento Golf Club, Vic.; The Boat House by the Lake, ACT; The Boathouse on Blackwattle Bay, NSW; The Criterion Restaurant, NSW; The George Public Bar, Vic.; The Grand National, NSW; The Manse Restaurant, SA; The Mixing Pot Restaurant, NSW; The Near East

Restaurant, Vic.; Tory's Seafood Restaurant, NSW; University & Schools Club, NSW; Villa D'Este Restaurant, WA; Volare Restaurant, Qld; Windows on the Bay, Vic.; Woodcocks Global Kitchen, NSW; Yarra Glen Grand Bistro, Vic.; Yarra Glen Grand Dining Room, Vic.

Red Wines

Allandale Mudgee Cabernet Sauvignon

Quality 🍷🍷½
Value ★★½
Grapes cabernet sauvignon
Region Mudgee, NSW
Cellar 2–8
Alc./Vol. 15.0%
RRP $17.70

Allandale's Bill Sneddon now sources fruit from other regions in New South Wales apart from the Hunter Valley home base, but he keeps the wines separate.

CURRENT RELEASE 1996 Is this the paddock they forgot to pick? The alcohol is 15 per cent, and the wine is so porty the grapes might have made better jam than wine. The bouquet has a bizarre blend of eucalyptus and jammy, berry smells; the palate has very big, overripe cordial flavours, and the acid sticks out, no doubt because they had to add a lot. Extraordinary stuff! We wouldn't like to predict its future.

Angove's Mondiale Shiraz Cabernet

Quality 🍷🍷🍷
Value ★★★
Grapes shiraz; cabernet sauvignon
Region Murray Valley, Vic. 80%; Padthaway, SA 20 %
Cellar 3
Alc./Vol. 13.0%
RRP $15.60 (S)

Boss John Angove is the fourth generation of the family to run this company. He's also a descendant of Dr A. C. Kelly, founder of Tintara (now Hardys) at McLaren Vale.

CURRENT RELEASE 1995 A respectable everyday drinking red, showing some development now, with soft, chocolatey, caramel and vanilla flavours. It's straightforward, smooth and well-balanced to taste, with some attractive fleshiness. Try it with barbecued lamb shish kebabs.

Annie's Lane Cabernet Merlot

This seems to have become a successful brand for Mildara Blass, after Quelltaler, Eaglehawk and others were abandoned. Maker David O'Leary.
CURRENT RELEASE 1996 Interesting combination of leafy and jammy fruit characters in this wine. There are porty elements and some vanilla from oak. It's full-bodied, with grainy tannins and good softness for drinkability. Try it with wild duck.

Quality	♥♥♥♥
Value	★★★★
Grapes	cabernet sauvignon; merlot
Region	Clare Valley, SA
Cellar	♦ 8
Alc./Vol.	13.5%
RRP	$15.00 ⑤

Arlewood Cabernet Sauvignon

Arlewood is a six-hectare vineyard in the Cowaramup area, established in 1988. The wines are made by Jurg Muggli at Chateau Xanadu.
CURRENT RELEASE 1995 Typical Margaret River herbal characters here, in tandem with a thumping, big, rustic, tannic palate structure. It smells of tomato bushes and oak, and it's not a wine of subtlety. It was obviously built with the cellar in mind, but it's a young vineyard so only time will tell how it develops. Try it with marinated buffalo.

Quality	♥♥♥?
Value	★★⊦
Grapes	cabernet sauvignon
Region	Margaret River, WA
Cellar	⬤ 2–5+
Alc./Vol.	13.5%
RRP	$21.80 ▮

Arrowfield Shiraz

This is the little brother of the '95 Trophy Shiraz (see last year's *Guide*) and is much less oaky, more approachable and drinks well young. The maker is Don Buchanan, whose previous winemaking gig was in Tasmania.
CURRENT RELEASE 1996 A typical Hunter red with its earthy, lightly leathery aromas, and smooth medium-bodied profile. Cherry and some spice notes come through, too. The tannins are supple on the finish. It will build typical Hunter gaminess with more age. Try it with duck.

Quality	♥♥♥?
Value	★★★⊦
Grapes	shiraz
Region	Hunter Valley, NSW
Cellar	♦ 5
Alc./Vol.	13.0%
RRP	$13.00 ⑤

Arrowfield Show Reserve Cabernet Sauvignon

Quality	♥♥♥♥
Value	★★★★
Grapes	cabernet sauvignon
Region	not stated
Cellar	➥ 2–8+
Alc./Vol.	13.0%
RRP	$21.30 $ ▌

The packaging tells us this was Highly Commended (the equivalent to a silver medal, but not a silver as it's given to an unfinished, unbottled and possibly unblended wine) at the Hobart Show.

CURRENT RELEASE 1994   Lots of oak here, and very tannic as well. It smells dusty, woodsy, earthy and meaty, and tastes rich, tannic and high in extract. There's plenty of flesh, and a savoury, oak-infused fruit flavour. It finishes slightly tough from the oak, and it needs more time. Then serve with aged parmesan cheese.

Ashton Hills Pinot Noir

Quality	♥♥♥♥
Value	★★★
Grapes	pinot noir
Region	Adelaide Hills, SA
Cellar	▌ 4
Alc./Vol.	12.7%
RRP	$35.00

This has filled out a little since last year's review, and has benefited from the extra age. It's the result of a very low crop (less than 2.5 kilograms per vine) due to the season. Maker Steve George.

Previous outstanding vintages: '94, '95

CURRENT RELEASE 1996   The colour is mid-purple–red and it smells of dark berries, earth and oak with mint and tomato-leaf high notes. As pinots go it's a light–middleweight. It has some pleasing extract on the palate, finishing smooth and savoury. Good with tuna.

Ashwood Grove Cabernet Sauvignon

Quality	♥♥♥
Value	★★★
Grapes	cabernet sauvignon
Region	Murray Valley, Vic.
Cellar	▌ 1
Alc./Vol.	13.5%
RRP	$12.50 $

This winery sent wine writers a pair of red boxer shorts with a picture of Marilyn Monroe attached. What does that say about the marketing genius behind it? Or what does it say about wine writers?

CURRENT RELEASE 1996   The colour is rather light and developed, and the dominant aroma is of herbal vegetal characters. The fragile fruit is backed up by a hearty wallop of wood, lending coffee and vanilla characters. Very much a drink-now red. It could raise some cheer around a smoky barbecue.

Ashwood Grove Murphy's Block Mourvèdre Shiraz

The address on the label is Wood Wood, Victoria, which is in the Sunraysia district on the Murray River. CURRENT RELEASE 1996 Don't look for a rich red here. The colour is a medium–light red–purple, and there are simple confectionery aromas, sweetish jammy flavours, and a light-bodied palate. It's a bit flimsy to keep, but makes a decent drink-now quaffing red. It could be chilled like a Beaujolais in summer. Food: chicken satays.

Quality	♟♟♟
Value	★★★ʳ
Grapes	mourvèdre; shiraz
Region	Murray Valley, Vic.
Cellar	▯ 1
Alc./Vol.	13.0%
RRP	$9.50 Ⓢ

Baileys 1920s Block Shiraz

Great old-fashioned style with loads of flavour and a surprising element of finesse. It's not as Neanderthal as the wines of the fifties and sixties, but there are echoes of the past. The company is part of Fosters Brewing nee Mildara Blass.
Previous outstanding vintages: '91, '92, '94
CURRENT RELEASE 1995 The colour is inky mulberry. The nose has ripe plum and earthy aromas. The palate is full-bodied and chewy with an impact of sweet concentrated plum flavours. The finish is characterised by some black-tea-like tannins and solid grip. It goes well with roast dija mutton.

Quality	♟♟♟♟ʟ
Value	★★★★
Grapes	shiraz
Region	Glenrowan, Vic.
Cellar	⟜ 4–10
Alc./Vol.	13.5%
RRP	$24.00

CURRENT RELEASE 1996 Rich, yet elegant. The colour is dark, and the nose has pepper spices and plum aromas. The palate is rich with middleweight fruit flavours. Dark cherry is the dominant element, and there are some inky tannins on a very sturdy finish. It needs more time and is well suited to a game pie.

Quality	♟♟♟♟
Value	4
Grapes	shiraz
Region	North East Vic.
Cellar	⟜ 2–8
Alc./Vol.	14.0%
RRP	$23.00

Balgownie Estate Cabernet Sauvignon

Quality	♟♟♟♟
Value	★★★★
Grapes	cabernet sauvignon
Region	Bendigo, Vic.
Cellar	▮ 4
Alc./Vol.	13.0%
RRP	$20.00 ▮

The vineyard was founded in 1969 by Stuart Anderson. These days Stuart is retired, but he still drives his Bugatti and plays the oboe. Maker Lindsay Ross.
Previous outstanding vintages: '76, '80, '86, '90, '92, '93, '94
CURRENT RELEASE 1995   Very solid Central-Victorian-style with a deep, dense colour and a pungent cabernet nose. There's also a hint of green leaf. The palate is medium-bodied with sweet blackberry fruit flavours, and the finish is tinder-dry with gripping tannins. Try it with a standing rib roast.

Quality	♟♟♟♟
Value	★★★★
Grapes	cabernet sauvignon
Region	Bendigo, Vic.
Cellar	▮ 5
Alc./Vol.	13.5%
RRP	$20.00 ▮

CURRENT RELEASE 1996   This is a big style that's typical of the region. The nose is a mixture of briar, blackberry and tar aromas. The solid palate has developed fruit flavours with blackberry and cherry as the major components. There's some sombre oak that adds tannin and grip to the finish. The wine would go well with an old-fashioned rib roast.

Balgownie Estate Shiraz

Quality	♟♟♟♟
Value	★★★
Grapes	shiraz
Region	Bendigo, Vic.
Cellar	▮ 3
Alc./Vol.	13.5%
RRP	$19.00 ▮

It's hard to credit that Mildara originally purchased Balgownie to take on the red wines from Wolf Blass! Then along came Jamiesons Run and, better still, along came the target. As a consequence, Balgownie is almost a forgotten thing. Maker Lindsay Ross.
Previous outstanding vintages: '76, '80, '86, '90, '91, '93
CURRENT RELEASE 1995   Great colour in this wine from Bendigo, but the nose has a slightly stewed vegetable character. The palate is quite rich with attractive sweet plum flavours, and there's a hint of pepper. The oak offers reasonable grip. It goes well with a pepper steak.

CURRENT RELEASE 1996 Comfort wine, red, rich and satisfying. The nose has a mixture of plums and spices with a background of oak. The palate is a heavyweight with strong plum and cherry flavours, and there's a hint of white pepper. The oak adds another dimension with attractive grippy tannins on a long finish. An each-way bet in the cellar–drink now stakes. Try it with an oxtail stew.

Quality	♥♥♥♥
Value	★★★★~
Grapes	shiraz
Region	Bendigo, Vic.
Cellar	5
Alc./Vol.	14.0%
RRP	$19.00

Balnaves Cabernet Sauvignon

You don't have to go far in the Coonawarra region to come across the name Balnaves. The major building in Penola is Balnaves store, and Doug Balnaves is a noted viticulturist and mechanical harvester contractor. So while the label might be new, the name's been around for quite a while.

CURRENT RELEASE 1995 A pleasant surprise from a vintage that tested the makers. The nose has blackberry and cherry aromas plus a savoury oak component. The medium-bodied palate has sweet blackberry fruit flavours, which are attended by spicy oak and fine-grained tannins on a long astringent finish. It's an impressive red that goes well with a cassoulet.

Quality	♥♥♥♥?
Value	★★★★★
Grapes	cabernet sauvignon
Region	Coonawarra, SA
Cellar	5
Alc./Vol.	13.0%
RRP	$22.00

Bannockburn Pinot Noir

Bannockburn's is without dispute one of the leading Australian pinots, albeit in an extreme style that shows some stalk character in its youth. This comes from a percentage of whole bunches in the fermenter.
Previous outstanding vintages: '84, '86, '88, '89, '90, '91, '92, '94, '95
CURRENT RELEASE 1996 Stalky undergrowth scents pervade the aroma at this early stage in the wine's life. In the mouth, it's sweetly fruity and pleasingly smooth, again with earthy, autumnal overtones: no way is this a simple tutti-frutti style. There's mild tannin to close, and it should reward cellaring for a year or three. Then serve with quail.

Quality	♥♥♥♥?
Value	★★★~
Grapes	pinot noir
Region	Geelong, Vic.
Cellar	5
Alc./Vol.	13.5%
RRP	$41.00

Bannockburn Serré Pinot Noir

Quality	♥♥♥♥⦇
Value	★★★
Grapes	pinot noir
Region	Geelong, Vic.
Cellar	▮ 4
Alc./Vol.	13.5%
RRP	$95.00

The fruit for this limited production comes from a close-planted vineyard. The viticulture is more like Burgundy than a typical Australian pinot planting, with interesting results. Maker Gary Farr.

Previous outstanding vintages: '91, '93

CURRENT RELEASE 1994   This is priced to compete with premier cru Burgundy, a comparison that holds water. It's very good indeed; a richly flavoured pinot that shows a typical Bannockburn stalk note in the bouquet, but that has fewer vegetal, undergrowth characters than the '93. There are gamy cherry flavours, and the palate has weight and authority. Very fine indeed. Try it with barbecued quail.

Banrock Station Shiraz Cabernet

Quality	♥♥♥
Value	★★★
Grapes	shiraz; cabernet sauvignon
Region	Riverland, SA
Cellar	▮ 2
Alc./Vol.	12.0%
RRP	$11.95

This is a no frills, airs or graces label that doesn't even run to a vintage on the label. The message is simple – drink the stuff. Part of the profits is donated to Landcare.

CURRENT RELEASE *non-vintage*   The nose has a hint of raspberry cordial aroma. The palate is light- to medium-bodied and there are sweet berry flavours which are dusted by light spices. The wood on the finish is discreet and gentle. A good BBQ style.

Barossa Valley Estate Ebenezer Cabernet Sauvignon Merlot

Quality	♥♥♥♥⦇
Value	★★★★⦆
Grapes	cabernet sauvignon; merlot
Region	Barossa Valley, SA
Cellar	▮ 4
Alc./Vol.	14.0%
RRP	$22.00 ▮

Ebenezer is a wine made from parcels of fruit grown by growers in the Barossa Valley. The wine would have been started by Colin Glaetzer, who was the winemaker at that time.

CURRENT RELEASE 1994   A very tasty wine. The nose is loaded with sweet berry aromas plus vanilla, and the palate is medium- to full-bodied. There are rich, sweet raspberry and cherry flavours, and these are matched by a mouthfilling texture. The oak weaves its spell with some drying tannins and prominent grip. It drinks well with osso bucco.

Bass Phillip Reserve Pinot Noir

This is the top-ranker of three pinots bottled by Bass Phillip's Phillip Jones, and although it's expensive and almost unprocurable, that doesn't stop people frothing at the mouth over it.
Previous outstanding vintages: '89, '94, '95
CURRENT RELEASE 1996   A wine that lives up to the hype. Very vivid dark purple–red colour, with clean spicy cherry and slightly peppery aromas and a hint of dark chocolate. It has great finesse, intensity and balance in the mouth, again with a hint of chocolate. Not a blockbuster, but a wine of complexity and subtlety. Serve it with barbecued quails.

Quality	♥♥♥♥♥
Value	★★★†
Grapes	pinot noir
Region	South Gippsland, Vic.
Cellar	▮ 7
Alc./Vol.	13.5%
RRP	$70.00

Batista Pinot Noir

This label looks very French in design, and the name sounds like it should be part of a revolution. The wine is a new label from Manjimup, Western Australia, and it's a very exciting debut.
CURRENT RELEASE 1996   The colour is dense, and the nose has dark cherry and plum aromas. The palate is solid and tight with strong plum and cherry flavours that are laced with spices. The finish offers solid tannins with loads of grip. The wine is big enough to handle a game pie.

Quality	♥♥♥♥♥
Value	★★★†
Grapes	pinot noir
Region	Manjimup, WA
Cellar	▮ 5
Alc./Vol.	13.5%
RRP	$34.00

Best's Great Western Shiraz

Best's is one of the oldest vineyards in Victoria, planted by Henry Best in 1866. His brother Joseph planted what became Seppelts across the highway.
Previous outstanding vintages: '85, '87, '88, '90, '91, '92, '94
CURRENT RELEASE 1995   This is a typical Best's shiraz: the oak handling is subtle; the nose is shy and takes time to 'come up' in the glass. There are cherry, raspberry and mint aromas, and the palate is quite rich and fleshy, with gentle tannins and a smooth, agreeable finish. It can be enjoyed now, but history shows it's likely to live 20 years. Try it with roast leg of goat.

Quality	♥♥♥♥↑
Value	★★★★
Grapes	shiraz
Region	Grampians, Vic.
Cellar	➘ 2–15+
Alc./Vol.	13.5%
RRP	$26.50 ▮

Best's Pinot Noir

Quality	♥♥♥꠹
Value	★★★
Grapes	pinot noir
Region	Grampians, Vic.
Cellar	➯ 1–4
Alc./Vol.	13.5%
RRP	$21.65

Best's has been producing pinot longer than most: its oldest vines date back to 1971. Maker Viv Thomson.
CURRENT RELEASE 1996 The colour is starting to show some development with a brick-red edge, and the aroma is of stewed plums. The wine has yet to build complexity; it needs time to soften a slight bitterness, which may be the result of some green stalky characters.

Bethany Cabernet Merlot

Quality	♥♥♥♥꠹
Value	★★★★꠹
Grapes	cabernet sauvignon; merlot
Region	Barossa Valley, SA
Cellar	▮ 3
Alc./Vol.	13.0%
RRP	$21.40

Everybody's best mate, this is a very affectionate style. The emphasis is on fruit, which is a positive trait of this very honest label.
CURRENT RELEASE 1996 The nose has ripe berry aromas and a hint of vanilla. The full-bodied palate is chockers with ripe, sweet berry flavour. There's raspberry and blackberry plus a touch of spice. The finish shows some gentle oak and soft cuddly tannins. It is ready to drink now, and the go is to try it with lasagne.

Bethany Shiraz

Quality	♥♥♥♥
Value	★★★★
Grapes	shiraz
Region	Barossa Valley, SA
Cellar	▮ 3
Alc./Vol.	13.5%
RRP	$21.40

This is a bounteous Mother Barossa wine – rich in flavour but somewhat inconclusive in terms of finish. Makers Geoff and Rob Schrapel.
CURRENT RELEASE 1996 The nose has ripe plum and cherry flavours. The palate is rich and full-bodied with ripe sweet fruit flavours that flood the mouth. The finish is soft and gentle with soft velvety tannins and understated acid. It drinks well with pasta and a meat sauce.

Black Rock Cabernet Sauvignon

Quality	♥♥♥
Value	★★꠹
Grapes	cabernet sauvignon
Region	not stated
Cellar	▮ 2
Alc./Vol.	13.0%
RRP	$16.00

This label doesn't refer to a bay suburb in Melbourne. It's a rather muddled presentation from Mildara Blass.
CURRENT RELEASE 1996 There are leaf and blackberry aromas on the nose. The middleweight palate has sweet blackberry flavour which is conjoined with some dry dusty tannins on a middle-length finish. A drink-now style that goes well with bangers and mash.

Bleasdale Shiraz

Obviously 1996 was a good year in the Langhorne Creek district. Bleasdale was established in 1850. Maker Michael Potts.

CURRENT RELEASE 1996 The colour is a deep red, and the nose has strong pepper–spice and plum aromas. The palate is intense with concentrated shiraz flavours and loads of spice. Some attractive oak gives this wine real backbone, and there's plenty of tannin grip. It will develop handsomely. Try it with venison.

Quality	ΥΥΥΥ?
Value	★★★★★
Grapes	shiraz
Region	Langhorne Creek, SA
Cellar	▮ 5
Alc./Vol.	14.0%
RRP	$17.90

Bloodwood Cabernet Sauvignon

They write a good newsletter at Bloodwood, it's often highly entertaining. See the address at the back of this book and put yourself on the mailing list.

CURRENT RELEASE 1994 The wine is starting to show bottle development. You pick up the first clue in the colour and then there are concentrated fruit aromas on the nose. The palate is medium-bodied with cherry and blackberry flavours. The finish has fine-grained tannins and a modest astringency. It drinks well with a mushroom risotto.

Quality	ΥΥΥΥ
Value	★★★★
Grapes	cabernet sauvignon
Region	Orange, NSW
Cellar	▮ 3
Alc./Vol.	12.4%
RRP	$18.00

Bloodwood Rosé of Malbec

Good to see people still having a go at a much-neglected style that's perfect for an Australian summer. Malbec makes a good vehicle for this style. Maker Stephen Doyle.

CURRENT RELEASE 1997 Party-frock pink it ain't, more a light ruby. The nose has sweet ripe berry aromas, and the delicate palate has some fleshy elements as well as sweet malbec flavours. These are balanced by soft acidity. Big chill makes it come to life. Drink mid-afternoon.

Quality	ΥΥΥ?
Value	★★★⋆
Grapes	malbec
Region	Orange, NSW
Cellar	▮ 1
Alc./Vol.	12.5%
RRP	$14.00

Boston Bay Cabernet Sauvignon

Quality	♥♥♥ℓ
Value	★★★ℓ
Grapes	cabernet sauvignon
Region	Eyre Peninsula, SA
Cellar	↓ 3
Alc./Vol.	12.8%
RRP	$20.50

They are making a stand against the cork problem at Boston Bay, hence this wine is bottled with a synthetic cork. We'll see more of this in future.

CURRENT RELEASE 1995   The nose has a hint of mint as well as blackberry aromas. The palate is medium-bodied and there are attractive blackberry flavours. The spice adds just that to the finish, which has some integrated oak. It drinks well now with braised steak.

Boston Bay Merlot

Quality	♥♥♥♥
Value	★★★★
Grapes	merlot
Region	Eyre Peninsula, SA
Cellar	↓ 3
Alc./Vol.	12.0%
RRP	$26.00

This is a pioneering venture by the Ford family. Graham 'Fordie' Ford is a splendid chap who takes wine – but not much else – seriously!

CURRENT RELEASE 1995   This wine is a bit of a find. It has a deep red colour, and the nose has a cherry-cordial quality. The palate is medium-bodied with dark cherry flavours, and there are attractive tannins on a lingering finish. It will cellar for the short term. Try it with a meat pie.

Quality	♥♥♥♥
Value	★★★★
Grapes	merlot
Region	Eyre Peninsula, SA
Cellar	↓ 3
Alc./Vol.	12.6%
RRP	$26.00

CURRENT RELEASE 1996   Very elegant wine that isn't without substance. The nose has rose-garden and red-berry aromas. The palate is medium-bodied with a tight fruit structure. There are spicy white cherries on a plum background, and the acid and tannins on the finish add structure and balance. Try it with scotch eggs.

Bowen Estate Shiraz

The Bowens believe the south of Coonawarra, where they are, has a slightly different climate to the north. They certainly pick their grapes later.

Previous outstanding vintages: '84, '87, '90, '91, '93, '94

CURRENT RELEASE 1996 A blinder of a shiraz! Doug Bowen has served up a great drink. It's tremendously complex, smelling gamy, spicy and vaguely animal, with mixed spices in the background. The flavour is terrifically intense, lively, bold and youthful, ending with nice firm tannins. It's a keeper. Enjoy it with lightly peppered steak.

Quality	🍷🍷🍷🍷🍷
Value	★★★★★
Grapes	shiraz
Region	Coonawarra, SA
Cellar	1–10+
Alc./Vol.	14.0%
RRP	$22.00

Bremerton Cabernet Sauvignon Shiraz Merlot

The vineyard is at Langhorne Creek and the wine is typical of the region. The winery was established in 1991.

CURRENT RELEASE 1995 The nose is ripe and plummy with gentle spice. The medium-bodied palate has sweet fruity redcurrant and ripe cherry flavours. The finish is soft with undemanding tannins. Decanting will enhance. This wine goes well with pasta and a meat sauce.

Quality	🍷🍷🍷½
Value	★★★★
Grapes	cabernet sauvignon; shiraz; merlot
Region	Langhorne Creek, SA
Cellar	3
Alc./Vol.	13.2%
RRP	$18.00

Bremerton Young Vine Estate Shiraz

Can you keep a secret? We don't suppose you can. It's interesting to see 'young vines' mentioned on a label. Makers don't normally admit to young vines. Never mind, this is a ripper.

CURRENT RELEASE 1996 The nose has spice and plum aromas, and the colour is a vibrant deep ruby. The palate is packed with fruit. It's sweet and luscious, and the finish shows some well-integrated oak and drying tannins. It should cellar well in the short term. Serve it with a rare T-bone steak.

Quality	🍷🍷🍷🍷½
Value	★★★★★
Grapes	shiraz
Region	Langhorne Creek, SA
Cellar	3
Alc./Vol.	13.8%
RRP	$17.50

Briar Ridge Hermitage

Quality	♟♟♟♟
Value	★★★★
Grapes	shiraz
Region	Hunter Valley, NSW
Cellar	🍷 6
Alc./Vol.	12.7%
RRP	$19.00

This is the latest venture by Karl Stockhausen. Karl is a wine icon in the Hunter Valley, where he was responsible for some of the legendary Lindemans four-bin-number series.

CURRENT RELEASE 1996   This wine shows the lineage. It has a deep ruby colour, and the nose is a mixture of plums, spice and leather. The palate is tight and restrained with plum and earthy flavours, and the wood adds structure and grip. It has far to go in the cellar, and is great with pasta and a meat sauce.

Bridgewater Mill Millstone Shiraz

Quality	♟♟♟♟
Value	★★★⋆
Grapes	shiraz
Region	McLaren Vale, SA
Cellar	🍷 5
Alc./Vol.	13.5%
RRP	$23.00

This is the house wine for one of Australia's best country restaurants. The Bridgewater Mill is a must-visit if you are in Adelaide.

CURRENT RELEASE 1995   This wine has a great vibrant colour with a range of hues from garnet to purple. The nose is spicy with plum and mulberry aromas. The palate is medium- to full-bodied with ripe berry fruit flavours and some attractive spices. These conjoin with solid oak on a long and grippy finish. It will reward those who are patient.

Brien Family Selection Shiraz Cabernet

Quality	♟♟♟⋆
Value	★★★⋆
Grapes	shiraz 53%; cabernet sauvignon 47%
Region	Macedon, Vic.
Cellar	🍷 3
Alc./Vol.	12.2%
RRP	$20.00

This is not necessarily an estate-grown wine, but it's a very friendly one. The grapes come from local vineyards. Maker Keith Brien of Cleveland.

CURRENT RELEASE 1996   The nose is all about fruit; there's a big berry aroma. The palate is medium-bodied with sweet blackberry fruit and briar-patch hints. The tannin on the finish is subdued and gentle. It drinks well now with a rabbit stew.

Brokenwood Cricket Pitch

There's no prize for guessing that the vineyard is planted on what used to be the Pokolbin cricket pitch. It's the marque's fighting brand. Maker Iain Riggs.

CURRENT RELEASE 1996 This wine has a deep colour, and the nose is laden with fruit and berry aromas. The palate is medium-bodied with rich, soft fruit flavours; raspberry and sweet cherry being the major ones. The tannins are clean and soft with hints of vanilla. It drinks well with steak and kidney pie.

Quality	⅋⅋⅋⅋⅋
Value	★★★★⯪
Grapes	merlot; cabernet sauvignon; shiraz
Region	Hunter Valley, NSW
Cellar	🍾 3
Alc./Vol.	13.0%
RRP	$23.00

Brokenwood Graveyard Vineyard

Winemaker Iain Riggs usually speaks softly and carries a big basket press. In the case of this wine he said, 'The Graveyard Shiraz has the stamp of terroir – it is the Hunter Valley'. He's absolutely right.
Previous outstanding vintages: '83, '85, '86, '88, '89, '90, '91, '93, '94, '95

CURRENT RELEASE 1996 The wine has the generosity that results when the weather has been kind. The nose has spice, vanilla and cherry aromas. The palate offers layers of flavour, including dark cherry, chocolate, earth and briar. These are supported by some lifted oak on a relatively gentle finish. It's very drinkable – try it with a rack of lamb with a mustard crust.

Quality	⅋⅋⅋⅋⅋
Value	★★★⯪
Grapes	shiraz
Region	Hunter Valley, NSW
Cellar	🍾 5
Alc./Vol.	13.0%
RRP	$50.00 (cellar door)

Brokenwood Shiraz

Iain Riggs, the winemaker at Brokenwood, is one of the superstars in the Australian winemaking firmament. He can take a bow.

CURRENT RELEASE 1996 The nose is rich and redolent of plums. The full-bodied palate has rich berry flavours and attractive spice, and the wood has been skilfully blended with the fruit flavours. There's plenty of grip and mouth-cleansing tannin. It will cellar well, and it cries out for a rare rump steak and horseradish sauce.

Quality	⅋⅋⅋⅋⅋
Value	★★★★⯪
Grapes	shiraz
Region	McLaren Vale, SA; Hunter Valley, NSW
Cellar	🍾 6
Alc./Vol.	13.5%
RRP	$26.00

Brokenwood Shiraz Rayner Vineyard

Quality	♀♀♀♀¿
Value	★★★¿
Grapes	shiraz
Region	McLaren Vale, SA
Cellar	╏ 7
Alc./Vol.	13.5%
RRP	$40.00 (cellar door)

The Rayner vineyard is located in McLaren Vale. The site at Blewitt Springs is 50 years old and the wine is available through cellar door or by mail order.
Previous outstanding vintages: '94
CURRENT RELEASE 1996   Great colour – deep, dark and lustrous. The nose is rich with a ripe plum and berry aroma. There's also loads of spice. The palate is medium- to full-bodied, with rich plum and raspberry fruit flavours. The finish shows off charred-oak characters and a persistent grip. It will cellar well and is great with an old-fashioned roast beef and Yorkshire pud.

Brookland Valley Merlot

Quality	♀♀♀♀¿
Value	★★★★¿
Grapes	merlot
Region	Margaret River, WA
Cellar	╏ 5
Alc./Vol.	14.3%
RRP	$19.00

This is now part of the BRL Hardy group. The marketing has stepped up a couple of notches, so you'll be hearing more about this label in future.
CURRENT RELEASE 1995   The nose has a spicy mixture of rosewater, cloves and a hint of earth. The palate is full-bodied with sweet cherry and berry flavours, which are interlinked with some discreet oak. The finish has soft fine-grained tannins and admirable length. Try it with rabbit stew.

Brown Brothers Barbera

Quality	♀♀♀
Value	★★★
Grapes	barbera
Region	King Valley, Vic.
Cellar	╏ 2
Alc./Vol.	13.0%
RRP	$15.15

Since the late 1960s Brown Brothers have maintained a healthy interest in diverse grape varieties. Some of the experiments have been more successful than others.
CURRENT RELEASE 1995   This is the first commercial vintage. It's in a light style with a slightly feral nose. The palate is light, with soft raspberry flavours that are tinged with tartness. There's acid and soft tannin on the finish. It drinks well with pasta.

Brown Brothers Everton

Proof positive that the Brown Brothers are not slaves to single-variety wines. This is a red fruit salad designed for early drinking at an affordable price.
CURRENT RELEASE 1996 The wine is quite stylish, with aromas of blackberry and hints of licorice. The palate is a mixture of flavours, including blackberry, redcurrant and a whisper of chocolate. There are soft tannins on a gentle finish. It drinks well now with spicy Sichuan duck.

Quality	♥♥♥♥
Value	★★★★
Grapes	cabernet sauvignon 39%; merlot 27%; shiraz 18%; malbec 9%; cabernet franc 7%
Region	North East Vic. & King Valley, Vic.
Cellar	▮ 2
Alc./Vol.	13.0%
RRP	$13.50

Brown Brothers Family Reserve Cabernet Sauvignon

The Family Reserve label is used for wine that is deemed to be near full-bottle development. As you would expect, you have to pay for the privilege.
CURRENT RELEASE 1991 The nose has obvious developed fruit aromas plus cedar and mint. The palate is a mellow mixture of cherry and redcurrant flavours with hints of chocolate. This is framed by some fine-grained tannins on a gentle finish. It's near the peak of development, so drink sooner rather than later. Try it with rare roast beef.

Quality	♥♥♥♥
Value	★★★
Grapes	cabernet sauvignon
Region	King Valley, Vic.
Cellar	▮ 2
Alc./Vol.	13.5%
RRP	$45.50

Brown Brothers King Valley Cabernet Sauvignon

The King Valley was originally a centre for growing tobacco and hops. The former is decidedly out of fashion, and the latter has migrated to Tasmania. Usher in the vines.
CURRENT RELEASE 1992 The nose is a pleasant mixture of cedar and mint aromas. The middleweight palate has sweet redcurrant fruit flavours and there are dusty oak sensations on the dry and astringent finish. It has obvious bottle development and drinks well now. Try it with lasagna.

Quality	♥♥♥
Value	★★★
Grapes	cabernet sauvignon
Region	King Valley, Vic.
Cellar	▮ 3
Alc./Vol.	13.0%
RRP	$36.85

Brown Brothers Merlot

Quality	♔♔♔
Value	★★★
Grapes	merlot
Region	King Valley, Vic.
Cellar	🍷 3
Alc./Vol.	13.5%
RRP	$18.50

This is a relatively new addition to the BB varietal arsenal. This is a good but not memorable wine, like many other single-variety examples in the marketplace.
CURRENT RELEASE 1996 The nose has a strong perfume with a hint of mint and redcurrant. The palate is medium-weight with cherry-ripe flavours, and there are discreet tannins on a supple finish. It's a drink-now style; try it with BBQ spare ribs.

Brown Brothers Tarrango

Quality	♔♔♔
Value	★★♔
Grapes	tarrango
Region	North East Vic.
Cellar	🍷 1
Alc./Vol.	12.5%
RRP	$11.90

This is a hybrid variety invented by the CSIRO to cope with warm climates. A quaffable style that makes for an affordable luncheon wine.
CURRENT RELEASE 1997   Vibrant colour, but the nose is not convincing. There's a strong vulcanised aroma that is quite offputting. The palate saves the day with ripe berry flavours and zesty acid on the finish. It can be served well-chilled and it goes with a salad niçoise.

BV Cabernets

Quality	♔♔♔
Value	★★★♔
Grapes	cabernet sauvignon; cabernet franc
Region	Bickley Valley, WA
Cellar	🍷 2
Alc./Vol.	13.5%
RRP	$16.50

Talk about French labels playing things close to their chest – this one's minimalist. Deduction says BV [sic] is short for the Bickley Valley in Western Australia.
CURRENT RELEASE 1996   The wine is a charmer with softness as the watchword. It's ready to go with a berry-laden nose. The palate is soft and uncomplicated. There are cherries and redcurrant flavours, and the tannin on the finish is soft. A good pasta-style wine.

Cambewarra Estate Chambourcin

This wine comes sealed with a synthetic cork. Judging by the neon purple colour, it does a good job of keeping the air out. Made at Tamburlaine.

CURRENT RELEASE 1997 It's a mystery why chambourcin is regularly priced over $20 – in this case, way over. The wine is very raw and unready. It has a meaty macerated smell, and the palate is acidic, rather thin and lacks both extract and fruit sweetness. A light-bodied, gamy wine with an unbelievably intense purple colour that stains the glass.

Quality	�♥♥
Value	★★
Grapes	chambourcin
Region	Shoalhaven, NSW
Cellar	➥ 1–3+
Alc./Vol.	12.8%
RRP	$28.00

Campbells The Barkly Durif

The old name of Rutherglen was apparently Barkly. A traditional name for a traditional wine. There's no other region in this country that is aligned with this obscure grape. Maker Colin Campbell.

CURRENT RELEASE 1995 This is just about port without being fortified! The dominant theme is raisins, almost like a liqueur muscat. Controlled oak allows prune-juice and raspberry-conserve smells to float from the glass. It tastes big and raunchy and a bit unsubtle. Despite the alcohol and raisin fruit, it lacks good dry red structure. Hard to know what to serve this with, but slow-braised venison is worth a go.

Quality	♥♥♥♥
Value	★★★
Grapes	durif
Region	Rutherglen, Vic.
Cellar	↑ 6+
Alc./Vol.	14.8%
RRP	$32.00

Canobolas-Smith Alchemy

One look at the label and the name alchemy makes sense: there's something mystical and magical happening in the vats chez Smith.

Previous outstanding vintages: '94

CURRENT RELEASE 1995 The colour is a full purple–red, and green sappy aromas abound. There's a touch of fennel-root, and stalky herbal flavours entwine with riper berry hints. The oak is very much in the background. The structure is tight and firm-ish, and it could repay some cellaring. Then serve with aged parmesan cheese.

Quality	♥♥♥♥
Value	★★★★
Grapes	cabernet sauvignon; cabernet franc; merlot
Region	Orange, NSW
Cellar	➥ 1–5+
Alc./Vol.	14.0%
RRP	$22.00 (cellar door)

Capel Vale Kinnaird Shiraz

Quality	♥♥♥♪
Value	★★↣
Grapes	shiraz
Region	Lower Great Southern, WA
Cellar	▮ 4
Alc./Vol.	12.5%
RRP	$48.00

This holds the record for the heaviest wine bottle we've ever dropped on our toe. We'd hate to unload a truck of the stuff. Makers Rob Bowen and Krister Jonsson fined it with free-range eggs!

CURRENT RELEASE 1996 Typical Mount Barker vegetal, herbal shiraz characters come to the fore in this new prestige selection. It shows some early development in a forward colour and earthy mellow characters, and it lacks a little in freshness. The profile is lean, with drying tannins and unusual, somewhat feral, herb–spice nuances. It has a slight spritz in the mouth. Goes with lamb medallions.

Capel Vale Merlot

Quality	♥♥♥♪
Value	★★↣
Grapes	merlot
Region	South-west Coastal Plain, WA
Cellar	▮ 3
Alc./Vol.	13.0%
RRP	$22.00

This sixth release of Capel Vale merlot was made from grapes grown at Capel. Maker Rob Bowen.

CURRENT RELEASE 1996   A pretty wine. The colour is medium red–purple and there are scents of strawberry, raspberry, fresh earth and a suggestion of leaves. The fruit is light-bodied and lean, soft but without a lot of concentration. It's ready to drink. Try it with veal.

Cape Mentelle Shiraz

Quality	♥♥♥♪
Value	★★★
Grapes	shiraz
Region	Margaret River, WA
Cellar	▮ 5
Alc./Vol.	14.0%
RRP	$24.00 ▮

Put this alongside the '95 version and you'd scarcely believe they came from the same producer: they're like chalk and cheese. That's seasonal variation, we guess.

Previous outstanding vintages: '86, '88, '90, '91, '93, '94, '95

CURRENT RELEASE 1996   This is a wild child, full of naughty smells and cheek. There are gamy, smoked herb, meaty characters that may reflect lees-contact or even a touch of sulfide. The palate is concentrated, fleshy and smooth with good firm tannins, plenty of power, fruit sweetness and length. It drinks beautifully already. One for fans of the feral. Try it with steak and kidney pie.

Cape Mentelle Trinders Cabernet Merlot

The Trinders vineyard is named after a school and a road in the vicinity of the main Cape Mentelle vineyard and winery on Wallcliffe Road, Margaret River. Maker John Durham.

Previous outstanding vintages: '94, '95

CURRENT RELEASE 1996 A tight, slightly austere wine with a cassis/blackberry nose and a slight burnt character on the finish. Plenty of fruit depth and concentration here ending in a firm tannin grip. A solid wine that could age well. Food: aged rump steak.

Quality	♀♀♀♀
Value	★★★ʀ
Grapes	cabernet sauvignon; merlot
Region	Margaret River, WA
Cellar	⬤ 1–10+
Alc./Vol.	14.5%
RRP	$21.35

Cape Mentelle Zinfandel

Zinfandel is a rare variety in Australia although it's prolific in California where it's the traditional workhorse. Makers John Durham and David Hohnen.

Previous outstanding vintages: '81, '82, '84, '88, '90, '91, '92, '93, '94, '95

CURRENT RELEASE 1996 Whacko: 16 per cent alcohol, and it doesn't show. All that means is the fruit and extract are so rich that it's all in amazingly good balance. The colour is like ink, and the nose is full of licorice, plum-jam, cherry and herb scents. The taste is massively deep and concentrated, with chocolate and aniseed joining in the chorus. It has enormous fruit sweetness and extraordinary length. A great zin. Should improve in the cellar and live till eternity – if you can keep your mitts off it. Food: steak and kidney pie.

Quality	♀♀♀♀♀
Value	★★★★ʀ
Grapes	zinfandel
Region	Margaret River, WA
Cellar	⬤ 10+
Alc./Vol.	16.0%
RRP	$30.00

Cassegrain Cabernet Merlot

Quality	♟♟♟
Value	★★★
Grapes	cabernet sauvignon; merlot
Region	Hastings Valley, NSW
Cellar	🍷 3
Alc./Vol.	12.9%
RRP	$18.90

The Cassegrain family, with typical Gallic bloody-mindedness, have pioneered the Port Macquarie area's 20th-century reawakening. Makers John Cassegrain and Glenn Goodall.

CURRENT RELEASE 1996   A light-bodied quaffer that some may find (as the label blurb says) a good antidote to the jammy monsters from warmer regions. A mild wine that will sit happily with many lighter foods. Try it with veal scaloppine.

Cassegrain Reserve Chambourcin

Quality	♟♟♟
Value	★★↟
Grapes	chambourcin
Region	Hastings Valley, NSW
Cellar	🍷 2
Alc./Vol.	13.2%
RRP	$23.60 🆅

The vines that produce this wine are grown biodynamically. That means no herbicides, pesticides, artificial fertilisers or fungicides – apart from copper and lime.

CURRENT RELEASE 1996   This has an unusually light colour for a chambourcin and smells oddly cheesy. There's an estery banana overtone as well. It's quite acidic, and it lacks fruit-sweetness, although it has much better palate structure than most chambourcins. Try it with vitello tonnato.

Castle Rock Pinot Noir

Quality	♟♟♟↟
Value	★★★
Grapes	pinot noir
Region	Great Southern, WA
Cellar	🍷 2
Alc./Vol.	13.0%
RRP	$18.40

Pinot from this region has turned a few heads in the past. Could Castle Rock be emerging as a pretender? The style is an improver.

CURRENT RELEASE 1996   The oak tends to dominate the fruit, with toasty and walnut-oil aromas. It simplifies the flavour and adds a note of hardness. It's a decent wine otherwise, and just needs some fine-tuning. Serve it with egg and bacon pie.

Chain of Ponds Novello Rosso

Few make a real effort with rosé in Australia, but when it's well done it can be a delight.

CURRENT RELEASE 1997 Vibrant young purple–red colour; cherry/plum and slightly herbal aromas with boiled-lolly overtones. Nice – and unusual too. The flavour is light, soft and dry, and it's easy to quaff. It has plenty of character, plus a little richness. *Bella* with antipasto.

Quality	🍷🍷🍷🍷
Value	★★★★
Grapes	grenache; sangiovese
Region	Adelaide Hills, SA
Cellar	2
Alc./Vol.	13.0%
RRP	$13.95

Chapel Hill Cabernet Sauvignon

Pam Dunsford reckons Coonawarra produces good cabernet in the warmer years, and McLaren Vale produces good cabernet in the cooler years. Hence, she blends the two.

Previous outstanding vintages: '88, '90, '91, '92, '95

CURRENT RELEASE 1996 A textbook cabernet: no green notes, no overt oakiness, no excessive alcohol, just layers of sweet ripe blackcurrant, cherry and blackberry flavour with a touch of spice. The palate has superb flavour and balance, smooth tannins and good length. Simply, sinfully, delicious. Goes great guns with Cheong Liew's pork hocks.

Quality	🍷🍷🍷🍷🍷
Value	★★★★½
Grapes	cabernet sauvignon
Region	McLaren Vale, SA 70%; Coonawarra, SA 30%
Cellar	1–15
Alc./Vol.	13.0%
RRP	$23.00

Chapel Hill Shiraz

Pam Dunsford is an ace when it comes to full-bodied reds. She has a state-of-the-art new winery in which to practise her perfectionism.

Previous outstanding vintages: '90, '94, '95

CURRENT RELEASE 1996 This is a baby that needs time, but it promises much. Spicy and oaky aromas mingle with a twist of black pepper. It's chunky and intense, with good viscosity and high extract. The oak is apparent but not overdone, and the tannins are persuasive on the finish. Cellar, then serve with beef casserole.

Quality	🍷🍷🍷🍷🍷
Value	★★★★
Grapes	shiraz
Region	McLaren Vale, SA
Cellar	2–12+
Alc./Vol.	13.5%
RRP	$25.50

Charles Melton Cabernet Sauvignon

Quality	♟♟♟♟
Value	★★★★
Grapes	cabernet sauvignon
Region	Barossa Valley, SA
Cellar	➥ 4–10+
Alc./Vol.	15.0%
RRP	$24.00 ▯

Never mind the ginormous alcohol: this is good stuff. Just use with care and apply sparingly. Maker Graham 'Charlie' Melton.

CURRENT RELEASE 1996 This is just a babe and deserves to do time in a dark place. The colour is deep, and the nose has sweet raspberry fruit plus herbal, leafy varietal nuances. The palate is biggish and strong with a firm tannin handshake. It comes alive in the mouth and the aftertaste lingers on and on. Top potential, and it's nice to see a young Barossa cab that isn't over-burdened with timber.

Charles Melton Nine Popes

Quality	♟♟♟♟
Value	★★★✦
Grapes	grenache; shiraz; mourvèdre
Region	Barossa Valley, SA
Cellar	▯ 6
Alc./Vol.	14.5%
RRP	$28.00 ▯

This is recorded more for curiosity's sake than anything, as it sold out long ago. A benchmark style that started the headlong rush to market 'GSM' blends. Maker Graham 'Charlie' Melton.

Previous outstanding vintages: '90, '91, '92, '93, '94, '95

CURRENT RELEASE 1996 Not the powerhouse some vintages have been, but a very smooth, rich, savoury red, which owes more to the old world than the new. Earthy, undergrowth, vaguely minty and toasty oak aromas; excellent concentration of mellowing, wood-matured rather than overtly oaky flavours; all backed with ripe, persistent tannins. Try it with oxtail stew.

Charles Melton Rose of Virginia

Most Australian rosés these days are much bigger wines than the classic French styles, with darker colour and more weight. It tallies with our obsession for bigness in all wine styles. Maker Graham 'Charlie' Melton.

CURRENT RELEASE 1998   A fuller style of rosé and con)sistently one of the best around. Medium–light purple–red colour, and a slightly stalky herbal grenache nose, that opens with aeration to reveal strawberries. A fuller-bodied rosé with a little well-judged sweetness. It's soft, fruity and eminently gluggable, but is at its best with food. Try it with antipasto.

Quality	♟♟♟♟
Value	★★★★
Grapes	grenache
Region	Barossa Valley, SA
Cellar	🍾 2
Alc./Vol.	12.5%
RRP	$14.00

Charles Melton Shiraz

Graham 'Charlie' Melton manages to get that extra little something into his reds which sets them apart from the ruck. This is a good example.

Previous outstanding vintages: most of them

CURRENT RELEASE 1995   Wonderful stuff: makes you want to burst into song (even if you're tone deaf, like one of the authors). Has already started to develop gamy, meaty, undergrowth nuances, and the bouquet really comes up in the glass. Great intensity on a tight-packed structure that's beautifully balanced, savoury and tannic for long keeping. Drinks well with venison stew.

Quality	♟♟♟♟♟
Value	★★★★
Grapes	shiraz
Region	Barossa Valley, SA
Cellar	🍾 10+
Alc./Vol.	14.0%
RRP	$28.00 🍾

CURRENT RELEASE 1996   Essence of Barossa shiraz: plum-pudding aromas mixed with coconut, mint and anise. Rich and very ripe, it's full-bodied but very smooth, with power and length. Masses of fruit uphold the tannin-oak balance. A rewarding drink, to go with beef and demiglaze.

Quality	♟♟♟♟♟
Value	★★★★
Grapes	shiraz
Region	Barossa Valley, SA
Cellar	🍾 10+
Alc./Vol.	14.0%
RRP	$28.00 🍾

Chateau Tahbilk Shiraz

Quality	♟♟♟
Value	★★★
Grapes	shiraz
Region	Goulburn Valley, Vic.
Cellar	🍷 5
Alc./Vol.	12.0%
RRP	$18.00 Ⓢ 🍷

Nostalgia reigns at Tahbilk: the red-wine style is quite old-fashioned, and that's no criticism. The Purbricks eschew fashion, and the wines have a distinctive style that resists the modern trend towards same-ishness. *Previous outstanding vintages: '71, '76, '80, '82, '85, '86, '90, '92, '93, '94*
CURRENT RELEASE 1995   The colour is fairly light and shows some development; the bouquet shows meaty shiraz fruit and some older wood characters. The palate has dusty, meaty and herbal flavours, and the finish has modest persistence. It's all about mellow fruit and isn't for oak-lovers. Would go well with rissoles.

Clarendon Hills Merlot

Quality	♟♟♟
Value	★★
Grapes	merlot
Region	McLaren Vale, SA
Cellar	➡ 2+
Alc./Vol.	14.0%
RRP	$120.00 🍷

Roman Bratasiuk has succeeded in capturing the attention of Robert Parker and numerous other fans by charging outrageous prices for his first releases. But the wines don't always stand up to close inspection.
CURRENT RELEASE 1996   The nose is all oak – albeit very smart French oak. There's a hint of talcum powder and some attractive flavour in the mouth, but it's overwhelmingly a wood flavour. The structure is tight and firm, closing with swatches of oak tannin. At least there's none of the greenness that besets so many Oz merlots. Extended breathing recommended; cellaring advised.

Cloudy Bay Pinot Noir

Quality	♟♟♟♟
Value	★★★
Grapes	pinot noir
Region	Marlborough, NZ
Cellar	🍷 4
Alc./Vol.	13.5%
RRP	$30.00

The first pinot from Cloudy Bay, where Kevin Judd et al. seem to excel at everything they attempt.
CURRENT RELEASE 1996   Tastes like a high-alcohol style: the nose is fumey and laden with brandied cherry (almost jammy), woodsy smells. It has a mouthfilling quality with a spirity warmth, lots of fruit and flavour, and high tannins. Not a wine of particular charm, but big and generous. Try it with roast duck.

Cobaw Ridge Shiraz

Is there a shiraz that's grown in a chillier spot than this? Cobaw is high (600 metres) in the Macedon Ranges. Maker Alan Cooper.

CURRENT RELEASE 1996 Nineteen-ninety-six was an ungenerous year in southern Victoria, and you'd have to like cold-climate shiraz to go for this. It has a peppery, dusty greenness and there's a lot of acid, which is accentuated by the leanness of the palate. It's light-bodied and a tad meagre, but the palate does have length and it goes much better with food than without. Try it with peppered salami.

Quality	♟♟♟
Value	★★★
Grapes	shiraz
Region	Macedon Ranges, Vic.
Cellar	▮ 4
Alc./Vol.	12.5%
RRP	$26.25

Cockfighters Ghost Pinot Noir

There's a link in ownership between the Hunter Valley's Poole's Rock and Pemberton's Smithbrook vineyards. Hence this brand straddles two disparate viticultural worlds. This one's made by John Wade.

CURRENT RELEASE 1996 A very decent pinot despite a slight volatile lift. Sweet strawberry fruit aromas and some cooked, hot-ferment characters add an extra dimension. It's medium-bodied, and has satisfying weight and palate texture. Could even improve with more age. Serve it with rare beef and wild mushrooms.

Quality	♟♟♟♟
Value	★★★★
Grapes	pinot noir
Region	Pemberton, WA 66%; Great Southern, WA 34%
Cellar	▮ 4
Alc./Vol.	13.6%
RRP	$20.70

Coldstream Hills Briarston

This is the early-drinking cabernet style from Coldstream, as opposed to the Reserve Cabernet Sauvignon. It's a quickly growing brand in what is one of the Yarra's fastest-growing wineries.

CURRENT RELEASE 1996 An attractively aromatic red, smelling leafy, herbal, dusty and berryish, and medium-bodied on the palate. It has a lively astringency and a touch of austerity that may be due to the uncooperative year, although it has an undeniable touch of class. Drink with veal cutlets.

Quality	♟♟♟♟
Value	★★★
Grapes	cabernet sauvignon; merlot; cabernet franc
Region	Yarra Valley, Vic.
Cellar	➥ 6+
Alc./Vol.	13.0%
RRP	$24.85

Coldstream Hills Pinot Noir

Quality	ŸŸŸŸ̈
Value	★★★⸀
Grapes	pinot noir
Region	Yarra Valley, Vic.
Cellar	🍷 3
Alc./Vol.	13.5%
RRP	$24.85 Ⓢ

The 1997 Yarra vintage was dry, warm and low-yielding, and the pinots may yet be judged superior to the excellent '96s. Makers James Halliday and Phil Dowell.
Previous outstanding vintages: '91, '92, '94, '96
CURRENT RELEASE 1997   This is a very attractive up-front, medium- to lighter-bodied pinot, which has delicious flavour and just lacks the power of the better '97 Yarra pinots. The colour is full purple–red; the aromas are of cherry fruit and spicy oak with a meaty, gamy, varietal character creeping in. There's tannin and richness, and the palate is smooth and very enjoyable now – with steak tartare.

Coldstream Hills Reserve Pinot Noir

Quality	ŸŸŸŸ̈
Value	★★★⸀
Grapes	pinot noir
Region	Yarra Valley, Vic.
Cellar	⊷ 1–5
Alc./Vol.	13.5%
RRP	$41.00

The vines in the suntrap bowl below the winery regularly provide the base material for this flagship wine. Makers Phil Dowell and James Halliday.
Previous outstanding vintages: '87, '88, '91, '92, '94
CURRENT RELEASE 1996   As usual, this shows quite marked oak influence as a youngster. The colour is a full red–purple, and there are stalk and oak aromas. The flavours are undeveloped, and there's good tannin grip which doesn't quite hide an attractive fruit sweetness. A well-structured pinot, but it needs time. Come back to it next year, and enjoy it with chargrilled quail.

Cowra Estate Cabernet Rosé

Quality	ŸŸŸŸ
Value	★★★★
Grapes	cabernet sauvignon
Region	Cowra, NSW
Cellar	🍷 1
Alc./Vol.	12.0%
RRP	$13.50 Ⓢ

Cowra Estate's head honcho, John Geber, never backward in coming forward, reckons rosé is the style of wine for this country and we should all be drinking his. Maker Simon Gilbert.
CURRENT RELEASE 1997   Spring/summer time is rosé time, sipping it chilled in an al fresco restaurant or at home on the deck amid the birds and bees. Light purple–red, this one has lollyish raspberry fruit aromas with hints of bubblegum and vanilla. It's light, soft and fruity to taste with just a little sweetness, but it ends dry. Easy to quaff with cold meats and salads.

Cowra Estate Classic Bat Cabernet Merlot

Proprietor John Geber is a cricket fanatic, hence the commemorative series of labels he's begun. This one features Victor Trumper.
CURRENT RELEASE 1996 A cabernet-based red of serious weight and extract. It has a deep red–purple colour and an oily appearance. The nose has concentrated dusty berry, earthy and oaky scents, and the cabernet berries come through again in the mouth. It's not a simple berry-fruit style; it's savoury and developed. The tannins have a slightly green edge. Try with lamb's fry and bacon.

Quality	♟♟♟❓
Value	★★★¼
Grapes	cabernet sauvignon; merlot
Region	Cowra, NSW
Cellar	➟ 1–5
Alc./Vol.	13.0%
RRP	$14.80

Cowra Estate Classic Bat Pinot Noir

How would the ghost of Victor Trumper feel if he knew he was selling wine these days? This is the first of a collection of cricket hero labels.
CURRENT RELEASE 1997   This is what the pundits call a dry-reddish pinot; in other words it's an acceptable red wine but has little pinot character. It has a relatively dark colour, and too much oak. Some cherry and stalk flavours come through, but the oak wins the battle, adding some hardness to the finish. Try it with crown roast of hare.

Quality	♟♟♟
Value	★★★
Grapes	pinot noir
Region	Cowra, NSW
Cellar	▮ 2
Alc./Vol.	12.5%
RRP	$15.75

Cranswick Estate Vignette Cabernet Merlot

A vignette is a fragment of grapevine with tendrils, leaves and bunches, as used in literature and the visual arts. Nice name. Maker Ian Hongell.
CURRENT RELEASE 1996   This is quite a gutsy red for the Riverina. It's an oak-driven style that has oily and sawn-timber aromas. It has respectable bodyweight and grippy, oaky tannins. The palate is gutsy and slightly hard. It goes better with food: try rissoles.

Quality	♟♟♟
Value	★★★
Grapes	cabernet sauvignon; merlot
Region	Riverina, NSW
Cellar	▮ 3
Alc./Vol.	12.5%
RRP	$12.00 Ⓢ

Crofters Cabernet Merlot

Quality	♀♀♀♀℔
Value	★★★★
Grapes	cabernet sauvignon; merlot
Region	Great Southern, WA
Cellar	➡ 1–10+
Alc./Vol.	14.0%
RRP	$21.65 Ⓢ 🍾

In a somewhat puzzling move, this red is on a higher plane than the Crofters whites – and the prices reflect it. Maker Paul Lapsley.

CURRENT RELEASE 1996   The only problem here is its youth. It's a slightly raw wine, the oak fairly evident and the palate sharp-edged with slightly hard fruit. It has a lively acid/tannin palate that gives an astringent finish and aftertaste, and it's packed with flavour and potential. Cellar it, then serve with steak diane.

Cullen Cabernet Sauvignon Merlot

Quality	♀♀♀♀♀
Value	★★★★★
Grapes	cabernet sauvignon 75%; merlot 20%; cabernet franc 5%
Region	Margaret River, WA
Cellar	➡ 3–15
Alc./Vol.	13.5%
RRP	$55.00 🍾

The vines are now 25 years old, and the back-label tells us they are dry-grown and low-yielding. Cullen's is a true estate winery where no compromises are made in the quest for quality. Maker Vanya Cullen.

Previous outstanding vintages: '84, '86, '90, '91, '92, '93, '94, '95

CURRENT RELEASE 1996   **Impressively dark purple–red colour with massive fruit concentration throughout. Signs of slow ageing point to a great future for this strapping red. It has marvellous fruit depth and optimal ripeness – not the slightest hint of green-leafy Margaret River character or under-ripeness. It's a sensational wine that will be much better when it peaks, in about a decade.**

PENGUIN BEST RED WINE

Dalry Road Cabernet Franc

Quality	♀♀♀℔
Value	★★★
Grapes	cabernet franc
Region	Yarra Valley, Vic.
Cellar	🍷 1
Alc./Vol.	13.5%
RRP	$15.00

This is the second label for Eyton on Yarra. It was minted to encompass fresh drink-now styles.

CURRENT RELEASE 1996   The colour is light ruby and the nose has fresh raspberry and rose-petal aromas. The palate is soft and fruity, with sweet cherry and strawberry flavours. These are followed by clean acid and minimalist oak. It drinks well and could use a little chill on a hot day. Serve with a pasta dish with a meat sauce.

d'Arenberg Red Ochre

The ochre from McLaren Vale was used as paint pigment for London pillar postboxes and buses. The wine is a fighting brand from d'Arenberg.
CURRENT RELEASE 1996   It has a brick-red colour and the nose is fruity with raspberry aromas. The palate is medium-bodied with sweet raspberry fruit and this is balanced by some soft tannins on a gentle finish. A good quaffing style that goes well with homemade baked beans.

Quality	♟♟♟
Value	★★★
Grapes	grenache 82%; shiraz 18%
Region	McLaren Vale, SA
Cellar	♙ 2
Alc./Vol.	14.0%
RRP	$9.90

d'Arenberg The Custodian Grenache

Only a third of this wine was aged in wood, and it was old wood, so it's very much the grape you're tasting. Maker Chester Osborn.
CURRENT RELEASE 1996   **This has a typical d'Arenberg nose: meaty, earthy, floral, spicy and very complex. It's a generous mouthful of warm, cuddly McLaren Vale flavour, with better fruit concentration and extract than most of its peers, due no doubt to very low yields. Strong tannin gives a mouth-puckering effect, and for that reason it's better with food than without. A heady drop that would wrestle with a hearty cassoulet.**

Quality	♟♟♟♟♟
Value	★★★★▶
Grapes	grenache
Region	McLaren Vale, SA
Cellar	➟ 1–10+
Alc./Vol.	14.5%
RRP	$21.35 ♟

PENGUIN BEST RED BLEND/ OTHER VARIETY

d'Arenberg The Footbolt Old Vine Shiraz

Give a marketing man his head and you're sure to get a lot of romantic and sometimes confusing names. This used to be simply Old Vine Shiraz.
CURRENT RELEASE 1996   The nose is spicy and there are hints of plums and pepper. The medium to full-bodied palate has hints of earth and iron tonic. The major flavours are raspberry and plum. The tannins on the finish fit well, making for a balanced wine with an attractive grip. Have it with spicy meatloaf.

Quality	♟♟♟♟♟
Value	★★★★
Grapes	shiraz
Region	McLaren Vale, SA
Cellar	➟ 2–6
Alc./Vol.	14.0%
RRP	$15.50

d'Arenberg The High Trellis Cabernet Sauvignon

Quality	♟♟♟⟨
Value	★★★⟨
Grapes	cabernet sauvignon
Region	McLaren Vale, SA
Cellar	➥ 2–6
Alc./Vol.	13.5%
RRP	$15.50

High Trellis is one of the original Osborn plots (the Osborn family started d'Arenberg) and the grapes are well above the ground. Maker Chester Osborn.

CURRENT RELEASE 1996   This is a feisty young wine bristling with stroppy tannins. The nose has strong berry aromas with hints of earth and licorice. The palate is medium to full-bodied with sweet raspberry and red-currant flavours. The tannins flood in like the ride of the Valkyrie, heavy and Wagnerian. Try it with smoked duck.

d'Arenberg The Peppermint Paddock Chambourcin

Quality	♟♟♟
Value	★★⟨
Grapes	chambourcin
Region	McLaren Vale, SA
Cellar	♟ 2
Alc./Vol.	14.0%
RRP	$15.50

Have d'Arenberg been looking over Brown Brothers' back fence and joined a varietal push? This variety is a French hybrid that resists downy and powdery mildew.

CURRENT RELEASE 1996   The wine has a grubby, earthy nose but the palate comes clean with lean berry flavours. There's plenty of clean acid on a dry finish. It drinks now and would be okay with chilli con carne.

d'Arenberg The Twenty-eight Road Mourvèdre

Quality	♟♟♟♟
Value	★★★★
Grapes	mourvèdre
Region	McLaren Vale, SA
Cellar	♟ 3
Alc./Vol.	14.0%
RRP	$15.00

Mataro by any other name, this is part of the growing trend to reinvent old styles. This wine won a gold medal at the Cairns wine show. Wonder what won the rum class?

CURRENT RELEASE 1996   The nose has strong berry aromas and a mineral and earth smell. The palate is full-bodied with a silky mouthfilling texture. There are strong berry flavours and distinctive blood plum flavours which are balanced by a warmth of acid and some attractive drying tannins. It's delightfully different, and cries out for a dish of rich devilled kidneys.

Deakin Estate Shiraz

The label was designed as a fighting brand and the original advertising was light-hearted, suggesting you should drink rather than think. Whatever – the wines are good value for money.

CURRENT RELEASE 1997 Good, deep colour and the nose offers a mixture of plum and spice aromas. The palate is medium-bodied with some rich cherry and plum flavours which are matched by soft tannins on a gentle finish. It drinks well now and goes well with bangers and mash.

Quality	🍷🍷🍷½
Value	★★★★
Grapes	shiraz
Region	Murray Valley, Vic.
Cellar	2
Alc./Vol.	13.5%
RRP	$9.95

De Bortoli Melba Barrel Select

This is the top of the De Bortoli red-wine tree. It's a very limited release blended from selected barrels. It seems De Bortoli has entered the 'Super Wine League'.

CURRENT RELEASE 1993 A complex wine with rich fruit flavours and plenty of tannin. The nose is a mixture of berries and wood, and the full-bodied palate is rich and complex. Although it has bottle-age, it gives the impression that there's far to go. There's considerable tannin grip on the long finish. Decant for best results. Try it with mushroom risotto.

Quality	🍷🍷🍷🍷½
Value	★★★
Grapes	cabernet sauvignon; shiraz; cabernet franc
Region	Yarra Valley, Vic.
Cellar	6
Alc./Vol.	13.0%
RRP	$56.00

De Bortoli Windy Peak Cabernet Shiraz Merlot

This is the fighting brand from the De Borts stable. It always represents value for money.

CURRENT RELEASE 1996 The nose has leaf, tobacco and berry aromas. The medium-bodied palate has sweet raspberry and cherry flavours, and these are adorned with some dusty oak on a soft finish that makes it easy to quaff. Try it with a designer pizza.

Quality	🍷🍷🍷½
Value	★★★½
Grapes	cabernet sauvignon; shiraz; merlot
Region	King & Yarra Valleys, Vic.
Cellar	3
Alc./Vol.	12.5%
RRP	$16.00

De Bortoli Windy Peak Pinot Noir

Quality	♟♟♟↿
Value	★★★↾
Grapes	pinot noir
Region	various, Vic.
Cellar	♦ 3
Alc./Vol.	12.5%
RRP	$16.00

They put a lot of winemaking effort into this drop. Barrel fermentation, minimal filtration etc. The result is a very perky wine.

CURRENT RELEASE 1997   The colour is a bright ruby and the nose is loaded with cherry and toasty oak aromas. The palate is medium-bodied with up-front fruit flavours and there are gentle tannins on the finish. It drinks well now with a chargrilled tuna.

De Bortoli Yarra Valley Cabernet Sauvignon

Quality	♟♟♟♟↿
Value	★★★★
Grapes	cabernet sauvignon
Region	Yarra Valley, Vic.
Cellar	♦ 5
Alc./Vol.	13.5%
RRP	$28.00

This is a very elegant style from the Dixon's Creek sub-region of the Yarra Valley. The team at De Bortoli are really hitting their straps.

CURRENT RELEASE 1995   The nose has blackberry, cigar-box and oak aromas. The palate is medium- to full-bodied with the emphasis on blackberry fruit flavours. The oak fits like the proverbial glove, giving a balanced tannin grip on the finish. It goes well with smoked kangaroo.

Quality	♟♟♟♟
Value	★★★↾
Grapes	cabernet sauvignon
Region	Yarra Valley, Vic.
Cellar	♦ 5
Alc./Vol.	13.0%
RRP	$29.00

CURRENT RELEASE 1996   About as cabernet as it gets – the nose is an exotic mix of berries, cigar-box and green leaf. The middleweight palate has intense cassis flavour and there's a shadow of cinnamon spice. The oak has been carefully handled, adding a savoury character and there are fine-grained tannins and medium grip. It needs time, but goes well with beef wellington.

De Bortoli Yarra Valley Pinot Noir

First, the bad news. MS has been up to his neck in this stuff – literally. He fell in when filming a video. The good news is, the wine wasn't ruined (alcohol kills germs). The wine was good enough to be the best pinot in last year's *Guide*.

CURRENT RELEASE 1996   This is an attractive and very drinkable wine (in spite of its handicaps). The nose has cherry, sap and smoke aromas. The medium to full-bodied palate is rich with dark cherry flavours with a hint of game. The oak is supportive rather than intrusive. It drinks very well now and is perfect for an exotic mushroom risotto – don't hold back on the morels.

Quality	?????
Value	★★★★
Grapes	pinot noir
Region	Yarra Valley, Vic.
Cellar	4
Alc./Vol.	13.0%
RRP	$29.00

CURRENT RELEASE 1997   Shows every sign of being the equal or better of the '96, but needs time. Closed, earth and undergrowth aromas, plenty of weight and assertive tannins. Cellar, then serve with pigeon pie.

Quality	?????
Value	★★★★
Grapes	pinot noir
Region	Yarra Valley, Vic
Cellar	1–5
Alc./Vol.	13.5%
RRP	$29.00

De Bortoli Yarra Valley Shiraz

Bless the De Borts: they're going from strength to strength. They picked up the much-touted Jimmy Watson Trophy last year, and the revamped restaurant in the Yarra Valley is winning great acclaim. Maker Steve 'Wally' Webber.

Previous outstanding vintages: '94

CURRENT RELEASE 1995   A tidy wine with a voluminous nose: there are loads of blackberry and cherry aromas, and notes of spice. The medium-bodied palate has blackberry flavours mixed with pepper–spice. There's well-integrated oak on a neat finish, with well-mannered tannin. It could handle an eye fillet with a reduction sauce.

Quality	????
Value	★★★★
Grapes	shiraz
Region	Yarra Valley, Vic.
Cellar	4
Alc./Vol.	13.0%
RRP	$30.00

Devil's Lair Margaret River

Quality	♟♟♟♟
Value	★★★★
Grapes	cabernet sauvignon; merlot; cabernet franc
Region	Margaret River, WA
Cellar	▮ 6
Alc./Vol.	14.0%
RRP	$28.00

The label refers to the fossils found in the district, but this is hardly a fossilised winery. It's actually a modern winery started by the bloke who also started the boutique brewing movement in Australia. Phil Sexton sold the brewery to Fosters and the winery to Southcorp. What's his next project?

CURRENT RELEASE 1995 A robust and stylish wine with a deep red–purple colour. The nose has blackberry and smoky-wood aromas. The palate is full-bodied and already quite complex with blackberry and cherry flavours. The oak is solid and supplies bracing tannins on a lingering finish. It should develop well. Serve with Peking duck.

Devil's Lair Pinot Noir

Quality	♟♟♟♟
Value	★★★★
Grapes	pinot noir
Region	Margaret River, WA
Cellar	▮ 6
Alc./Vol.	14.0%
RRP	$29.00

Margaret River and pinot noir are not common currency, but this is an interesting example that seems to suggest there should be more of this variety in the region.

CURRENT RELEASE 1996 The colour is a bright cherry-red, and the nose has strawberry and cherry aromas with a slight hint of earth. The medium- to full-bodied palate has cherry flavours and a touch of green stalks. The finish is long with just a hint of bitterness, but this is balanced by a warmth of alcohol. Have it with mushroom risotto.

Dromana Estate Pinot Noir

According to MS, this capricious grape variety has a rather precious reputation on the Mornington Peninsula. It's good to find a wine of substance. Maker Garry Crittenden.
CURRENT RELEASE 1997   The wine is succulent and satisfying. There are tobacco and coffee aromas underscored by ripe fruit. The palate is mouthfilling and sweet, with ripe fruit flavours dominated by cherry and adorned with some earthy truffle flavours. The finish has acid and dry tannins on the finish. It goes well with devilled kidneys.

Quality	♥♥♥♥?
Value	★★★★
Grapes	pinot noir
Region	Mornington Peninsula, Vic.
Cellar	↑ 5
Alc./Vol.	13.5%
RRP	$28.00

Elderton Cabernet Sauvignon

Elderton was the middle name of Samuel Tolley, a member of the ubiquitous Tolley winemaking family, who was the vineyard's first owner.
Previous outstanding vintages: '94
CURRENT RELEASE 1996   The cork was deeply soaked by wine – not a good sign for ageing. A gutsy, rather extractive style which shows the Elderton hallmark of generous vanillan oak over blackberry, ripe cabernet fruit. The finish is aggressive with acid and tannin, and it needs time. Serve with rabbit pie.

Quality	♥♥♥?
Value	★★★
Grapes	cabernet sauvignon
Region	Barossa Valley, SA
Cellar	➡ 1–5+
Alc./Vol.	14.0%
RRP	$21.30 Ⓢ ▮

Elderton Command Shiraz

'Your wish is our command', so rang the sales pitch of the late Neil Ashmead. The company is run today by Lorraine Ashmead, and the wines are made at Peter Lehmann.
CURRENT RELEASE 1994   Perhaps the best vintage yet for this Barossa blockbuster. It shows some development in colour and nose. A very complex bouquet of rich sweet plum, cherry and toasty oak is reflected on the palate. It's oaky, but not excessively so. Finishes with great length and a warmth from alcohol. A good match for gourmet hamburgers.

Quality	♥♥♥♥?
Value	★★★★
Grapes	shiraz
Region	Barossa Valley, SA
Cellar	↑ 8+
Alc./Vol.	14.0%
RRP	$41.00 ▮

Elderton Merlot

Quality	♥♥♥⁊
Value	★★⋆
Grapes	merlot
Region	Barossa Valley, SA
Cellar	▮ 4
Alc./Vol.	14.0%
RRP	$31.20 ▮

Elderton has survived the crisis precipitated by the sudden death of co-founder Neil Ashmead, and has settled back into stride with his widow Lorraine at the helm.

CURRENT RELEASE 1996   Why do wine producers get a rush of blood to the head when setting merlot prices? This is typical Elderton in its dominant vanillan, toasty oak nose, and rich fleshy chocolate/vanilla palate flavour. Oak-reliant, but a decent drink. Try it with braised beef.

Elderton Shiraz

Quality	♥♥♥⁊
Value	★★★
Grapes	shiraz
Region	Barossa Valley, SA
Cellar	➟ 2–8
Alc./Vol.	14.5%
RRP	$21.30 ▮

The wine world was saddened by the passing of Neil Ashmead in 1997, who did so much to establish a high profile for this marque.

Previous outstanding vintages: '86, '88, '90, '91, '92, '94

CURRENT RELEASE 1996   A gutsy, slightly extractive Barossa shiraz, which has tremendous colour and an alarmingly minty/herbal nose. In the mouth it's somewhat thick and rough, with stalky tannins that turn bitter on the end-palate. It needs time, and its ultimate quality is obscure. Marinated buffalo fillet would suit.

Evans & Tate Barrique 61 Cabernet Merlot

Quality	♥♥♥
Value	★★★
Grapes	cabernet sauvignon; merlot
Region	Pemberton, Margaret River & other, WA
Cellar	▮ 4
Alc./Vol.	13.0%
RRP	$19.60 Ⓢ

This is E & T's QDR, or quaffing dry red. It's about 30 per cent Margaret River.

Previous outstanding vintages: '95

CURRENT RELEASE 1996   Sweet American oak lends a floral, pretty note to the nose, and it's fairly light in weight and lean in profile. A decent ready-drinking red, without a great deal of richness. Sweet oak lends a major helping hand. Serve it with meatballs.

Evans & Tate Cabernet Sauvignon

There have been few '95 reds from this region that haven't hit our tender spot. Watch for the '96, too: it looked like a ripper in the tank.

CURRENT RELEASE 1995 A big, brawny, powerhouse of a cabernet with a roasted, toasted nose that recalls chestnuts and hazelnuts. The fruit aromas are subdued, buried deep in the wine, and they need time to reveal themselves. In the mouth it has impressive extract and tannin grip. Liberal oak has been skilfully applied. It's a brooding giant, to cellar or serve with aged cheeses.

Quality	🍷🍷🍷🍷½
Value	★★★★
Grapes	cabernet sauvignon
Region	Margaret River, WA
Cellar	2–8
Alc./Vol.	13.0%
RRP	$30.00

Evans & Tate Gnangara Shiraz

This used to be regarded as an everyday-drinking red. That was before the price topped $18. Maker Brian Fletcher.

CURRENT RELEASE 1996 The nose is shy and retiring. There are earthy, vanilla hints and the wine is pretty light in every regard. There's pleasant flavour and balance, and it's ready to drink without further ado. It would suit pasta with salsicce.

Quality	🍷🍷🍷
Value	★★½
Grapes	shiraz
Region	various, WA
Cellar	2
Alc./Vol.	13.0%
RRP	$18.40

Evans & Tate Margaret River Merlot

Brian Fletcher is a dedicated winemaker, and he plays the big-kids' game. His reds are built with weight and structure.

CURRENT RELEASE 1995 This is a serious attempt to make a merlot with guts and structure. Generous helpings of wood have been employed in the process. The colour is deep and the aromas are of dusty, oaky developed characters, together with ripe berry and leafy overtones. Vanillan oak is evident on the palate, where the wine is decidedly savoury and drying, with some acid/tannin astringency that needs time to soften. Try it with venison sausages.

Quality	🍷🍷🍷🍷½
Value	★★★½
Grapes	merlot
Region	Margaret River, WA
Cellar	1–6+
Alc./Vol.	13.0%
RRP	$30.00

Evans & Tate Margaret River Shiraz

Quality	🍷🍷🍷🍷
Value	★★★
Grapes	shiraz
Region	Margaret River, WA
Cellar	➡ 2–6+
Alc./Vol.	13.0%
RRP	$30.00 🍸

This is an estate-grown wine – from E & T's Redbrook vineyard in the Willyabrup sub-region. Maker Brian Fletcher.

Previous outstanding vintages: '86, '88, '90, '91, '92, '93, '94

CURRENT RELEASE 1995   This is a big red, fashioned around lots of oak. The nose is spicy with shiraz fruit but also with layers of toasty oak and earthy, possibly barrel-ferment, characters. There's a hint of tar, and it's tight, firm, oaky and unready on the palate. Cellar, then drink with aged hard cheeses.

Eyton Cabernets

Quality	🍷🍷🍷◗
Value	★★★
Grapes	cabernet sauvignon; cabernet franc; merlot
Region	Yarra Valley, Vic.
Cellar	🍸 5
Alc./Vol.	12.8%
RRP	$19.00

Eyton is a modern complex on the Maroondah Highway, which incorporates a restaurant and a tower with a good view of the vineyards. Maker Matt Aldridge.

CURRENT RELEASE 1995   Quite an oaky wine, which smells of spices, cherry and toasted wood. The palate opens with smoky oak notes and savoury flavours, finishing with fresh acid. More than just simple fruit, but the acid level seems high. It needs food: try it with lamb kebabs.

Eyton Pinot Noir

Quality	🍷🍷🍷
Value	★★★
Grapes	pinot noir
Region	Yarra Valley, Vic.
Cellar	🍸 2
Alc./Vol.	13.0%
RRP	$19.70

Eyton on Yarra is not a boat race, but a winery. The year 1996 wasn't great in southern Victoria, and there's a lot of greenness in some of the wines. Maker Matt Aldridge.

CURRENT RELEASE 1996   This has a medium–light colour and smells very green and stalky. The palate is hollow and austere with a lack of warmth and sweetness. It needs food. It should go with lamb cutlets and pesto sauce.

Fiddlers Creek Cabernet Shiraz

This is a soft drinkable style that won't break the bank. The fiddlers were gold-mining prospectors trying to strike it rich.
CURRENT RELEASE 1996   The nose has a whiff of spice with sweet berry aromas. The medium-weight palate has sweet berry flavours, mainly cherry and raspberry, and there's a light dusting of oak on the finish. It's a drink-now style and it's right with pasta.

Quality	♟♟♟♟
Value	★★★⊁
Grapes	cabernet sauvignon; shiraz
Region	Pyrenees, Vic.
Cellar	↓ 2
Alc./Vol.	12.0%
RRP	$9.95

Fire Gully Pinot Noir

This is the second label of blue-chip Margaret River winery, Pierro. The wines are made from bought-in grapes. Maker Dr Mike Peterkin.
CURRENT RELEASE 1996   This has good depth of red–purple colour, and a shy meaty pinot aroma that opens up to reveal nicely ripened scents of brandied cherry with a faint whiff of stalks. Clean and fresh, it has a mara-schino cherry taste, and the fruit more than balances some fine-grained tannins. Goes well with roast pheasant.

Quality	♟♟♟♟
Value	★★★★
Grapes	pinot noir
Region	Margaret River, WA
Cellar	↓ 4+
Alc./Vol.	14.0%
RRP	$16.40

Flanagan's Ridge Cabernet Sauvignon

This is a new label for the Mildara Blass group. It comes from a new vineyard in the Koppamurra region north of Coonawarra. Given the nature of the vintage, it's a very promising debut. Maker David O'Leary.
CURRENT RELEASE 1995   The nose has strong red-currant aromas on a background of tobacco leaves. The palate is medium-bodied with rich, sweet blackberry fruit flavours that are followed by dry dusty tannins on a lingering finish. Try it with pink lamb chops.

Quality	♟♟♟♟
Value	★★★★
Grapes	cabernet sauvignon
Region	Koppamurra, SA
Cellar	↓ 4
Alc./Vol.	12.5%
RRP	$20.00 (restaurants only)

Fox Creek JSM Shiraz Cabernets

Quality	🍷🍷🍷🍷
Value	★★★★
Grapes	shiraz; cabernet sauvignon; cabernet franc
Region	McLaren Vale, SA
Cellar	▮ 5
Alc./Vol.	14.0%
RRP	$18.40

J.S.M. are the initials of an early McLaren Vale pioneer, James Stanley Malpas, who established Roseworthy College in 1873. Maker Sparky Marquis.

CURRENT RELEASE 1996   This is very well made, with an interesting zest for life. The nose has berry and spice aromas. The palate is already complex, with strong cherry and cassis flavours and lashings of spice. The wood adds another dimension, and the fine-grained tannins give some extra zing on a grippy finish. It has plenty of potential and needs a hearty beef casserole to set it off.

Garden Gully Shiraz

Quality	🍷🍷🍷🍷
Value	★★★★
Grapes	shiraz
Region	Grampians, Vic.
Cellar	▮ 4
Alc./Vol.	13.0%
RRP	$18.00 (cellar door) ▮

This vineyard, beside the Western Highway between Ararat and Great Western, was first planted in 1952. Former Great Western winemakers Warren Randall (Manning Park) and Brian Fletcher (Evans & Tate) own it and supervise the winemaking.

CURRENT RELEASE 1994   This is a boots-and-all red for those who like traditional gutsy flavours and aren't fussed about elegance. There's a wintergreen/eucalypt touch, and the tannins are grainy, persistent and a tad domineering. Try it with a mixed grill.

Geoff Merrill Cabernet Merlot

Quality	🍷🍷🍷
Value	★★★
Grapes	cabernet sauvignon; merlot; cabernet franc
Region	McLaren Vale & Coonawarra, SA; Goulburn Valley, Vic.
Cellar	▮ 2
Alc./Vol.	13.0%
RRP	$18.00 $

Geoff Merrill is taking a lower profile than he used to. The reason? He sells most of his wine offshore and spends a lot of time flitting around the world.

CURRENT RELEASE 1995   Typical of the maker, the colour is of a lighter shade and the wine is smooth and easy on the palate. The nose is strong on vanilla, and toasty oak flavours reappear in the mouth. The body is light to medium, and it would drink well with veal scaloppine.

Geoff Merrill Shiraz

Geoff Merrill's Stratmer Wine Co. has vineyards at McLaren Vale and Coonawarra. Mount Hurtle is his volume brand and Geoff Merrill the premium label. Chief winemaker is Goe DiFabio.

CURRENT RELEASE 1994   This is different for McLaren Vale. It has some restraint – it's not a 'let's-go-for-the-jugular' style. The colour is medium red–purple, and the nose offers dusty, meaty, plum aromas. The palate is tight and rustic with good flavour, grip and length. It drinks well now, with gourmet bangers.

Quality	♟♟♟♟
Value	★★★★
Grapes	shiraz
Region	McLaren Vale, SA
Cellar	▮ 4
Alc./Vol.	13.5%
RRP	$18.00

Geographe Grand One Cabernet Merlot

This is the flagship red of the Vincorp group, headed up by ex-Virgin Hills winemaker Mark Sheppard in Kyneton, Victoria.

CURRENT RELEASE 1996   Smells and tastes like a cold-climate central Victorian. The colour is only medium intensity, and the nose has a rank vegetal character that hints at tomato and ketchup. The palate has concomitant hollowness, and finishes with an unbalanced tannin grip.

Quality	♟♟♟
Value	★★
Grapes	cabernet sauvignon; merlot
Region	Central Victoria
Cellar	▮ 2
Alc./Vol.	12.0%
RRP	$32.65 ▮

Geographe Red One Shiraz

The subscript is 'classic dry red', but what does that really mean? This company has a Red One, a White One and a Grand One. Did they get the idea from De-Bortoli's Noble One?

CURRENT RELEASE 1997   It's just a babe, but was obviously designed as a light-bodied, low-tannin, early-drinking red. The colour is lightish, and the aroma presents red fruits, herbs and green tinges. In the mouth it's simple, light and raspberry-like. Quaff with spaghetti marinara.

Quality	♟♟♟
Value	★★★
Grapes	shiraz
Region	not stated
Cellar	▮ 2
Alc./Vol.	12.5%
RRP	$15.00

Giesen Canterbury Reserve Pinot Noir

Quality	🍷🍷🍷🍷🍷
Value	★★★★
Grapes	pinot noir
Region	Canterbury, NZ
Cellar	🍷 5+
Alc./Vol.	13.5%
RRP	$41.00

Marcel Giesen's winery is in the cool Canterbury region of the South Island. He sources grapes from Marlborough for some wines. Maker Rudi Bauer.
CURRENT RELEASE 1996   The colour shows some early development, and the nose features a fabulous perfume of sweet cherry, vanilla and 'forest floor'. A wine of tremendous charm, it doesn't rely on oak or stalk character. The structure is impressive, with lovely fruit sweetness plus a well-judged tannin grip. Superb now, but should improve in the short term. Serve with Peking duck.

Gilberts Shiraz

Quality	🍷🍷🍷🍷
Value	★★★
Grapes	shiraz
Region	Great Southern, WA
Cellar	➤ 1–6+
Alc./Vol.	13.0%
RRP	$21.00 🍷

This is a tiny 5-hectare vineyard at Mount Barker, so the wines are inevitably hard to find. The wines are contract-made at Plantagenet and the quality is always good.
CURRENT RELEASE 1995   The colour is vivid purple–red and the nose is a bracingly youthful rush of cherry, spice and coconutty oak. There's good concentration, although the oak and tannins are a little assertive. It will be better in a year or so. Then serve with barbecued hamburgers.

Glaetzer Bishop Shiraz

Quality	🍷🍷🍷
Value	★★⊁
Grapes	shiraz
Region	Barossa Valley, SA
Cellar	🍷 5
Alc./Vol.	14.0%
RRP	$25.60

Nothing churchy about this wine: Judith Glaetzer was originally a Bishop. It's the second-string Glaetzer shiraz. Colin Glaetzer was at Barossa Valley Estate for 10 years before they decided to do their own thang.
CURRENT RELEASE 1996   The nose displays slightly unintegrated coconutty oak, and the palate is grippy and somewhat un-together. It may just need a little time to settle down. Serve it with German sausage.

Glaetzer Shiraz

Colin and Judith Glaetzer started their own label in 1996. The wines are made at Barossa Vintners, a new bulk-wine producer in Tanunda where Colin is wine-maker. The shiraz comes from Elmor Roehr's vineyard – he of the original E & E.

CURRENT RELEASE 1996   Mint is a feature of many '96 Barossa shirazes, and this has plenty. It's relatively gently wooded, which is an asset. The wine is a smart debut for the Glaetzers, showing heaps of aroma and satisfying weight of ripe, sweet berry fruit along with supple tannins. Drink with kassler.

Quality	▼▼▼▼
Value	★★★
Grapes	shiraz
Region	Barossa Valley, SA
Cellar	➤ 1–8+
Alc./Vol.	14.0%
RRP	$32.00 ▮

Goundrey Cabernet Merlot

It's so innocent, it's kinda cute. Each label has the words 'A Fine Wine' on the front label. Are people really persuaded by such exhortations?

CURRENT RELEASE 1996   It's a basic cab blend, revealing the lesser material used. The nose has acrid peppery and leafy capsicum characters, and there are Ribena flavours too. The palate is just adequate: lean, light-bodied and somewhat hollow as it shows either young-vine or less-ripe cool-climate origins. Try it with a Big Mac.

Quality	▼▼▼
Value	★★★
Grapes	cabernet sauvignon; merlot
Region	Great Southern, WA
Cellar	▮ 3
Alc./Vol.	13.0%
RRP	$15.60

Goundrey Reserve Cabernet Sauvignon

Jack Bendat is a businessman who bought Goundrey on a whim. But it worked out fine: he caught the wine bug along the way and is now hell-bent on turning it into a large and outstanding producer.

CURRENT RELEASE 1994   This is a rich, chunky wine, which makes much of highly toasted oak. It has good density of flavour, and smooth but ample tannins. It's a satisfying red to drink now, but it promises to improve with ageing. Try it with barbecued, butterflied leg of lamb. ▶

Quality	▼▼▼▼?
Value	★★★▸
Grapes	cabernet sauvignon
Region	Lower Great Southern, WA
Cellar	▮ 8
Alc./Vol.	13.2%
RRP	$23.00 ▮

Quality 🍷🍷🍷🍷🍷
Value ★★★★
Grapes cabernet sauvignon
Region Lower Great Southern, WA
Cellar 10
Alc./Vol. 13.9%
RRP $24.60

CURRENT RELEASE 1995 A powerful, opulent red with aromas of mulberry, blackcurrant and stylish French oak. The palate has generous fruit sweetness, richness and dimension. It has a lovely flavour and structure. It's drinking well already with food, but it has a long future. Serve it with pink venison cutlets.

Goundrey Reserve Shiraz

Quality 🍷🍷🍷🍷½
Value ★★★★
Grapes shiraz
Region Lower Great Southern, WA
Cellar 8+
Alc./Vol. 12.5%
RRP $23.00

The Mount Barker region has thrown up some scrumptious shirazes over the years. Here's another one.
CURRENT RELEASE 1996 The colour is dark blood-red, and the nose has plums and spices. Thankfully the French and American oak is in check. There's also a hint of licorice, and the palate is intense with spicy/berry fruit/oak flavours. Goes well with lamb chops.

Gramps Cabernet Merlot

Quality 🍷🍷🍷
Value ★★★
Grapes cabernet sauvignon; merlot
Region not stated
Cellar 2
Alc./Vol. 13.0%
RRP $15.75 (S)

In days of yore, before the Orlando name was coined, the company was known as Gramps, after the founding family.
CURRENT RELEASE 1995 Not especially cabernet-ish, this wine has deep plummy fruit and sappy oak aromas, and the oak chimes in again on the finish, which is somewhat assertive and green. Drink now, with bangers and mash.

Grant Burge Cameron Vale Cabernet Sauvignon

Quality 🍷🍷🍷½
Value ★★★
Grapes cabernet sauvignon
Region Barossa Valley, SA
Cellar 5
Alc./Vol. 13.5%
RRP $19.70

Grant Burge's cellar-door sales at Rowland Flat is very picturesque, but it doesn't have a winery attached. He makes the wines elsewhere.
CURRENT RELEASE 1996 Sweet, ripe blackberry and blackcurrant aromas show the variety to good effect. There are spicy and jammy aromas too. It's not as rich or long in the mouth as we've come to expect from this brand, but it's a very good drink nonetheless. Serve it with pork sausages.

Grant Burge Filsell Shiraz

Burge's Filsell vineyard is in the Lyndoch area at the southern end of the Barossa. Many of the vines are quite old, and it also supplies much of his Meshach material. CURRENT RELEASE 1996 A rich, ripe-fruity, typical Barossa shiraz, with plenty of coconutty American oak but not nearly as woody as the Meshach. Sweet, chunky, vanillan – it's a lovely smooth drink right now, but it should also cellar well. Drink it with Barossa mettwurst.

Quality	♟♟♟♟♟
Value	★★★★
Grapes	shiraz
Region	Barossa Valley, SA
Cellar	↓ 10+
Alc./Vol.	14.0%
RRP	$19.70

Grant Burge Hillcot Merlot

It's interesting to note that the best merlots produced in Australia so far are from warmer-climate areas where the grapes ripen properly. But the dearest ones are mostly from cooler climates. It doesn't add up. CURRENT RELEASE 1996 Nice wine! It has generous, rich, ripe fruit aromas – sweet and blackberryish. There are lots of legs in the glass, and the palate shows alcohol and glycerol texture. Sweet fruit flavour abounds. It's also a wine with backbone. Drinks well now, with rissoles.

Quality	♟♟♟♟
Value	★★★★
Grapes	merlot
Region	Barossa Valley, SA
Cellar	↓ 4
Alc./Vol.	13.0%
RRP	$18.00

Grant Burge Meshach Shiraz

Meshach William Burge was winemaker Grant Burge's great-grandfather, the one who settled in the Barossa. The price has skyrocketed in recent years, no thanks to shameless ramping by *Winestate* magazine.
Previous outstanding vintages: '88, '90
CURRENT RELEASE 1994 Sumptuous stuff! One of the best Meshachs so far. The bouquet is a riot of plums, mint and spices. It's oaky, but not excessively so, beautifully integrated and smooth. The flavours are marvellously rich, sweet and opulent. It has great concentration and balance. Truly in Grange class. Try it with osso bucco.

Quality	♟♟♟♟♟
Value	★★★
Grapes	shiraz
Region	Barossa Valley, SA
Cellar	⬱ 2–12+
Alc./Vol.	14.0%
RRP	$70.00 ↓

Grant Burge Rubycind

Quality	♔♔♔♔
Value	★★★
Grapes	pinot noir
Region	Barossa Valley, SA
Cellar	▲ 1
Alc./Vol.	13.0%
RRP	$17.25

Nice wine, snappy bottle – pity about the name. This is Burgie's marketing department gone troppo and out to lunch.

CURRENT RELEASE 1997   Perhaps best described as a light Beaujolais style, this is a summer red with the bonus of pinot flavour. It has a medium rosé colour, a nose of cherry skins and pips, and a light simple cherry/strawberry flavour. As a chillable quaffer, it would be better without the touch of acid/tannin astringency on the finish. Best with food: try antipasto.

Grant Burge Shadrach Cabernet Sauvignon

Quality	♔♔♔♔
Value	★★★
Grapes	cabernet sauvignon
Region	Coonawarra & Barossa Valley, SA
Cellar	➥ 1–8+
Alc./Vol.	13.5%
RRP	$41.00 ▮

Meshach, Shadrach and Abednego were the three Jews delivered by God from King Nebuchadnezzar's fiery furnace (or did God's PR department make that one up?). Grant Burge has the first two covered, but the third may be somewhat less marketable.

CURRENT RELEASE 1994   Unusual, but loaded with character. The colour isn't all that deep, but the nose reveals jammy ripe smells and strong minty herbaceous and fruit-cake aromas. It's full-bodied to taste, rich and youthfully astringent; quite tannic and old-fashioned. You need to like minty reds. Try it with roast lamb and mint sauce.

Greenock Creek Cabernet Sauvignon

Quality	♔♔♔♔
Value	★★★
Grapes	cabernet sauvignon
Region	Barossa Valley, SA
Cellar	▲ 3
Alc./Vol.	14.6%
RRP	$28.70 ▮

The Waughs of Greenock Creek believe in getting their grapes super-ripe, hence they're always strong in alcohol. Their vineyard is near Seppeltsfield in one of the warmest parts of the Barossa.

CURRENT RELEASE 1995   Smells of blackberry jam, as a result of overripe fruit. The palate is very fruit-sweet and warming from the alcohol, and it lacks subtlety. Many will love it as a youngster for its exuberant fruit. Not very food-friendly, but try beef with a rich reduction sauce.

Greenock Creek Seven Acre Shiraz

This winery is owned by Michael and Annabelle Waugh, who bought an elderly vineyard in the Greenock district near Seppeltsfield.

Previous outstanding vintages: '94

CURRENT RELEASE 1995   This is a monster, true to the maker's style. It has heaps of alcohol and masses of flavour. The colour is very deep and dark, and it smells like a Christmas pudding! Sweet cherry, plum, raisin and licorice elements all combine in a solid crescendo of flavour and tongue-coating tannin. It's quite astringent now and needs patience. Cellar, then drink it with a hearty beef casserole.

Quality	♟♟♟♟♟
Value	★★★┝
Grapes	shiraz
Region	Barossa Valley, SA
Cellar	➰ 2–10+
Alc./Vol.	14.8%
RRP	$32.80 ▯

The Green Vineyards Cabernets

The philosophy is to make cool-climate wines from fruit from the various Victorian regions and give them minimal handling and filtration.

CURRENT RELEASE 1994   There's no doubting the cool-climate origins. This is a typical medium-bodied cabernet with a strong tobacco and cigar-box aroma on the nose. The major flavour on the palate is redcurrant, and there's a notable amount of natural tannin on the finish. It will drink well with beef olives.

Quality	♟♟♟◗
Value	★★★┝
Grapes	cabernet sauvignon 80%; merlot 20%
Region	Geelong, Vic.
Cellar	▯ 3
Alc./Vol.	13.2%
RRP	$20.00 ▯

The Green Vineyards Port Phillip Pinot (Macedon)

The name says it all, really. The winery is in Upper Beaconsfield, which is south-east of Melbourne overlooking Western Port Bay, and the fruit comes from Macedon in the north-east. How Port Phillip fits in is a moot point. Maker Dr Sergio Carlei.

CURRENT RELEASE 1996   The colour is a mid-brick red and the nose has a sappy component combined with strawberry aromas and a hint of mint. The medium-bodied palate has sweet fruit flavours ranging from strawberry and cherry and there's a hint of stalk character. The finish has dry tannins, thanks to the French oak.

Quality	♟♟♟◗
Value	★★★
Grapes	pinot noir
Region	Macedon, Vic.
Cellar	▯ 3
Alc./Vol.	13.1%
RRP	$19.00 ▯

Grosset Gaia

Quality	🍷🍷🍷🍷🍷
Value	★★★★½
Grapes	cabernet sauvignon 75%; cabernet franc 20%; merlot 5%
Region	Clare Valley, SA
Cellar	2–12+
Alc./Vol.	13.5%
RRP	$39.50

Gaia is the 'earth mother', and if this is her milk, we'd like to adopt her as our honorary mum. Maker Jeffrey Grosset.

Previous outstanding vintages: '90, '91, '92, '93, '94, '95

CURRENT RELEASE 1996 An absolute cracker! The skilled hand of Grosset weaves its spell again. It's a red wine of great concentration and balance, showing nothing out of place; just heaps of sweet ripe fruit, slight toastiness from oak, terrific structure to hold it for long keeping, and marvellous cabernet style. Serve with rare beef.

Grosset Reserve Pinot Noir

Quality	🍷🍷🍷🍷
Value	★★★
Grapes	pinot noir
Region	Adelaide Hills, SA
Cellar	1–4+
Alc./Vol.	13.0%
RRP	$26.00

It's the only Grosset pinot, so why the word Reserve? Maybe it's a reference to the tiny quantity: just 200 cases were produced. It's grown in the Piccadilly Valley.

Previous outstanding vintages: '94, '95

CURRENT RELEASE 1996 There's a greenness to this wine that polarises tasters, some seeing it as unripe and others admiring its aromatic attributes. Whatever the case, there's evidence of whole-bunch fermentation – stalks included – and the nose reminds one of cut capsicums. The profile is lean and somewhat austere, and the finish is quite astringent. Cellar it, then serve with pigeon.

Quality	🍷🍷🍷🍷🍷
Value	★★★½
Grapes	pinot noir
Region	Adelaide Hills, SA
Cellar	1–5+
Alc./Vol.	13.5%
RRP	$49.50

CURRENT RELEASE 1997 A mass of contradictions, this wine. It smells of capsicum and stalks with a lacing of undergrowth, opening up with air to reveal some hints of cherry. It tastes very lively and intense, with spicy and ripe sweet berry flavours and a very persistent finish. A delicious drink, despite the green character, which may be a whole-bunch ferment character that will mellow in time. Try Peking duck.

Hanging Rock Cabernet Sauvignon Merlot

The cabernet sauvignon comes from the King Valley and Bendigo. The merlot was grown at Mount Duneed. Hanging Rock winery was established in 1982.
CURRENT RELEASE 1996   A light leafy style with soft fruit characters. There are green-leaf, tobacco and redcurrant aromas. The palate is light- to medium-bodied with sweet redcurrant flavours, which are matched by some fine-grained tannins on a balanced finish. Bake a beef wellington and enjoy.

Quality	♟♟♟♟
Value	★★★⯪
Grapes	cabernet sauvignon; merlot
Region	Bendigo & Geelong, Vic.
Cellar	◊ 3
Alc./Vol.	12.5%
RRP	$23.00

Hanging Rock Highlands Victoria Pinot Noir

The grapes were grown at Lockwood in the Central Highlands of Victoria. The wine was made at Hanging Rock. Maker John Ellis.
CURRENT RELEASE 1996   The colour is a bright pale crimson. The nose is sappy with some soft strawberry aromas. The lightweight palate has a clean strawberry fruit flavour with a hint of cherry pip. The finish is characterised by fresh acid and gentle grip. It could be served slightly chilled, if you wish, with a tuna salad.

Quality	♟♟♟♟
Value	★★★
Grapes	pinot noir
Region	Central Highlands, Vic.
Cellar	◊ 3
Alc./Vol.	12.5%
RRP	$23.00

Hanging Rock The Jim Jim Merlot

This is the last of a pretty short line. The vines have been grubbed out, and after you've tasted the wine you'll agree it was a wise decision: merlot wasn't meant for the region. It's been replaced with pinot noir.
CURRENT RELEASE 1995   The colour is a deep crimson and the nose has strong raspberry aromas. The palate fails to deliver, being light and thin with strong impressions of unripe fruit. There's high acid on the finish. Drink now with BBQ chops.

Quality	♟♟♟
Value	★★★
Grapes	merlot
Region	Macedon, Vic.
Cellar	◊ 2
Alc./Vol.	12.0%
RRP	$20.00

Hanging Rock Victoria Shiraz

Quality	🍷🍷🍷🍷
Value	★★★★
Grapes	shiraz
Region	Macedon, Vic.
Cellar	2–6
Alc./Vol.	13.5%
RRP	$22.00

In this district the weather is the key factor to the style and health of the wine. This is on the cool-climate margin and a sunny year is needed to get the grapes ripe. Maker John Ellis.

CURRENT RELEASE 1996 A ripe year for once, and the results are very pleasing. It's still obviously a cool-climate wine but there's some flesh on the acid bones. The nose has cherry and plum aromas and there's a waft of black pepper. Dark cherry flavours dominate the palate and there's plenty of acid and drying tannin on the finish. Elegance is the watchword. Try it with a steak and mushroom pie.

Happs Cabernet Merlot

Quality	🍷🍷🍷🍷
Value	★★★½
Grapes	cabernet sauvignon 65%; merlot 35%
Region	Margaret River, WA
Cellar	4
Alc./Vol.	13.8%
RRP	$24.00

Happs have two vineyards, one at Dunsborough and the other at Karridale in the Margaret River region. They were established in 1978 and there's a total of 32 hectares under vines.

CURRENT RELEASE 1996 Great colour: a spectacular bright ruby red greets the eye. The nose is a mixture of mint, cedar and berry aromas. The palate is medium-bodied and the merlot adds berry flavours and flesh to the cabernet's bones. The finish shows drying tannins and a reasonable grip. It drinks well now and would suit roast lamb.

Happs Merlot

Erland Happ is an interesting chap given to writing complicated missives. MS, being a bear of very little brain, is bothered by big words. Quoth the bothered bear, 'Erland, stick to your day job, you do that very well.'

Previous outstanding vintages: '84, '85, '91, '93

CURRENT RELEASE 1995 This is a big, Rubenesque style that has plenty of flesh. The nose is a portent of things to come – it has abundant sweet berry and rose-petal aromas, and a decidedly animal overtone that bothered HH more than MS. The palate is a fruit bomb that explodes in the mouth. It's sweet and silky, with rich redcurrant and cherry flavours. There's subtle oak on the finish; perhaps a little more would add extra structure but the wine is an impressive drink as it stands. Try it with rabbit and mushroom stew.

Quality	♟♟♟♟?
Value	★★★ʳ
Grapes	merlot
Region	Margaret River, WA
Cellar	▮ 4
Alc./Vol.	14.5%
RRP	$33.00

Hardys Bankside Shiraz

Here's one from the 'twilight zone' part of the Hardys portfolio. Where it fits is relatively obscure, but the Bankside cellars on the banks of the Torrens burned down in 1905. Having no location in the portfolio it becomes just another brand.

CURRENT RELEASE 1996 The wine is rich – almost to the point of being sweet. The nose has a strong raspberry aroma. The palate hints at sugar, and there are very ripe berry flavours. These are followed by some soft velvety tannins on a gentle finish. Good with a casserole or stew.

Quality	♟♟♟
Value	★★ʳ
Grapes	shiraz
Region	McLaren Vale, SA
Cellar	▮ 2
Alc./Vol.	12.5%
RRP	$17.00

Hardys Eileen Hardy Shiraz

Quality	♟♟♟♟♟
Value	★★★★
Grapes	shiraz
Region	McLaren Vale & Padthaway, SA
Cellar	⬌ 5–10
Alc./Vol.	14.5%
RRP	$60.00

A Jimmy Watson Memorial Trophy winner and more medals than Stormin' Norman. This label is always reserved for the best red of the year. This is a very attractive wine.
Previous outstanding vintages: '70, '71, '75, '76, '79, '81, '82, '86, '87, '88, '90, '91, '93, '94
CURRENT RELEASE 1995   The nose has strong blackberry aromas and savoury oak smells. The full-bodied palate has a velvety texture and strong blackberry flavour. This is enhanced by a vanilla lift, thanks to the American oak. There's plenty of grip on the long finish and the tannin is very fine-grained. It has far to go and the alcohol is substantial. Try it with a roast saddle of hare.

Hardys Hunter Ridge Shiraz

Quality	♟♟♟♟
Value	★★★★
Grapes	shiraz
Region	Hunter Valley, NSW
Cellar	▮ 3
Alc./Vol.	13.0%
RRP	$14.95

Wouldn't the Hunter Ridge be the Brokenback range? This is BRL Hardys' presence in the Hunter Valley. Stand by for the wine from the new vineyards in the ACT.
CURRENT RELEASE 1997   Fairly typical of the region. The nose has some lifted raspberry aromas and hints of earth and leather. The medium-bodied palate is full of berry flavours and these are matched by some gentle oak on a soft finish. It's easy to drink, and goes well with a humble Irish stew.

Hardys Insignia Cabernet Sauvignon Shiraz

Quality	♟♟♟♟
Value	★★★★
Grapes	cabernet sauvignon; shiraz
Region	not stated
Cellar	▮ 1
Alc./Vol.	13.0%
RRP	$12.95 Ⓢ

Pull on the gloves sluggo, this is a fighting brand. It won't bother the likes of Aussie Joe Bugner but the bank manager will be pleased at the thrifty price.
CURRENT RELEASE 1995   Very drinkable style that has changed little since the last review. The nose has warm, sweet berry aromas. The light palate has raspberry and plum flavours and there's discreet tannin on a soft finish. Quaff it now with some bangers and mash.

Hardys Nottage Hill Cabernet Shiraz

This is a fighting brand made to celebrate Tom Nottage, who spent 60 years before the mast at Hardys' cellars.
CURRENT RELEASE 1997 The wine is soft, light and drinkable. There's a spicy nose with soft fruit aromas. The palate is light with some simple sweet fruit flavours and there's demure oak on a soft finish. Try it with BBQ chump chops.

Quality 🍷🍷🍷
Value ★★★
Grapes cabernet sauvignon; shiraz
Region various, SA
Cellar 🍾 2
Alc./Vol. 13.0%
RRP $8.95

Hardys Padthaway Cabernet Sauvignon

BRL Hardy have a considerable investment in this region, and they have minted a mid-price label.
CURRENT RELEASE 1995 The nose is a mixture of leaf, briar and berry smells. The medium- to full-bodied palate has sweet cassis flavours and tinges of spices. These are matched by some attractive oak and drying tannins on a balanced finish. A style that would suit a beef casserole.

Quality 🍷🍷🍷🍷
Value ★★★★
Grapes cabernet sauvignon
Region Padthaway, SA
Cellar 🍾 4
Alc./Vol. 14.0%
RRP $ 17.95

Hardys Stamps of Australia Shiraz Cabernet Sauvignon

This is a commercial style that was made for drinking rather than thinking. It's not one for collectors.
CURRENT RELEASE 1997 The wine has sweet berry aromas on the nose and the medium-bodied palate carries on the sweetness. The redcurrant flavours are followed by some discreet tannins. It's very drinkable, perfect with a meat pie.

Quality 🍷🍷🍷
Value ★★★
Grapes shiraz; cabernet sauvignon
Region South East Australia
Cellar 🍾 1
Alc./Vol. 12.5%
RRP $12.00

Hardys Thomas Hardy Cabernet Sauvignon

Quality	♟♟♟♟♟
Value	★★★
Grapes	cabernet sauvignon
Region	Coonawarra, SA
Cellar	➥ 3–10
Alc./Vol.	14.0%
RRP	$60.00 🍾

This is the big gun from BRL Hardy. It's an outstanding wine by any measure but the price is daunting. Life is expensive in the fast lane.

Previous outstanding vintages: '89, '90, '91, '92

CURRENT RELEASE 1993   The nose has classic developed cassis aromas and savoury oak. The medium- to full-bodied palate offers ripe blackberry flavour and there are tall timbers on the palate. It is highly tannic and there's abundant grip. It needs time in the cellar and buffalo steaks are the go.

Hardys Tintara Grenache

Quality	♟♟♟♟♟
Value	★★★★⊢
Grapes	grenache
Region	McLaren Vale, SA
Cellar	🍾 6
Alc./Vol.	14.5%
RRP	$23.00

This marks the full revival of this Cinderella variety. The packaging sets it apart, but the contents confirm that grenache is back with gusto.

CURRENT RELEASE 1995   The colour is dense, and the nose has strong raspberry and spicy aromas. The palate is sweet and succulent with rich berry flavours, which are balanced by lively spices on a well-balanced finish. It should cellar, but why bother? It drinks very well now, and is a terrific match with squab casserole.

Hardys Tintara Shiraz

Quality	♟♟♟♟♟
Value	★★★★★
Grapes	shiraz
Region	McLaren Vale, SA
Cellar	🍾 10
Alc./Vol.	14.5%
RRP	$24.00

Great old–new packaging, with a very impressive (and no doubt expensive) bottle. The wine is wonderfully old-fashioned and comforting – a nostalgia trip for those old enough to remember this style and a new adventure for younger wine buffs.

CURRENT RELEASE 1995   The colour is deep and rich. The nose is loaded with ripe fruit aromas from berries and plums. The palate is mouthfilling and silky; it has rich fruit tinged with spice. This is matched by some soft gentle tannins, and there's a warmth of alcohol. It drinks well now, but it can be cellared with confidence. Try it with saltbush mutton. ▸

CURRENT RELEASE 1996 This is keeping the faith as far as the style is concerned. It's a bit brutal at the moment – put it down to the brashness of youth. The nose has loads of spices and peppers. The palate is mouthfilling and slippery. There are sweet berry flavours and slabs of tannin. It is very rich and full-flavoured. It is a steak-and-eggs style with no beg pardons.

Quality	♟♟♟♟?
Value	★★★★
Grapes	shiraz
Region	McLaren Vale, SA
Cellar	➡ 3–10
Alc./Vol.	14.5%
RRP	$25.00

Haselgrove H Reserve Shiraz

This is the top of the line for this maker. The marque has connections with McLaren Vale and Coonawarra. Maker Nick Haselgrove.

CURRENT RELEASE 1996 The nose is dominated by oak. There are charcoal, vanilla and butterscotch aromas. The palate is full-bodied with dark cherry and plum flavours, and these are overshadowed by some high-toned toasty oak. There's also a warmth of alcohol. Will the oak dominance settle with time? We will have to wait and see.

Quality	♟♟♟♟?
Value	★★★★
Grapes	shiraz
Region	McLaren Vale, SA
Cellar	▮ 5
Alc./Vol.	14.0%
RRP	$35.00

Henschke Abbotts Prayer

Your prayers will be answered The elevation of the vineyard is 550 metres, so picking takes place late in the season. In this case the grapes were harvested late in May.
Previous outstanding vintages: '90, '91, '92, '93, '94
CURRENT RELEASE 1995 A divine wine with an abundant nose featuring cedar, cassis, mint and leaf aromas. The palate is rich but elegant; there are strong blackberry flavours with a dusting of spices. Merlot adds some fleshy characters. The finish shows off some well-tailored oak and smoky characters. It should be cellared but try it now if you can't wait with an oxtail stew.

Quality	♟♟♟♟?
Value	★★★↟
Grapes	cabernet sauvignon 52%; merlot 42%; cabernet franc 6%
Region	Lenswood, SA
Cellar	➡ 2–6
Alc./Vol.	13.5%
RRP	$51.00

Henschke Cyril Henschke Cabernet Sauvignon

Quality	♟♟♟♟
Value	★★★
Grapes	cabernet sauvignon; merlot; cabernet franc
Region	Eden Valley, SA
Cellar	➥ 10+
Alc./Vol.	14.0%
RRP	$67.00 ▮

Cyril Henschke was the current winemaker's (Stephen's) father, a distinguished winemaker himself, who died tragically in 1979 whereupon Stephen decided to name a wine after him.

Previous outstanding vintages: '86, '88, '90, '91, '92, '93

CURRENT RELEASE 1994   A somewhat challenging style that has polarised tasters. It has an exaggerated cassis, mulberry and dark-chocolate aroma, almost Ribena-like. The palate has a sweet/acidic effect with some porty overtones and a little hollowness in the middle. A style that has many devotees, but HH has misgivings. Try it with roast leg of lamb.

Henschke Giles Pinot Noir

Quality	♟♟♟♟♟
Value	★★★
Grapes	pinot noir
Region	Lenswood, SA
Cellar	▮ 5
Alc./Vol.	13.5%
RRP	$37.00

This vineyard is the inspiration of Prue Henschke, who's in charge of the viticulture. This region seems eminently suited to pinot noir. Maker Stephen Henschke.

CURRENT RELEASE 1997   A very convincing wine with a deep colour and a cherry, mint and truffle nose. The palate is rich with sweet cherry and plum flavours. There's also some mint flavour. This is balanced by discreet oak, which adds a charred character, and the acid makes a firm contribution. It goes well with quail stuffed with wild rice.

Henschke Hill of Grace

An icon in Australian wine, second only to Grange in stature. The biggest difference is that much less of it is produced. It comes from a single discrete vineyard. Maker Stephen Henschke.

Previous outstanding vintages: '82, '86, '88, '89, '90, '91

CURRENT RELEASE 1992 This has been eked out over two years because of the tiny quantity of '93 to come. It's an extraordinary wine, tremendously complex and now starting to soften nicely with age. The colour is deep, still with a purple tinge, and the nose shows lots of coffee and toasted oak influences with a beguiling earthy undergrowth element. There are echoes of the Rhone Valley in this wine. It's tremendously elegant in the mouth – not a Barossa blockbuster at all. Great wine to serve with aged Reggiano.

Quality	🍷🍷🍷🍷🍷
Value	★★★
Grapes	shiraz
Region	Eden Valley, SA
Cellar	10+
Alc./Vol.	14.1%
RRP	$130.00

Henschke Keyneton Estate

This used to be the poor cousin to Mount Edelstone but can quite often surprise and eclipse its relative. It's no longer at a 'poor relative' price.

Previous outstanding vintages: '82, '84, '86, '90, '92, '93, '94

CURRENT RELEASE 1995 This is lighter than usual when it comes to the weight of fruit. It has a mid-ruby colour, and the nose has strong berry aromas plus some earthy notes. The medium-bodied palate has ripe fruit flavours and a high level of complexity. There are some fine-grained tannins and persistent grip on the finish. It works well with roast lamb and mint sauce.

Quality	🍷🍷🍷🍷½
Value	★★★½
Grapes	shiraz; cabernet sauvignon; merlot
Region	Eden Valley, SA
Cellar	4
Alc./Vol.	13.5%
RRP	$29.00

CURRENT RELEASE 1996 This is a little more elegant than usual with a nose full of ripe berry, leaf and smoky oak. The medium-bodied palate has sweet raspberry and blackberry fruit flavours, and these are matched by some oak which bestows fine-grained tannins, making for a tinder-dry finish. If you drink it now, try it with devilled kidneys.

Quality	🍷🍷🍷🍷½
Value	★★★★
Grapes	shiraz; cabernet sauvignon; merlot
Region	Eden Valley & Barossa Valley, SA
Cellar	4
Alc./Vol.	13.0%
RRP	$33.00

Henschke Mount Edelstone

Quality	♟♟♟♟♟
Value	★★★★
Grapes	shiraz
Region	Eden Valley, SA
Cellar	▮ 10+
Alc./Vol.	14.2%
RRP	$48.00 ▮

Edelstone is more like a hill than a mountain, and Hill of Grace isn't even a hill. Oh well, everything is relative. The wines are certainly worth climbing for.
Previous outstanding vintages: '78, '80, '84, '86, '88, '90, '91, '92, '93
CURRENT RELEASE 1994   One of the best Edelstones in some years, this is a powerhouse, a beautiful drop of shiraz. The nose has meaty, gamy and beef-stock nuances. The palate has powerful flavours of berries, herbs, game and even a hint of spice, plus mouth-puckering tannins and an incredibly long finish. The intense fruit shines through the masses of tannin and it really sings. Yummy stuff to have with beef wellington.

Heritage Cabernet Malbec

Quality	♟♟♟♟
Value	★★★★
Grapes	cabernet sauvignon; merlot
Region	Barossa Valley, SA
Cellar	▮ 3
Alc./Vol.	12.5%
RRP	$14.50

The proprietor is Steve Hoff, aka 'Hoop', a very likeable chap who works for other wine companies on contract and who still finds time to make wine under his own label.
CURRENT RELEASE 1995   Soft and yummy, this wine is very easy to drink. The nose has strong fruity aromas with a hint of raspberry. The palate is medium-bodied and soft, with some juicy berry flavours plus a hint of plum. The wood on the finish adds support, but doesn't intrude. Perfect for your next pasta disaster.

Heritage Cabernet Sauvignon

Quality	♟♟♟♟
Value	★★★★
Grapes	cabernet sauvignon
Region	Barossa Valley, SA
Cellar	▮ 3
Alc./Vol.	13.0%
RRP	$15.95

Steve Hoff is a large chap, almost in the man-mountain league, but for all the size he makes some very elegant wines.
CURRENT RELEASE 1996   This wine is an interesting joust between fruit and oak. The nose has blackberry and toasty wood. The medium-bodied palate has cherry and blackberry flavours but the oak is never far away. There are lots of caramel, vanilla and toast flavours, and the tannins supply a grippy finish. The wine goes well with lamb.

Heritage Shiraz

The Hoff family is a talented bunch: Steve's brother, Jack, is a senior captain flying 747s and Steve's partner is the local GP. Steve also moonlights at Saltram during the night shift.

CURRENT RELEASE 1996 A very soft style with the emphasis on fruit. The nose has ripe plum and vanilla aromas. The palate continues the plum theme and there's a touch of spice. The tannin is benign with a gentle grip. It drinks well now with pasta in a meat sauce.

Quality	🍷🍷🍷½
Value	★★★
Grapes	shiraz
Region	Barossa Valley, SA
Cellar	2
Alc./Vol.	12.5%
RRP	$17.95

Hillstowe Buxton Cabernet Merlot

Buxton Forbes Laurie pioneered viticulture on the Fleurieu Peninsula south of McLaren Vale, South Australia. He planted his first vines in the 1850s. The family is still in the grapegrowing business.

CURRENT RELEASE 1994 The wine has a deep purple colour, and the nose has merlot rose-petal aromas with a hint of undergrowth. The medium-bodied palate has some sweet blackberry fruit flavours. There are black-tea-like tannins on the finish. Have it with steak and kidney.

Quality	🍷🍷🍷🍷
Value	★★★★
Grapes	merlot 55%; cabernet sauvignon 45%
Region	McLaren Vale, SA
Cellar	3
Alc./Vol.	14.0%
RRP	$18.00

Hillstowe Mary's Hundred Shiraz

This wine honours Mary Laurie, South Australia's first registered female vigneron and winemaker. Hillstowe is located in Hahndorf.

CURRENT RELEASE 1996 The wine has a brilliant ruby colour and the nose offers berry, iron and earth smells. The elegant palate has an impressive dark cherry flavour with a hint of chocolate. Black-tea-like tannins at the finish, which is long and lingering. The wine would go well with seared kangaroo fillets.

Quality	🍷🍷🍷🍷
Value	★★★½
Grapes	shiraz
Region	Fleurieu Peninsula, SA
Cellar	8
Alc./Vol.	14.0%
RRP	$32.00

Hillstowe Udy's Mill Pinot Noir

Quality	♟♟♟
Value	★★↾
Grapes	pinot noir
Region	Adelaide Hills, SA
Cellar	▮ 2
Alc./Vol.	13.5%
RRP	$28.00

This is a small 3.2-hectare vineyard in the Adelaide Hills adjacent to Adelaide. The outlet for cellar-door sales is located in Hahndorf. Makers Chris Laurie and Martin Shaw.

CURRENT RELEASE 1995　The wine has a medium brick red colour. The nose is sappy with some stalk aromas. The palate is a little fruit-shy, and the sappy stalk characters dominate the finish. It has plenty of acid. Try it with veal stew.

Hollick Cabernet Sauvignon Merlot

Quality	♟♟♟♟
Value	★★★★
Grapes	cabernet sauvignon; merlot
Region	Coonawarra, SA
Cellar	▮ 3
Alc./Vol.	13.0%
RRP	$18.50

This is the fighting brand in the Hollick stable. It's made for relatively early and easy drinking. Coonawarra via Tuscany (not really!), but there are echoes of Italy in the structure of this wine.

CURRENT RELEASE 1996　The colour is deep ruby and the nose has blackberry and raspberry aromas. The palate is medium-bodied with raspberry fruit flavours and a hint of tartness. This is followed by well-tailored oak and some fine-grained tannins. There's also plenty of acid in evidence. This is a drink-now style that would be good with spaghetti and meatballs.

Hollick Ravenswood

Quality	♟♟♟♟♟
Value	★★★★
Grapes	cabernet sauvignon
Region	Coonawarra, SA
Cellar	➤ 2–8
Alc./Vol.	13.5%
RRP	$51.00

This is the top of the Hollick totem, and it's a wonderful Coonawarra cabernet sauvignon. It's only released when the vintage conditions permit the requisite quality.

CURRENT RELEASE 1994　The nose is full of blackberries and spices. The palate is substantial, with rich blackberry fruit flavours and a mouthfilling texture. The oak is very well integrated, with fine-grained tannins and persistent grip. It's the complete package. A very appealing drink, perfect with roast duck.

Holm Oak Pinot Noir

This is a Tasmanian label that's respected for its red wines. The vineyard was established in 1983, and there are 6 hectares under vine. Maker Nicholas Butler.

CURRENT RELEASE 1995 A light style with a pale red–pink colour. The nose has sweet strawberry aromas, and the palate continues the strawberry theme. It's light- to medium-bodied, and there's strong acid on a long finish. It drinks well now, and could be served chilled if you so desire. Try it with roast pork.

Quality	🍷🍷🍷
Value	★★★
Grapes	pinot noir
Region	Tas.
Cellar	🍾 3
Alc./Vol.	12.5%
RRP	$24.00

Houghton Cabernet Sauvignon

Houghton is the largest winery in Western Australia. It was established in 1836 and the annual production is 300 000 cases per annum. Maker Paul Lapsley.

CURRENT RELEASE 1996 This is about as cabernet as you can get. The nose has capsicum, cassis and smoky wood aromas. The medium-bodied palate doesn't want for flavour: it's intense with cherry and redcurrants, and these are grafted on to some well-tuned oak on a grippy finish. It drinks well now. Try it with smoked lamb chops.

Quality	🍷🍷🍷🍷
Value	★★★★★
Grapes	cabernet sauvignon
Region	various, WA
Cellar	🍾 3
Alc./Vol.	13.0%
RRP	$11.95

Houghton Cygnet

A cygnet is a young swan, and this is an early-picked cabernet sauvignon. But it all falls apart when the grapes don't come from the Swan Valley. Never mind, chill and don't think.

CURRENT RELEASE 1997 This is a rosé by another name, a leafy little number with all the ills that befall juvenile cabernet. It's a pretty pink colour and herbal aromas dominate the nose. The palate is an essay in berry flavours, and there are some clean acid characters on the finish. Chill out and serve it as an afternoon drink.

Quality	🍷🍷🍷
Value	★★★
Grapes	cabernet sauvignon
Region	Frankland River, WA
Cellar	🍾 1
Alc./Vol.	10.0%
RRP	$11.95

Houghton Jack Mann

Quality	♥♥♥♥
Value	★★★
Grapes	cabernet sauvignon; malbec; shiraz
Region	Mount Barker & Frankland River, WA
Cellar	➡ 2–12+
Alc./Vol.	13.5%
RRP	$50.00

Jack Mann was part of Western Australia's wine history. In the process he became a winemaking icon, so it's fitting that the Houghton flagship should bear his name. CURRENT RELEASE 1994   Little change since last year. The nose is almost jammy with some cassis and cedar aromas. The palate is generous, with strong berry flavours that wrestle with substantial tannins, which really give the tastebuds a workout. It needs plenty of time locked away in the cellar. Trot it out with a squab pie with a wholemeal crust.

Houghton Wildflower Ridge Shiraz

Quality	♥♥♥
Value	★★★
Grapes	shiraz
Region	Swan Valley, WA
Cellar	▮ 2
Alc./Vol.	14.0%
RRP	$14.50

This is another commercial label that takes the middle ground in BRL Hardys' portfolio. It was made for early drinking. CURRENT RELEASE 1996   Attractive fruit here: the nose has a pepper and capsicum quality. The palate is medium-bodied with a mixture of ripe cherry and berry flavours, and there's a light dusting of wood that makes the finish dry-cleansing. It's ready to go; try it with pasta and a meat sauce.

Howard Park Cabernet Sauvignon Merlot

Quality	♥♥♥♥
Value	★★★
Grapes	cabernet sauvignon; merlot
Region	Great Southern, WA
Cellar	➡ 3–11
Alc./Vol.	13.5%
RRP	$60.00

This is a rich person's sport: the wine is very classy, but the price seems to go up as the level in the bottle goes down. CURRENT RELEASE 1995   It's a youngster at the moment, with a complex nose. There are wild cherry and raspberry aromas, plus a hint of undergrowth. The palate is tight with blackberry and cassis flavours, and the oak is solidly wedded to the fruit. Purists may quibble at the level of volatile acidity, but it has length and style. It needs time, then serve with devilled kidneys.

Ingoldby Cabernet Sauvignon

There have been Ingoldbys in McLaren Vale since the turn of the century. This company is part of Mildara Blass these days.
CURRENT RELEASE 1996 **This label has proven tremendous value for money in recent times. The colour is a faultless purple–red, and it smells of sweet ripe blackberries and blackcurrants with the oak well under control. The flavour is very elegant and speaks of cabernet sauvignon: sweet ripe berry fruit, beautifully harmonised oak and tannins, and a satisfying aftertaste. Drinks beautifully now and will keep. Serve it with beef bourguignon.**

Quality	ΨΨΨΨ℟
Value	★★★★★
Grapes	cabernet sauvignon
Region	McLaren Vale, SA
Cellar	🍶 10+
Alc./Vol.	13.0%
RRP	$14.80 Ⓢ

Innisfail Pinot Noir

This tiny vineyard and winery are at Batesford, on the Ballarat Road near Geelong. Pinot specialist Gary Farr makes the pinot up till it's had its malolactic, then Ron Griffiths takes it home to his own winery.
CURRENT RELEASE 1996 This reveals its cool-year origins in a peppery, spicy, lightly cherry-fruit aroma. The colour is mid-purple–red, and the palate is firm and tight as a drum. There's some tannin austerity. It could use a little more fruit sweetness, but it's a good effort nonetheless. Serve with mild pork sausages.

Quality	ΨΨΨ℟
Value	★★★
Grapes	pinot noir
Region	Geelong, Vic.
Cellar	🍶 2
Alc./Vol.	13.5%
RRP	$18.00 (cellar door)

Jamiesons Run

This label is ten years old and an outstanding success in terms of brand building. The red begat a chardonnay, and they went overseas to great acclaim. Ever since then, Mildara Blass have been looking for another hit label.
CURRENT RELEASE 1996 Right on track, this is a very drinkable and undemanding style. There are smoky oak aromas and strong berry smells. The middleweight palate has sweet cherry and plum flavours, and there's a hint of vanilla. The finish offers modest grip, making the wine a very enjoyable quaff. Try it with a piece of eye fillet steak.

Quality	ΨΨΨΨ
Value	★★★★
Grapes	cabernet sauvignon;
	shiraz; merlot;
	cabernet franc
Region	Coonawarra, SA
Cellar	🍶 3
Alc./Vol.	13.0%
RRP	$15.00

Jamiesons Run Reserve

Quality	¶¶¶¶
Value	★★★
Grapes	cabernet sauvignon; shiraz
Region	Coonawarra, SA
Cellar	▮ 5
Alc./Vol.	13.0%
RRP	$38.00

Looks like Jamiesons Run had a promotion. There has certainly been a lot of effort spent on the presentation, right down to a specially embossed bottle. Maker the gifted Gavin Hogg.

CURRENT RELEASE 1995   The wine is a remarkable effort for a difficult vintage. There are spice and berry aromas with domineering toasty oak. The medium-bodied palate is elegant with blackberry and plum fruit flavours. Expensive oak has clearly been used, and there are toast and vanilla flavours. The grip is very impressive and it goes well with kangaroo.

Jeanneret Shiraz

Quality	¶¶¶¶
Value	★★★★
Grapes	shiraz
Region	Clare Valley, SA
Cellar	▮ 8+
Alc./Vol.	13.2%
RRP	$18.00 ▮

Ben Jeanneret is one of the newer brigade at Clare, making a promising start with riesling as well as shiraz. The grapes came from Stanley Flat.

CURRENT RELEASE 1996   Herbal, minty aromas pervade, and these are backed up by berry and vanilla flavours. It has a rich and chunky profile, and the tannins are as smooth as silk, although abundant. Plenty of bang for your buck here. Enjoy it with seared kangaroo fillet.

Jim Barry McCrea Wood Shiraz

Quality	¶¶¶¶¶
Value	★★★★
Grapes	shiraz
Region	Clare Valley, SA
Cellar	▮ 4
Alc./Vol.	13.5%
RRP	$43.00

The McCrea Wood was a property originally purchased by Jim Barry. This wine is near the top of the Barry tree. Maker Mark Barry.

CURRENT RELEASE 1995   The colour is an impressive deep mulberry stain, and the nose has a mixture of berries, plums and spices. The palate is rich with sweet plum and dark cherry flavours. Oak adds to the structure and provides grip for the finish. It's a rich style that drinks well with pan-fried kangaroo.

Jindalee Shiraz

The label comes from a company in Geelong but the fruit comes from the Murray Valley.

CURRENT RELEASE 1997 The wine is an old-fashioned style which probably would have been labelled as a 'claret' in days of yore. The nose is dominated by American oak. The palate is light- to medium-bodied with soft raspberry flavours. There's oak dominating the finish. It's very quaffable and probably needs no further bottle age. Try it with spaghetti bolognaise.

Quality	🍷🍷🍷
Value	★★★
Grapes	shiraz
Region	Murray Valley, SA
Cellar	2
Alc./Vol.	13.5%
RRP	$ 13.00

Joadja Vineyards Southern Highlands Berrima Cabernet Malbec

Just as well this isn't a talking book because there would be trouble pronouncing the name of this new vineyard. It started production in 1990.

CURRENT RELEASE 1995 A very minty style with some eccentricities that add to the overall charm. (It won't be everyone's cup of cabernet.) There's a string-eucalypt aroma on the nose, and the medium-bodied palate has dark cherry flavours and hints of mint. The finish shows well-integrated oak. Try it with devilled kidneys.

Quality	🍷🍷🍷½
Value	★★★
Grapes	cabernet sauvignon; malbec
Region	Berrima, NSW
Cellar	4
Alc./Vol.	12.4%
RRP	$18.00

Kangarilla Road Cabernet Sauvignon

This is the former Stevens Cambrai winery. It's now owned by the O'Briens – Kevin O'Brien was head of the Australian Wine Export Council until lately.

CURRENT RELEASE 1996 The nose is slightly edgy, with a minty/eucalyptus note and an earthiness that pervades the wine. The palate is straightforward and rustic and finishes with grippy tannins. Serve with sautéed calf's liver.

Quality	🍷🍷🍷
Value	★★★
Grapes	cabernet sauvignon
Region	McLaren Vale, SA
Cellar	4+
Alc./Vol.	12.3%
RRP	$18.00

Kangaroo Island Vines Florance Cabernet Merlot

Quality 🍷🍷🍷🍷
Value ★★★½
Grapes cabernet sauvignon; merlot
Region Kangaroo Island, SA
Cellar 2–6+
Alc./Vol. 13.0%
RRP $20.50

Kangaroo Island is a large chunk of land off the coast just south of Adelaide. The vineyard is at Cygnet River and was established by the Amadio family of Chain of Ponds.

CURRENT RELEASE 1996 Concentration is the key word here. The colour is dark and blackish, and the nose is dense with latent blackcurrant and oak scents. This bigness and extraction are evident on the palate as well. Hearty, oaky and dense, it has astringent tannin and needs time before broaching. Solid stuff! Try it with casserole.

Katnook Estate Cabernet Sauvignon

Quality 🍷🍷🍷🍷🍷
Value ★★★★
Grapes cabernet sauvignon
Region Coonawarra, SA
Cellar 3–10+
Alc./Vol. 13.5%
RRP $40.00

PENGUIN BEST CABERNET SAUVIGNON

What a year 1996 was for cabernet in Coonawarra. It seems to run in two-year cycles. Witness the fine wines from '86, '88, '90, '94, '96. Maker Wayne Stehbens.

Previous outstanding vintages: '90, '91, '92, '94

CURRENT RELEASE 1996 **Classic Katnook style: heaps of cleverly infused oak flavour and tannin, and dense blackcurrant fruit welded to the smartest French oak. The result is a chunky, concentrated red in ultra-modern style. It's a blinder right now, but will be even better in a few years when the oak will have completely integrated. Try it with venison casserole. NB: The price has risen $10 in one vintage!**

Katnook Estate Merlot

Quality 🍷🍷🍷½
Value ★★½
Grapes merlot
Region Coonawarra, SA
Cellar 4
Alc./Vol. 13.0%
RRP $34.50

We're constantly amazed at the prices people charge for merlot, and can only assume it's because merlot grapes are scarce. Or else it's Petrus envy.

CURRENT RELEASE 1996 This is nothing startling, at least not as eye-bugging as the price. It has a developed mellow leafy mulberry nose, with a hint of gaminess and some blackcurrant. It's fairly light, but has pleasant berryish flavours on a fruit-driven, smooth, ready-drinking structure. Try it with veal boscaiola.

Katnook Estate Odyssey Cabernet Sauvignon

Winemaker Wayne Stehbens is on record as saying he puts this among the world's top 25 cabernets. Phew! Modesty forbids us to comment.

CURRENT RELEASE 1992 Thirty months (count 'em) in new French oak barriques has left its mark on this six-year-old. There's a lot of oak influence, but the wine has swallowed it up beautifully. It has a rich, chunky, chewy texture and real concentration. It's full-bodied, densely knit, smooth and very long, with good ripe tannins. Give it time and it will be terrific. Breathe well, and serve with boeuf bordelais.

Quality	🍷🍷🍷🍷🍷
Value	★★★
Grapes	cabernet sauvignon
Region	Coonawarra, SA
Cellar	2–10+
Alc./Vol.	13.5%
RRP	$75.00

Kingston Estate Merlot

Amazingly, this won a gold medal at the '97 Hobart Show. It's a good wine, but *that* good? Perhaps there wasn't much else in its class.

Previous outstanding vintages: '96

CURRENT RELEASE 1997 Fresh, simple but bell-clear cherry fruit aromas that are clean and cheerful. It's soft and light-bodied, lacking somewhat in structure and intensity, but as a drink-now luncheon red with pasta, it's hard to go past. Drink, don't keep.

Quality	🍷🍷🍷½
Value	★★★★
Grapes	merlot
Region	Murray Valley, SA
Cellar	2
Alc./Vol.	13.0%
RRP	$14.00 (S)

Kingston Estate Reserve Petit Verdot

Winemaker Bill Moularadellis figured that most of the world's petit verdot is grown in places like Bordeaux that are too cold. What it needs is heat, and yes: it does get nice and ripe in the Riverland.

CURRENT RELEASE 1996 This is a bold statement in style and price as well as choice of grape. It's a whopper, pumped up with copious amounts of oak and tannin. The colour has that frightening black tint, and the palate is very dry and grippy. Either drink it with something hearty, like venison, or cellar it – but for how long is anyone's guess.

Quality	🍷🍷🍷🍷½
Value	★★★
Grapes	petit verdot
Region	Murray Valley, SA
Cellar	1–5+
Alc./Vol.	13.5%
RRP	$35.00

Kingston Estate Reserve Shiraz

Quality	♟♟♟♟
Value	★★★
Grapes	shiraz
Region	Murray Valley, SA
Cellar	▭ 1–5+
Alc./Vol.	13.5%
RRP	$30.00 ▯

You can't say the folk at Kingston Estate aren't having a go. They believe in the Riverland, and their expensive Reserves are the dearest things to come out of this poor-relation region.

CURRENT RELEASE 1996   Like the petit verdot, this is a fearsomely tannic drop, rather oaky at this stage and seeming to need time; however, just how bottle-age will affect it is unclear, as it's a pioneering style. Cedary, vanillan, spicy, very dry and somewhat planky. Cellar, then serve with a mild chilli con carne.

Knappstein Cabernet Merlot

Quality	♟♟♟♟
Value	★★★★
Grapes	cabernet sauvignon; merlot
Region	Clare Valley, SA 75%; Adelaide Hills 25%, SA
Cellar	▮ 7
Alc./Vol.	13.0%
RRP	$21.30 ▯

Andrew Hardy has added his own stamp to the Knapp-stein wines ever since he was promoted to the job of winemaker from his *alma mater*, Petaluma.

CURRENT RELEASE 1996   This contains some Adelaide Hills fruit, but where does all that mint come from? A real Peppermint Pattie, but much more than that – fine French oak and berry fruit perfumes, real elegance and subtle tannins adding just the right amount of grip. Fresh and clean, with potential to improve. Food: beef stroganoff.

Knappstein Enterprise Cabernet Sauvignon

Quality	♟♟♟
Value	★★★
Grapes	cabernet sauvignon
Region	Clare Valley, SA 86%; Adelaide Hills, SA 14%
Cellar	▭ 2–10
Alc./Vol.	13.0%
RRP	$29.90 ▯

With the new lease of life given to this winery by the Petaluma ownership and Andrew Hardy as winemaker, they've resurrected the old Enterprise name for the flag-ship reds.

CURRENT RELEASE 1995   This is a big, bold, butch, typical Clare style with hints of gumleaf/mint and herbal fruit, older oak aromas and a fairly astringent finish. The acid pokes through a bit. Give it time, then serve with pan-fried calves' liver.

Knappstein Enterprise Shiraz

The lovely old stone building in the heart of Clare where
Tim Knappstein founded the winery that bears his name
was once a brewery – the Enterprise brewery. Maker
Andrew 'The Ox' Hardy.
CURRENT RELEASE 1995 This limited (1100-case)
bottling was all aged (unusually) in French oak. It's a
dark and brooding monster: a big, rich, strongly
built, old-fashioned style with lots of oak, tannin and
guts. It smells like creosote and is swingeingly astringent.
It benefits from extended breathing. Cellar! Then have
it with a juicy steak.

Quality	🍷🍷🍷🍷?
Value	★★★⸶
Grapes	shiraz
Region	Clare Valley, SA
Cellar	5–10+
Alc./Vol.	14.5%
RRP	$29.90

Krondorf Family Reserve Cabernet Sauvignon

Who are they kidding? There's no family associated with
Krondorf. Another example of marketers inventing
history as they go along.
CURRENT RELEASE 1995 A tight and slightly austere
low-alcohol style, with a modicum of elegance to it. It
has subdued toasty-oak and blackcurrant fruit aromas,
and is taut, tense and firm in the mouth. It's still a
reserved youngster and needs time. Goes well with beef
olives.

Quality	🍷🍷🍷🍷
Value	★★★⸶
Grapes	cabernet sauvignon
Region	various, SA
Cellar	2–6+
Alc./Vol.	12.0%
RRP	$17.60 Ⓢ

Kumeu River Merlot Cabernet

Mike Brajkovich was the first Kiwi to pass the Master
of Wine exam, which just means he passed an exam set
by Poms. His more important qualification is that after
three years' study he graduated dux of oenology at Roseworthy Agricultural College, but does anyone ever
mention that?
CURRENT RELEASE 1996 A heavily worked middleweight red that avoids the green characters prevalent in
New Zealand reds. Instead, it has savoury secondary
characters of walnut, earth, toasty oak and spices. It has
a gamy, slightly rustic style, and the finish is very dry.
It has a lot of oxidative (as opposed to fruity) characters.
Goes well with braised beef.

Quality	🍷🍷🍷?
Value	★★★⸶
Grapes	merlot; cabernet franc; malbec
Region	Auckland, NZ
Cellar	5+
Alc./Vol.	13.0%
RRP	$24.00

Laanecoorie

Quality	ŶŶŶŶ𝟁
Value	★★★★𝗋
Grapes	cabernet sauvignon; cabernet franc; merlot
Region	Maryborough, Vic.
Cellar	➥ 2–5
Alc./Vol.	12.5%
RRP	$19.00

The label is a bit of fun because the name means 'the land of the big kangaroos'. Spot the roo. The vineyard is owned by John McQuilten. Maker John Ellis (contract).

CURRENT RELEASE 1996   The colour is deep ruby, and the nose has strong berry aromas with a hint of mint and lavender. The medium-bodied palate is quite complex. There are raspberry and ripe cherry flavours, which are married to bracing French oak. There are fine-grained tannins and astringent acid on the finish. Try it with kangaroo – what else?

Lakes Folly Cabernets

Quality	ŶŶŶ𝟁
Value	★★𝗋
Grapes	cabernet sauvignon 70%; petit verdot 10%; shiraz 10%; merlot 10%
Region	Hunter Valley NSW
Cellar	➥ 2–6
Alc./Vol.	12.0%
RRP	$25.00

This is more than just cabernet, it's a Bordeaux blend with a varietal interloper in the form of shiraz. It sports a very impressive and expensive cork.

CURRENT RELEASE 1995   The colour is a deep ruby and the nose has some pungent leaf and herb aromas with underlying berry character plus a suspicion of sulfides. The palate is medium-bodied with redcurrant fruit flavours which are followed by some very dry and astringent tannins. It's a hard wine that may soften with time. Try it with roast veal.

Lavender Bay Pinot Noir

Quality	ŶŶŶ𝟁
Value	★★★
Grapes	pinot noir
Region	Mornington Peninsula, Vic.
Cellar	▮ 3
Alc./Vol.	12.3%
RRP	$21.30

This is another developing label and the fourth vintage from the Mornington Peninsula in Victoria. It's a pretty wine by name and nature.

CURRENT RELEASE 1996   The colour is a medium red–purple. The nose has lush berry aromas, dominated by strawberry and cherry. The medium-bodied palate is soft, with sweet strawberry flavours. The finish is also soft and has gentle tannins. It drinks well now with smoked chicken.

Leasingham Bin 56 Cabernet Malbec

This is a long-standing bin number that has always been associated with easy and early drinking.
CURRENT RELEASE 1996   The nose is very fruity with ripe berry and developed fruit flavours. The palate is not as fruity as the nose would suggest. There are sweet berry flavours and the oak on the finish adds some firming tannin. This wine has a cellar life ahead. It goes well with steak and eggs.

Quality	♥♥♥♥
Value	★★★⊦
Grapes	cabernet sauvignon; malbec
Region	Clare Valley, SA
Cellar	▮ 5
Alc./Vol.	13.0%
RRP	$19.95

Leasingham Bin 61 Shiraz

This is a tough wine that needs time to come together. It was made to attract attention on the show circuit.
Previous outstanding vintages: '90, '91, '92, '93, '94
CURRENT RELEASE 1995   Very little change since last year. The colour is deep and the nose has plum and briar-patch aromas. The medium- to full-bodied palate is chunky with loads of concentrated plum flavour, vanilla and spice. There's substantial grip on the finish. It's not subtle, but you know you are having a drink. Serve with beef wellington.

Quality	♥♥♥♥⸳
Value	★★★★
Grapes	shiraz
Region	Clare Valley, SA
Cellar	➥ 4–10
Alc./Vol.	13.0%
RRP	$19.95

Leasingham Classic Clare Cabernet Sauvignon

The winemaker is very adroit at lobbying management to increase his oak budget. The result is easily detected in these wines. Maker Richard Rowe.
Previous outstanding vintages: '91, '92, '93, '94
CURRENT RELEASE 1995   Apart from the price, not much change since the last review; perhaps a little mellowing around the edges. The toasty charred oak still dominates the nose and there are mulberry and blackberry aromas. The palate is succulent with rich berry flavours and the oak adds a tannic dimension to the finish. It goes well with aged cheddar.

Quality	♥♥♥♥♥
Value	★★★★
Grapes	cabernet sauvignon
Region	Clare Valley, SA
Cellar	➥ 2–12
Alc./Vol.	13.5%
RRP	$32.00

Leasingham Classic Clare Shiraz

Quality	???????
Value	★★★★
Grapes	shiraz
Region	Clare Valley, SA
Cellar	▮ 5
Alc./Vol.	13.5%
RRP	$32.00

This is a much-decorated label and it gets the goods as far as winemaking treatment is concerned. It has already started to throw a substantial crust.
Previous outstanding vintages: '91, '92, '93, '94
CURRENT RELEASE 1995 The nose is marked by toasty, charred oak as well as plum and berry aromas. The palate is full-bodied with sweet cherry and plum flavours which are augmented by cinnamon and other spices. There's vanilla on the finish and some toasty elements. The grip is marked and the wine goes well with a veal and mushroom pie.

Leasingham Domain Shiraz

Quality	???????
Value	★★★★★
Grapes	shiraz
Region	Clare Valley, SA
Cellar	▮ 5
Alc./Vol.	13.5%
RRP	$18.00

This is an ever-reliable style even when the vintage going gets tough. Maker Richard Rowe.
CURRENT RELEASE 1995 The colour is a vibrant ruby and the nose has a strong spice aroma as well as berry and plum. The full-bodied palate has rich mulberry and cherry flavours, and these are followed by some soft tannins and moderate grip. It drinks very well now and teams well with a game pie.

Leconfield Cabernet

Quality	????
Value	★★★
Grapes	cabernet sauvignon; merlot; petit verdot; cabernet franc
Region	Coonawarra, SA
Cellar	▮ 4
Alc./Vol.	13.0%
RRP	$25.00

This vineyard/winery was established by the late Sid Hamilton in 1974. Since then the production has developed to 16 000 cases per annum. Maker Ralph Fowler.
CURRENT RELEASE 1996 Very polished style that has elegance and panache. The nose has blackberry and floral notes like violets and herbs. The medium-bodied palate offers attractive berry character and blackberry flavour. This is tuned by some swank oak that adds an impressive tannin grip. Try it with BBQ spare ribs.

Leconfield Shiraz

Would have expected a bigger wine given the nature of the vintage. This is an elegant herbal style with loads of spice but not a lot of flesh. This seems out of step with other wines in the district. Maker Ralph Fowler.

CURRENT RELEASE 1996 The nose has capsicum and herbs. The palate is medium-bodied with soft sweet plum flavours which are also attended by some earthy characters and a sprinkle of pepper. There are fine-grained tannins on the finish. Try it with pink lamb.

Quality	🍷🍷🍷½
Value	★★★½
Grapes	shiraz
Region	Coonawarra, SA
Cellar	🍾 3
Alc./Vol.	13.0%
RRP	$17.90

Leydens Vale Cabernet Sauvignon

Cabernet does good in them thar blue Pyrenees hills. The blue colour is supposed to happen in the afternoon when the gum trees give off volatile oils. It's a nice story.

CURRENT RELEASE 1996 Great fruit impact here; the varietal concentration is typical of the region. The colour is deep and the nose has blackberry and smoky oak aromas. The palate is full-bodied with an intense blackberry fruit flavour which is followed by some chalky dry oak on a lingering finish. Try it with seared kangaroo on a sweet potato mash.

Quality	🍷🍷🍷🍷
Value	★★★★
Grapes	cabernet sauvignon
Region	Pyrenees, Vic.
Cellar	🍾 4
Alc./Vol.	14.0%
RRP	$18.00

Leydens Vale Pinot Noir

In this region someone should blow pinot noir up! It's okay for bubbly but doubtful as far as table wine is concerned.

CURRENT RELEASE 1995 This wine has an earthy nose with some underlying strawberry aromas. The palate is medium- to light-bodied, with soft strawberry flavours and some firm acid on the gentle finish. It drinks well now. Serve it with a pork and veal terrine.

Quality	🍷🍷🍷
Value	★★★
Grapes	pinot noir
Region	Pyrenees, Vic.
Cellar	🍾 3
Alc./Vol.	13.5%
RRP	$18.00

Leydens Vale Shiraz

Quality	♟♟♟♟
Value	★★★★
Grapes	shiraz
Region	Pyrenees, Vic.
Cellar	▲ 4
Alc./Vol.	13.0%
RRP	$18.00

It's all about marketing flim-flam: Leyden was one of the original settlers in the district and this is the middle tier of the Blue Pyrenees/Remy trilogy.
CURRENT RELEASE 1996   A spicy drop. The nose offers obvious wood aromas plus mint and berry aromas. The palate is medium- to full-bodied with ripe cherry and plum flavours, and the finish is dry with fine-grained tannins and a chalky sensation. Try it with spicy meatloaf.

Lindemans Padthaway Vineyard Cabernet Merlot

Quality	♟♟♟♟
Value	★★★★
Grapes	cabernet sauvignon; pinot noir
Region	Padthaway, SA
Cellar	▲ 3
Alc./Vol.	13.0%
RRP	$17.00

There are good reasons why these varieties work well together, and in this region they can elevate the standard of the wines. This is a good example of how well they go together.
CURRENT RELEASE 1994   A style that is developing well. There's a hint of leaf on the nose and the fruit is mainly redcurrant in terms of aroma. The medium-bodied palate offers sweet red and blackberry flavours and the finish has some well-integrated tannin that dries the mouth. It goes well with pink lamb chops.

Lindemans Padthaway Vineyard Pinot Noir

Quality	♟♟♟♟
Value	★★★★
Grapes	pinot noir
Region	Padthaway, SA
Cellar	▲ 3
Alc./Vol.	12.5%
RRP	$17.00

Why don't we expect the earth to move with this wine? Padthaway is a broad hectare dedicated to balancing production and quality. It makes good wines that are sometimes memorable.
CURRENT RELEASE 1997   Bright cherry-red colour and a strawberry nose are good hints of what's to come. The light- to medium-bodied palate has sweet berry flavours and there's clean acid on a well-balanced finish. It goes well with chargrilled tuna.

Lowe Merlot

Winemaker David Lowe was the grapesmith at Rothbury before he branched out on his own. As a consequence he nose the vineyards of the region backwards (pun intended).

CURRENT RELEASE 1997 A light elegant wine that has obvious varietal character. The nose has concentrated fruit aromas as well as some rose-petal perfume. The palate is light- to medium-bodied with soft raspberry fruit flavours and a hint of green leaves. The finish has a slight stalk quality. The wine goes well with pasta in a meat sauce.

Quality	♈♈♈
Value	★★★
Grapes	merlot
Region	Hunter Valley, NSW
Cellar	3
Alc./Vol.	12.3%
RRP	$21.85

Lowe Orange Red

Sounds funny, but Orange is the district. The company was established in 1987 and production is a modest 1000 cases per annum. Maker David Lowe.

CURRENT RELEASE 1996 There's a strong mint aroma on the nose and the palate is medium-bodied with sweet berry flavours of admirable complexity. The discreet oak on the finish adds subtle grip. It drinks well now with a lamb and barley casserole.

Quality	♈♈♈♈
Value	★★★
Grapes	cabernet sauvignon; cabernet franc; merlot
Region	Orange & Hunter Valley, NSW
Cellar	4
Alc./Vol.	12.2%
RRP	$21.85

Luigi Riserva

This is a new label from what used to be called the Warrenmang vineyard near Moonambel. Luigi Bazzani is the proprietor. He's a noted restaurateur and the vineyard also features a plush resort. It's the place to stay when you visit the district.

CURRENT RELEASE 1991/1997 Yes that's right, this is a blend of two years, and the result is a remarkable wine. The nose shows mature fruit aromas plus a measure of savoury oak. The palate is rich with a juicy texture and sweet fruit flavours that border on being porty. The finish shows some mellow oak and soft tannins. It goes well with osso bucco.

Quality	♈♈♈♈♈
Value	★★★
Grapes	merlot; cabernet sauvignon; shiraz
Region	Pyrenees, Vic.
Cellar	5
Alc./Vol.	14.0%
RRP	$55.00

Maglieri Cabernet Sauvignon

Quality	ΨΨΨ𝒾
Value	★★★
Grapes	cabernet sauvignon
Region	McLaren Vale, SA
Cellar	➡ 1–5+
Alc./Vol.	13.5%
RRP	$17.70 ⑤ 🍾

Maglieri, the lambrusco king, has come from the shadows to stand tall among the great shiraz makers of Australia in recent years. With cabernet, he's still working on the style.
CURRENT RELEASE 1995   Lovely colour! A dense, royal purple–red robe. Has good weight, depth and richness, but way too much oak for our liking. It gives a dominant coconut aroma and a tough oaky tannin finish to the palate. No doubt it will have its admirers, and time will very likely soften and subdue the oakiness.

Quality	ΨΨΨΨ
Value	★★★★ꜰ
Grapes	cabernet sauvignon
Region	McLaren Vale, SA
Cellar	🍾 7+
Alc./Vol.	14.0%
RRP	$17.70 ⑤ 🍾

CURRENT RELEASE 1996   A solid citizen that improves on the '95. It might not have definitive cabernet character, but it's a flavoursome savoury, middleweight with some earthy, drying tannins to close. The colour is deep, and there are plum and cherry fruit characters. Serve with wild duck.

Maglieri Shiraz

Quality	ΨΨΨΨ𝒾
Value	★★★★★
Grapes	shiraz
Region	McLaren Vale, SA
Cellar	🍾 8+
Alc./Vol.	14.0%
RRP	$17.25 ⑤

In five years, this deceptively large McLaren Vale producer has burst to the forefront of the shiraz pack. Winemaker is John Loxton and consultant, Pam Dunsford.
Previous outstanding vintages: '90, '91, '93, '95
CURRENT RELEASE 1996   The '95 blitzed the International WINE Challenge in London and this is a worthy successor. An impressively dark colour, and rich aromas of well-married oak, dusty berry, coconut and licorice. The palate is spicy and tightly focused, with lovely fruit/oak sweetness despite a firm tannin grip to close. Try it with buffalo fillet.

Maglieri Steve Maglieri Shiraz

This eponymously named bottling is this maker's reserve wine. Both it and the standard '95 did tremendously well at various judgings. Maker John Loxton.

CURRENT RELEASE 1995 A classic regional shiraz style: an enormously deep, youthful colour and a voluminous bouquet of licorice, ripe plum, blackberry and oak. It's a big, fruit-sweet, exaggerated style – so concentrated it's thick on the tongue. It's opulent and lush, with shovelfuls of tannin to close. Great stuff, and terrific with rump steak.

Quality	🍷🍷🍷🍷🍷
Value	★★★★
Grapes	shiraz
Region	McLaren Vale, SA
Cellar	3–10+
Alc./Vol.	14.0%
RRP	$34.50

Majella Cabernet

Majella is grapegrower Brian Lynn's foray into the world of winemaking. Majella now has a cute little cellar-door sales outlet off V & A Lane, Coonawarra.

CURRENT RELEASE 1996 Wood has been pushed to the limit here, but the wine has the legs to age and it will come into balance. The colour is dark and brooding, and there are glimpses of blackcurrant among the oaky notes. It tastes sweetly ripe and very varietal. It's intense and long on the palate and the finish has youthful astringency. Cellar, then serve with rare beef.

Quality	🍷🍷🍷🍷½
Value	★★★½
Grapes	cabernet sauvignon
Region	Coonawarra, SA
Cellar	2–12+
Alc./Vol.	13.5%
RRP	$28.70

Majella Shiraz

The Lynn family has only recently begun to make wine, although its vineyards were planted 30 years ago. Maker Bruce Gregory.

CURRENT RELEASE 1996 A crackerjack Coonawarra shiraz! A tremendously intense, spicy, blackberry style, which is not oaky or excessively alcoholic. A wine of great depth, yet a wine of elegance and harmony. There's a hint of mint among the berries and spices. Fine indeed, and a long-term keeper. Enjoy a glass or two with seared kangaroo backstraps.

Quality	🍷🍷🍷🍷🍷
Value	★★★★★
Grapes	shiraz
Region	Coonawarra, SA
Cellar	12+
Alc./Vol.	13.2%
RRP	$24.80

Majella The Mallea

Quality	惷惷惷惷惷
Value	★★★★★
Grapes	shiraz; cabernet sauvignon
Region	Coonawarra, SA
Cellar	➡ 2–15+
Alc./Vol.	13.3%
RRP	$45.00 🍾

This is the first bottling of a special selection from the best Majella vines. It's said to be the same vineyard that provided much of the fruit for the early Wynns John Riddochs. Grower Brian Lynn. Maker Bruce Gregory.
CURRENT RELEASE 1996   Ring the bells: a new star is born. This is a tremendous wine, marvellously deep and concentrated yet also showing the great elegance for which Coonawarra is rightly famed. Deep brooding colour; dark-berry and stylish oak aromas; tightly structured, intensely flavoured and incredibly long on the aftertaste. This is a great wine in the making. Cellar, then serve with hard cheeses.

Martinborough Vineyard Pinot Noir

Quality	惷惷惷惷惷
Value	★★★★↾
Grapes	pinot noir
Region	Martinborough, NZ
Cellar	🍾 5
Alc./Vol.	13.5%
RRP	$41.00

Larry McKenna has carved out a great reputation for Martinborough pinot. He's unarguably one of the leading exponents in the southern hemisphere.
Previous outstanding vintages: '86, '88, '91, '94
CURRENT RELEASE 1996   Marvellous perfumes of maraschino cherries. It's sweet and ripe with no greenness, and the oak is tucked away in the background. Tight structure, with mouth perfumes of red fruits and roses, and delicacy and length. A wine of charm and style rather than brute force. Serve with beef carpaccio.

The McAlister

Quality	惷惷惷惷惷
Value	★★★★↾
Grapes	cabernet sauvignon 60%; cabernet franc 4%; merlot 34%; petit verdot 2%
Region	Gippsland, Vic.
Cellar	🍾 7
Alc./Vol.	13.0%
RRP	$35.00

This is the only wine from a small vineyard adjacent to the Sale airforce base. According to the owner Peter Edwards, during pruning you risk sunburn on the roof of your mouth because the aerobatic stunt team, the Roulettes, are usually practising. The wine is pretty special also.
CURRENT RELEASE 1995   The nose has a strong vinous aroma. It has blackberry, briar and cigar-box smells. The palate is complex, with a Bordeaux-like structure. The oak and fruit conjoin to make a solid style. Blackberry is the major flavour and there's attractive black-tea-like tannin on a grippy finish. It's great with rare roast beef.

McLarens On The Lake Cabernet Shiraz

Strange that none of the wines under this label is straight McLaren Vale. Could be a comment on the rising price of grapes in the Vale. Maker Andrew Garrett (the real one).

CURRENT RELEASE 1996 The colour has good depth and hue, and the nose has a gamy meaty overtone which might offend some. It airs to reveal some berry character, and there's good depth of flavour for the price. It doesn't win prizes for finesse and the finish is a tad hard, but it's fair value for money. Food: kofta kebabs.

Quality	🍷🍷½
Value	★★★
Grapes	cabernet sauvignon; shiraz
Region	south-eastern Australia
Cellar	2
Alc./Vol.	13.0%
RRP	$11.50 ($)

McWilliams Barwang Cabernet Sauvignon

The '94 of this took out the Penguin Wine of the Year Award two years ago. It's a vineyard with great potential, although seasonal variations are apparent.

Previous outstanding vintages: '93, '94

CURRENT RELEASE 1996 Fragrant cabernet fruit welded to toasty but tidy oak here. The palate has good focus and structure, and although it's only medium- to full-bodied, the tannins are balanced and it has some elegance. Short-term cellaring will improve it. Try it with pink lamb chops.

Quality	🍷🍷🍷🍷½
Value	★★★★
Grapes	cabernet sauvignon
Region	Hilltops, NSW
Cellar	1–8+
Alc./Vol.	13.5%
RRP	$18.00 ($)

McWilliams Barwang Shiraz

Barwang was an established vineyard at Young, on the western side of the Great Dividing Range in New South Wales when McWilliams bought it. Makers Jim Brayne and Russell Cody.

Previous outstanding vintages: '90, '91, '92, '93, '94

CURRENT RELEASE 1996 Charred oak perfumes the bouquet here. There's a fragrance, too, but it's mainly oak-derived. In the mouth, it's lean and graceful, with good intensity, but it just lacks the overt shiraz spice that typifies the best Barwangs. And the oak is getting in the road at this stage. Try BBQ rissoles.

Quality	🍷🍷🍷🍷
Value	★★★½
Grapes	shiraz
Region	Hilltops, NSW
Cellar	1–5+
Alc./Vol.	13.5%
RRP	$18.00 ($)

McWilliams Hanwood Cabernet Sauvignon

Quality	♟♟♟
Value	★★★
Grapes	cabernet sauvignon
Region	Riverina, NSW
Cellar	🍶 2
Alc./Vol.	13.0%
RRP	$10.20 ⑤

Each of the Hanwood wines has a different Aboriginal painting on the label. Mouton Rothschild eat your heart out.

CURRENT RELEASE 1996   A lighter purple–red hue echoes the light-bodied structure of this drink-now budget red. It has moderate intensity, leafy mulberry and blackcurrant aroma and flavour, and some wood aromatics. It's light and herbaceous, and is a good quaffer at the price. Try it with meat pie and tomato sauce.

McWilliams John James McWilliam Shiraz

Quality	♟♟♟
Value	★★★
Grapes	shiraz
Region	not stated
Cellar	🍶 2
Alc./Vol.	12.5%
RRP	$12.00 ⑤

J. J. McWilliam was the founder. He didn't initially set up shop at Griffith but at Junee, which was where the railway line from Victoria ran out at the time.

CURRENT RELEASE 1996   The shiraz has a little more weight and strength than the cabernet under the same label. It has a light but spicy nose, reflecting the variety. It's lightly wooded and not very complex. The palate is soft and light- to medium-bodied, with a degree of richness and substance. It fills the mouth admirably. Try it with pork sausages and mash.

McWilliams Mount Pleasant Merlot

Quality	♟♟♟
Value	★★★
Grapes	merlot
Region	Hunter Valley, NSW
Cellar	🍶 3
Alc./Vol.	13.5%
RRP	$14.00 ⑤

Merlot in the Hunter? Why not? It may never produce the Great Australian Merlot, but they can have fun trying. Maker Phillip Ryan.

CURRENT RELEASE 1996   The bouquet proffers coco-nutty new oak and leafy fruit aromatics. The palate has reasonable depth of flavour, and acid chimes in on the finish. It's light-bodied and drinks well young. Try it with veal saltimbocca.

Merrivale Tapestry Shiraz

This is the occupation of ex-Normans chief winemaker Brian Light, whose family has a history of grapegrowing in the Vale.

CURRENT RELEASE 1995   A lovely mouthful of classic McLaren Vale shiraz. A voluptuous style, with generous jammy overripe fruit, blackberry flavours and spicy oak. That big fruit is full and rather broad on the palate, and it seems to lack a little in terms of structure. Goes down a treat with venison cutlets.

Quality	♟♟♟♟
Value	★★★★
Grapes	shiraz
Region	McLaren Vale, SA
Cellar	▍ 5+
Alc./Vol.	13.5%
RRP	$19.70 ▌

Milburn Park Reserve Cabernet Sauvignon

This is from the Alambie Wine Co., which also delivers Salisbury wines. This brand is a couple of bucks dearer and a year older, with more guts. Maker Bob Shields.

CURRENT RELEASE 1996   This is a lighter-bodied red that tries hard to be something sterner. The colour is full purple–red, and it smells of cherry-pip and plum-skin. The finish carries a fair grip, and there are prune-juice flavours in the mouth. It's slightly flimsy and needs food. Try it with spaghetti bolognaise.

Quality	♟♟♟
Value	★★★
Grapes	cabernet sauvignon
Region	Murray Valley, Vic.
Cellar	▍ 3
Alc./Vol.	12.0%
RRP	$12.00 ⑤

Mildara Blass Stellar Shiraz

'And she's buying a stairway to heaven . . .' Is this a bid for the star-struck, Led-Zeppelin-loving baby boomers?

CURRENT RELEASE 1996   The nose is all ripe plums and dark chocolate, and it's a no-frills, straightforward, ready-drinking red. It has decent balance, and the flavour has some length. A very respectable drop to partner lasagne.

Quality	♟♟♟
Value	★★★★
Grapes	shiraz
Region	not stated
Cellar	▍ 3
Alc./Vol.	12.0%
RRP	$10.15 ⑤

Mildara Coonawarra Cabernet Sauvignon

Quality	♟♟♟♟
Value	★★★★
Grapes	cabernet sauvignon
Region	Coonawarra, SA
Cellar	▮ 5
Alc./Vol.	12.5%
RRP	$21.20 Ⓢ

Mildara makes this wine in a style that's elegant, moderate in alcohol strength, and picked earlier than many of the modern Coonawarra cabernets. Maker Gavin Hogg.
Previous outstanding vintages: '63, '79, '81, '86, '88, '90, '91, 92
CURRENT RELEASE 1995   An impressive wine for the vintage, this has a restrained blackcurrant/dark berry elegance, coupled with classy oak. The palate has good concentration and length. There's a degree of finesse, and the wine appears to have good ageing potential. It deserves pink lamb with mint sauce.

Miranda Mirrool Creek Cabernet Shiraz

Quality	♟♟♟
Value	★★★★
Grapes	cabernet sauvignon; shiraz
Region	Riverina, NSW
Cellar	▮ 2
Alc./Vol.	13.0%
RRP	$9.20 Ⓢ

The garish label cannot be ignored. It has a windmill and a glaring sun, so you could say it evokes an image of rural Australia.
CURRENT RELEASE 1997   This is very good value, something we've come to expect from the various Miranda labels. While the colour is fairly light, it has decent flavour and character for the price. It smells of toasted oak and is light-bodied and somewhat firm in the mouth, with a dominant flavour of vanilla. There's fruit and tannin also, and it goes down well with a steak sandwich.

Miranda Rovalley Ridge Grey Series Shiraz

Quality	♟♟♟♟
Value	★★★★⸕
Grapes	shiraz
Region	Barossa Valley & Eden Valley, SA
Cellar	▮ 4
Alc./Vol.	13.0%
RRP	$14.20 Ⓢ

The name is quite a mouthful. The Riverina-based company, Miranda, bought the former Rovalley winery from the Liebich family, then added a ridge to it, which seems to be the fashion.
CURRENT RELEASE 1995   This has a somewhat light colour, but don't be put off. It has good depth and weight of flavour in the mouth. There are dusty cherry, slightly developed aromas and cherry-ripe flavours that are balanced with a good grip. It drinks well now with pork chops.

Mitchell Cabernet Sauvignon

The Mitchells have over 60 hectares of vineyards at Watervale and Sevenhill. Maker Andrew Mitchell.

CURRENT RELEASE 1995   A savoury, old-fashioned red, with discreet wood and developing fruit, into which a trace of volatility intrudes. It has a big structure with a quite astringent tannin finish. A food wine: it needs a hearty game casserole to balance all that tannin.

Quality	????
Value	★★★
Grapes	cabernet sauvignon
Region	Clare Valley, SA
Cellar	⬤ 1–8
Alc./Vol.	13.5%
RRP	$22.00 Ⓢ ▮

Mitchell The Growers Grenache

Some love this thumping high-alcohol grenache style, but HH is a dissenting voice. However, you can't argue that it's not very different to the other Mitchell reds.

CURRENT RELEASE 1997   There's no oak in this wine, according to the label. It has a sweet nose of spices, cherries and berries, and the palate is terrifically sweet with hot alcohol burning the finish. There's also some bitter astringency. It's an over-the-top style that polarises drinkers. Serve with lamb's fry and onions.

Quality	???
Value	★★★
Grapes	grenache
Region	Clare Valley, SA
Cellar	▮ 4
Alc./Vol.	15.0%
RRP	$15.00

Mitchelton Reserve Cabernet Sauvignon

Mitchelton is a serious producer with 142 hectares of vineyards. It's part of the Petaluma group these days, and no longer makes cask or cheapo wines. Makers Don Lewis and Alan George.

CURRENT RELEASE 1995   This is a shy, shrinking violet – a wallflower. But ask her out and she knows how to party! The nose is subdued and reticent, but the palate is a different matter. Nutty, toasty oak under-currents and rich dark berry flavours combine with asser-tive tannin to make a powerful, structured wine with a big future. It needs air to show its wares. Better still, cellar it. Then serve with braised venison.

Quality	?????
Value	★★★★
Grapes	cabernet sauvignon
Region	Goulburn Valley & others, Vic.
Cellar	⬤ 2–8+
Alc./Vol.	12.5%
RRP	$23.80 ▮

Monichino Merlot

Quality	🍷🍷🍷🍷
Value	★★★★½
Grapes	merlot
Region	Goulburn Valley, Vic.
Cellar	5
Alc./Vol.	13.0%
RRP	$14.75

For a low-profile winery that's somewhat outside the region, Monichino's makes some pretty decent wines. Carlo Monichino migrated from Asti, in Piedmont, and started his vineyard in 1962.

CURRENT RELEASE 1996 A full-bodied merlot, this has ripe fruit character and quite a lot of smoky, banana-like oak. It has good freshness and a lively, deep, lasting flavour that fills the mouth. The structure is tight and it lingers for a long time on the finish. An impressive wine! Try it with duck.

Monichino Shiraz

Quality	🍷🍷🍷
Value	★★★
Grapes	shiraz
Region	Katunga, Vic. 70%; Bendigo, Vic. 30%
Cellar	1–5+
Alc./Vol.	13.9%
RRP	$14.75

This is a family affair at Katunga, north of the Goulburn Valley, where there are 25 hectares of vines planted. Maker Carlo Monichino.

CURRENT RELEASE 1995 There's a baked, hot-climate character on the nose and a hint of sump-oil. It has tannin to lose: the finish is very astringent, but there's also a lot of flavour. Unsubtle, old-fashioned red wine. Serve with saltbush mutton.

Montana Reserve Merlot

Quality	🍷🍷🍷½
Value	★★½
Grapes	merlot
Region	Marlborough, NZ
Cellar	4
Alc./Vol.	13.0%
RRP	$28.70

Why put 'barrique matured' on an expensive merlot label? It would be worth talking about were it *not* matured in small wood. Maker Jeff Clarke and team.

CURRENT RELEASE 1996 The colour is only of medium depth, and the bouquet is shy and dusty. There's some lollyish fruit in the mouth and it's fairly straightforward in character. There's a surprising tannin kick to the finish, and the balance is somewhat askew. Try it with pan-fried veal.

Montrose Barbera

Barbera was planted in the Montrose vineyards along with sangiovese and nebbiolo by the winery's founder, Transfield, a construction company run by Italians.

CURRENT RELEASE 1996   There are spicy, peppery and raspberry fruit aromas coupled with a hint of wood. The palate is smooth, round and fruit-sweet. The tannins are soft and gentle, and the character of the wine is excitingly different. Drinks well as a youngster. Try it with BBQ quail.

Quality	▼▼▼▼ᵭ
Value	★★★★
Grapes	barbera
Region	Mudgee, NSW
Cellar	▮ 2
Alc./Vol.	13.0 %
RRP	$20.00

Montrose Black Shiraz

Rockford was first to employ the phrase 'black shiraz' on labels. Others, including McGuigan Brothers and Montrose, followed suit. Maker Robert Paul.

CURRENT RELEASE 1995   It has a very spicy bouquet: cloves, cinnamon and five-spice are suggested. The style is medium-bodied and lean with an oaky aftertaste. It's fair value for money and it goes well with chipolatas.

Quality	▼▼▼ᵭ
Value	★★★⭒
Grapes	shiraz
Region	Mudgee, NSW
Cellar	▮ 4
Alc./Vol.	13.5%
RRP	$16.00 Ⓢ

Montrose Cabernet Sauvignon

This won a gold medal at the Cowra Show in the winter of '96, presumably as an unfinished wine. Maker Robert Paul.

Previous outstanding vintages: '94

CURRENT RELEASE 1995   Another example of the good value for money in Montrose wines. This is quite oaky, but it also has abundant sweet ripe berry flavour and richness. The bouquet is earthy, walnutty and woodsy, and shows lots of oak-maturation character. It has a tannin grip to finish, and is starting to drink well, but don't be in a hurry to rip out the cork. Serve it with roast duck.

Quality	▼▼▼▼
Value	★★★★
Grapes	cabernet sauvignon
Region	Mudgee, NSW
Cellar	▮ 8+
Alc./Vol.	12.5%
RRP	$16.00 Ⓢ ▮

Montrose Sangiovese

Quality	♟♟♟♟
Value	★★★★★
Grapes	sangiovese
Region	Mudgee, NSW
Cellar	▮ 3
Alc./Vol.	13.5 %
RRP	$20.00

Montrose has had several Italian varieties in its Mudgee vineyards for 20 years. Only lately has it begun to market them solo, thanks to the efforts of winemaker Robert Paul. They are being sold mainly in restaurants.
CURRENT RELEASE 1996   This is different, and as you might hope; it has an individuality all of its own. Very exciting stuff: lovely sweet, but well-modulated, dried cherry aroma with a hint of undergrowth and gaminess. It's not obscured by obvious oak, and has a purity of expression that is a joy to behold. Great with Italian taleggio cheese. More, please!

Moondah Brook Cabernet Sauvignon

Quality	♟♟♟♟
Value	★★★★★
Grapes	cabernet sauvignon
Region	Frankland River, WA
Cellar	⬤ 2–10+
Alc./Vol.	13.5%
RRP	$19.00 ⑤ ▮

Moondah Brook is at Gingin, north of Perth, but most of the grapes for this wine are now sourced from the cooler parts of southern Western Australia. Maker Paul Lapsley.
CURRENT RELEASE 1996   A very oaky young wine, but it appears to have the fruit and structure to age. In fact, there's little doubt the wine will come into balance given a couple of years. The colour is deep and dark, and it smells of fresh-sawn timber. The palate is dry and firmly structured, and the blackcurrant cabernet fruit peeps through with extended breathing. It has good richness and extract. Serve with aged cheddar.

Moorebank Merlot

Quality	♟♟♟
Value	★★▸
Grapes	merlot
Region	Hunter Valley, NSW
Cellar	▮ 2
Alc./Vol.	12.5%
RRP	$24.50 (500 ml)

The packaging struts design flair, and the wines are quite expensive (this is the equivalent of $36.75 a full bottle). But is there substance as well as style?
CURRENT RELEASE 1997   The colour is a medium–light purple–red, and it smells of mint and eucalyptus. There's a slight hollow in the middle, and the acid shows on the finish. A pleasant drink with some redeeming aromatic features. Try it with pasta al funghi.

Moss Brothers Cabernet Merlot

When Moss Brothers set up just down the road from Margaret River pioneer Moss Wood, it must have looked mighty strange. In fact, it's their real name. Maker David Moss.

CURRENT RELEASE 1996   There's some typical regional greenness in this wine, together with dark cherry and chocolate flavours. In the mouth there's some astringency with decent fruit/oak flavours, all lifted by a little volatility. Try it with pasta with ham and pesto.

Quality	▼▼▼↑
Value	★★↑
Grapes	cabernet sauvignon; merlot
Region	Margaret River, WA
Cellar	▮ 5
Alc./Vol.	13.0%
RRP	$24.60

Moss Brothers Moses Rock Red

Moses Rock is a landmark on the coast not far from the winery. This is a fruit-salad blend from Margaret River.

CURRENT RELEASE 1996   The colour is fairly light and the aromas are of green fruit, herbal, leafy, stalky notes predominating. It's lean and medium-weight, with fairly rough tannins to finish. A rustic red that should wash down well-charred BBQ bangers nicely.

Quality	▼▼▼
Value	★★★
Grapes	merlot; pinot noir; grenache; shiraz; cabernet franc
Region	Margaret River, WA
Cellar	▮ 3
Alc./Vol.	13.0%
RRP	$17.00

Mountadam Cabernet Sauvignon

Mountadam doesn't produce a straight cabernet every year – it usually finds its way into The Red cabernet merlot. Maker Adam Wynn.

CURRENT RELEASE 1994   This is a solid, extractive, heavily worked red wine, with a big, tannic palate and robust structure. The nose has mellowing herbal, aniseed and mulberry fruit characters; the palate has stalky, wintergreen flavours and a rustic grip. Try it with well-herbed gourmet hamburgers.

Quality	▼▼▼
Value	★★↑
Grapes	cabernet sauvignon
Region	Eden Valley, SA
Cellar	➙ 1–5
Alc./Vol.	13.0%
RRP	$32.80 ▮

Mountadam Pinot Noir

Quality	♟♟♟♟
Value	★★★
Grapes	pinot noir
Region	Eden Valley, SA
Cellar	▮ 5
Alc./Vol.	14.0%
RRP	$32.00

Adam Wynn's pinots are sometimes criticised for lacking pinot character, whatever that is. On the plus side, they don't have the green characters of so many cool-climate southern efforts.

Previous outstanding vintages: '91, '93

CURRENT RELEASE 1996   A top year for Mountadam pinot. This brilliant wine has a full red–purple colour – nothing washed-out or rusty-looking here. It smells sweet and ripe of cherries and plums, and has terrific intensity in the mouth with a long finish. It has the requisite fruit sweetness, which builds to a silkily sumptuous level when you use it to chase a mouthful of something appropriate, such as ham and spinach quiche.

Mount Horrocks Shiraz

Quality	♟♟♟♟♟
Value	★★★★
Grapes	shiraz
Region	Clare Valley, SA
Cellar	▮ 10
Alc./Vol.	13.5%
RRP	$30.50

Stephanie Toole manages this Clare Valley brand and makes the wines with the help of her partner, Jeffrey Grosset. This is her first-ever shiraz, and what a debut!

CURRENT RELEASE 1996   Wonderful stuff, and all the better for being matured in French rather than ubiquitous American oak. It has an inviting perfume of clean, spicy, floral, almost fruity/talcum-like/aromatic, oak. It develops minty, sweet ripe berry aromas with breathing. The palate has a sweet entry, intense flavour with tightness, and an elegance that bodes well for cellaring. Enjoy it with peppered steak.

Mount Langi Ghiran Shiraz

Langi has quickly established itself as one of the greatest shirazes in Australia, a wine of power, complexity, charm – and longevity. And we're thrilled to say it achieves all this without obvious oak. Maker Trevor Mast.

Previous outstanding vintages: '84, '86, '88, '89, '90, '91, '92, '94, '95

CURRENT RELEASE 1996   A blinder of a wine! Very youthful colour, and marvellous pepper–spice cool-area aromas, with the oak well in check. The entry is lively and fresh; the palate is positively frisky, with marvellous intensity, weight and balance. Although cool and spicy, it has fruit sweetness and lacks nothing in palate length. A great wine! Serve with pride.

Quality	♟♟♟♟♟
Value	★★★★★
Grapes	shiraz
Region	Grampians, Vic.
Cellar	🍷 15+
Alc./Vol.	13.5%
RRP	$40.00 🍷

Mount Mary Cabernets Quintet

Mount Mary is planted on the same grey clay-loam soils that the de Castellas swore by in the 19th century. The original vines are now more than 25 years old, although there's been a lot of replanting in recent years.

Previous outstanding vintages: '77, '82, '84, '86, '88, '90, '91, '94

CURRENT RELEASE 1995   The quintessence of Yarra Valley cabernet. Full purple–red colour; pristine black-currant/dark berry aromas, with no trace of greenness or overt oak. Very intense flavour, fine and discreet, with marvellous balance and length. A very tidy wine that should age superbly. Try it with roast leg of lamb.

Quality	♟♟♟♟♟
Value	★★★★
Grapes	cabernet sauvignon 41%; cabernet franc 23%; merlot 23%; malbec 7%; petit verdot 6%
Region	Yarra Valley, Vic.
Cellar	🍷 10+
Alc./Vol.	12.0%
RRP	$52.00 (cellar door) 🍷

Mount Mary Pinot Noir

Quality	♟♟♟♟♟
Value	★★★★
Grapes	pinot noir
Region	Yarra Valley, Vic.
Cellar	♟ 5+
Alc./Vol.	13.5%
RRP	$52.00 (cellar door)

Only a tiny amount of pinot is made here every year and as far as supplying the market goes, it doesn't begin to touch the sides. Makers John Middleton and Mario Marson.

Previous outstanding vintages: '82, '84, '85, '86, '88, '91, '92, '94

CURRENT RELEASE 1995   The colour is not deep, but as is often the case with pinot, that's no indication of quality. This is a highly perfumed pinot, with cherry/strawberry aromas but no oak or stalk characters. The taste is refined – delicate yet intense – with tight structure, focus and great length. A benchmark style. Serve with duck confit.

Mount Pleasant Philip

Quality	♟♟♟♟
Value	★★★★
Grapes	shiraz
Region	Hunter Valley, NSW
Cellar	♟ 2
Alc./Vol.	12.0%
RRP	$15.00 Ⓢ

Hunter shiraz is arguably the most determinedly individual wine style in Australia, and McWilliams is one of the most traditional. Maker Phil Ryan.

CURRENT RELEASE 1993   An idiosyncratic, typical Hunter regional style of shiraz. The colour is fairly light and developed; the bouquet shows earth, undergrowth and gamy notes, and recalls mushrooms and beef stock. The palate is light-bodied, soft and very easy to drink, with light gentle tannins. The taste is savoury rather than fruity, and it's complex and food-friendly. Great with mushroom risotto.

Mount Pleasant Rosehill Vineyard Shiraz

This property was bought by Hunter winemaking legend Maurice O'Shea in 1945. The wines are never big; they're always elegant and deceptively long-lived. Maker Phillip Ryan.

CURRENT RELEASE 1995 The colour is still a youthful cherry-red. The nose shows some coconut/vanilla oak and cherry–plum fruit, and the taste is medium-weight, nicely balanced, dry and savoury with some tannin and oak dryness. It benefits from breathing. A lovely drink now, but it will repay cellaring where it will build the gamy, leathery, slightly feral complexities typical of the region. From an excellent year, it should become a classic.

Quality	♆♆♆♆♆
Value	★★★★
Grapes	shiraz
Region	Hunter Valley, NSW
Cellar	🍶 15
Alc./Vol.	12.5%
RRP	$21.30 ⓢ

Mount William Pinot Noir

Mount William is very boutique, with a 6-hectare vineyard and just five wines. They are made at nearby Cope-Williams.

CURRENT RELEASE 1995 The colour has already developed a brick shade and the nose has interesting feral, gamy and vegetal characters. The palate reveals some greenness, and there's prominent acid on the finish. It needs food, so try it with barbecued quails.

Quality	♆♆♆♆
Value	★★★
Grapes	pinot noir
Region	Macedon Ranges, Vic.
Cellar	🍶 2
Alc./Vol.	13.0%
RRP	$23.00

NDC Shiraz

The initials stand for Newell Davis Cowan and this is the reserve label for Eyton on Yarra. It's a bloody marvellous wine.

CURRENT RELEASE 1995 The nose has abundant grape and plum aromas plus some exotic spice. The palate is medium-bodied and very complex; there are berry and plum flavours, which are laced with pepper and spices. These are wedded to some very attractive oak, which imparts plenty of tannin grip. It drinks well now but should become more complex after a decade. It would suit a venison dish.

Quality	♆♆♆♆♆
Value	★★★★
Grapes	shiraz
Region	Yarra Valley, Vic.
Cellar	🍶 5
Alc./Vol.	12.5%
RRP	$27.00

The Nobbies Pinot Noir

Quality	ŸŸŸŸ
Value	★★★★
Grapes	pinot noir
Region	Gippsland, Yarra Valley, Vic.
Cellar	▯ 3
Alc./Vol.	13.0%
RRP	$22.00

The wine has attracted plenty of hype yet it presented in the glass as a pinot noir by another name. MS takes the blame, and probably shows a bias.

CURRENT RELEASE 1996   The nose has strawberry and cherry aromas and the medium-bodied palate has ripe strawberry flavours. These are followed by some reserved tannins and solid acid on a clean finish. It drinks well now with pan-fried quail.

Normans Chais Clarendon Cabernet Sauvignon

Quality	ŸŸŸ⸮
Value	★★★
Grapes	cabernet sauvignon
Region	McLaren Vale, SA
Cellar	▯ 3
Alc./Vol.	12.5%
RRP	$22.00

This is the top of the Normans' tree. Pity about the rather pretentious name. It's a bit like calling the Shield abode Chateau Rat Shack.

CURRENT RELEASE 1995   The nose is a mixture of leaf, oak and perfumed berry aromas. The palate is medium-bodied with sweet redcurrant and cherry fruit flavours. This is linked with some classy oak on a balanced finish that features fine-grained tannins. Try it with meatloaf.

Notley Gorge Cabernet Merlot

Quality	ŸŸŸ⸮
Value	★★★
Grapes	cabernet sauvignon; merlot
Region	Tas.
Cellar	▯ 3
Alc./Vol.	12.5%
RRP	$19.50

This Tasmanian wine comes from Glengarry and shows cool-climate characters. It was established in 1983. Maker Andrew Hood (contract).

CURRENT RELEASE 1995   The nose has a strong tobacco-leaf aroma, and the palate is light- to medium-bodied with some soft raspberry and redcurrant flavours. These are matched by some very fine tannins and persistent grip. It's a well-balanced style, but you've got to like cool-climate reds. Try it with chicken.

Notley Gorge Pinot Noir

The vineyard was established in 1983 in the northern foothills of Notley Fern Gorge in the Western Tamar Valley.

CURRENT RELEASE 1995 The wine is quite light, with a pale brick-red colour and a soft strawberry nose with hints of earth and leaves. The palate offers sweet strawberry flavours. Fresh acid makes for a refreshing finish. It goes well with roast quail.

Quality	▼▼▼
Value	★★★
Grapes	pinot noir
Region	Tas.
Cellar	▮ 2
Alc./Vol.	12.5%
RRP	$19.50

Oakridge Reserve Cabernet Sauvignon

Winemaker Mike Zitzlaff says this comes off red soils on the southern side of the Yarra Valley. They're more fertile soils than the traditional grey loams in the main part of the Valley.

Previous outstanding vintages: '90, '91, '94

CURRENT RELEASE 1995 This is a complex wine that shows off some sophisticated oak handling. There are toasty, gamy, smoked-oyster characters and oak has been liberally applied. It's of elegant weight without a lot of structure, but the flavours are delicious and beautifully balanced. It's hard to see it improving long-term, but it drinks well now with rare beef fillet.

Quality	▼▼▼▼▼
Value	★★★★
Grapes	cabernet sauvignon 95%; merlot 5%
Region	Yarra Valley, Vic.
Cellar	▮ 5+
Alc./Vol.	12.3%
RRP	$35.00

Oakridge Reserve Merlot

The 'Let's-put-out-a-hatful-of-expensive-merlot' craze has truly gone off the rails. The syndrome is particularly virulent in the Yarra Valley.

CURRENT RELEASE 1995 This is a nice wine, but we fail to see why it should be priced at $90. It smells of mulberries and asparagus, and tastes very sweet and fruity/oaky, but so far it's not complex. The palate is round and smooth, and it's easy to drink young. While it has abundant fruit and oak flavours it lacks structure, and it's hard to see it doing much with age. It would drink well with duck.

Quality	▼▼▼▼
Value	★★
Grapes	merlot
Region	Yarra Valley, Vic.
Cellar	▮ 3+
Alc./Vol.	13.5%
RRP	$90.00

Old Station Watervale Shiraz Grenache

Quality	♟♟♟♟
Value	★★★
Grapes	shiraz; grenache
Region	Clare Valley, SA
Cellar	♦ 3
Alc./Vol.	13.8%
RRP	$17.50

The brand is owned by former Sydney retailers Bill and Noel Ireland. The vineyard was planted in 1926 beside the now-defunct Watervale rail station. Maker David O'Leary.

CURRENT RELEASE 1996   A fresh, youthful, spicy style, which should put steam back in the boiler. It's peppery and herbal, and has a lolly character from the grenache. There's no obvious wood, and the texture is quite viscous. It's medium- to light-bodied, soft and quaffable in a light Côtes-du-Rhone style. Serve with vitello tonnato.

Paringa Estate Pinot Noir

Quality	♟♟♟♟♟
Value	★★★★
Grapes	pinot noir
Region	Mornington Peninsula, Vic.
Cellar	⊷ 1–6+
Alc./Vol.	13.5%
RRP	$30.00 (cellar door)

Lindsay McCall shares with Stoniers' Tod Dexter the title of king of pinot noir on the Mornington Peninsula. *Previous outstanding vintages: '88, '90, '91, '92, '93, '95*

CURRENT RELEASE 1997   This is possibly the best yet from Paringa. It's a massive wine, showing concentration in every regard: colour, aroma and palate. The bouquet is terrifically complex with fruit-cake characters, some smart toasty oak and deep dark berry fruits. All this is faithfully translated onto the powerful, lingering palate. Needs time: a monumental effort. Cellar and serve with Chinese honey-glazed pork.

Parker Estate First Growth

John Parker was one of the founding partners in Hungerford Hill. He recently carved off half of his Coonawarra vineyard and sold it to Peppertree, which makes his wine. A winery is currently being built on the land. NB: Last year's *Guide* mistakenly reviewed the '93 as the '94 vintage.

Previous outstanding vintages: '88, '91, '94

CURRENT RELEASE 1996   The best First Growth yet. Good now, but promising much in the cellar, it has great purity of blackberry/blackcurrant fruit, well integrated with smart French oak. Superbly fragrant, elegant palate flavours with fruit-sweet ripeness and liberal oak. A seamless wine and the epitome of Coonawarra. Great with rare roast beef and all the trimmings.

Quality	ΨΨΨΨΨ
Value	★★★★
Grapes	cabernet sauvignon; merlot; cabernet franc
Region	Coonawarra, SA
Cellar	▮ 15
Alc./Vol.	13.5%
RRP	$63.00

Patterson's Shiraz

This is a small-production (1000 cases) vineyard and winery that was established in 1982 by Sue and Arthur Patterson. In their day job they are chalkies.

CURRENT RELEASE 1996   The colour is deep and the nose has some black pepper and dark cherry flavours. The palate is medium-bodied and tight with some hard cherry flavours and pepper spices. The tannins are green and astringent. It might live long but the gains probably won't be spectacular. Try it with casseroled kid.

Quality	ΨΨΨΐ
Value	★★★
Grapes	shiraz
Region	Great Southern, WA
Cellar	▮ 5
Alc./Vol.	12.0%
RRP	$22.00

Paul Osicka Cabernet Sauvignon

Is mint a fault? Some think it is, while others enjoy the character. This wine will put your views to the test. Maker Paul Osicka.

CURRENT RELEASE 1996   They don't come much more minty than this! It's not unattractive but the quirk is marked. The palate also shows a trace of mint with blackberry flavours. The body is medium in terms of weight and there's some well-structured tannin on the finish. The acid remains high and clean. It's a neat wine that goes well with a beef and onion pie.

Quality	ΨΨΨΨ
Value	★★★★
Grapes	cabernet sauvignon
Region	Goulburn Valley, Vic.
Cellar	▮ 5
Alc./Vol.	13.0%
RRP	$22.20

Paul Osicka Shiraz

Quality	♈♈♈♈
Value	★★★★
Grapes	shiraz
Region	Goulburn Valley, Vic.
Cellar	▮ 5
Alc./Vol.	13.0%
RRP	$22.20

The vineyard and winery were established in 1955. In the formative decades all the production was sold in bulk to merchants like Crittendens and Seabrooks.

CURRENT RELEASE 1996   Mega mint on the nose, which also has dark cherry and spice aromas. The medium-bodied palate is clean and tight with dark cherry flavours. The oak slips in without a pause, adding fine-grained tannins. It goes well with a beef and Guinness pie.

Pauletts Polish Hill River Cabernet Merlot

Quality	♈♈♈♈♈
Value	★★★★⋆
Grapes	cabernet sauvignon 88%; merlot 12%
Region	Clare Valley, SA
Cellar	▮ 5
Alc./Vol.	13.5%
RRP	$21.00

Neil 'Darkie' Paulett is a charming chap and a very talented winemaker. The view from his cellar door is spectacularly enchanting.

CURRENT RELEASE 1996   The colour is deep, and the nose has pungent aromas with loads of berry and rose-petal character. There's also a background of spice. The medium- to full-bodied palate has complexity and length. Blackberry is the major flavour, and there's a hint of pepper–spice. Fine-grained tannins round out the finish adding plenty of grip. Try it with roast saddle of hare.

Pauletts Polish Hill River Shiraz

Quality	♈♈♈♈
Value	★★★★
Grapes	shiraz
Region	Clare Valley, SA
Cellar	▮ 4
Alc./Vol.	13.5%
RRP	$22.00

The vineyard was established in 1983 and the production is 12 000 cases. Clare Valley shiraz is making a big claim to fame.

CURRENT RELEASE 1996   The nose is powerful with shiraz and oak aromas. The palate is complex with hints of chocolate, plums and pepper. It's medium-bodied but also quite rich. The wood on the finish gives a vanilla touch, and it's well balanced against the weight for fruit. It should age well. A rare roast beef and Yorkshire pud would suit it nicely.

Pegasus Bay Pinot Noir

The vineyard was established in 1992 and has an annual production of around 15 000 cases.

CURRENT RELEASE 1996 The wine is a tight little number that has undergrowth and earthy aromas on the nose. The medium-bodied palate is understated, with some muted cherry flavours followed by assertive acid on the finish. It responds to breathing and suits stir-fried lamb straps.

Quality	♟♟♟♟
Value	★★★
Grapes	pinot noir
Region	Canterbury, NZ
Cellar	🍷 2
Alc./Vol.	13.0%
RRP	$28.00

Penfolds Bin 128 Coonawarra

Is this the last of the regional Penfolds Bin numbers? It's a brave try under difficult vintage conditions.
Previous outstanding vintages: '71, '78, '80, '82, '86, '88, '90, '91, '92, '93, '94
CURRENT RELEASE 1995 The nose has some charming berry, leather and leaf characters. The medium- to light-bodied palate offers sweet cherry and raspberry flavours, and the oak plays a sympathetic part imparting dusty dry tannins. Good work, and it is beaut with beef and mushroom pie.

Quality	♟♟♟♟
Value	★★★★
Grapes	shiraz
Region	Coonawarra, SA
Cellar	🍷 3
Alc./Vol.	12.5%
RRP	$20.50

Penfolds Bin 389 Cabernet Shiraz

This is a very famous bin number that stands the test of time. The 1995 vintage was Wednesday's child in terms of ripening conditions, so this wine is a triumph for the wine cobblers.
Previous outstanding vintages: '66, '71, '80, '83, '87, '90, '91, '92, '94
CURRENT RELEASE 1995 The colour is a healthy red/purple and the nose has plum, meat and spice aromas. The medium- to full-bodied palate offers sweet ripe fruit flavours with cherry and plum flavours and there's a typical Penfolds oak treatment on the finish. Loads of zip and grip with nutmeg and vanilla spice. It should cellar for the medium term. Try it with steak and eggs.

Quality	♟♟♟♟
Value	★★★★
Grapes	cabernet sauvignon; shiraz
Region	various, SA
Cellar	🍷 4
Alc./Vol.	13.0%
RRP	$27.90

Penfolds Bin 407 Cabernet Sauvignon

Quality	♟♟♟♟
Value	★★★★
Grapes	cabernet sauvignon
Region	various, SA
Cellar	▲ 4
Alc./Vol.	13.0%
RRP	$24.00 ⑤

This is a late starter in the bin number range, which started in 1990. It's being touted on the label as the 'benchmark' for Australia's cabernet sauvignon. What happened to Bin 707?

CURRENT RELEASE 1995   This is a leaner example, thanks to the vintage conditions. The nose has a distinct leaf aroma plus blackberries. The medium-bodied palate is a tad fruit-shy but there's complexity, and blackcurrant flavour dominates. The tailored oak works well. Serve it with braised steak and onions.

Penfolds Clare Estate

Quality	♟♟♟♟♟
Value	★★★★★
Grapes	merlot; cabernet sauvignon; cabernet franc
Region	Clare Valley, SA
Cellar	▲ 5
Alc./Vol.	12.5%
RRP	$22.55

What a difference a year makes! This vintage came good in many regions and it reflects in the quality and flavour. Great to see this region in the correct light.

CURRENT RELEASE 1996   The nose has savoury barrel storage-shed smells and crushed berry aromas. The palate is medium- to full-bodied and there are lashings of sweet fruit flavour. Froggy oak adds to the complexity but doesn't steal the scene. Nice grip and it drinks well. Try it with Peking duck.

Penfolds Grange

Australia's most famous wine has never had more competition for that distinction. Rich, concentrated, oaky old-vine shirazes are being produced by a host of makers in various regions. But judging by price and hoopla, Grange still has the edge. It is still the only real internationally collectable Australian wine and as such it's in the same league as the top Bordeaux. Maker John Duval and team.

Previous Outstanding Vintages: '52, '53, '55, '62, '63, '66, '71, '76, '83, '86, '88, '90, '91

CURRENT RELEASE 1993 A very good Grange. It seems slightly forward in colour and perhaps lacks some of the immense length we expect from Grange, but this is a case of splitting hairs. Trademark toasty oak contributes to the gamy, earthy, undergrowth bouquet and there are traces of cassis, prune, plum, licorice and black olive to smell. It is smooth and supple despite a very full body, and assertive tannin provides a drying grip to the finish. A savoury style that's built around oak. Grange lovers will not be disappointed. Serve it with aged cheddar.

Quality	🍷🍷🍷🍷🍷
Value	★★½
Grapes	shiraz
Region	Barossa Valley & Coonawarra, SA
Cellar	5–15+
Alc./Vol.	13.5%
RRP	$200–$250

Penfolds Kalimna Bin 28

Do us a favour – Kalimna is a vineyard in the Barossa Valley, so how come the grapes for Bin 28 come from all over the shop? Is it part of the Southcorp plot to make Chairman Mao suits at various price levels?

Previous outstanding vintages: '71, '82, '83, '86, '87, '88, '90, '91, '92, '93, '94

CURRENT RELEASE 1995 The wine has a musty (but not corked) nose with some leather and berry aromas. The palate is medium-bodied with sweet berry flavours but a certain hollowness. The wood redeems with some drying tannins. There's not a lot of room for improvement, so drink now. Try it with spaghetti bolognaise.

Quality	🍷🍷🍷
Value	★★★
Grapes	shiraz
Region	Barossa, Padthaway, Langhorne Creek, McLaren Vale and Clare Valley, SA
Cellar	3
Alc./Vol.	$13.00
RRP	$20.00

Penfolds Koonunga Hill Shiraz Cabernet Sauvignon

Quality	🍷🍷🍷
Value	★★★
Grapes	shiraz; cabernet sauvignon
Region	not stated
Cellar	3
Alc./Vol.	13.5%
RRP	$12.50 (S)

This is the ever-reliable people's wine. It's a bit like a Vee Dub, it usually gets you there with a minimum of fuss. Unfortunately the price is creeping up into non-Volks realm.

CURRENT RELEASE 1996 This is a relatively lean Penfolds style. The nose has aromatic berry characters with a hint of spice. The palate is medium-bodied with sweet redcurranty and cherry flavours. The tannin is gentle and non-threatening. It is a good savoury-mince-on-toast style.

Penfolds Old Vine Shiraz Mourvèdre Grenache

Quality	🍷🍷🍷🍷
Value	★★★★
Grapes	shiraz; mourvèdre; grenache
Region	Barossa Valley, SA
Cellar	6
Alc./Vol.	13.5%
RRP	$23.50

For all the buzzwords on this label, it is a resurrection of the old Bin 2 that fell out of fashion in the 1970s along with the Barossa Valley.

CURRENT RELEASE 1995 The wine is rich and soft with an emphasis on fruit. There are strong plum aromas and hints of spice. The full-bodied palate has sweet raspberry and plum flavours, and these are wedded to some attractive oak which adds caressing tannins. It goes well with a steak and kidney pie.

Penfolds Rawson's Retreat

Quality	🍷🍷🍷
Value	★★★½
Grapes	cabernet sauvignon; shiraz; ruby cabernet
Region	various, SA
Cellar	1
Alc./Vol.	13.0%
RRP	$10.00 (S)

Why did Rawson attack in the first place? This wine is classified as 'Penfolds entry level wine'. It is ranked in the top five best-selling wines under $10.00. Perhaps that makes it a fighting brand.

CURRENT RELEASE 1997 As you would expect, the earth doesn't move but you get a very good quaff. The nose has sweet fruit and spice aromas. The palate is fruity and the finish shows some benign tannin. Try it with bangers and mash.

Penfolds St Henri Shiraz

This much-revered label is starting to bulk up a bit: there's more tannin and structure. Once second only to Grange, it has since been eclipsed by 707, Magill Estate et al.

CURRENT RELEASE 1993 The nose has typical Penfolds ripe fruit aromas and toasty oak. The full-bodied palate has ripe plum fruit flavours, hints of earth and leathery overtones. There are fine-grained tannins on a long dry finish. It's one for the long haul. Try it with bratwurst.

Quality 🍷🍷🍷🍷
Value ★★★★
Grapes shiraz
Region various SA
Cellar 5
Alc./Vol. 13.5%
RRP $39.50

CURRENT RELEASE 1994 This is a great drink and you'll be sorry when the bottle is empty. There are ripe plum and spice aromas on the nose. The palate is full-bodied with rich plum flavours and hints of earthy characters. There's a succulent quality which is framed by some gentle tannins and well-integrated oak. Serve with osso bucco.

Quality 🍷🍷🍷🍷½
Value ★★★★½
Grapes shiraz & cabernet sauvignon
Region various, SA
Cellar 6
Alc./Vol. 13.5%
RRP $39.50

Penley Estate Cabernet Sauvignon

Penley is Pen-folds and Tol-ley joined together. If you know your Australian winemaking history you'll appreciate the significance. Kym Tolley is a descendant of Dr Penfold.

Previous outstanding vintages: '92, '94

CURRENT RELEASE 1995 The wine is a very good try in a difficult year. The nose has strong blackberry aromas plus a hint of spice. The medium-bodied palate is slightly hollow and blackberry. The finish shows some fine-grained tannins and a hardness in the grip. It goes well with a mushroom risotto.

Quality 🍷🍷🍷🍷
Value ★★★
Grapes cabernet sauvignon
Region Coonawarra, SA
Cellar 5
Alc./Vol. 13.0%
RRP $50.00

Penley Estate Hyland Shiraz

Quality	♥♥♥⬗
Value	★★★
Grapes	shiraz
Region	Coonawarra, SA
Cellar	▯ 3
Alc./Vol.	12.5%
RRP	$18.00

This is the fighting brand for Penley Estate. At the price it won't really slug it out with the likes of Wynns just down the road. Maker Kym Tolley.

CURRENT RELEASE 1996   The nose is a mixture of fresh plum, leaf and fermentation aromas. The medium-bodied palate has attractive plum flavours, which are matched by some white pepper spice. The oak plays a distant supporting role. It drinks well now with a designer pizza.

Penley Estate Shiraz Cabernet

Quality	♥♥♥⬗
Value	★★★
Grapes	shiraz; cabernet sauvignon
Region	Coonawarra, SA
Cellar	▯ 4
Alc./Vol.	13.5%
RRP	$25.00

Kym Tolley has thrown a bucket of money at this project which started from virgin terra rossa soil in 1988.

CURRENT RELEASE 1995   This is a tough wine. There's a strong wet bracken or undergrowth aroma on the nose. The medium-bodied palate is a little fruit-shy; there are blackberry and plum flavours but these are masked by heavy tannins on an assertive finish. It might settle with time. Try it with smoked lamb.

Penley Phoenix Cabernet Sauvignon

Quality	♥♥♥⬗
Value	★★★⬗
Grapes	cabernet sauvignon
Region	Coonawarra, SA
Cellar	▯ 3
Alc./Vol.	12.5%
RRP	$ 20.50

A phoenix was a mythical Arabian bird that built its nest with spices, and flapped its wings so hard they caught fire. After self-immolation it rose again from the ashes. The Phoenix refers to Tolley's first company, the Phoenix Winemaking and Distilling company.

CURRENT RELEASE 1996   The wine is a light and like-able style with a blackberry aroma on the nose with a hint of green leaf. The light to medium palate has some charming blackberry flavours and the tannins on the finish are soft and discreet. This wine drinks well now. Serve with a designer pizza.

Pepper Tree Wines Cabernet Sauvignon, Cabernet Franc, Merlot

Another Coonawarra that is sold in the Hunter Valley. This takes a leaf out of the Brokenwood manual and refuses to be a prisoner of the vineyard or region. The company has 50 hectares in the Hunter and 10 hectares in Coonawarra.

CURRENT RELEASE 1996 This is a very elegant style that has been blended for maximum complexity. The nose has ripe berry aromas and toasty oak smells. The medium-bodied palate is complex, with attractive blackberry and cherry flavours. These are matched by fine-grained tannins on a grippy finish. It should suit pink lamb.

Quality	??????
Value	★★★★ト
Grapes	cabernet sauvignon; cabernet franc; merlot
Region	Coonawarra, SA
Cellar	▮ 4
Alc./Vol.	13.0%
RRP	$18.50

Pepper Tree Wines Classics Reserve

Contact *www.ozemail.com.au/peppetw* if you want to know more. Interesting how the classic differs from its cousin – same blend, tad more alcohol and a lot more money. Maker Chris Cameron.

CURRENT RELEASE 1996 Big colour and a very seductive nose with a lot of perfumed cabernet franc influence. The palate has a strong blackberry flavour and a juicy mouthfilling texture. The finish is overwhelmed by the fruit and the tannins seem mild and gentle. There's modest grip. It's well matched by some smoked turkey breast.

Quality	??????
Value	★★★
Grapes	cabernet sauvignon; merlot; cabernet franc
Region	Coonawarra, SA
Cellar	▮ 4
Alc./Vol.	13.4%
RRP	$33.00

Pepper Tree Wines Merlot

This is the face of the modern Hunter Valley, which is as much about tourism as it is about wine. The grapes come from Coonawarra. The presentation is pretty fancy, right down to the embossed bottle.

CURRENT RELEASE 1996 The colour is a deep purple and the nose has mulberry and blackberry aromas. The palate is substantial with sweet berry characters and loads of flavour. These are matched by some fine-grained tannins on a grippy finish. It should cellar well and goes well with venison sausages.

Quality	?????
Value	★★★★
Grapes	merlot
Region	Coonawarra, SA
Cellar	▮ 6
Alc./Vol.	14.1%
RRP	$45.00

Petaluma Coonawarra

Quality	?????
Value	★★★★
Grapes	cabernet sauvignon; merlot
Region	Coonawarra
Cellar	➛ 2–7+
Alc./Vol.	13.3%
RRP	$42.00 ▮

Maker Brian Croser cut back on the industry politics, committees and globe-trotting statesmanship to return to hands-on winemaking, but now he's back fighting taxes as president of the Winemaker's Federation.
Previous outstanding vintages: '79, '82, '88, '90, '91, '92, '93, '94
CURRENT RELEASE 1996   The label notes that the wine is unfiltered, which is an attempt to maximise the flavour. The nose has cherry aromas and a hint of mint, lantana and leaves. The medium-bodied palate is tightly structured and there are some dark cherry flavours as well as blackberry notes. The oak has a toasty character and the finish has plenty of grip. It needs more time in the bottle and would go well with a lamb and barley pie.

Peter Lehmann Clancy's

Quality	????
Value	★★★★⋆
Grapes	shiraz; cabernet sauvignon; cabernet franc; merlot
Region	Barossa Valley, SA
Cellar	▮ 3
Alc./Vol.	13.5%
RRP	$14.50

Some marketing boffin has been tinkering again. The wine is no stranger to these pages but the label has been completely changed. Why? Maker Andrew Wigan.
CURRENT RELEASE 1996   The nose is rich with leaf, mint and ripe fruit. The palate is sweet with dark cherry and plum flavours, and there's a hint of earth. The wood gives a dusty effect to the tannin on the finish. It's a pretty package that drinks well now. Try it with lamb and barley broth.

Peter Lehmann Grenache

Quality	???
Value	★★★
Grapes	grenache
Region	Barossa Valley, SA
Cellar	▮ 1
Alc./Vol.	14.5%
RRP	$18.00

It seems grenache has become a fashion statement that can't be denied, particularly in the Barossa Valley. Here's yet another example.
CURRENT RELEASE 1997   The colour is light ruby and the nose has a strong raspberry aroma plus a hint of sweetness. The palate is simple with sweet raspberry-jam flavours. The tannin on the finish is soft and gentle. It's dial-a-pizza style.

Peter Lehmann Mentor

What makes this multiple blend a Mentor is unclear. Could it be that the old vines give wisdom to the blend? They are in the sub-regions of Stonewell, Angaston, Ebenezer and Light Pass.

CURRENT RELEASE 1993   The wine is a very fruity drop with a strong berry aroma on the nose. The palate is supple and sweet, with ripe blackberry and dark cherry flavours. The wood is carefully blended with a brace of dry tannins and persistent grip. It drinks well now and the wine goes well with roast goose.

Quality	♟♟♟♟♟
Value	★★★★⊢
Grapes	cabernet sauvignon; malbec; shiraz; merlot
Region	Barossa Valley, SA
Cellar	▮ 4
Alc./Vol.	13.5%
RRP	$22.50

Peter Lehmann Shiraz

Lordy, lordy – look at the fancy bottle. It looks cheap, and goes against the laws of shiraz and convention. Never mind, it's what's in the glass that counts.

CURRENT RELEASE 1996   The nose is typical Barossa abundance with rich plum, spice and pepper aromas. The palate is medium- to full-bodied with sweet ripe cherry and plum flavours and well-tailored oak. There's plenty of grip and the fine-grained tannins dry the mouth. Goes well with beef casserole.

Quality	♟♟♟♟♟
Value	★★★★⊢
Grapes	shiraz
Region	Barossa Valley, SA
Cellar	▮ 6
Alc./Vol.	14.0%
RRP	$17.00

Phantom's Lake Cabernet Shiraz

Is this a case of running something up the flagpole to see if anyone salutes? It has more flash than substance. Mildara Blass get the blame.

CURRENT RELEASE 1995   It's a drinkable commercial style with a bright ruby colour. The nose has soft berry aromas, and there are pleasant raspberry flavours on a medium-bodied palate. The tannin on the finish has a dry dusty quality. It drinks well now with a meat pie.

Quality	♟♟♟
Value	★★★
Grapes	cabernet sauvignon 75%; shiraz 25%
Region	Glenrowan; Barossa Valley; McLaren Vale
Cellar	▮ 2
Alc./Vol.	13.0%
RRP	$14.50

Pikes Clare Valley Cabernet

Quality	♟♟♟♟
Value	★★★★
Grapes	cabernet sauvignon 95%; cabernet franc 5%
Region	Clare Valley, SA
Cellar	➠ 2–6
Alc./Vol.	13.5%
RRP	$23.00

This wine is from the Polish Hill River sub-region of Clare. Neil Pike is an old hand in the region: don't ever let him con you into a game of golf!

CURRENT RELEASE 1996 It has a rich ruby colour, and the nose has blackberry and iron-tonic aromas. This ferric influence is also detected on the palate, which has a strong berry flavour and a medium to full body. The oak on the finish is discreet but supportive, and the tannin is soft. Try it with steak and kidney.

Pikes Reserve Shiraz

Quality	♟♟♟♟♟
Value	★★★⊬
Grapes	shiraz
Region	Clare Valley, SA
Cellar	▮ 8+
Alc./Vol.	14.0%
RRP	$42.00

The Pike brothers are quiet achievers in the Clare district. Winemaker Neil looks after the property, while Andrew is head viticulturist with Southcorp.

Previous outstanding vintages: '94

CURRENT RELEASE 1995 Less gutsy than many in Clare, where the approach often seems to be the bigger the better. Make no mistake: this is an opulent, warmly flavoured red, smoothly succulent and brimming with cherry and blackberry fruit. The oak, largely French these days, is commendably well balanced, and the alcohol doesn't do a flame-out on the finish. A very smart wine. Serve with aged cheeses.

Pikes Shiraz

Quality	♟♟♟♟
Value	★★★★
Grapes	shiraz
Region	Clare Valley, SA
Cellar	▮ 4
Alc./Vol.	14.0%
RRP	$23.00

The label has become a bit of classy design: it's elegant and understated. The wine tends to be more exuberant and both make a handsome package. Maker Neil Pike.

CURRENT RELEASE 1996 The spice is nice and there's plenty of it! The colour has the typical Clare density, and the nose is full of spicy plum with a whiff of oak. The palate is about bold berry flavours, with a hint of earth and aniseed. The oak is subtle and engages the fruit without overpowering the flavour. It should cellar well, and it's great with venison.

Plunkett Blackwood Ridge Pinot Noir

Don't know what to make of the label; it's certainly not for everybody. Include MS out.
CURRENT RELEASE 1996   This is a standard-issue pinot noir with a light ruby colour. The nose is a mixture of strawberry and sap aromas. The medium-bodied palate has simple strawberry fruit flavours, and there's a zap of acid and some discreet oak. It drinks well now with char-grilled quail.

Quality	????
Value	★★★⊦
Grapes	pinot noir
Region	Strathbogie, Vic.
Cellar	▮ 3
Alc./Vol.	13.0%
RRP	$20.00

Plunkett Strathbogie Ranges Cabernet Merlot

The winery was established in 1980. There are two vine-yards: 3.6 hectares at Avenel and 52 hectares at Strath-bogie on a hilltop location. Maker Sam Plunkett.
CURRENT RELEASE 1996   It has a deep ruby colour and a strong nose full of blackberry and rose-petal aromas. The middleweight palate is succulent with rich sweet berry flavours, and these are adorned by some classy oak on a dry and gripping finish. It should cellar well and it responds to decanting. Serve with a duck terrine.

Quality	????
Value	★★★★
Grapes	cabernet sauvignon; merlot
Region	Strathbogie, Vic.
Cellar	▮ 5
Alc./Vol.	12.6%
RRP	$22.30

Port Phillip Estate Pinot Noir

'And the beat goes on . . .' The hunt for the definitive great Australian pinot noir goes on, and much of the intensity is centred on the Mornington Peninsula.
CURRENT RELEASE 1997   Very smart wine with a con-vincing deep-ruby colour. The nose is packed with emphatic ripe berry aromas. The medium-bodied palate has a rich dark-cherry flavour and some toasty high-toned oak. There are fine-grained tannins that supply plenty of grip on the finish. It should age gracefully and well. Try it with roast squab and wild rice.

Quality	?????
Value	★★★★⊦
Grapes	pinot noir
Region	Mornington Peninsula, Vic.
Cellar	▮ 6
Alc./Vol.	14.0%
RRP	$23.00

Portree Damask

Quality	▼▼▼▼
Value	★★★★
Grapes	cabernet franc
Region	Macedon, Vic.
Cellar	▮ 3
Alc./Vol.	11.3%
RRP	$13.95 (cellar door)

Up here for thinking . . . This rosé is called Damask after a family of roses, traditionally credited with the best perfume. Maker Ken Murchison.

CURRENT RELEASE 1997   This is as close to an Anjou rosé style as we can recall seeing in Oz. In fact it's better than most Anjous we've tried. Very lively herbaceous/raspberry aromas; intense and clean as a whistle. The palate really sings, with some sweetness well balanced by the zing of high natural acidity. Very intense. It goes well with barbecued baby octopus.

Preece Cabernet Sauvignon

Quality	▼▼▼
Value	★★★
Grapes	cabernet sauvignon
Region	various, Vic.
Cellar	▮ 2
Alc./Vol.	13.0%
RRP	$14.50 Ⓢ

Whether the Australian winemaking icon Colin Preece would have been impressed with having his name on this style of wine is debatable.

CURRENT RELEASE 1996   The wine is a commercial style with a light berry aroma on the nose. The medium-bodied palate has cherry and raspberry flavours, and there are soft tannins on the finish. It's a quaffing style that goes well with a pizza.

Redgate Cabernet Franc

Quality	▼▼▼▼?
Value	★★★★
Grapes	cabernet franc
Region	Margaret River, WA
Cellar	▮ 5
Alc./Vol.	14.7%
RRP	$28.00

There's no use carving wine rules in stone. For example, 'cabernet franc should not be the major component of a blend or stand alone'. As soon as that is done, along comes a wine to disprove the rule.

CURRENT RELEASE 1995   Smooth and silky with attitude, this wine has plenty of grunt but manages to retain finesse. The nose is highly seductive, with loads of perfume. The palate is rich with a mouthfilling texture and a strong redcurrant flavour. The finish doesn't disappoint because there's plenty of tannin and length. A stylish wine that needs a robust dish like liver and bacon in a reduction sauce.

Redgate Cabernet Sauvignon

Textbook stuff except for the label (in the eyes of MS), which has the inevitable red gate as a centrepiece. According to a survey at cellar doors, people like it like that. For the record, the gate leads to the beach. Maker Andrew Forsell.

CURRENT RELEASE 1995   The mojo is working with this one; it's quintessential Margaret River. The nose is a mix of cassis and briar aromas. The palate is lean but not mean, there are complex cassis and cherry flavours, and the oak strikes a dark minor chord. It has some heavy fine-grained tannins and plenty of grip. It fits well with Peking duck.

Quality	♥♥♥♥
Value	★★★★
Grapes	cabernet sauvignon 86%; cabernet franc 12%; merlot 2%
Region	Margaret River, WA
Cellar	▮ 5
Alc./Vol.	13.4%
RRP	$28.00

Redgate Shiraz

Shiraz tends to be forgotten in these parts where cabernet tends to be king. It's a pity because shiraz can be a star if it's handled properly. Redgate have the clues.

CURRENT RELEASE 1995   This wine has plenty of verve. The nose is assertive with lots of stewed plum and spices. The palate is very generous, flooding the mouth with rich cherry and plum flavours that are garnished with cinnamon and cloves. Pepper is also there, and this leads on to some grippy tannins on a long finish. It needs time and goes well with a guineafowl pie.

Quality	♥♥♥♥?
Value	★★★★
Grapes	shiraz
Region	Margaret River, WA
Cellar	➤ 2–6+
Alc./Vol.	14.2%
RRP	$29.30

Red Hill Estate Pinot Noir

Red Hill is one of the more ambitious ventures on the Peninsula. It was founded in 1989 and produces 6000 cases per year. Maker Jenny Bright.

CURRENT RELEASE 1997   A wine with structure and good colour. The nose has ripe cherry and sap aromas. The medium-bodied palate is already quite complex with cherry and blood plum flavours. These are matched by some discreet oak and fresh acid. The wine should develop well and is amigos with chargrilled quail.

Quality	♥♥♥♥?
Value	★★★★
Grapes	pinot noir
Region	Mornington Peninsula, Vic.
Cellar	▮ 4
Alc./Vol.	13.4%
RRP	$25.00

Redman Coonawarra Cabernet Sauvignon

Quality	ŢŢŢĭ
Value	★★ĭ
Grapes	cabernet sauvignon
Region	Coonawarra, SA
Cellar	▬ 5
Alc./Vol.	12.5%
RRP	$25.00

Cabernet sauvignon was a late arrival in the Redman portfolio. In the beginning there was shiraz, which was originally called 'claret'.
CURRENT RELEASE 1996 The nose has a strong mixture of mint and spices on a background of red-currant fruit. The palate is elegant with raspberry and redcurrant flavours, and there's a blast of oak on a tannic finish. It would go well with smoked lamb.

Redman Coonawarra Shiraz

Quality	ŢŢŢĭ
Value	★★★
Grapes	shiraz
Region	Coonawarra, SA
Cellar	▬ 3
Alc./Vol.	12.5%
RRP	$17.00

This is an historic label that was first minted in 1966 when the original Rouge Homme was sold. It was the start of the independent labels on the terra rossa strip. Maker Bruce 'Redders' Redman.
CURRENT RELEASE 1996 The nose is sappy with soft berry aromas. The medium-bodied palate is relatively straightforward, with plum flavours and a touch of spice. The oak is unobtrusive and the finish soft. A good wine with pasta.

Reynella Cabernet Sauvignon

Quality	ŢŢŢŢ
Value	★★ĭ
Grapes	cabernet sauvignon
Region	McLaren Vale, SA
Cellar	➥ 3–7
Alc./Vol.	14.0%
RRP	$37.00

Lovely old-fashioned wine but it's a pity about the new-fangled price. BRL Hardy are not alone in high prices but enjoying fine red wine is becoming a rich person's sport.
CURRENT RELEASE 1995 Big and rich with plenty of grunt, but there are no brutal elements. The nose is rich with strong berry fruit and loads of spices. The palate is rich with a sweet blackberry flavour and a mixture of spices. There are black-tea-like tannins on a firm finish. It needs hearty food like oxtail stew.

Reynella Shiraz

When all else fails, go back to tried-and-true methods. Low-tech winemaking techniques like open fermenters and basket-pressing have helped to restore the glory of this historic label.

Previous outstanding vintages: '92, '93, '94

CURRENT RELEASE 1995 There's an abundance of riches in this wine. The nose has ripe-plum, capsicum, cinnamon and pepper aromas. The palate is mouthfilling with sweet plum and berry characters. The tannin is soft, with a caressing grip, and there's the warmth of alcohol with attendant sweetness. Try it with a spicy meat loaf.

Quality	🍷🍷🍷🍷½
Value	★★½
Grapes	shiraz
Region	McLaren Vale, SA
Cellar	➡ 2–7
Alc./Vol.	14.0%
RRP	$37.00

Ribbon Vale Estate Cabernet Sauvignon

This winery and vineyard were established in 1977, when the region was just starting to be noticed around the wine world. The production is around 4000 cases. Maker Mike Davies.

CURRENT RELEASE 1995 A tough style that needs time. At the moment, austerity is the watchword. The colour is deep and the nose is closed. There are some briar aromas and blackberry smells. The palate has blackberry flavours and leafy characters. The oak and fine-grained tannins make for an astringent finish. It goes well with a seared Scotch fillet steak.

Quality	🍷🍷🍷½
Value	★★★½
Grapes	cabernet sauvignon
Region	Margaret River, WA
Cellar	➡ 2–6
Alc./Vol.	13.0%
RRP	$19.75

Ribbon Vale Estate Cabernet Sauvignon Merlot

This is the second of the reds; the dash of merlot makes a big difference to the drinkability.

CURRENT RELEASE 1995 Much more approachable than the cabernet because the merlot puts some flesh on its bones. The nose has strong perfumed fruit aromas, and there's a hint of rose garden and lavender to add interest. The medium-bodied palate is sweet with some attractive raspberry flavours, and there are some black-tea tannins on the finish. A style that would suit a beef burgundy.

Quality	🍷🍷🍷🍷
Value	★★★★
Grapes	cabernet sauvignon 48%; merlot 37%; cabernet franc 15%
Region	Margaret River, WA
Cellar	🍾 4
Alc./Vol.	13.0%
RRP	$19.75

Riddoch Cabernet Shiraz

Quality	♟♟♟
Value	★★★
Grapes	cabernet sauvignon; shiraz
Region	Coonawarra, SA
Cellar	▐ 2
Alc./Vol.	12.5%
RRP	$17.70 ⑤

Another commercial style from Coonawarra. There seems to be a growing trend towards wines with a high leaf-mulch character – too bad.

CURRENT RELEASE 1996   The nose has a leafy, wet bracken aroma and hints of wood. The palate is light-to medium-bodied with some sweet redcurrant fruit flavours that are followed by discreet oak and high acidity. Serve with gnocchi and a meat sauce.

Riddoch Shiraz

Quality	♟♟♟
Value	★★★
Grapes	shiraz
Region	Coonawarra, SA
Cellar	▐ 2
Alc./Vol.	13.0%
RRP	$17.70 ⑤

This is the middle-of-the-road Coonawarra shiraz that is made to drink when young. Pity it doesn't live up to the promise of the year's vintage conditions.

CURRENT RELEASE 1996   The nose has a strong mulched-leaf component as well as spice and powdery oak. The fruit makes a late entrance on the palate, which is medium-bodied, and there are some attractive sweetness and raspberry fruit flavours. The oak on the finish is gentle but there's some firm acidity. Try it with savoury mince.

R L Buller & Son Cabernet Sauvignon

Quality	♟♟♟
Value	★★★
Grapes	cabernet sauvignon
Region	Swan Hill, Vic.
Cellar	▐ 4
Alc./Vol.	13.0%
RRP	$17.95

It's sad to note the death of Richard 'Dick' Buller, who was one of the great winemakers of Rutherglen. Maker Richard Buller Jr.

CURRENT RELEASE 1996   The colour is a vibrant ruby, and the nose has a slightly stewed berry aroma with a hint of yeast. The palate has sweet raspberry fruit flavours with hints of dark cherry. There are black-tea-like tannins on an astringent finish. It needs more bottle-age. Try it with T-bone steak and eggs.

R L Buller & Son Calliope Shiraz

Don't fall over when you read the alcohol content, this is the famous Rutherglen red style that you don't see all that often in modern times. It's nice to get some in a glass once in a while. This is a museum release.
CURRENT RELEASE 1991 Wow, time has done this wine a favour. It must have been a brute when young but now it's a lovely drink. The colour is youthful and dark. The nose has spicy plum aromas. The palate is full-bodied with rich ripe berry flavours floating on a solid raft of tannin. There's plenty of grip on the impressive finish. It needs a chargrilled aged steak and all the trimmings.

Quality	♟♟♟♟
Value	★★★
Grapes	shiraz
Region	North East Vic.
Cellar	🍷 5
Alc./Vol.	16.0%
RRP	$39.00

R L Buller & Son Victoria Classic

This tri-blend was made to drink now. A classic it ain't, but the maker is hoping it will become the top of the pops. Maker Richard Buller Jr.
CURRENT RELEASE 1996 The nose is dominated by ripe berry aromas and the palate is light to middleweight with sweet, soft berry fruit flavours. Raspberry seems to dominate, and the tannins on the finish are soft. The mouth is left with a dry, dusty sensation. It is a good outdoors' style with BBQ chops.

Quality	♟♟♟
Value	★★★
Grapes	shiraz; grenache; malbec
Region	Murray Valley, Vic.
Cellar	🍷 2
Alc./Vol.	13.6%
RRP	$11.00

Robertson's Well Cabernet Sauvignon

The search for another Jamiesons Run goes on. It's all part of 'the run it up the flagpole and see if anyone salutes' culture at Fosters nee Mildara Blass. Maker 'Gifted Gavin' Hogg.
CURRENT RELEASE 1996 A very tidy wine which is a tango between oak and fruit. There's a hint of vanilla on the cassis-laden nose. The medium-bodied palate has sweet blackberry fruit flavours and a tinge of spice. The wood gives a good account of itself and there's abundant tannin on a grippy finish. A good each-way bet, cellar or drink. Try it with chargrilled lamb fillets.

Quality	♟♟♟♟
Value	★★★★
Grapes	cabernet sauvignon
Region	Coonawarra, SA
Cellar	🍷 4
Alc./Vol.	13.0%
RRP	$18.00

Rosemount Balmoral Syrah

Quality	❦❦❦❦❦
Value	★★★❦
Grapes	shiraz
Region	McLaren Vale, SA
Cellar	⬤ 8
Alc./Vol.	13.5%
RRP	$49.00

Why not shiraz? That's marketing, folks, but it remains big McLaren Vale shiraz, whatever the label says.
CURRENT RELEASE 1995 Big wood statement here: loads of high-tone Yankee oak and just enough fruit to make a convincing package. The colour is deep, dark plum. The nose has high-toned vanilla and sawdust aromas, plus underlying fruit. The palate has a solid weight of fruit (less than the previous vintage), and the oak steals the scene with a marked note of vanilla. There are grippy tannins on the finish, which is dry and astringent. Serve with strong cheddar.

Rosemount Coonawarra Cabernet Sauvignon

Quality	❦❦❦❦
Value	★★★★
Grapes	cabernet sauvignon
Region	Coonawarra, SA
Cellar	⬤ 4
Alc./Vol.	13.5
RRP	$28.00

Considering the weather trials and tribulations, this wine turned out very well. Rosemount have plantings very close to Penola on terra rossa soil.
CURRENT RELEASE 1995 The wine has a mulberry nose with hints of cigar box and leaf. The medium-bodied palate has rich blackberry fruit flavours and a silky mouth-feel. The oak works well with a persistent grip. Serve with doner kebab.

Rosemount Grenache Shiraz

Quality	❦❦❦
Value	★★★
Grapes	grenache; shiraz
Region	not stated
Cellar	⬤ 2
Alc./Vol.	13.0%
RRP	$12.00 Ⓢ

It seems you're no longer in the red game if you don't have some grenache in the arsenal.
CURRENT RELEASE 1997 A quaffing style that has a brick-red colour and a leafy nose on a backdrop of raspberry. The medium-bodied palate offers blood plum and raspberry flavours tinged with spice. There are gentle tannins on a modest finish. Drink now with spaghetti bolognaise.

Rosemount GSM

The GSM stands for Grenache, Syrah, Mourvèdre, which is becoming a more common blend these days. It seldom makes earth-shattering wines.
Previous outstanding vintages: '94
CURRENT RELEASE 1995 The colour is a mid-brick-red, and the nose is dominated by sweet raspberry grenache odours. The palate has very sweet berry flavours, and the tannins on the finish are soft and lingering. Try it with oxtail.

Quality	♟♟♟♟
Value	★★★★
Grapes	grenache; shiraz; mourvèdre
Region	McLaren Vale, SA
Cellar	▮ 3
Alc./Vol.	13.5%
RRP	$19.00

Rosemount Mountain Blue Shiraz Cabernet Sauvignon

This label is becoming a jewel in the Rosemount tiara. The grapes come from Mudgee and prove this is a much underrated region.
Previous outstanding vintages: '94
CURRENT RELEASE 1995 The wine has beautiful balance with a deep mulberry-stain colour. The nose is a complicated mix of spicy shiraz and blackberry cabernet aromas. The medium- to full-bodied palate continues the complexity with ripe berry flavours lifted by spice. The finish shows a mixture of oaks and persistent tannin grip. It drinks well with mildly spicy beef sausages.

Quality	♟♟♟♟♟
Value	★★★★
Grapes	shiraz; cabernet sauvignon
Region	Mudgee, NSW
Cellar	➡ 2–6
Alc./Vol.	13.5%
RRP	$35.00

Rosemount Orange Vineyard Cabernet Sauvignon

The wine is almost as delicate and certainly as tasteful as the elegant labelling. This is an exciting project that shows much promise.
CURRENT RELEASE 1994 This wine is an elegant style with a perfumed cassis aroma. The medium-bodied palate is already quite complex with a mixture of berry flavours, and these are married with some dry dusty oak. The finish is long and astringent with plenty of grip. It should cellar in the medium term, and it's good with a mixed grill.

Quality	♟♟♟♟
Value	★★★★
Grapes	cabernet sauvignon
Region	Orange, NSW
Cellar	▮ 5
Alc./Vol.	13.5%
RRP	$25.00

Rosemount Shiraz Cabernet Sauvignon

Quality	♟♟♟♟
Value	★★★★ɩ
Grapes	shiraz; cabernet sauvignon
Region	not stated
Cellar	▮ 2
Alc./Vol.	12.5%
RRP	$12.00 ⑤

This a cheap and cheery commercial style that's fun to drink. It usually manages to squeak a few medals on the show circuit.

CURRENT RELEASE 1997   The nose has a hint of leaf as well as spice and plum flavours. The medium-bodied palate has attractive plum and dark cherry flavours and there are mouth-caressing tannins on a gentle finish. It drinks well with a designer pizza.

Rosemount Show Reserve Shiraz

Quality	♟♟♟♟
Value	★★★★
Grapes	shiraz
Region	Orange, NSW; McLaren Vale, SA
Cellar	▮ 5
Alc./Vol.	13.0%
RRP	$28.00

This highly decorated wine makes the best of both worlds when it comes to cool and temperate climates. Judging by the show gongs it's a recipe for success.

CURRENT RELEASE 1995   The nose is a triumph of fruit aromas: it's ripe sweet berries all the way and there are some heady spice aromas. The palate is full of ripe fruit, and there are plums and cherries dusted with cinnamon. The finish is a little anticlimactic, with the oak playing a background role. It drinks well now with aged ox rump steak.

Rosemount Traditional

Quality	♟♟♟♟ɩ
Value	★★★★ɩ
Grapes	cabernet sauvignon; merlot; petit verdot
Region	McLaren Vale, SA
Cellar	▮ 4
Alc./Vol.	13.0%
RRP	$18.00

In Australian terms what's traditional about a blend with petit verdot? Never mind, this is a very fine drink so let's found a new tradition.

CURRENT RELEASE 1995   The nose has a strong berry aroma and an attractive grace note of oak. The medium- to full-bodied palate is complex with several dark berry flavours like cherry, mulberry, blackberry and raspberry. These are framed by a grippy oak finish that adds tannins and length. It drinks very well now. Try it with a turkey breast in a rich reduction sauce.

Rothbury Estate Brokenback Shiraz

This is the top of the Rothbury line and shows a certain regional style. The Hunter Valley is a difficult place to grow grapes but shiraz is usually a pleasant surprise.
Previous outstanding vintages: '89, '91, '93, '94
CURRENT RELEASE 1995 The nose is perfumed with a strong berry aroma and loads of spice. The palate is medium-bodied yet intense, with cherry and plum flavours laced with pepper. These are framed by toasty vanillan oak. There's an attractive grip and leathery characters. It goes well with a beef casserole.

Quality	♟♟♟♟♟
Value	★★★★
Grapes	shiraz
Region	Hunter Valley, NSW
Cellar	♙ 5
Alc./Vol.	12.5%
RRP	$23.00

Rothbury Estate Hunter Valley Shiraz

Founder Len Evans used to complain of lack of representation in the pages, but judging by the lack of communication, we concluded he wasn't really interested. The new management tends to be overenthusiastic. Maker Adam Eggins.
CURRENT RELEASE 1996 The nose has plum, leather and spice aromas. The palate is complex with plum, spice and pepper flavours. There's also a suggestion of blackberry and this is aided by some American oak that adds a vanilla flavour to the finish. It drinks well with pink lamb chops.

Quality	♟♟♟♟
Value	★★★★
Grapes	shiraz
Region	Hunter Valley, NSW
Cellar	♙ 3
Alc./Vol.	12.5%
RRP	$15.00

Rothbury Estate Mudgee Shiraz

Where's the mud? This is clean and neat, with plenty of wholesome flavour. It's part of a regional range that's priced to be a fighting brand.
CURRENT RELEASE 1996 The nose has a strong mint element as well as spice and berry aromas. The medium-bodied palate has a strong black cherry flavour which is balanced pepper and toasty oak. Give it time. Serve with a pepper steak.

Quality	♟♟♟♟
Value	★★★★
Grapes	shiraz
Region	Mudgee, NSW
Cellar	♙ 5
Alc./Vol.	12.5%
RRP	$11.00

Rotherhythe Cabernet Sauvignon

Quality	♟♟♟♟
Value	★★★★
Grapes	cabernet sauvignon
Region	Tamar Valley, Tas.
Cellar	▮ 5+
Alc./Vol.	12.5%
RRP	$25.00

The vineyard was planted in 1976 and it now produces 2500 cases. Cellar door is by appointment only.
CURRENT RELEASE 1992 Still pretty youthful in spite of the bottle-age. It has some developed fruit characters as well as green-leaf aromas. The medium-bodied palate has sweet fruit flavours – mainly blackberry – and there's a hint of spice. The tannin on the finish is assertive, and there's evidence of high acid. It should develop further. Try it with veal chops.

Rotherhythe Pinot Noir

Quality	♟♟♟♟♟
Value	★★★★
Grapes	pinot noir
Region	Tamar Valley, Tas.
Cellar	▮ 4
Alc./Vol.	13.0%
RRP	$33.00

What's a nice pinot noir like you doing in a place like this? Actually Tasmania is the right place for pinot noir and this wine bears witness. Maker Meadowbank (contract).
CURRENT RELEASE 1994 The colour is a mid-brick red and the nose has sappy qualities as well as cherry aromas. The palate is complex with cherry and wild berry flavours, hints of earth and meat. There's plenty of acid on the finish, which displays impressive length. The balance is equally impressive and it's great with a mushroom risotto.

Rouge Homme Coonawarra Shiraz Cabernet

Quality	♟♟♟
Value	★★★
Grapes	shiraz; cabernet sauvignon
Region	Coonawarra, SA
Cellar	▮ 3
Alc./Vol.	13.0%
RRP	$14.00 Ⓢ

The wine reflects the nature of the vintage in the district. It's a straightforward drink-now style that's easy to like.
CURRENT RELEASE 1995 The nose has redcurrant and leafy aromas. The palate is light- to medium-bodied. The major flavour is blackberry, and there's a light spice of oak. The finish shows plenty of acid. It's good with savoury mince on toast. ▶

CURRENT RELEASE 1996   The wine is a handsome style that has been well put together. It is a drink-now style with sweet berry and vanilla-oak aromas. The palate is medium-bodied and there's some intense blackberry fruit flavour. This is matched by some tinder-dry oak on a grippy finish. It sells at a bargain price. Try it with a rabbit terrine.

Quality	♟♟♟♟
Value	★★★★
Grapes	shiraz; cabernet sauvignon
Region	Coonawarra, SA
Cellar	▮ 4
Alc./Vol.	13.0%
RRP	$14.00 Ⓢ

Rowan Pinot Noir

Rowan was one of the pioneers in the Yarra Valley. It's not necessarily the second label to St Huberts.
CURRENT RELEASE 1997   As to be expected, this is a soft, succulent style with an emphasis on drinkability. The nose has sweet berry-fruit aromas and a hint of sap. The palate is light with sweet strawberry fruit flavours, followed by some clean, soft acid. Try it chilled with chargrilled ocean trout.

Quality	♟♟♟
Value	★★★
Grapes	pinot noir
Region	not stated
Cellar	▮ 2
Alc./Vol.	13.0%
RRP	$16.00

Rufus Stone Cabernet Sauvignon

It seems the ancient Tyrrells were crook shots. An errant arrow from Sir Walter Tyrrell knocked off King William (Rufus) and the spot is marked with a stone.
CURRENT RELEASE 1996   The wine comes from Coonawarra and is very typical of the region, with the emphasis on berries. The nose has a strong Ribena aroma and there's intense blackcurrant fruit on the medium-bodied palate. The finish has some new oak characters and fine-grained tannins. It goes well with pink spring lamb.

Quality	♟♟♟♟
Value	★★★★
Grapes	cabernet sauvignon
Region	Coonawarra, SA
Cellar	▮ 4
Alc./Vol.	13.0%
RRP	$19.00

Rufus Stone Shiraz

Quality	♟♟♟♟
Value	★★★★
Grapes	shiraz
Region	McLaren Vale, SA
Cellar	▮ 4
Alc./Vol.	13.2%
RRP	$19.00

To continue the Tyrrell and errant arrow story (see previous entry), the culprit fled to France and lived in exile. Perhaps that's where the family became interested in making wine. Maker Bruce Tyrrell and team.

CURRENT RELEASE 1996   This is a solid style with plenty of grunt. The nose is a mixture of spicy plums and vanilla. The medium-bodied palate shows concentrated plum and berry flavours laced with spice. These are followed by some dusty vanilla oak and fine-grained tannins on the finish. It goes well with a rich osso bucco.

Saddlers Creek Equus Shiraz

Quality	♟♟♟♟
Value	★★★⁑
Grapes	shiraz
Region	McLaren Vale, SA
Cellar	⟷ 1–8
Alc./Vol.	13.5%
RRP	$25.00 (cellar door)

Everyone's doin' it. Truckin' McLaren Vale red up to the Hunter, that is. A pity: Hunter shiraz can be very good too. Maker John Johnson.

CURRENT RELEASE 1996   No mistaking the provenance of this rich, voluptuous shiraz. The nose is dominated by vanillan American oak; the taste is rich and full with smooth, dark-chocolate, vanilla and plum flavours and loads of fruit sweetness. It needs time to swallow up its oak, then serve with game pie.

Salisbury Cabernet Merlot

Quality	♟♟♟♟
Value	★★★★
Grapes	cabernet sauvignon; merlot
Region	Murray Valley, Vic.
Cellar	▮ 3
Alc./Vol.	12.0%
RRP	$10.00 Ⓢ

Salisbury sounds very English: you can almost hear the plum in the mouth and a long drawn-out first syllable.

CURRENT RELEASE 1997   Minty, crushed-leaf and raspberry scents combine to make an attractive young aroma. In the mouth it has lively, crisp, leafy and berry flavours in a light-bodied, well-balanced structure. Soft and light enough to drink when young. Goes with veal saltimbocca.

Salisbury Cabernet Sauvignon

These reds are released at the same age as the Salisbury whites, and are intended for current drinking. They are certainly at their best young.
CURRENT RELEASE 1996 A light-bodied, simple red wine. It has an impressively youthful purple colour and simple cherry-like fruit aromas. It lacks typical cabernet character, and has a little firmness from tannin on the finish. Drink now – with shish kebabs.

Quality	♟♟♟
Value	★★★ｷ
Grapes	cabernet sauvignon
Region	Murray Valley, Vic.
Cellar	🍷 2
Alc./Vol.	12.0%
RRP	$9.35 Ⓢ

CURRENT RELEASE 1997 A lightly wooded, simple red wine for current drinking. It smells of cherry, plum and green herbs. It's fruit-driven and lacks maturation character. The tannins are light and the flavours undemanding. It's very quaffable, and goes well with san choy bow.

Quality	♟♟♟
Value	★★★ｷ
Grapes	cabernet sauvignon
Region	Murray Valley, Vic.
Cellar	🍷 2
Alc./Vol.	12.0%
RRP	$10.00 Ⓢ

Salitage Pinot Noir

Monster pinot is the trademark of this Pemberton district vineyard, with prices to match. Maker Patrick Coutts.
CURRENT RELEASE 1996 The wine is showing development all round, but it's full of character. There are smells of earth, sap, caramel and burnt meat – more appealing than it may sound! The palate is big with plenty of fruit-sweetness and warmth from alcohol. The tannins are persistent and flavour floods the mouth. It's good with pink lamb chops.

Quality	♟♟♟♟？
Value	★★★
Grapes	pinot noir
Region	Pemberton, WA
Cellar	🍷 3+
Alc./Vol.	14.0%
RRP	$34.50

Saltram Classic Cabernet Sauvignon

This is a fighting varietal, which could come from anywhere. Saltram is a Barossa firm, but when it doesn't say Barossa on the bottle, you can bet it's not Barossa fruit.
CURRENT RELEASE 1996 The colour is rather weak. It smells of herbs (parsley, basil), and there's a faint hint of cherry on the palate. It's light-bodied and not at all like the Saltram reds of yore. 'Classic' it ain't. A simple quaffing light red that's fair value for the price.

Quality	♟♟♟
Value	★★★
Grapes	cabernet sauvignon
Region	not stated
Cellar	🍷 2
Alc./Vol.	12.5%
RRP	$11.80 Ⓢ

Saltram Mamre Brook Cabernet Sauvignon

Quality	ㅜㅜㅜㅜ⸍
Value	★★★★
Grapes	cabernet sauvignon
Region	Barossa Valley, SA
Cellar	➥ 3–12+
Alc./Vol.	14.0%
RRP	$19.00 ⑤ 🍾

Until this vintage, Mamre Brook was a cabernet shiraz blend. Now they've split the varieties into a straight cabernet and a straight shiraz. Both are pretty spectacular. Maker Nigel Dolan.

CURRENT RELEASE 1996   This is a big brute that needs to be locked up for a while to calm its savage instincts. The colour is very dark and thick; the nose is powerfully concentrated with stacks of toasty vanillan oak and darkberry fruit. It has massive palate flavour, which is very oaky, tannic and unready. Put it down and in a few years it'll go nicely with beef casserole.

Saltram Mamre Brook Shiraz

Quality	ㅜㅜㅜㅜ
Value	★★★⸍
Grapes	shiraz
Region	Barossa Valley, SA
Cellar	➥ 1–7+
Alc./Vol.	13.5%
RRP	$19.00 ⑤ 🍾

Maker Nigel Dolan is the son of a former Saltram winemaker of the '50s and '60s, Brian 'Skip' Dolan. The company is now part of the Fosters group.

CURRENT RELEASE 1996   Toasty, charred oak dominates the nose at present and needs time to settle down. There's good cherry and plum shiraz flavour underneath, and this surfaces on the palate where it has lovely fruit-sweetness and supple tannin. Give it a couple of years and you'll have a gem. Serve with grilled lamb chops.

Saltram No. 1 Shiraz

Quality	ㅜㅜㅜㅜ⸍
Value	★★★
Grapes	shiraz
Region	Barossa Valley, SA
Cellar	➥ 2–10+
Alc./Vol.	14.0%
RRP	$30.50 ⑤ 🍾

This label was traditionally reserved for the best shiraz of the harvest in days of yore. It was resurrected a few years ago. Maker Nigel Dolan.

CURRENT RELEASE 1995   A big, solid Barossa fraulein. It's chock-full of character, if a trifle oak-dominated at the moment. The aromas are toasty-oak-led, with vanilla and plum notes. Rich, and ample in the mouth, it has swatches of tannin and good length, and promises much for the future if cellared. Try it with beef with a reduction sauce that includes a splash of the wine.

CURRENT RELEASE 1996   Overwhelming American oak dominates at present, but the wine has the stuffing to rise above it and make a great bottle in years to come. A powerful coconut, green mint and toasty nose, with lots of mint, raw oak and undeveloped berry flavours on the palate. An impressive wine that should have a big future. Aged cheddar here.

Quality	♥♥♥♥?
Value	★★★
Grapes	shiraz
Region	Barossa Valley, SA
Cellar	➥ 2–15+
Alc./Vol.	14.0%
RRP	$30.50 Ⓢ ▮

Sandalford Shiraz

These wines are made by Bill Crappsley, formerly of Evans & Tate, one of the West's most experienced winemakers.
CURRENT RELEASE 1996   Somewhat advanced development here – in colour and flavour. The bouquet is peppery and stalky, with herbal and earthy development. The palate is a leaner style with cool-grown pepper–spice characters. It lacks a little on the finish. A decent red to serve with Irish stew.

Quality	♥♥♥?
Value	★★★
Grapes	shiraz
Region	Mt Barker & Margaret River, WA
Cellar	▮ 5
Alc./Vol.	12.5%
RRP	$20.50

Sand Hills Vineyard Shiraz

Here's one straight out of left-field. It's a boutique vineyard and winery at Forbes in the New South Wales central ranges. They have 11 hectares under vine.
CURRENT RELEASE 1996   Sandhills mean low-yielding vines, no? Whatever the case, this is an impressive effort. The colour is mid-purple–red, and it smells of ripe cherries with fruit taking centre stage. It tastes sweet and ripe, with echoes of blackberry jam and a hint of licorice. The finish has firm tannins and good length. It could be cellared. Try it with aged cheddar.

Quality	♥♥♥♥
Value	★★★★⸴
Grapes	shiraz 90%; cabernet sauvignon 10%
Region	Lachlan Valley, NSW
Cellar	▮ 5+
Alc./Vol.	12.5%
RRP	$15.00 (cellar door)

Scarpantoni Cabernet Sauvignon

Quality	ŸŸŸŸ?
Value	★★★★★
Grapes	cabernet sauvignon
Region	McLaren Vale, SA
Cellar	�‣ 3–10+
Alc./Vol.	14.0%
RRP	$17.00 🍶

We record this as a matter of duty. It was in such demand that it sold out after a few weeks. And full marks to the punters who managed to get some: great value like this doesn't come around often!

CURRENT RELEASE 1996   This opens up with breathing and needs air to show its best. Somewhat meaty at first, it develops a rich, very ripe, sweet fruit nose and flavour that's very much the opulent McLaren Vale style. The colour is raw purple, and it's fruit-driven, with great depth of dark berry flavour. It desperately needs time to develop complexity and mellowness, so cellar it! Then drink with braised venison.

Seaview Cabernet Sauvignon

Quality	ŸŸŸ
Value	★★★⭒
Grapes	cabernet sauvignon
Region	mainly McLaren Vale, SA
Cellar	➣ 1–6
Alc./Vol.	13.5%
RRP	$13.80 ⑤

This is the 45th vintage of Seaview Cab. It was established by Edwards & Chaffey in 1951, exactly 100 years after George Pitches Manning bought the land and planted the original vineyard.

CURRENT RELEASE 1996   The colour is a promising dark shade, and the nose has a plummy quality that doesn't really remind one of cabernet. The palate is fairly plain, but it offers decent flavour for the money and it ends with some aggressive tannin. It could use some short-term cellaring. Try it with rissoles.

Seaview Grenache

Quality	ŸŸŸ?
Value	★★★
Grapes	grenache
Region	Barossa Valley & McLaren Vale, SA
Cellar	🍶 3
Alc./Vol.	13.5%
RRP	$13.75 ⑤

A few years ago the wayward Seaview announced it was going back to basing its reds on McLaren Vale grapes. Now it's strayed into the Barossa again.

CURRENT RELEASE 1996   Spicy, earthy grenache perfumes mingle with camphor-mint hints that come through on the palate also. It's a good drink at a fair price: plenty of fruit and flavour, and smooth tannins to close. Drinks well now with pressed tongue.

Seaview Shiraz

Not all the Seaview wines are from McLaren Vale these days. Check the label and you'll see this one is. Maker Steve Clarkson.

CURRENT RELEASE 1996 True to form, this is a decent everyday drinking red that won't break the bank. The nose has spicy, woodsy scents; the body is light to medium. The profile is slightly angular and it has some astringency on the finish. Suits pork spare ribs.

Quality	🍷🍷🍷
Value	★★★★½
Grapes	shiraz
Region	McLaren Vale, SA
Cellar	5
Alc./Vol.	13.5%
RRP	$13.80 ($)

Seppelt Dorrien Cabernet Sauvignon

The degree of oak Seppelt uses in its reds, and to some degree its whites, is one of the great mysteries of the wine world. Why would you deliberately do that to good fruit, year after year?

CURRENT RELEASE 1993 The dense colour has a brick-red edge, which is a sign of premature ageing. It smells of oak: raw oak high notes, and vanilla and chocolate flavours from fruit–oak interactions. It's rich and thickly textured in the mouth, and the oak chimes in with an astringent finish. Needs more cellar time, then team it with heavily charred BBQ meats.

Quality	🍷🍷🍷🍷
Value	★★½
Grapes	cabernet sauvignon
Region	Barossa Valley, SA
Cellar	2–8+
Alc./Vol.	13.5%
RRP	$44.30 ($)

Seppelt Drumborg Cabernet Sauvignon

Drumborg is a wild and woolly place in the cool southern Victorian climate near Portland. Maker Ian McKenzie and team.

CURRENT RELEASE 1993 The year 1993 marked a difficult season in the cooler parts and this is starting to show considerable age development. It's also still tremendously oaky. There are earthy, dusty characters mingling with porty and licorice undertones. The oak flavour and tannins reassert themselves on the finish, and the mid-palate seems hollow and lacking fruit. Best served with food, such as aged cheddar.

Quality	🍷🍷🍷½
Value	★★½
Grapes	cabernet sauvignon
Region	western Victoria
Cellar	4
Alc./Vol.	12.5%
RRP	$37.75

Seppelt Great Western Vineyard Shiraz

Quality 🍷🍷🍷🍷
Value ★★★
Grapes shiraz
Region Great Western, Vic.
Cellar 5+
Alc./Vol. 13.5%
RRP $36.00

The grapes come from a small patch of old vines right in front of the winery at Great Western, and this wine follows a fine tradition of superb shirazes. Maker Ian McKenzie and team.

Previous outstanding vintages: '54, '62, '67, '71, '85, '86, '88, '91, '92

CURRENT RELEASE 1993 Cool-year spice and slight vegetal characters distinguish this vintage. It shows some maturity already, and the gamy, spicy, slightly licorice aromas recall the Rhone Valley. It's a leaner style with some acid showing through, and it already drinks well. Serve with lamb's fry and bacon.

Seppelt Harpers Range Cabernet Sauvignon

Quality 🍷🍷🍷½
Value ★★★
Grapes cabernet sauvignon
Region Geelong, Mornington Peninsula & Great Western, Vic.
Cellar 1–5
Alc./Vol. 13.5%
RRP $17.70 (S)

This is part of the Seppelt Victorian portfolio. They buy grapes from a large number of cooler Victorian vineyards to cobble these wines together.

CURRENT RELEASE 1994 Rather green flavours detract from this wine. The colour is starting to show some aged tints, and the nose has crushed-leaf and capsicum aromas. The palate is lean and somewhat meagre, but has a firm tannin grip. More age could help. Then serve with a mild lamb curry.

Seppelt Sunday Creek Pinot Noir

This is a triumph for winemaker Ian McKenzie, and the packaging is nothing if not eye-catching. The '96 version won the value award at the '98 Sydney Wine Show (best gold medal red under $15).

Previous outstanding vintages: '96

CURRENT RELEASE 1997   Absolutely delicious: the best Seppelt pinot so far. Surprisingly deep colour; pristine cherry fruit nose lifted by stylish and well-handled French oak. A complex, layered wine with oodles of sweet cherry flavour and lovely silky texture. Plenty of weight and some well-judged soft tannins. A brilliant wine that's beaut with Cantonese salt spice pork.

Quality	♟♟♟♟♟
Value	★★★★★
Grapes	pinot noir
Region	Drumborg & Strathbogie Ranges, Vic.; Tumbarumba, NSW
Cellar	▮ 5
Alc./Vol.	13.0%
RRP	$17.80 Ⓢ

PENGUIN BEST PINOT NOIR

Seppelt Terrain Series Cabernet Sauvignon

This is a new range by Seppelt, made for inexpensive everyday drinking. Why terrain? It couldn't be a reference to terroir, because the grapes come from all over the shop. Maybe it's the abstract soil depicted on the label.

CURRENT RELEASE 1996   Excellent value at this modest (and often discounted) price. It has excellent depth of colour, and a noseful of dark berry, cassis and toasted oak. The cabernet character comes rocketing through. The palate has plain but pleasant fruit of some sweetness and modest depth, and the finish is somewhat tannic. It needs food, so try it with lamb chops.

Quality	♟♟♟♟
Value	★★★★
Grapes	cabernet sauvignon
Region	not stated
Cellar	▮ 4
Alc./Vol.	13.0%
RRP	$11.65 Ⓢ

Seppelt Terrain Series Shiraz

This is what the Americans term a fighting varietal. It's in a very competitive price bracket.

CURRENT RELEASE 1996   A clean, well-made wine that won't move the earth but that will give you a lot of satisfaction for your ten bucks. Lifted, sweet cherry aroma; straight up-and-down fruit-driven palate that is medium-bodied and that ends with a pleasing tannin handshake. Serve it with tomato and eggplant lasagne.

Quality	♟♟♟
Value	★★★★
Grapes	shiraz
Region	not stated
Cellar	▮ 3
Alc./Vol.	13.0%
RRP	$11.65 Ⓢ

Seville Estate Cabernet Sauvignon

Quality	掌掌掌掌掌
Value	★★★★
Grapes	cabernet sauvignon
Region	Yarra Valley, Vic.
Cellar	🍷 10
Alc./Vol.	13.0%
RRP	$29.50

Seville is on the cooler southern side of the Yarra Valley and the vines are planted on rich red–brown soils. Maker Alastair Butt.

CURRENT RELEASE 1995   A lovely ripe cabernet full of blackcurrant and cherry fruit aromas, with no greenness – just clean, finely crafted pristine Yarra style. Elegance and length on a grand scale. Try it with roast leg of lamb.

Seville Estate Shiraz

Quality	掌掌掌掌
Value	★★★
Grapes	shiraz
Region	Yarra Valley, Vic.
Cellar	🍷 7
Alc./Vol.	12.5%
RRP	$44.30

Seville has a proud tradition of shiraz stretching back into the early 1970s. It has been a beacon of the variety in a district where remarkably little shiraz is planted.
Previous outstanding vintages: '76, '78, '80, '85, '86, '88, '90, '91, '92, '93, '94, '95

CURRENT RELEASE 1996   A finer style of shiraz crammed with cool-grown white-pepper and fresh spice aromas, and real elegance on the palate. Perhaps not as powerful as the superb '95, but a goodie all the same. Serve with spicy gourmet hamburgers.

Sharefarmers Red

Quality	掌掌掌
Value	★★★
Grapes	merlot 56%; malbec 35%; cabernet sauvignon 9%
Region	Coonawarra, SA
Cellar	➥ 1–5+
Alc./Vol.	13.4%
RRP	$18.00

Pending the decision of the Geographic Indications Committee on the defining of the Coonawarra boundary, this is still boldly labelled 'Coonawarra'. It's a borderline case.

CURRENT RELEASE 1996   The colour is a healthy dark purple–red, and there are aromas of cherry, aniseed, herbal mint and dusty oak. The herbal flavours permeate a fairly straightforward palate, which is light in weight but which has a firm finish. Designed for bistro use. Try it with chipolatas.

Shottesbrooke Merlot

Nick Holmes has built a winery and smart tasting room for Shottesbrooke at McLaren Vale. The name comes from the place in England where his family hails from. **CURRENT RELEASE 1996** A decent wine, but it looks as though it would have been better if harvested riper. The colour is of medium depth, the nose has fairly straight raspberry, grassy, stalky characters, and the palate is light-bodied and structured on acid. Try it with pigeon or quail.

Quality	▼▼▼
Value	★★★
Grapes	merlot
Region	McLaren Vale, SA
Cellar	▮ 3
Alc./Vol.	12.5%
RRP	$18.00

Skillogalee Shiraz

This is a real humdinger from one of the lower-profile wineries of the Clare Valley. The owners are David and Diana Palmer, who also run a restaurant that is a must for lunch. **CURRENT RELEASE 1996** A very youthful wine that needs time to mellow a little, but that has all the ingredients for a superb bottle of red. Dense colour, powerful peppermint and dark berry aromas, and a palate that's strong, rich and very flavoursome. Superb depth and grip as well as plenty of extract. A quintessential Aussie shiraz. Enjoy it with rare kangaroo backstraps.

Quality	▼▼▼▼▼
Value	★★★★▸
Grapes	shiraz
Region	Clare Valley, SA
Cellar	▬ 2–10+
Alc./Vol.	12.5%
RRP	$27.00 ▮

Smithbrook Merlot

The first merlot from this vineyard, which was recently purchased by the Petaluma group. **CURRENT RELEASE 1995** A lumberjack's wine. The colour is nice and dark, and the wine has good depth and intensity, but it's a pity it's totally dominated by oak. There are also some undergrowth characters and a twinge of volatility, and the wine certainly has length. But it's wood *über alles*. Even when checked daily for a week, the wood did not give up. Try it with smoked lamb.

Quality	▼▼▼▸
Value	★★▸
Grapes	merlot
Region	Pemberton, WA
Cellar	▬ 3+
Alc./Vol.	13.5%
RRP	$28.70

Stanley Brothers Black Sheep

Quality	ŶŶŶ℩
Value	★★★★
Grapes	shiraz; cabernet; grenache; merlot
Region	Barossa Valley, SA
Cellar	▮ 3
Alc./Vol.	14.0%
RRP	$14.50 (cellar door)

Every family has a black sheep, according to Lindsay Stanley, so everyone has a reason to buy a bottle of this affordable blended red. Sound thinking that pays off at the till.

CURRENT RELEASE *non-vintage* This blend of '97 and '96 is lighter and demands less attention than the up-scale Stanley reds. It has an attractive spicy, peppery aroma, and is smooth and nicely balanced for ready-drinking with – what else? – mutton. Serve it with roasted brisket.

Stanley Brothers John Hancock Shiraz

Quality	ŶŶŶŶ℩
Value	★★★ʳ
Grapes	shiraz
Region	Barossa Valley, SA
Cellar	▮ 7+
Alc./Vol.	14.5%
RRP	$24.00 ▮

Who the heck was John Hancock, we hear you ask. According to winemaker Lindsay Stanley, he was a signatory to the American Declaration of Independence. Since then, a 'John Hancock' has come to mean a signature of any sort. The one on the label is a replica of the original.

CURRENT RELEASE 1996 Typical rich, minty, spicy Barossa shiraz with the fruit to the fore, rather than the oak, as is the case with many of its peers. Very good palate: it's fruit-sweet and quite persuasive in the tannin department. It promises to age well, although it's a beaut drink now – with shish kebabs.

Stephen John Cabernet Sauvignon

Quality	ŶŶŶ℩
Value	★★★
Grapes	cabernet sauvignon
Region	Clare Valley, SA
Cellar	� 2–6+
Alc./Vol.	12.0%
RRP	$20.00 ▮

Traugott Benjamin John arrived in the colony of South Australia in 1845, and gave rise to a whole tribe of little Johns. Stephen and his brother Phillip of Lindemans are two of them.

CURRENT RELEASE 1995 The John family are coopers and they love oak. Here's one for wood-lovers: it's a decent mouthful of dry red, but the toasty oak character is all-pervading. The palate is smooth and savoury with drying tannins on the finish. Give it a year or two, then serve it with smoked beef.

Stephen John Shiraz

The John family boasts 150 years' involvement in the South Australian wine industry. Stephen's brother Phillip is Lindemans' chief winemaker and their father's cooperage, A. P. John, is one of the biggest in Australia. CURRENT RELEASE 1996 Tremendous colour here, and the nose is equally vivid: wafting gumleaf/wintergreen scents that will polarise tasters. Indeed, the wine has a thread of greenness throughout, falling away towards the finish, which has some acid and tannin astringency. It needs time. Then serve with saddle of hare.

Quality	▼▼▼?
Value	★★★
Grapes	shiraz
Region	Clare Valley, SA
Cellar	➥ 2–6+
Alc./Vol.	13.0%
RRP	$18.50 ▮

St Hallett Faith Shiraz

They're a religious lot in the Barossa winemaking fraternity – not. This is named after the church and school that's next to one of the vineyards. Maker Stuart Blackwell.
CURRENT RELEASE 1995 A good foil for the Old Block, this is a leaner style with less obvious oak. The nose is dusty and earthy, with plum warm-area shiraz notes. Some dark chocolate chimes in on the palate. It's a rustic, fruit-driven, but fairly developed, style. It goes well with cheese.

Quality	▼▼▼▼
Value	★★★▸
Grapes	shiraz
Region	Barossa Valley, SA
Cellar	▮ 5
Alc./Vol.	13.0%
RRP	$19.70 ▮

St Hallett Old Block Shiraz

This was one of the first Barossa shirazes to reignite interest in the grape and make a feature of old vines. Maker Stuart Blackwell.
Previous outstanding vintages: '86, '88, '90, '91, '93
CURRENT RELEASE 1994 Cherry aromas have toasty oak, vanilla and nutmeg-like overtones, and the palate is medium-weight and leaner than we've come to expect from this marque. A good wine, but it doesn't raise the roof. Is it a case of expectations being too high? Well, we did try several bottles. Goes well with braised pork hock.

Quality	▼▼▼▼
Value	★★▸
Grapes	shiraz
Region	Barossa Valley & Eden Valley, SA
Cellar	▮ 6+
Alc./Vol.	13.5%
RRP	$39.50 ▮

St Huberts Cabernet Merlot

Quality	♥♥♥
Value	★★ґ
Grapes	cabernet sauvignon; merlot
Region	Yarra Valley, Vic.
Cellar	↓ 4
Alc./Vol.	13.0%
RRP	$21.00 Ⓢ

This is a proud old Yarra Valley name, which is now part of the Mildara Blass juggernaut. The blend is always a lighter, more forward wine than the straight cabernet. CURRENT RELEASE 1996 Slightly green leafy cabernet aromas greet the nose. The palate has some intensity, but again greenish notes dominate. It's light- to medium-bodied and still undeveloped, finishing with harsh, possibly slightly green, tannins. Try it with lamb and mint sauce.

St Huberts Pinot Noir

Quality	♥♥♥
Value	★★ґ
Grapes	pinot noir
Region	Yarra Valley, Vic.
Cellar	↓ 3
Alc./Vol.	12.0%
RRP	$21.00 Ⓢ

It's almost as if St Huberts has been downgraded in the Mildara hierarchy: these days the wines seldom hit the heights. CURRENT RELEASE 1997 A rather green pinot, even considering the excellent vintage. It has good depth of youthful purple–red colour, and the nose and palate are dominated by green stalky characters. It's a very straightforward pinot which has some depth to it, but the greenness chimes in again on the finish.

St Leonards Wahgunyah Shiraz

Quality	♥♥♥ґ
Value	★★★
Grapes	shiraz
Region	Rutherglen, Vic.
Cellar	➡ 1–5
Alc./Vol.	13.0%
RRP	$20.00 🍾

This winery is now under the Brown Brothers umbrella, together with All Saints. The reds share an oaky similarity. CURRENT RELEASE 1995 The wine has very good colour – deep red–purple – but the nose is dominated by aggressive, coconutty American oak. The toasty sweet-oak flavour reappears in the mouth, and it's a little one-dimensional. Will age bring it into balance? We suspect few buyers will give it enough cellaring time to find out. Food: charred BBQ steak.

Stonyfell Metala Original Plantings Shiraz

Begun in 1994, this special reserve bottling is made from fruit off the vines of the Old Block and Cellar Block – all centenarians – planted in 1894 and 1891. Maker Nigel Dolan.

Previous outstanding vintages: '94

CURRENT RELEASE 1995   From a famous Langhorne Creek property, this is serious stuff. It has concentrated flavour that's chunky and very deep in the mouth, with ample sweet fruit. It also has trademark Langhorne Creek mint on the nose together with chocolatey, berry and smoky nuances. It can be enjoyed now, but six to 10 years should see it peaking, and history suggests it should last for 20 years. Try it with aged parmesan cheese.

Quality	素素素素素
Value	★★★★★
Grapes	shiraz
Region	Langhorne Creek, SA
Cellar	➡ 2–20
Alc./Vol.	14.0%
RRP	$24.00

CURRENT RELEASE 1996   A wonderful wine! Not at all oaky, it smells of berry jam, mint, plum, prune and licorice, and it still shows some of the rawness of youth. The palate is sweet from masses of very ripe fruit, and the concentration and length are mightily impressive. Already complex, it can only grow more so. Try it with aged parmigiana reggiano.

Quality	素素素素素
Value	★★★★★
Grapes	shiraz
Region	Langhorne Creek, SA
Cellar	➡ 2–20
Alc./Vol.	14.0%
RRP	$24.00

Stonyfell Metala Shiraz Cabernet

This is a wine with a past. Unusual, but it's an ancient vineyard and the wines have always been made by other people. The line began in the sixties.

Previous outstanding vintages: '71, '83, '84, '86, '92, '93, '94

CURRENT RELEASE 1995   An old-fashioned style, with older wood characters, it smacks of slightly rougher-than-usual handling (a South Australian in-joke). It has toasty, dry, savoury flavours and grainy tannin to finish, and the aftertaste lingers well. It's a food wine, which would go well with satays.

Quality	素素素素
Value	★★★★
Grapes	shiraz; cabernet sauvignon
Region	Langhorne Creek, SA
Cellar	6+
Alc./Vol.	13.6%
RRP	$16.00 Ⓢ

Tait Wines Bush Vine Grenache

Quality	♥♥♥♥
Value	★★★★
Grapes	grenache
Region	Barossa Valley, SA
Cellar	▮ 2
Alc./Vol.	13.7%
RRP	$12.00 (cellar door)

The Taits are making an impressive debut in winemaking, but be warned: they don't shrink away from alcohol in their reds.

CURRENT RELEASE 1997 This is a charming, fruit-driven grenache that pitches between rosé and beaujolais weight and has been made without significant oak input. Bright cherry-red colour; simple, clean berry/spice characters on the nose and palate. The finish has some alcohol warmth and the tannins are very mild. Takes a chill well, and quaffs easily now. Enjoy it with egg and bacon pie.

Tait Wines Shiraz

Quality	♥♥♥♥
Value	★★★★
Grapes	shiraz
Region	Barossa Valley, SA
Cellar	▮ 6
Alc./Vol.	14.8%
RRP	$16.00 (cellar door)

The Tait family, based at Lyndoch, have been involved in the Barossa wine industry for over a century as coopers. They've only recently started to market wine. Maker David Tait.

CURRENT RELEASE 1996 Lots of oak has been employed here, and the effect is a vanilla aroma and a hint of almost rancio oak-aged character. The high alcohol strength shows on the nose and palate. It's very full and rich, with some heat in the aftertaste. A cuddly, rustic Barossa red that has good concentration of prune and raisin flavours, and a long follow-through. Try it with peppered steak.

Taltarni Cabernet Sauvignon

There are not many winemakers in Australia who can claim to be a 'ninth-generation winemaker'. You'd think by now he'd get it right! Only joking, Dominique Portet – take a bow.

Previous outstanding vintages: '77, '78, '79, '81, '82, '84, '86, '88, '90, '93, '94

CURRENT RELEASE 1995 The wine is fine with a strong cassis aroma on the nose. The palate is medium-bodied with some complex fruit flavours dominated by blackberry fruit flavours. Then comes the typical B&D Madam Lash Taltarni oak treatment that bestows black-tea tannins on a powerful finish. Give it time in the bottle and serve it with seared kangaroo fillets.

Quality	♟♟♟♟
Value	★★★★
Grapes	cabernet sauvignon
Region	Pyrenees, Vic.
Cellar	🍷 7
Alc./Vol.	$12.7%
RRP	$27.00

Taltarni Merlot

This variety is a deadset teaser. Often 'the cheque is in the mail' where body and flavour are concerned.

CURRENT RELEASE 1995 The colour shows much promise, being dense and bright. The nose tweaks the tease factor and then comes the palate, which starts with sweet ripe fruit, and then . . . an anticlimax, a flat spot that is followed by firm oak tannins on a lingering finish. Time might add more complexity. It goes well with a hearty cassoulet.

Quality	♟♟♟♟
Value	★★★★
Grapes	merlot
Region	Pyrenees, Vic.
Cellar	🍷 5
Alc./Vol.	13.2%
RRP	$30.00

Taltarni Merlot Cabernet

No pain, no gain – not when it comes to wine, and happily, this is a painless wine that is very easy to drink. It has some Italian qualities and a high gluggability factor.

CURRENT RELEASE 1996 The nose is fruity with sweet berry smells and some chalky oak. The palate is medium-bodied with sweet cherry and raspberry flavours, and the oak is gentle with a modest grip. Drink now on a sunny afternoon with an antipasto platter.

Quality	♟♟♟♟
Value	★★★★
Grapes	merlot; cabernet sauvignon
Region	Pyrenees, Vic.
Cellar	🍷 2
Alc./Vol.	12.6%
RRP	$18.00

Taltarni Shiraz

Quality	♟♟♟♟
Value	★★★℣
Grapes	shiraz
Region	Pyrenees, Vic.
Cellar	▮ 5
Alc./Vol.	13.2%
RRP	$26.00

The Rhone comes to Moonambel or should that be the other way around? There's no doubt about the grape variety in this bottle.

CURRENT RELEASE 1995   The colour is rich ruby, and the nose has spice and ripe berry aromas. The full-bodied palate manages to retain decorum, and the fruit is intense cherry and berry flavoured. The spice adds that Rhône touch. The grip is quite substantial, but the balance is retained. Serve with casserole of kid.

Quality	♟♟♟♟℣
Value	★★★★
Grapes	shiraz
Region	Pyrenees, Vic.
Cellar	▮ 5
Alc./Vol.	13.2%
RRP	$26.00

CURRENT RELEASE 1996   This is a poised wine with loads of style. The age of reason is well past the yardarm at Taltarni; elegance is the watchword. The nose is an explosion of spices and ripe berry aromas. The medium-bodied palate is packed with cinnamon, plum and blackberry flavours, and these are dusted with black pepper. Well-tailored oak adds fine-grained tannins to the finish. It goes well with BBQ lamb backstraps.

Taltarni Special Reserve Cabernet Sauvignon

Quality	♟♟♟♟
Value	★★
Grapes	cabernet sauvignon
Region	Pyrenees, Vic.
Cellar	▮ 10+
Alc./Vol.	13.0%
RRP	$75.00

They've got to be kidding with the price tag! The wine costs an arm and half a leg, and will take aeons to attain maturity. Maker Dominique Portet.

CURRENT RELEASE 1992   The nose has a strong blackberry aroma. The palate is tight with some blackberry flavour that's overshadowed by strong tannins. The finish offers mega-grip with black-tea-like tannins. It's probably spent extra time in wood; it needs time in the bottle. Serve it with pan-fried kangaroo.

Tapestry Bin 338 Shiraz

Young and frisky; an exciting style. It was with trepidation that the cork was pulled because of the youth, but sometimes this is a benefit. The label design is pretty uninspired.

CURRENT RELEASE 1997 The nose is abundant with ripe fruit flavours, black pepper and allspice. The palate is medium-bodied and complex. There are some plum and cherry flavours and the spices add grace notes to the score. The finish has strong grip and fine-grained tannins. It's a very well-structured wine, right for a mixed grill.

Quality	🍷🍷🍷🍷
Value	★★★★
Grapes	shiraz
Region	McLaren Vale, SA
Cellar	2–5
Alc./Vol.	13.5%
RRP	$20.60

Tapestry Bin 388 Cabernet Sauvignon

This is an elegant style that is very complex, a tapestry indeed. It's a family winery started by the Light family. Maker Brian Light.

CURRENT RELEASE 1996 The nose is a mixture of mint, vanilla, violets and berries. The palate has a strong mulberry, blackberry flavour with a hint of chocolate. It is medium-bodied. The finish shows well-tuned vanilla and coconut oak. It drinks well now with rare eye-fillet steak.

Quality	🍷🍷🍷½
Value	★★★½
Grapes	cabernet sauvignon
Region	McLaren Vale, SA
Cellar	3
Alc./Vol.	12.5%
RRP	$20.50

Tarchalice Magna Carta Shiraz

The company is now being run by Robin and Phil Shaw who originally came from Melbourne. Robin gained wine experience working for the Australian Wine Club.

CURRENT RELEASE 1996 Great colour and a very rich, ripe plum nose on a background of spice. The full-bodied palate has plenty of plum flavours and there are attractive spices. There's an impressive weight of fruit, and the soft tannins on the finish contribute to the overall balance. It drinks well now and is great with a cassoulet.

Quality	🍷🍷🍷🍷
Value	★★★★
Grapes	shiraz
Region	Barossa Valley, SA
Cellar	3
Alc./Vol.	13.6%
RRP	$18.00

Tarchalice Cabernet Franc

Quality	🍷🍷🍷½
Value	★★★½
Grapes	cabernet franc
Region	Barossa Valley, SA
Cellar	3
Alc./Vol.	12.0%
RRP	$17.00

An old name with a new life. The management has changed and we can expect some exciting developments.

CURRENT RELEASE 1995 Very fruity and vinous nose with lots of perfume and rose-petal elements and hints of spice. The medium-bodied palate offers a developed fruit flavour with mellow raspberry characters. The tannin on the finish is mild but cleansing. It is a great pasta-style wine.

Tarchalice Shiraz Cabernet

Quality	🍷🍷🍷🍷
Value	★★★★
Grapes	shiraz; cabernet sauvignon
Region	Barossa Valley, SA
Cellar	4
Alc./Vol.	13.5%
RRP	$16.50

How do you pronounce the name? It's been round for yonks, but most people fumble or pass over it on a wine list. The winery does a lot of mail order, which means pronouncing the name isn't necessary.

CURRENT RELEASE 1996 The wine is elegant but shows substance. It's finer than the usual blockbuster from the Barossa. The nose is vinous and spicy, with some cherry and berry characters. The medium-bodied palate has ripe plum flavours and these are matched by some fine-grained tannins on an astringent finish. It's a good wine for rare roast beef and a bit of Yorkshire pud.

Tatachilla Merlot

Quality	🍷🍷🍷🍷🍷
Value	★★★★★
Grapes	merlot
Region	McLaren Vale, SA
Cellar	4
Alc./Vol.	13.0%
RRP	$22.00

This wine is getting the accolades it deserves on the show circuit. It's better structured than the usual straight merlot. Maker Michael Fragos.

CURRENT RELEASE 1996 The colour is deep ruby, and the nose has mulberry, spice and floral notes. The palate is medium- to full-bodied. There are sweet berry flavours, which are intermingled with some fine-grained tannins. It has excellent grip. Try it with devilled kidneys.

Terrace Vale T Cabernet Sauvignon

You have to look hard to discover the vintage on the label, which features a large letter 'T' and the words 'a letter worth opening'. The copywriter shouldn't give up his or her day job!

CURRENT RELEASE 1996 The colour is a rich ruby, and the nose is a mixture of redcurrant and green-leaf aromas. The palate is medium-bodied with sweet redcurrant fruit flavours. The finish has modest tannins and a hint of green stalk. Try it with spare ribs.

Quality	🍷🍷🍷
Value	★★★
Grapes	cabernet sauvignon
Region	Hunter Valley, NSW
Cellar	2
Alc./Vol.	13.8%
RRP	$19.00

Thistle Hill Zinfandel

This is an odd bod (varietally speaking) from a small maker that was established in 1976. There are 11 hectares under vines. Maker David Robinson.

CURRENT RELEASE 1995 It's no shrinking violet; the colour is a deep brick-red and the nose is highly perfumed with violets and raspberry. The palate is mouthfilling with tart raspberry flavours. There's a big whack of tannin on the finish. It has an affinity with wild duck.

Quality	🍷🍷🍷
Value	★★★
Grapes	zinfandel
Region	Mudgee, NSW
Cellar	3
Alc./Vol.	14.0%
RRP	$24.00

Tim Adams Cabernet

Tim Adams, who always credits his grapegrowers on the back label, uses a basket press to get the last drops of good stuff out of his grapes.

CURRENT RELEASE 1996 A solid Clare style, which is unready now and which demands patience. It has impressive sweet ripe berry aromas. Big fruit is evident throughout and there's some acid/tannin astringency on the afterpalate. The healthy aggression of youth is here in abundance. Try it with barbecued kangaroo.

Quality	🍷🍷🍷🍷
Value	★★★★
Grapes	cabernet sauvignon 90%; cabernet franc 10%
Region	Clare Valley, SA
Cellar	2–10+
Alc./Vol.	13.0%
RRP	$17.25

Tim Adams The Fergus

Quality	♈♈♈♈
Value	★★★★
Grapes	cabernet sauvignon; cabernet franc; shiraz; malbec
Region	Clare Valley, SA
Cellar	🍷 3
Alc./Vol.	14.5%
RRP	$18.00

The name comes from the grower, Fergus Mahon. Tim Adams has a policy of acknowledging the source of his fruit. The 1996 model was awarded the best blend in last year's guide.

Previous outstanding vintages: '94, '95, '96

CURRENT RELEASE 1997 Even more alcohol than usual but the flavour is a little subdued. The nose has mint and ripe berry smells. The palate is medium-bodied with a slight hollow. The major flavour is dark cherry and there are hints of earth. The finish offers soft tannins and a warmth of alcohol. It drinks well with a designer pizza.

Tim Gramp Shiraz

Quality	♈♈♈♈♈
Value	★★★⊢
Grapes	shiraz
Region	McLaren Vale, SA
Cellar	➥ 1–8+
Alc./Vol.	14.5%
RRP	$25.40 🍾

The label is an enigmatic statement that could be a stairway to heaven. Whatever, there's no enigma about the wine, which is a very honest red. Maker Tim Gramp.

CURRENT RELEASE 1996 This is a big earth mother of a shiraz. The nose has strong spices and a hint of porty spirit. The palate is full-bodied with juicy shiraz fruit and rich ripe plum flavours. These are followed by astringent tannins and a warmth of alcohol. It would be great with a game pie.

Tipperary Hill Cabernets

Quality	♈♈♈♈♈
Value	★★★★★
Grapes	cabernet sauvignon; cabernet franc
Region	Maryborough, Vic.
Cellar	🍷 4
Alc./Vol.	12.5%
RRP	$28.00

The vineyard is a tiny 2 hectares, so it pays to be on the mailing list. The stocks produced won't exactly flood the wine shops.

CURRENT RELEASE 1995 This is a lovely wine with plenty of style. It has a brilliant colour, and the nose is all perfumes and berries. The palate is complex with raspberry, blackberry and cherry flavours that are laced with spices. The wood fits perfectly, adding fine-grained tannins and length to the finish. It will be fun to watch in the cellar. Try it with roast squab.

CURRENT RELEASE 1996   A lighter and leaner style which seems to reverse the vintage trends. The colour is a deep ruby, and the nose has cherry, berry and leaf aromas. The medium-weight palate has dark cherry flavours and a hint of green tannin. The finish is astringent with plenty of acid. Try it with a mince pie.

Quality	▼▼▼▽
Value	★★★⋆
Grapes	cabernet sauvignon; cabernet franc
Region	Maryborough, Vic.
Cellar	▮ 3
Alc./Vol.	12.5%
RRP	$28.00

Tipperary Hill Estate Shiraz

The wine comes from the Maryborough district in Victoria, which in turn is a sub-region of Bendigo. The vineyard was established in 1985. Maker Paul Flowers.
CURRENT RELEASE 1996   It's a very youthful style with a vibrant ruby colour with tinges of violet. The nose is spicy with some floral notes and berry smells. The medium-bodied palate is tight with some attractive fruit. Dark cherry is the major flavour, and there's plenty of acid on the finish. It also has some assertive oak. It's but a youngster. Have it with venison sausages.

Quality	▼▼▼▽
Value	★★★⋆
Grapes	shiraz
Region	Maryborough, Vic.
Cellar	▬ 2–4
Alc./Vol.	12.4%
RRP	$28.00

Tisdall Shiraz Cabernet

This company used to be a bright new star in the wine firmament but today is part of the Mildara/Blass conglomerate and a very diminished brand in the marketplace.
CURRENT RELEASE 1996   Ripe, drinkable style that won't break the bank. The nose has plum and cherry aromas. The palate is relatively simple, with sweet berry flavours that are followed by gentle tannins and discreet oak. Try it at a BBQ and avoid the burned chops.

Quality	▼▼▼▽
Value	★★★★
Grapes	shiraz; cabernet sauvignon
Region	not stated
Cellar	▮ 3
Alc./Vol.	13.0%
RRP	$12.00

Tollana Bin TR 16 Shiraz

Quality 🍷🍷🍷🍷
Value ★★★★½
Grapes shiraz
Region Eden Valley, SA
Cellar 4
Alc./Vol. 13.0%
RRP $18.00 (S)

One of the most underestimated and overlooked wines on the planet. The brand seems ever-reliable and is now realistically priced. Maker Neville Falkenberg.

CURRENT RELEASE 1996 This is an elegant style with a hint of mint on the plummy nose. The medium-bodied palate has sweet ripe fruit flavour that is lifted by pepper and spice. The oak adds a subtle tannin to the lingering finish. It drinks well now and is very compatible with roast duck.

Tollana Bin TR 222 Cabernet Sauvignon

Quality 🍷🍷🍷🍷½
Value ★★★★½
Grapes cabernet sauvignon
Region Eden Valley, Adelaide Hills, SA
Cellar 3
Alc./Vol. 13.5%
RRP $18.00 (S)

Herr Wolfgang Blass pioneered this wine before he left Tolley Scott and Tolley and became a solo act. It was a very definite sign of things to come. These days Neville Falkenberg carries on the tradition.

Previous outstanding vintages: '82, '84, '87, '88, '90, '91, '92, '93

CURRENT RELEASE 1996 Well-made and stylish wine with an engaging sandalwood and cedar nose and blackberry aromas. The palate is quite complex with attractive redcurrant and blackberry flavours that are framed by charred oak. There are also hints of mint and chocolate to add to the complexity. There are soft tannins on a lingering finish which make the wine very drinkable. Serve it with oxtail.

Tollana Show Reserve Shiraz

Quality 🍷🍷🍷🍷
Value ★★★½
Grapes shiraz
Region Eden Valley, SA
Cellar 4
Alc./Vol. 13.0%
RRP $21.00

According to the back label the show reserve label has been developed to recognise wines from 'exceptional' vintages. In most areas 1995 was the pits.

CURRENT RELEASE 1995 The wine has a heavily oak-influenced nose with plum, berry, white pepper and chocolate aromas. The medium-bodied palate is rich with shiraz flavour, and the oak offers soft astringent tannins. It is *bella* with stirfried beef.

Tuck's Ridge Pinot Noir

Tuck's Ridge was established in 1988 and by Mornington Peninsula standards is rather large, with 26.5 hectares under vines. Maker Daniel Greene.
CURRENT RELEASE 1996   A straightforward wine that couldn't be called complex. The nose has strawberry aromas and a hint of sap. The medium-bodied palate has a simple strawberry flavour and there's evidence of barrel-ferment character. The finish has discreet oak and obvious acid. Drink it now with veal schnitzel.

Quality	▼▼▼
Value	★★★
Grapes	pinot noir
Region	Mornington Peninsula, Vic.
Cellar	▮ 2
Alc./Vol.	12.3%
RRP	$22.00

Turramurra Estate Pinot Noir

This is a new label from the Mornington Peninsula. What does the label mean? We'll leave that up to you.
CURRENT RELEASE 1996   The colour is dark cherry or plum, and the nose has strawberry aromas with floral notes. The palate is almost shiraz-like, with plum and cherry flavours, and the oak on the finish makes a perfect fit. Serve it with duck.

Quality	▼▼▼▼
Value	★★★
Grapes	pinot noir
Region	Mornington Peninsula, Vic.
Cellar	▮ 3
Alc./Vol.	12.9%
RRP	$32.00

Tyrrell's Eclipse Pinot Noir

You have to read the back label to know what this is going to eclipse. (It's named after a mail ship, which used to ply between Maitland and Sydney circa 1820.)
CURRENT RELEASE 1996   The colour is a pale brick-red, and the nose is sappy with hints of strawberry. The palate is medium-bodied and has a sweet strawberry centre. There are gentle, silky tannins on the finish. It goes well with pink lamb.

Quality	▼▼▼▼
Value	★★★★
Grapes	pinot noir
Region	Hunter Valley, NSW
Cellar	▮ 3
Alc./Vol.	13.0%
RRP	$22.00

Voyager Estate Cabernet Sauvignon Merlot

Quality	ỲỲỲỲ
Value	★★★
Grapes	cabernet sauvignon; merlot
Region	Margaret River, WA
Cellar	⬥ 2–8
Alc./Vol.	13.7%
RRP	$28.00

This is a must-visit when you're in Margaret River. It's safe to say you've never seen anything like it: Cape Dutch architecture, massive dams and a touch of South Africa.

CURRENT RELEASE 1994   The wine has a deep colour, and the nose is a mixture of blackberry, undergrowth and a hint of smoke. The palate is tight with blackberry fruit flavours, and the tannin has a solid black-tea-like quality. It has a slightly hard edge that might soften with time. Try it with pan-fried kangaroo.

Waimarama Estate Cabernet Merlot

Quality	ỲỲỲỲ
Value	★★★
Grapes	cabernet sauvignon; merlot
Region	Hawkes Bay, NZ
Cellar	▮ 4
Alc./Vol.	12.5%
RRP	$26.25

This estate is widely touted as one of the better cabernet producers in New Zealand. It's a recently established (1988) venture by the Loughlin family.

CURRENT RELEASE 1995   High-quality toasty oak teams up with leafy fruit in this definite cool-climate cabernet style. Look hard and you'll find some sweet berry flavour too. A lean, lively, lighter style that has plenty of varietal character and drinks well right now. Goes well with duck.

Wandin Valley WVE Reserve Cabernet Sauvignon

Quality	ỲỲỲỲ
Value	★★★⊦
Grapes	cabernet sauvignon
Region	Hunter Valley, NSW
Cellar	⬥ 2–8+
Alc./Vol.	13.2%
RRP	$24.35 ▮

Wandin Valley is in the Lovedale sub-region of the Lower Hunter, and is run by the Davern family of *A Country Practice* fame. Maker Geoff Broadfield.

CURRENT RELEASE 1996   A serious red, but the high-toast American oak is somewhat domineering and doesn't sit too tidily with the blackcurrant cabernet fruit. Dense-looking colour; concentrated vanilla/chocolate and coffee nose; ripe and warm with just a hint of leafiness; good body and length. The acid sticks out a bit. Some age should soften its astringency. Then serve it with rare beef.

Wantirna Estate Cabernet Merlot

This family vineyard and winery is at Wantirna South, in outer Melbourne. Winemaker Maryann Egan, daughter of founders Reg and Tina, recently quit Domaine Chandon and returned to work there.
CURRENT RELEASE 1995 A very fine Yarra Valley wine, happily avoiding the green characters of some prior vintages. It's a lighter style in weight, and has tremendous purity of cabernet-like sweet berry fruit with a kiss of oak and the gentlest leafiness. Clean, fragrant and stylish. Wins with subtlety rather than brute force. Try it with veal cutlets.

Quality	?????
Value	★★★★
Grapes	cabernet sauvignon; merlot
Region	Yarra Valley, Vic.
Cellar	➥ 5+
Alc./Vol.	12.5%
RRP	$36.00

Warrenmang Estate Shiraz

When it comes to red wines, Warrenmang has a history of whoppers. And they tend to age slowly and for the long term. This is no exception. Maker Simon Clayfield.
Previous outstanding vintages: '82, '85, '89, '94
CURRENT RELEASE 1996 Here's an awesome Pyrenees shiraz. It shouts concentration in every regard: deep colour; powerful, young, inky, spicy, cool-area nose with a lacing of mint. Very tight and undeveloped in the mouth, it has taut structure and firm, dry, serious tannins which are well balanced by fruit and bode well for ageing. It begs to be cellared. Food: beef wellington.

Quality	?????
Value	★★★★
Grapes	shiraz
Region	Pyrenees, Vic.
Cellar	➥ 2–12+
Alc./Vol.	14.5%
RRP	$30.50 ▌

Warrenmang Grand Pyrenees

Warrenmang is one of the earlier Pyrenees wineries and is owned by Luigi Bazzani, a restaurateur who not surprisingly runs an excellent restaurant at Warrenmang.
CURRENT RELEASE 1995 The colour is deadly serious: impenetrable purple–red. It's a concentrated wine in every regard, with a powerful berry-fruit, slightly gum leafy nose and oak that is still slightly apart. The palate is lively and fresh to the point of being raw, with astringent tannins. It needs a lot of time. Cellar, then serve with BBQ kangaroo.

Quality	????
Value	★★★
Grapes	cabernet sauvignon; cabernet franc; merlot; shiraz
Region	Pyrenees, Vic.
Cellar	➥ 3–15+
Alc./Vol.	13.5%
RRP	$32.15 ▌

Waterwheel Cabernet Sauvignon

Quality	🍷🍷🍷🍷
Value	★★★★
Grapes	cabernet sauvignon
Region	Bendigo, Vic.
Cellar	1–8+
Alc./Vol.	13.5%
RRP	$16.00

Great value springs regularly from this Bendigo district winery, located at Bridgewater-on-Loddon. The Cumming family grow excellent cherries and tomatoes as well as grapes.

Previous outstanding vintages: '90, '91, '92, '94, '95

CURRENT RELEASE 1996 Cherry aromas couple with vanilla oak on the bouquet, and it has sweet fruit, fleshiness and good texture in the mouth. It has some grip and impressive length, although the vanilla is assertive at present. Try it with venison stew.

Waterwheel Shiraz

Quality	🍷🍷🍷🍷🍷
Value	★★★★★
Grapes	shiraz
Region	Bendigo, Vic.
Cellar	10+
Alc./Vol.	14.5%
RRP	$16.00

PENGUIN BEST SHIRAZ

The waterwheel of the name refers to the old flour mill that stands on the Loddon River near the winery, a relic of a bygone era. Maker Peter Cumming.

CURRENT RELEASE 1996 **Another superb wine at a give-away price from the lithe and mercurial Peter Cumming. It has a nice dark colour, and a rich nose of berries, vanilla and chocolate, well tinged with American oak. It has ample power and depth of flavour. It lingers long on the finish with a twist of licorice and a nice tight grip. Goes a treat with rare kangaroo.**

Wendouree Shiraz

Quality	🍷🍷🍷🍷½
Value	★★★★½
Grapes	shiraz
Region	Clare Valley, SA
Cellar	4–12+
Alc./Vol.	13.5%
RRP	$26.00 (ex-winery)

Wendouree is so sought-after these days that the phone is mostly off the hook and the annual release sells out in a matter of days. Custodians Tony and Lita Brady. Maker Stephen George.

Previous outstanding vintages: '83, '86, '90, '91, '92, '93, '94, '95

CURRENT RELEASE 1996 This is a monster which is generously endowed with everything (except perhaps oak). The colour is deep and dark; the nose is strong with warm, cherry, spicy aromas and some alcohol lift. It's a tad heavy in the mouth, big and broad-shouldered, with a definite tannin grip and a little toughness. It needs age, and hearty food. Try beef wellington.

Westend Three Bridges Cabernet Sauvignon

This is the new premium label for the old Calabria winery in Griffith's 'west end'. Maker Bill Calabria.

CURRENT RELEASE 1996   The colour is nice and deep, and the nose has a minty, herbal character that's almost medicinal in intensity. The palate has reasonable depth and grip with a hint of the mythical cabernet dough-nut – a slight hollow in the mid-palate. Serve it with well-herbed rissoles.

Quality	♥♥♥
Value	★★★
Grapes	cabernet sauvignon
Region	Riverina, NSW
Cellar	▐ 4
Alc./Vol.	13.5%
RRP	$16.95

The Willows Shiraz

This is a refreshing change from the so-called 'Super Barossa Shiraz', which is brimming in alcohol and bound by American oak. This wine retains some subtlety. Maker Peter Scholz.

CURRENT RELEASE 1995   It's already complex with a spicy plum aroma on the nose. The middleweight palate has sweet berry flavours and lifted spices. The wood is an integral part of the composition. There are fine-grained tannins and grip on the finish, which make for a balanced wine. Serve with smoked kangaroo and sweet-potato mash.

Quality	♥♥♥♥
Value	★★★★
Grapes	shiraz
Region	Barossa Valley, SA
Cellar	▐ 5
Alc./Vol.	13.5%
RRP	$19.50

The Wilson Vineyard Zinfandel

The label states you should approach this wine with 'an open mind and a strong cheese'. Add to that a strong head, given the alcohol in this table wine.

CURRENT RELEASE 1997   The nose has strong berry and earth aromas. The palate shows a high level of sweet-ness and jammy characters. Raspberry is the major flavour, and there are some soft tannins on a clean finish. It's an oddball, which goes well with Peking duck.

Quality	♥♥♥
Value	★★★
Grapes	zinfandel
Region	Clare Valley, SA
Cellar	▐ 3
Alc./Vol.	16.6%
RRP	$18.30 (375 ml)

Wirra Wirra Church Block

Quality ??? (3½ glasses)
Value ★★★
Grapes cabernet sauvignon 50%; shiraz 30%; merlot 20%
Region McLaren Vale, SA
Cellar 5
Alc./Vol. 13.5%
RRP $19.70

This has often impressed as being a pretty average sort of wine selling at a premium price. However, it's always well-made and tasty in an easy-to-drink mould.

CURRENT RELEASE 1996 A decent red that sells well in bistros, where its approachable style is right at home. There are herbal and spicy aromas, thanks to the two main varieties (cabernet and shiraz), and a little earthiness. The weight is medium to full and it has smooth tannins. One of the best Church Blocks for some years. Try it with a mixed grill.

Wirra Wirra Original Blend Grenache Shiraz

Quality (4½ glasses)
Value ★★★★
Grapes grenache; shiraz
Region McLaren Vale, SA
Cellar 6+
Alc./Vol. 14.5%
RRP $19.70

This is the sort of strapping stuff the Vales used to export by the shipload in the good ol' days (late last century). Only today the winemaking's much better. Maker Ben Riggs.

CURRENT RELEASE 1996 Wow! This is sterling stuff. Tremendous depth of flavour, very spicy and rich, yet it still seems to be holding more in reserve. The palate has a tight-fisted tannin grip, and it's packed with berry and spice flavours. A genie in a bottle. Cook up a rich venison stew and enjoy.

Wirra Wirra RSW Shiraz

Quality (4 glasses)
Value ★★★
Grapes shiraz
Region McLaren Vale, SA
Cellar 1–7+
Alc./Vol. 13.5%
RRP $33.00

RSW stands for Robert Strangways Wigley, the founder of the original W2, whose old winery Greg and Roger Trott revived. Maker Ben Riggs.

Previous outstanding vintages: '92, '94

CURRENT RELEASE 1995 A big gutsy number with slightly stewy flavours, the aroma recalling prune juice. A robust and fairly tannic wine that perhaps lacks a little refinement. Generous, honest shiraz flavour. Serve it with game meats.

Wisson Lake Pinot Noir

The samples arrived out of the blue – this winery at Piccadilly in the Adelaide Hills simply doesn't exist in any directory or learned tome. Last year there was one new winery licence every week, making it very difficult to keep track of developments.

CURRENT RELEASE 1995 The wine has a pale colour and an earthy, meaty nose. There's also a cherry aroma. This is the major flavour on the light-to-medium palate, which has elegance and style. There's plenty of acid on the finish. A drink-now style that would suit casseroled quail.

Quality	🍷🍷🍷½
Value	★★★½
Grapes	pinot noir
Region	Adelaide Hills, SA
Cellar	3
Alc./Vol.	13.7%
RRP	$22.00

Wolf Blass Yellow Label Cabernet Shiraz

Whatever happened to Herr Wolfgang Blass? Well, in between trips to the track and managing a stable of horseflesh, he runs the Wolf Blass Foundation and waves the flag for the company overseas.

CURRENT RELEASE 1996 This is the wine that did it all for Blassie, but it's very much the junior these days. It smells very woody, with toasty, charred timbery aromas. The palate has abundant oak and drying tannins, but not a lot of fruit. A rustic drop that often dips as low as $13. Goes well with a steak sandwich.

Quality	🍷🍷🍷
Value	★★★
Grapes	cabernet sauvignon; shiraz
Region	not stated
Cellar	4
Alc./Vol.	13.0%
RRP	$16.00 (S)

Woolshed Cabernet Shiraz Merlot

Woolshed is a new budget line from the Wingara group (Katnook, et al.). There's a touch of woolshed or barnyard about the wine, too.

CURRENT RELEASE 1996 The colour is fairly light and the nose has a feral whiff: a gamy, meaty, earthy complexity. There's some coconut oak and cabernet leafy/raspberry character. It's fairly light and basic on the palate. A decent quaffer to have with pasta and a mushroom-based sauce.

Quality	🍷🍷🍷
Value	★★★
Grapes	cabernet sauvignon; shiraz; merlot
Region	Coonawarra, SA
Cellar	2
Alc./Vol.	12.5%
RRP	$15.00 (S)

Wynns Cabernet Sauvignon

Quality	♟♟♟♟⧗
Value	★★★★
Grapes	cabernet sauvignon
Region	Coonawarra, SA
Cellar	▮ 10+
Alc./Vol.	12.5%
RRP	$22.00 Ⓢ

Some fine cabernets have been made at Wynns under the hardworking Black Label since Wynns turned the corner in 1982. Maker Peter Douglas.
Previous outstanding vintages: '62, '71, '76, '82, '85, '86, '88, '90, '91, '93, '94
CURRENT RELEASE 1995 No John Riddoch was bottled from '95, so it's all in here. A good wine, especially given the vintage. Vivid purple–red colour, and vibrant young blackcurrant cabernet fruit-led aromas with a hint of leafiness. Fine but intense palate, with smooth tannin and ready drinkability. Good, but not outstanding. Try it with pink leg of lamb.

Wynns Cabernet Shiraz Merlot

Quality	♟♟♟♟
Value	★★★★
Grapes	cabernet sauvignon; shiraz; merlot
Region	Coonawarra, SA
Cellar	▮ 4
Alc./Vol.	12.5%
RRP	$17.00 Ⓢ

The red sash gets smaller as time passes, but the style and quality remain steady. This is the drink-now bistro red of the Wynns portfolio. Maker Peter Douglas.
CURRENT RELEASE 1995 A truckload of oak-derived vanilla adorns the nose. Blackberry, blackcurrant fruit shines through on the palate, with the cabernet component carrying the torch. Good fruit sweetness, and it drinks well now. There's nothing to be gained by cellaring it. Serve it with lamb fillets with pesto sauce.

Wynns Michael Shiraz

Quality	♟♟♟♟⧗
Value	★★★
Grapes	shiraz
Region	Coonawarra, SA
Cellar	➡ 4–15+
Alc./Vol.	13.0%
RRP	$74.00 ▮

Wynns didn't produce a Michael in 1995 because it was a lesser year in Coonawarra – especially for shiraz. Maker Peter Douglas.
Previous outstanding vintages: '90
CURRENT RELEASE 1994 There's a heap of toasted oak involved in this wine, but the complexity of its bouquet indicates there's a lot more to it than just wood. Impressive weight and length, firm oaky tannins. Quite massive in every regard. Needs a lot of time. (By the way, the '90 is just starting to drink beautifully.) Serve with osso bucco.

Wynns Shiraz

In the best years in Coonawarra, the bread-and-butter wines are outstanding and such is the case with this large-production number in '96. It has the legs to cellar, too.

Previous outstanding vintages: '86, '88, '90, '91, '93, '94

CURRENT RELEASE 1996 Peter Douglas has put together another impressive shiraz. The vibrant cherry, berry fruit is augmented by a dash of smoky, toasty oak. Full-bodied and well-structured for drinking or keeping, it has intense flavour and represents great value, especially when discounted. Osso bucco is obligato.

Quality	♟♟♟♟⁀
Value	★★★★⟆
Grapes	shiraz
Region	Coonawarra, SA
Cellar	▮ 8
Alc./Vol.	12.5%
RRP	$16.00 Ⓢ

Xanadu Cabernet Reserve

Reserved for judgement probably because this is a young and thorny style that needs a step in faith to see if it matures into a gem.

CURRENT RELEASE 1995   This is the top of the Xanadu line, and a typically elegant Margaret River style. The nose is starting to show some bottle development but with talcum powder–oak qualities. The palate has red-currant flavours and a tight structure. There are assertive tannins on a grippy finish. It's a little belligerent at the moment. Serve it with venison.

Quality	♟♟♟♟
Value	★★★
Grapes	cabernet sauvignon
Region	Margaret River, SA
Cellar	➡ 2–7
Alc./Vol.	13.5
RRP	$57.00

Xanadu Cabernet Sauvignon

This is a very elegant style from Margaret River. Elegance doesn't mean it lacks intensity. The same could be said for the proprietor, Conor Lagan.

CURRENT RELEASE 1996   The nose has cassis and briar qualities. The medium-bodied palate has blackberry and spice flavours, and there are some black-tea-like tannins on a grippy finish. It is well-balanced with an impressive level of complexity. Try with casseroled quail.

Quality	♟♟♟♟
Value	★★★★
Grapes	cabernet sauvignon
Region	Margaret River, WA
Cellar	▮ 5
Alc./Vol.	13.5%
RRP	$33.00

Yalumba Oxford Landing Cabernet Shiraz

Quality 🍷🍷🍷
Value ★★★½
Grapes cabernet sauvignon; shiraz
Region Murray Valley, SA
Cellar 🍾 2
Alc./Vol. 12.5%
RRP $8.85 (S)

Some of the best value-for-money wines in Australia come from the Murray River Valley, like this one.

CURRENT RELEASE 1996 The colour is a healthy, full red–purple and the nose shows charred wood plus leafy herbal fruit aromas. It's a light-bodied, ready-drinking quaff. No great power or length here, but it's decent value at the price, which is often discounted. Serve with fast food.

Yalumba Oxford Landing Merlot

Quality 🍷🍷🍷
Value ★★★
Grapes merlot
Region Murray Valley, SA
Cellar 🍾 1
Alc./Vol. 12.5%
RRP $8.85 (S)

Oxford Landing is named after a place on the Murray River where stock drovers used to stop to give their sheep or cattle a drink.

CURRENT RELEASE 1996 This is a decent drink at the price, but the green-fruit characters are surprising, considering the hot climate where the grapes were grown. The nose has green-leaf, capsicum/green-bean aromas, and the palate is light in weight and smoothly quaffable. It airs to develop some attractive undergrowth, berry and earthy characters. Food: spaghetti bolognaise.

Yalumba Reserve Shiraz

Quality 🍷🍷🍷🍷½
Value ★★★★½
Grapes shiraz
Region Barossa Valley, SA
Cellar 🍾 8
Alc./Vol. 14.0%
RRP $19.70 (S) 🍾

This a *real* Reserve – the old Yalumba Family Reserve label has been discontinued. Maker Brian Walsh and team.

CURRENT RELEASE 1994 This is almost a caricature of Barossa shiraz. The nose is all sweet, ripe, jammy fruit and chocolatey characters laced with coconut/vanilla American oak. It's very oaky and needs time to settle down, but there's so much sweet plummy voluptuous fruit that it's a safe bet. Serve with jugged hare.

Yalumba The Octavius

The story is that the first vintages were aged only in octaves (very small barrels) of new well-seasoned American oak, but this is no longer so. Maker Simon Adams. *Previous outstanding vintages: '90, '91, '92, '93*
CURRENT RELEASE 1994   After a more balanced, spicy '93, this is just oak, oak and more oak. And very heavily charred, caramelised wood at that. It's hard to detect anything but wood at this stage, so we suspend final judgement and recommend it be tasted again in a couple of years. A big, solid wine with heavy tannins. Cellar!

Quality	🍷🍷🍷🍷
Value	★★★
Grapes	shiraz
Region	Barossa Valley, SA
Cellar	➥ 3–8+
Alc./Vol.	14.0%
RRP	$45.00

Yarra Burn Pinot Noir

Yarra Burn is part of the BRL Hardy group. It was purchased from founders David and Christine Fyffe in 1995. Maker David Fyffe.
CURRENT RELEASE 1997   The colour is impressively dark and youthful. It smells fresh and undeveloped, with spicy oak to the fore, which is backed up by concentrated ripe fruit. It has terrific palate structure and a rich, fleshy texture. Potential plus. Cellar, then serve with crown roast of hare.

Quality	🍷🍷🍷🍷🍷
Value	★★★★★
Grapes	pinot noir
Region	Yarra Valley, Vic.
Cellar	➥ 1–5+
Alc./Vol.	13.5%
RRP	$18.00

Yarra Edge Cabernets

These wines are made at Yering Station by Tom Carson, and the vineyard is in the Coldstream area. Cellar door sales are at Yering Station, too.
CURRENT RELEASE 1994   This is a big red – rich and deep – with a dark colour, and concentrated flavour and tannin in the mouth. Power and cellarability aren't in doubt, but whether the tannin will tend to remain assertive and demand that it be drunk with food is a moot point. Try it with a hearty steak and chips.

Quality	🍷🍷🍷🍷?
Value	★★★★
Grapes	cabernet sauvignon 70%; merlot, cabernet franc & malbec 30%
Region	Yarra Valley, Vic.
Cellar	8+
Alc./Vol.	13.5%
RRP	$24.00

Yarra Ridge Cabernet Sauvignon

Quality	♟♟♟
Value	★★⊱
Grapes	cabernet sauvignon 90%; merlot 10%
Region	Yarra Valley, Vic.
Cellar	♦ 3
Alc./Vol.	12.5%
RRP	$21.00 Ⓢ

The year 1996 was a reasonable pinot noir vintage, but it won't go down as a great year for cabernet in the Yarra. Maker Rob Dolan.

CURRENT RELEASE 1996 The nose has a lifted aromaticity, but the dominant notes are herbal: dusty, vegetal and unripe. The palate is lean and austere with a firm and somewhat unbalanced tannic finish. It lacks mid-palate fruit sweetness, but it will have its admirers. Try it with mild Thai green curry.

Yarra Ridge Reserve Pinot Noir

Quality	♟♟♟♟
Value	★★★
Grapes	pinot noir
Region	Yarra Valley, Vic.
Cellar	➥ 1–5
Alc./Vol.	13.5%
RRP	$39.50

Reserve bottlings are all the rage at present, which must be an indicator of prosperous times, as they are invariably expensive (and difficult to find).

CURRENT RELEASE 1997 This epitomises the modern style of Oz pinot: very dark-coloured, with lashings of new oak character and masses of vibrant cherry fruit. It has plenty of weight and length, and it will be interesting to see if it develops complexity with age. Tends to polarise tasters. Food: duck à l'orange.

Yarra Valley Hills Log Creek Cabernet Sauvignon

Quality	♟♟♟
Value	★★★
Grapes	cabernet sauvignon
Region	Yarra Valley, Vic.
Cellar	♦ 4
Alc./Vol.	13.0%
RRP	$22.00

This company draws grapes from three small vineyards in the Yarra Valley: Kiah Yallambee, Log Creek and Warranwood. Maker Martin Williams.

CURRENT RELEASE 1995 An interesting wine that smells somewhat meaty from a marriage of generous toasty oak and slightly green herbal fruit. It's lean and medium-bodied with some astringency to finish. It would go with well-charred barbecued kebabs.

Yering Station Cabernet Sauvignon Merlot

This marque, developed by the Dominguez family of Sydney banking fame, is now owned by the brothers Rathbone, who also sell agricultural chemicals. Maker Tom Carson.

CURRENT RELEASE 1995 Attractive ripe dark berry and cherry flavours laced with a well-judged hint of new oak pervade the wine. The finish shows some firm tannin, which could benefit from a few years' cellaring to soften. A high-quality wine and further evidence that Yering Station is on the way up. Try it with minted lamb.

Quality	▼▼▼▼▼
Value	★★★★☆
Grapes	cabernet sauvignon; merlot
Region	Yarra Valley, Vic.
Cellar	▮ 10
Alc./Vol.	12.5%
RRP	$17.50

Yering Station Pinot Noir

The new winery at this historic property is a sight to behold. Napa Valley comes to the Yarra! It's both grand and functional and, being dug into the hillside, it doesn't dominate the landscape.

CURRENT RELEASE 1997 Perhaps the best pinot yet from this relatively new producer. A fine wine, it has a lighter purple–red hue, and aromas of spices and cherry that are clear and precise. The taste is smooth and soft and deceptively full in the mouth. It avoids stalky or overt oaky accents. It is balanced and long. Enjoy it with beef carpaccio.

Quality	▼▼▼▼▼
Value	★★★★
Grapes	pinot noir
Region	Yarra Valley, Vic.
Cellar	▮ 5
Alc./Vol.	13.5%
RRP	$19.50

Yering Station Pinot Noir Rosé ED

What does ED stand for? Why, extra dry, of course! It's a subtle reminder that, historically, most Australian rosés have been to some degree sweet.

CURRENT RELEASE 1997 This style of wine is inevitably produced by doing a *saignée* on pinot noir; that is, some juice is 'bled' off to concentrate a pinot noir and make a serious dry red. The 'bled' juice happens to make a fine rosé style. The colour is pale pink, and it has a delicately smoky/cherry aroma and flavour, without sugar sweetness but with excellent balance. Deliciously drinkable with many lighter foods, such as smoked salmon.

Quality	▼▼▼▼▼
Value	★★★★
Grapes	pinot noir
Region	Yarra Valley, Vic.
Cellar	▮ 1
Alc./Vol.	13.5%
RRP	$18.40

Zema Estate Cabernet Sauvignon

Quality	♟♟♟♟♟
Value	★★★★
Grapes	cabernet sauvignon
Region	Coonawarra, SA
Cellar	▮ 7
Alc./Vol.	13.8%
RRP	$19.00

Le Patron, Demetrio 'Bludda' Zema, is a colourful character brimming with the joy of living. He takes great delight in mangling the English language, and his conversation is peppered with words like 'bludda' and 'bast'. May you have good fortune and meet him at the cellar door.

Previous outstanding vintages: '84, '86, '88, '92, '94

CURRENT RELEASE 1996   The nose has sweet and succulent blackberry aromas plus hints of vanilla and toast. The palate has a mouthfilling quality. It has plenty of flavour with sweet cassis and blackberry flavours adorned with some fine-grained tannins and a gentle grip. Try it with rare roast beef.

Zema Estate Cluny

Quality	♟♟♟♟♟
Value	★★★★★
Grapes	cabernet sauvignon 65%; merlot 15%; cabernet franc 12%; malbec 8%
Region	Coonawarra, SA
Cellar	▮ 6
Alc./Vol.	13.3%
RRP	$19.00

This is a Bordeaux-style blend from a now not-so-small family vineyard in the cradle of great Australian reds. Makers Matt and Nick Zema.

CURRENT RELEASE 1996   The nose has strong berry aromas. The palate is rich with plenty of sweet fruit flavour, including dark cherry and blackberry. These are framed by some graceful oak that offers fine-grained tannins and lasting grip. It drinks well with casserole of quail.

Zema Estate Shiraz

Quality	♟♟♟♟
Value	★★★★
Grapes	shiraz
Region	Coonawarra, SA
Cellar	➡ 2–6
Alc./Vol.	13.5%
RRP	$19.00

The Zema holdings are growing apace. The new vineyard on the terra rossa soil will be in full production this year. Hopefully they will help satisfy a growing market demand.

Previous outstanding vintages: '84, '86, '88, '92, '94

CURRENT RELEASE 1996   This one is so young it almost throws a tantrum in the mouth. It has strong pepper and concentrated berry aromas. The palate is soft and sweet, but this is counterbalanced by some firm oak on a very virile finish. The tannin is astringent and drying, and it also shows outstanding length.

White Wines

Alkoomi Frankland River Riesling

Western Australia's Great Southern region may have a markedly different climate to the Clare, but it's also an outstanding riesling area. Some say it ranks alongside Eden Valley and the Clare.

CURRENT RELEASE 1997 This is a backward, undeveloped riesling with a pale hue and shy, bready, mineral aromas. The nose is restrained but with an underlying intensity. The palate is vivacious, with all the desirable attributes: finesse, life, length and balance. Drinks beautifully now, but history shows it will repay at least 10 years in a cool dark place. Drink with West Australian marron.

Quality	♟♟♟♟♟
Value	★★★★★
Grapes	riesling
Region	Great Southern, WA
Cellar	🍾 10+
Alc./Vol.	12.0%
RRP	$18.20

All Saints Chardonnay

All Saints is a winery, not a church, although you'd never guess it isn't a castle, the first time you set eyes on it. Made at Brown Brothers.

CURRENT RELEASE 1997 Slightly volcanic sulfur dioxide nose which needs time to settle down. There are lanolin and woolly aromas in the bouquet, which should show more fruit in time. The taste is fairly straightforward with light wood influence and a drying finish. Drink from the end of 1998, with smoked cod.

Quality	♟♟♟
Value	★★★
Grapes	chardonnay
Region	Rutherglen, Vic.
Cellar	🍾 4
Alc./Vol.	14.0%
RRP	$16.80

All Saints Riesling

Quality	♟♟♟♟♟
Value	★★★★★
Grapes	riesling
Region	Rutherglen, Vic.
Cellar	◊ 5+
Alc./Vol.	12.5%
RRP	$13.60

Rutherglen/Wahgunyah is probably not top of your list of riesling areas, but this is a real eye-opener! Made by Terry Barnett at Brown Brothers.
CURRENT RELEASE 1997 A most impressive riesling, smelling of delicate lime/citrus fruit and turning rich, full and smooth yet with no lack of finesse in the mouth. Excellent depth of fruit, a well-judged trace of sweetness but dry to finish, and a deep, long follow-through. Goes well with Murray perch.

Amberley Estate Chenin

Quality	♟♟♟
Value	★★★
Grapes	chenin blanc
Region	Margaret River, WA
Cellar	◊
Alc./Vol.	12.5%
RRP	$15.20

This is a sugary wine aimed at the masses, and is probably one of the biggest-selling wines in all of Margaret River. They've dropped the 'blanc' off the name this year.
CURRENT RELEASE 1997 Powder-puff aromas that are lightly floral and shy. It has a very sweet entry in the mouth, which then broadens on the mid-palate. Lacks strength of flavour and with all that sugar, is hard to treat as a serious wine. Will please the tourist-bus crowds.

Amberley Estate Semillon Sauvignon Blanc

Quality	♟♟♟♟
Value	★★★★
Grapes	semillon; sauvignon blanc
Region	Margaret River, WA
Cellar	◊ 5
Alc./Vol.	12.5%
RRP	$18.70

Amberley is one of the bigger producers at Margaret River, and the winemaking, under Eddie Price, is always competent.
Previous outstanding vintages: '95, '96
CURRENT RELEASE 1997 A delicate, restrained style with some finesse. The nose is herbal and lemony, and lightly toasty from barrel fermentation. The palate has delicacy, a racy structure and tangy acid. It's near bone-dry and is a more-ish and very pleasing drink. Try it with prawns and aioli.

Andrew Garrett Chardonnay

This won a gold medal in the Melbourne Show in 1997, and two trophies at Brisbane this year. We can't see what the fuss is about.
CURRENT RELEASE 1997 The colour is medium–full yellow and there are dominant coconut oak aromas as well as creamy, peachy notes. It smells a bit like bourbon barrels. It's very light on the tongue, and has modest intensity and length. The finish is slightly hot and astringent. Try it with deep-fried prawns.

Quality	ΨΨΨ
Value	★★★
Grapes	chardonnay
Region	not stated
Cellar	🍾 1
Alc./Vol.	13.5%
RRP	$15.60

Andrew Garrett Riesling

The Mildara Blass home-brand these days, but the quality is good and occasionally outstanding in its modest price-range.
CURRENT RELEASE 1997 A commendable riesling which is much better than quaffing standard. The dry grass/straw aromas are gathering some toastiness and although it doesn't have a lot of floral aromatics, the palate shows good fruit concentration and length. Just a hint of sweetness fills it out. It goes well with grilled flounder.

Quality	ΨΨΨΨ
Value	★★★★★
Grapes	riesling
Region	not stated
Cellar	🍾 4
Alc./Vol.	12.5%
RRP	$14.00 Ⓢ

Angoves Mondiale

Groovy labelling is the way of the future, if not the present, and this is Angoves's attempt to win the hearts and minds of the fashionable set.
CURRENT RELEASE 1997 A very broad, overblown style which smells of fig jam, toffee and other confections. The flavour starts off big, but is all up-front and falls away quickly. Unsubtle, but some will like it. We recommend a big chill, and serve with Thai fish cakes.

Quality	ΨΨΨ
Value	★★ᵏ
Grapes	sauvignon blanc; chardonnay; semillon
Region	87% Padthaway, 13% Murray Valley, SA
Cellar	🍾 1
Alc./Vol.	11.0%
RRP	$15.60 Ⓢ

Annie's Lane Chardonnay

Quality	🍷🍷🍷½
Value	★★★★
Grapes	chardonnay
Region	Clare Valley, SA
Cellar	2
Alc./Vol.	13.5%
RRP	$14.10

The grapes were 70% from the Polish Hill River subregion and 30% from Watervale. Maker David O'Leary.

CURRENT RELEASE 1997 A workman – like chardonnay with toasty, coconutty aromas and a rich, slightly sweet/juicy palate that borders on the clumsy. There's some alcohol heat in the finish and it has some pleasing flavour complexity. Good value and goes with chicken satay.

Annie's Lane Riesling

Quality	🍷🍷🍷½
Value	★★★½
Grapes	riesling
Region	Clare Valley, SA
Cellar	3
Alc./Vol.	13.0%
RRP	$14.00 (S)

This is the main label emanating from the Quelltaler Clare Valley winery these days. The Annie in question would be very surprised if she knew a wine had been named after her.

CURRENT RELEASE 1996 A straightforward riesling with earthy, bracken and dusty aromas. It's starting to show some development and is probably at a difficult, in-between stage. A good drink, however, and invitingly priced. Goes well with skate.

Quality	🍷🍷🍷🍷
Value	★★★★
Grapes	riesling
Region	Clare Valley, SA
Cellar	4
Alc./Vol.	12.0%
RRP	$14.00 (S)

CURRENT RELEASE 1997 A soft, up-front riesling that's made to be drinking at its best young. It smells floral with a trace of doughy, bready fermentation esters. The palate is full and rich with a hint of sweetness and a nice long carry. Acidity gives it just enough bite. Serve with yabby tails.

Annie's Lane Semillon

The old Quelltaler vineyard has long produced outstanding semillon, although it's been bottled under various brand names over the years. There's a component of barrel fermentation in it.
CURRENT RELEASE 1997 The dusty, lemony aromas are typical semillon and bottle-age has yet to make an appearance. It's a lean, narrow-profile dry white with lemony and lightly herbal flavours, and the acidity adds freshness to the finish. Understated and with good persistence, it drinks well with pan-fried flounder with lemon juice.

Quality	♟♟♟♟
Value	★★★★
Grapes	semillon
Region	Clare Valley, SA
Cellar	🍷 6+
Alc./Vol.	13.0%
RRP	$14.10

Arlewood Sauvignon Blanc Semillon

Arlewood is a very small vineyard in the Willyabrup subregion. The wines are contract-made by Mike and Jan Davies.
CURRENT RELEASE 1997 This is a soft, slightly syrupy style with some sweetness and a bouquet that recalls lemon essence. There's a hint of wood and the structure is broad with fully ripe flavours. Very much a drink-now style. Try it with lemon chicken.

Quality	♟♟♟
Value	★★★
Grapes	sauvignon blanc; semillon
Region	Margaret River, WA
Cellar	🍷 1
Alc./Vol.	13.5%
RRP	$17.90

Arrowfield Chardonnay

Arrowfield makes several chardonnays. This is the standard issue, a blend of vineyards and regions. Maker Don Buchanan.
CURRENT RELEASE 1996 There are some green elements in the herby aroma that recall parsley and crushed vine leaves. Oak is not really apparent, and the wine is light-bodied and a fraction wispy. Try it with a caesar salad.

Quality	♟♟♟
Value	★★★
Grapes	chardonnay
Region	not stated
Cellar	🍷 1
Alc./Vol.	13.0%
RRP	$13.15 Ⓢ

Arrowfield Hunter Valley Semillon

Quality	♟♟♟¿
Value	★★★
Grapes	semillon
Region	Hunter Valley, NSW
Cellar	▯ 3
Alc./Vol.	12.4%
RRP	$17.25 Ⓢ

This Japanese-owned winery was once part of an impo-rotant thoroughbred horse stud. It's located in the Upper Hunter.

CURRENT RELEASE 1996   American oak gives a decid-edly peppermint toothpaste aroma to this wine, over herbal and lemony fruit. There is some richness to the palate and it has good weight and length, even if a little oaky.

Arrowfield Show Reserve Semillon

Quality	♟♟♟¿
Value	★★★
Grapes	semillon
Region	Hunter Valley, NSW
Cellar	▯ 1
Alc./Vol.	13.0%
RRP	$21.30 Ⓢ

The winemaker these days is Don Buchanan, a seasoned campaigner who used to work for Krondorf before heading off to pursue cool-climate viticulture in Tasmania.

CURRENT RELEASE 1994   The full yellow colour betrays both oak ageing and bottle-age. It's a developed, oaky style, full of toasty and coconutty aromas. In the mouth it's big and full-on with masses of up-front flavour but without great length. For lovers of big, devel-oped dry whites. Try it with roast chicken.

Ashton Hills Chardonnay

Quality	♟♟♟¿
Value	★★★
Grapes	chardonnay
Region	Adelaide Hills, SA
Cellar	➾ 1–5
Alc./Vol.	13.0%
RRP	$31.00

The vineyard was owned by winemaker Steve George's in-laws, Sophie and Peter Van Rood. Recently, George became a part-owner. He makes the wines at other peo-ple's wineries.

CURRENT RELEASE 1996   A very delicate wine, with a light yellow colour and shy, fruit-driven straw/hay aromas. The winemaking complexities are there but very subtle. It needs time to show its true colours. Cellar, then serve it with snapper quenelles.

Ashton Hills Riesling

Riesling does well in the Adelaide Hills. You can bet your bottom dollar they'll plant more of it when the riesling revival hits. Maker Stephen George.

Previous outstanding vintages: '89, '90, '91, '93, '94, '96

CURRENT RELEASE 1997 A typically delicate youngster which needs time to prove its worth. Fine, cool-grown bath-powder aromatics; high-toned flowery, appley scents. Delicate, soft apple and mineral flavours with some flowery mouth-aromas. Clean, dry, lively finish. Great with caesar salad.

Quality	🍷🍷🍷🍷½
Value	★★★★
Grapes	riesling
Region	Adelaide Hills, SA
Cellar	🍾 8+
Alc./Vol.	13.0%
RRP	$22.00

Ashwood Grove Chardonnay

Ashwood Grove is named after a plantation of trees planted by a certain green-thumbed Lady Hamilton.

CURRENT RELEASE 1996 Ripeness doesn't seem to have been a problem here. The wine has sweet-cooked smells of fig jam and apricot compote. The palate structure is soft and fat, and could use more acid. A good-value dry white: drink up before it broadens any further. Serve with smoked salmon.

Quality	🍷🍷🍷
Value	★★★
Grapes	chardonnay
Region	Murray Valley, Vic.
Cellar	🍾
Alc./Vol.	12.5%
RRP	$12.50 ($)

Auldstone Riesling

An estate-grown wine from the Taminick area in the Warby Ranges, Glenrowan, Victoria.

CURRENT RELEASE 1996 A riesling with training wheels from a region more noted for its heroic reds and rich fortifieds. Subdued bouquet with earthy, dusty notes. The palate is broad, weighty and quite sweet. It could work with a mild fish curry.

Quality	🍷🍷½
Value	★★★
Grapes	riesling
Region	North East Victoria
Cellar	🍾 1
Alc./Vol.	12.5%
RRP	$13.00 (cellar door)

Austin's Barrabool Chardonnay

Quality	ҮҮҮҮ̊
Value	★★★ᵏ
Grapes	chardonnay
Region	Geelong, Vic.
Cellar	▮ 4
Alc./Vol.	12.5%
RRP	$25.00 (ex-vineyard)

This Waurn Ponds, Geelong-district producer has its wines made by John Ellis at Hanging Rock. It's tiny at the moment, but the Austins have just planted more vines in the Moorabool Valley.

CURRENT RELEASE 1996   Impressive stuff: butterscotch and grapefruit to sniff, cool-grown delicacy, refined and tight, delicious flavour and balance. Enjoyable now, but it could reward keeping too. Try it with scallops.

Babich Sauvignon Blanc

Quality	ҮҮҮҮ̊
Value	★★★★ᵏ
Grapes	sauvignon blanc
Region	Marlborough, NZ
Cellar	▮ 2
Alc./Vol.	13.0%
RRP	$15.25

This firm is one of the pioneers, established by the Babich family in 1916. It has persevered and these days produces around 80 000 cases per annum. Maker Neil Culley.

CURRENT RELEASE 1997   A very polished style with none of the excesses. The nose has a strong tropical fruit aroma and there are also herbal notes in the background. Pineapple, passionfruit and gooseberry dominate the palate; fresh acid adds balance to the finish. It can be served well-chilled, and goes well with green-lip mussels.

Badger's Brook Chardonnay

Quality	ҮҮҮ̊
Value	★★★★
Grapes	chardonnay
Region	Yarra Valley, Vic.
Cellar	▮ 3
Alc./Vol.	13.2%
RRP	$14.00 ▮ Ⓢ

This is a new label from the Yarra Valley – Coldstream, to be precise.

CURRENT RELEASE 1996   The nose is gentle with varietal chardonnay aromas. The medium-bodied palate offers melon and nectarine flavours. This is balanced by a dry finish that lingers in the mouth. It seems to be best near room temperature. Salmon patties are the go with this wine.

Baldivis Estate Chardonnay

This is a West Australian wine with lots of class. The venture started in 1982, and the production is in the order of 6000 cases. Maker Jane Gilham.

CURRENT RELEASE 1996 The nose is complex with attractive oak aromas that include nuts, toast and cashew. There are also tropical fruit flavours and nectarines. The palate has a creamy texture, and several fruit flavours combine to make an impact on the palate. The wood is very well integrated, and the finish is dry and satisfying. It can be served with a medium chill. Try it with raw tuna.

Quality	?????
Value	★★★★
Grapes	chardonnay
Region	South West Coastal Plains, WA
Cellar	◈ 5
Alc./Vol.	13.2%
RRP	$20.50

Baldivis Estate Semillon Sauvignon Blanc

There has been a big improvement in the quality of wines under this label. Indeed, they are now turning out very tidy wines.

CURRENT RELEASE 1997 This is a very pungent wine with a strong herbal component – on both the nose and the palate. There are also tropical fruit characters and hints of mango and peaches in the mix. It can survive a big chill, and a plate of fish and chips wouldn't be a hardship.

Quality	????
Value	★★★★
Grapes	semillon; sauvignon blanc
Region	South West Coastal Plains, WA
Cellar	◈ 2
Alc./Vol.	13.2%
RRP	$15.00

Balnaves Chardonnay

Balnaves might be a newish label, but the name isn't new in the Coonawarra district. The family have been in the grapegrowing business for years. Maker Peter Bissell.

CURRENT RELEASE 1996 There's a curious menthol note on the nose, which could be a function of the oak. The palate is full-bodied with excellent mouth-feel, and there are peach and melon flavours. The oak adds a very dry element to the finish. It wouldn't want to be too cold. Try it with ocean trout.

Quality	????
Value	★★★⟨
Grapes	chardonnay
Region	Coonawarra, SA
Cellar	◈ 3
Alc./Vol.	13.4%
RRP	$18.00

Bannockburn Chardonnay

Quality	♛♛♛♛♛
Value	★★★★★
Grapes	chardonnay
Region	Geelong, Vic.
Cellar	🍷 10
Alc./Vol.	13.5%
RRP	$41.00

This vineyard had its own Battle of Bannockburn in 1997–98, with the death of founder Stuart Hooper followed by a devastating hailstorm. Maker Gary Farr.
Previous outstanding vintages: '88, '90, '91, '92, '94, '95
CURRENT RELEASE 1996 A real mind-bender. Very complex, with such fine harmony that no single characteristic dominates. It has that intangible quality which means that more and more unfolds as the wine sits in the glass, warming and interacting with the air. Yet another superb chardonnay from a leading maker. Serve with lobster.

Bannockburn SRH Chardonnay

Quality	♛♛♛♛♛
Value	★★★
Grapes	chardonnay
Region	Geelong, Vic.
Cellar	🍷 5+
Alc./Vol.	13.5%
RRP	$95.00

This reserve wine, made in tiny quantity, commemorates the founder and owner of Bannockburn Vineyards, Stuart Hooper, who died in early 1998. He was one of nature's gentlemen. Maker Gary Farr.
CURRENT RELEASE 1994 Great wine that lobs right into the league of the '95 Leeuwin and Yattarna. A tremendously complex chardonnay with more Burgundy-like character than either of the above. Golden coloured, and powerfully flavoured with toasted hazelnut. It's mealy, with creamy aromas and a hint of honey. The palate is extraordinary, concentrated, monumental. The archetypal red drinker's white. Serve with lobster.

Banrock Station Semillon Chardonnay

Quality	♛♛♛
Value	★★★
Grapes	semillon; chardonnay
Region	Riverland, SA
Cellar	🍷 1
Alc./Vol.	11.5%
RRP	$7.95 ⓢ

This is a straightforward economy wine from the Riverland. It doesn't carry a vintage.
CURRENT RELEASE *non-vintage* The nose is a mixture of gooseberry and herb aromas. The medium-bodied palate offers grapey flavours and the finish is dry and dusty. The wine can be served well-chilled. Try it with Friday night's fish and chips.

Basedow Chardonnay

Barossa chardonnays tend to be battleships rather than destroyers. They are usually generous and can take lashings of wood to give them backbone.

CURRENT RELEASE 1996 Thumping style with lots of wood. The nose has a smoky aroma plus loquat and quince fruit. The palate is full-bodied with ripe peach and quince flavours. These contest some fairly brutal oak on a very firm finish. Whether the oak will soften is a matter for time in the bottle. Don't over-chill. Try it with rabbit and mushroom stew.

Quality	🍷🍷🍷
Value	★★★
Grapes	chardonnay
Region	Barossa Valley, SA
Cellar	4
Alc./Vol.	13.5%
RRP	$16.50

Basedow Eden Valley Riesling

Basedow have gone further afield for their riesling source. It used to come from the home base, Barossa Valley.

CURRENT RELEASE 1996 The nose has strong citrus aromas, with hints of bottle development and kerosene. The palate has a full impact of lime and other citrus flavours, and a mouthfilling texture. Clean, crisp acid balances the finish. It can be served well-chilled, and goes well with curry puffs.

Quality	🍷🍷🍷🍷
Value	★★★★
Grapes	riesling
Region	Eden Valley, Vic.
Cellar	3
Alc./Vol.	11.5%
RRP	$14.00

Basedow Oscar's White Burgundy

This is a real bargain that has cellar potential and instant appeal. The style was pioneered by Doug 'Dingo' Lehmann, and these days the winemaking mantle resides on the shoulders of Grant Burge.

CURRENT RELEASE 1996 It's a well-wooded Barossa semillon with oak, hay and a hint of lanolin on the nose. The palate is full-bodied with gooseberry and citrus flavours, and these are intermingled with some extractive oak flavours. It has a firm finish and drinks well near room temperature. A plate of roast pork and baked spuds won't hurt.

Quality	🍷🍷🍷🍷
Value	★★★★★
Grapes	semillon
Region	Barossa Valley, SA
Cellar	3
Alc./Vol.	13.0%
RRP	$14.50

Beresford Chardonnay

Quality	♥♥♥♥
Value	★★★★
Grapes	chardonnay
Region	Padthaway, McLaren Vale, SA
Cellar	🍷 4
Alc./Vol.	13.5%
RRP	$16.00

Good wine at a realistic price. This is a well-made chardonnay using fruit from Padthaway and McLaren Vale. Maker Rob Dundon.

CURRENT RELEASE 1997   The nose has obvious wood plus some peach aromas. The medium-bodied palate has peach and nectarine flavours. Wood makes for a long dry finish. Don't over-chill. Try it with pan-fried veal in lemon sauce.

Bethany Semillon

Quality	♥♥♥♥
Value	★★★★
Grapes	semillon
Region	Barossa Valley, SA
Cellar	🍷 3
Alc./Vol.	12.5%
RRP	$16.00

This is a barrel-fermented style made from Barossa fruit. The Schrapel family have long been growers in the Bethany district, which was the first settlement in the Valley. Maker Geoff Schrapel.

CURRENT RELEASE 1997   The wine has an interesting damp straw nose and the wood doesn't intrude. The palate has a creamy texture and lemon and lychee flavours. The wood fills out the finish and adds dry tannins. It should be served with a medium chill with zucchini and goat's cheese soufflé.

Black Rock McLaren Vale Chardonnay

Quality	♥♥♥♥
Value	★★★★
Grapes	chardonnay
Region	McLaren Vale, SA
Cellar	🍷 4
Alc./Vol.	13.5%
RRP	$14.50

At first glance you'd think the wine came from a bayside suburb of Melbourne. But it's all McLaren Vale – rich and generous of flavour and gentle in nature. It's also Mildara Blass looking for the second coming of Jamiesons Run.

CURRENT RELEASE 1996   The nose has strong peach aromas and there's a hint of wood. The palate is peachy with a hint of nectarine, and there's plenty of wood in the background. The finish is dry and cleansing. Old-fashioned roast chicken does good!

Bleasdale Sandhill Verdelho

The grapes were grown in the Sandhill Vineyard in Langhorne Creek. Bleasdale used to sell flagons to Noah. It was established in 1850.
CURRENT RELEASE 1996 The nose has honeysuckle and tropical fruit aromas. The palate is rich with melon, guava and tropical fruit flavours, and the finish adds some drying qualities. It will probably age well. It needs to be served well-chilled, and would go well with salmon patties.

Quality	♥♥♥↑
Value	★★★↑
Grapes	verdelho
Region	Langhorne Creek, SA
Cellar	▮ 4
Alc./Vol.	13.0%
RRP	$15.60

Bloodwood Riesling

Established in 1983 by Rhonda and Stephen Doyle, who are obviously far-sighted pioneers in the rapidly expanding Orange Region.
CURRENT RELEASE 1997 The wine has strong citrus aromas with hints of toast and yeast. The palate has attractive mouth-feel and acute lemon citrus flavours. There's medium-strength acid on the finish, and the wine can be served well-chilled. Try it with a summer salad.

Quality	♥♥♥↑
Value	★★★↑
Grapes	riesling
Region	Orange, NSW
Cellar	▮ 3
Alc./Vol.	12.5%
RRP	$16.00

Blue Pyrenees Estate Chardonnay

This wine comes from the Pyrenees region near Avoca. The Remy Martin Co. in France own and operate the vineyard, which was originally planted with grapes for brandy.
CURRENT RELEASE 1996 The colour is pale straw, and the nose has strong varietal aromas accompanied by wood smells. The palate is medium-bodied. Peach and nectarine flavours dominate, and there's a dusting of oak. The finish is dry and long. It should be served near room temperature with a plate of sushi.

Quality	♥♥♥↑
Value	★★↑
Grapes	chardonnay
Region	Pyrenees, Vic.
Cellar	▮ 3
Alc./Vol.	13.5%
RRP	$21.00

Boston Bay Chardonnay

Quality	♟♟♟♟
Value	★★★★
Grapes	chardonnay
Region	Eyre Peninsula, SA
Cellar	🍷 3
Alc./Vol.	12.8%
RRP	$19.00

This is a pioneering venture on the Eyre Peninsula near Port Lincoln. The Ford family are to blame; they're thoroughly charming folk.

CURRENT RELEASE 1996   The wine is equally charming. The nose has peach and melon aromas, and there are also some smoky oak characters. The medium-bodied palate is rich with peach and nectarine flavours. Some charred oak completes the picture on the finish. Don't over-chill. Try it with pork chops.

Brands Coonawarra Chardonnay

Quality	♟♟♟♟
Value	★★★★
Grapes	chardonnay
Region	Coonawarra, SA
Cellar	🍷 3
Alc./Vol.	13.0%
RRP	$19.00

Brands were one of the first to peruse this variety in Coonawarra. They have persisted where many others have tried and become disenchanted.

CURRENT RELEASE 1996   The nose is smoky with a background of peach and nectarine. The palate is full-bodied and rich. There's a strong peach flavour, and this is matched by some assertive oak that adds a blast of vanilla flavour. It needs more time in the bottle. Don't over-chill. It works well with smoked cod.

Brands Coonawarra Riesling

Quality	♟♟♟
Value	★★★
Grapes	riesling
Region	Coonawarra, SA
Cellar	🍷 2
Alc./Vol.	10.5%
RRP	$16.00

This is one from the blue: Brands Laira is known for red wines and chardonnay. The riesling is something of a smoky. Makers Jim and Bill Brand.

CURRENT RELEASE 1994   The nose has citrus and apricot aromas. The palate has soft lime flavours with a hint of bottle development. The finish still exhibits a high degree of acid. It can be served well-chilled. It's good with scallops.

Bremerton Langhorne Creek Verdelho

Don't let the label turn you off: this winery makes some very good wines under the rather lacklustre banner.

CURRENT RELEASE 1997   Yet another example of this perplexing variety (it's difficult to get a handle on it). The nose has herbs, sap and nutty aromas. The palate offers loquat, honey and tropical fruit flavours. The finish is crisp and clean. It can be served with a medium chill, and some smoked turkey breast.

Quality	♟♟♟
Value	★★★
Grapes	verdelho
Region	Langhorne Creek, SA
Cellar	♦ 3
Alc./Vol.	13.0%
RRP	$18.00

Brian Barry Juds Hill Riesling

Brian Barry is one of the doyens of the Australian wine industry. He first captured public attention with a cold-fermented red that won the Jimmy Watson Trophy in 1982.

CURRENT RELEASE 1996   A very honest riesling from the Clare Valley. It has typical citrus aromas plus floral notes on the nose. The palate is rich with lime and lemon flavours, which are matched by crisp acid on a clean, lingering finish. It can be served well-chilled. Try it with oysters natural.

Quality	♟♟♟♟
Value	★★★★
Grapes	riesling
Region	Clare Valley, SA
Cellar	♦ 3
Alc./Vol.	12.5%
RRP	$16.00

Briar Ridge Chardonnay

This Hunter Valley wine shows the talents of its maker. It's a tight style that should develop well. Makers Karl Stockhausen and Neil McGuigan.

CURRENT RELEASE 1997   The nose has obvious oak as well as peach and varietal aromas. The palate has a creamy texture, with peach and melon the dominant flavours. There's obvious French oak on a tight finish. It's a wine with impressive length. Try it with a chicken and mushroom pie.

Quality	♟♟♟♟
Value	★★★★
Grapes	chardonnay
Region	Hunter Valley, NSW
Cellar	♦ 4
Alc./Vol.	13.2%
RRP	$17.00

Briar Ridge Early Harvest Semillon

Quality	♥♥♥♥
Value	★★★★
Grapes	semillon
Region	Hunter Valley, NSW
Cellar	▮ 5
Alc./Vol.	11.0%
RRP	$17.00

Regulation stuff. This has been picked early so the alcohol level is low. It should do well in the cellar.

CURRENT RELEASE 1997 The nose has some citrus and damp straw aromas, and the palate has gooseberry and citrus flavours. There's abundant acid on a dry, clean finish. It needs time in the bottle. Serve reasonably well-chilled. Try it with pan-fried veal in a light lemon sauce.

Briar Ridge Hand Picked Chardonnay

Quality	♥♥♥♥
Value	★★★★
Grapes	chardonnay
Region	Hunter Valley, NSW
Cellar	▮ 4
Alc./Vol.	12.5%
RRP	$18.00

According to the back label hand-picking 'maximises the fruit intensity and eliminates oxidation'. Translation: it's more gentle than machine-picking, but on the downside hand-pickers can't work in the dark when it's cool.

CURRENT RELEASE 1997 Barrel fermentation is very evident. The nose smells of damp wood and underlying grape aromas. The palate is full-bodied and buttery, with peach flavours dominating. The finish is very dry and dominated by oak. A medium chill will thrill. Have it with a veal terrine.

Briar Ridge Semillon

Quality	♥♥♥♥
Value	★★★★
Grapes	semillon
Region	Hunter Valley, NSW
Cellar	⬤ 2–6
Alc./Vol.	12.8%
RRP	$17.00

Karl Stockhausen was a Hunter Valley legend at Lindemans; he's back in the saddle (if he ever really dismounted) under this label.

CURRENT RELEASE 1997 At this stage of development the wine remains shy and reserved. The nose has wet hay and citrus aromas. The palate is austere with a continuation of the citrus, and the acid is crisp and clean. It's a wine for the future. Chill well and serve with pipis in a black bean sauce.

Bridgewater Mill Chardonnay

Technically this is the house wine for a splendid restaurant at Bridgewater in the Adelaide Hills. The wine is nationally distributed but the best setting for it is the balcony beside the turning waterwheel. Maker Brian Croser.

CURRENT RELEASE 1996 There is plenty of varietal character on both the nose and the palate. It has abundant peach aromas and there are also hints of wood and barrel-ferment characteristics. The palate is rich with a buttery texture. It's peaches *über alles* and there's plenty of dry dusty oak. A beautifully balanced wine; serve with a modest chill. Try it with pan-fried quail.

Quality	🍷🍷🍷🍷
Value	★★★★
Grapes	chardonnay
Region	Clare Valley, Adelaide Hills, SA
Cellar	🍾 4
Alc./Vol.	13.3%
RRP	$20.00

Bridgewater Mill Sauvignon Blanc

There's more to the mill than just a waterwheel; the food is some of the best fare in the land and it easily outguns many fine city restaurants.

CURRENT RELEASE 1997 The nose has a strong tropical fruit component. The palate has a mixture of gooseberry, passionfruit and pawpaw flavours, and these are framed by some crisp acid on a long tingling finish. It's a great summer style because it can take a big chill. Serve with a niçoise salad.

Quality	🍷🍷🍷🍷
Value	★★★★
Grapes	sauvignon blanc
Region	Coonawarra, Clare Valley, Adelaide Hills, SA
Cellar	🍾 2
Alc./Vol.	12.5%
RRP	$18.00

Brindabella Hills Riesling

Roger Harris was a research scientist with CSIRO before he fell in love with the grape.

CURRENT RELEASE 1997 There are lime aromas on the nose and the palate is a mixture of lemon and limes. There's some crisp acid on the finish. It can be served very well-chilled. Try it with whitebait fritters.

Quality	🍷🍷🍷🍷
Value	★★★★
Grapes	riesling
Region	Canberra district, NSW
Cellar	🍾 5
Alc./Vol.	12.5%
RRP	$13.50 (cellar door)

Brokenwood Gewürztraminer

Quality 🍷🍷🍷🍷½
Value ★★★★
Grapes gewürztraminer
Region McLaren Vale, SA
Cellar 3
Alc./Vol. 11.0%
RRP $14.00 (375 ml)

Here's a good way to use an unpopular variety of grapes. This is a late-picked style made by the 'cut cane' method, and is not Botrytis affected.

CURRENT RELEASE 1996 It has a fragrant nose with violet and honeysuckle aromas. The palate is luscious with sweet-honeyed fruit flavours that have a mouth-filling texture. There's plenty of bracing acid on a crisp finish. It can be served well-chilled with a summer pudding.

Brokenwood Graveyard Chardonnay

Quality 🍷🍷🍷🍷½
Value ★★★★
Grapes chardonnay
Region Hunter Valley, NSW
Cellar 4
Alc./Vol. 13.5%
RRP $30.00 (cellar door)

One of the authors had one foot in it at vintage time 1998 (two actually). Though we will all come to it some time, we commend it to you. Makers Iain Riggs and Dan Dineen.

CURRENT RELEASE 1997 Nothing necrotic about this, it's deadly serious stuff. The best wine under this label yet, and there's well-integrated fruit/oak on the nose with a toasty, nutty aroma. The palate has cashew nut chardonnay flavours with some finesse and good length. Serve with roast chicken.

Brokenwood Semillon

Quality 🍷🍷½
Value ★★★½
Grapes semillon
Region Hunter Valley, NSW
Cellar 2–6
Alc./Vol. 11.0%
RRP $22.00

Here's one for the punters, and we mean those who like a flutter. It could turn into a gem with bottle-age but only time will tell.

CURRENT RELEASE 1997 Very youthful Hunter style and the nose seems to be playing truant. The palate is a pleasant shock with sweet-honeyed lemon and grassy fruit flavours. The finish has plenty of cleansing acid. It can be served with a medium chill but the best is yet to come; cellaring is a must. Try it with oysters natural.

Brookland Valley Sauvignon Blanc

The wine comes from Margaret River and it has a power of flavour combined with freshness. With the BRL Hardy distribution engine we should see more of this label.

CURRENT RELEASE 1997 The colour is a bright lemon yellow and the nose has cut-grass aromas. There are tropical fruits, kiwifruit and gooseberry on the palate, and the finish shows some fresh acid. It's a drink-now style, ideal for mussels poached in a drop of the same wine.

Quality	♈♈♈♈
Value	★★★★
Grapes	sauvignon blanc
Region	Margaret River, WA
Cellar	🍶 2
Alc./Vol.	13.1%
RRP	$18.00

Brown Brothers Family Reserve Chardonnay

It might be reserved, but the family is willing to share. Very generous, these brothers.

CURRENT RELEASE 1994 It's a rich style and the wood still bristles through the mix. The nose has peach and lychee aromas. The palate is rich with sweet peach flavours and a hint of nectarine. The wood is never very far away and some might find it intrusive at this stage. The wine should be served at room temperature. Try it with kassler and lentils.

Quality	♈♈♈♈
Value	★★★★
Grapes	chardonnay
Region	King Valley, Vic.
Cellar	🍶 4
Alc./Vol.	13.5%
RRP	$30.55

Brown Brothers Family Reserve King Valley Riesling

The Family Reserve label is used for aged wines and these are released when they are deemed to be near the peak. They are usually sold to restaurants.

CURRENT RELEASE 1995 There is evidence of some bottle development with a deeper colour and a hint of kero on the nose. The palate is dominated by lime, and there's a suggestion of noble rot influence. The acid on the finish adds crispness and freshness. Serve well-chilled with smoked trout.

Quality	♈♈♈♈
Value	★★★⋆
Grapes	riesling
Region	King Valley, Vic.
Cellar	🍶 3
Alc./Vol.	12.5%
RRP	$18.95

Brown Brothers King Valley Gewürztraminer

Quality	🍷🍷🍷½
Value	★★★½
Grapes	gewürztraminer
Region	King Valley, Vic.
Cellar	🍾 2
Alc./Vol.	13.5%
RRP	$16.30

It has taken a long time, but retailers and restaurateurs are reporting increased demand for this variety. Perhaps consumers are looking for a change from chardonnay.

CURRENT RELEASE 1997 This is a pungent style with plenty of alcohol for an aromatic wine. The nose has a strong lychee aroma and some floral notes. The palate has a hint of sweetness and tropical fruit, with clean acid on the finish. It can be served well-chilled, and would go nicely with Vietnamese tamarind soup.

Brown Brothers King Valley Riesling

Quality	🍷🍷🍷½
Value	★★★½
Grapes	riesling
Region	King Valley, Vic.
Cellar	🍾 2
Alc./Vol.	12.5%
RRP	$14.70

As improbable as it sounds, is the King Valley too fertile? Some argue this is the case and that it promotes vigour problems and high yields. Brown Brothers have strict contracts with growers to keep the yields low to maximise the flavour.

CURRENT RELEASE 1997 The nose has a mixture of lime and lavender aromas. There's also a faint hint of kero. The palate continues the lime theme and there's fresh acid on the finish. A crisp style that goes with prawn tempura.

Brown Brothers King Valley Sauvignon Blanc

Quality	🍷🍷🍷🍷
Value	★★★½
Grapes	sauvignon blanc
Region	King Valley and others, Vic.
Cellar	🍾 2
Alc./Vol.	12.0%
RRP	$17.60

The label reads King Valley and the majority of the grapes come from that district, but there are also elements from Milawa and Whitlands vineyards. Maker Terry Barnett.

CURRENT RELEASE 1997 Nice nose, tropical fruits and a shaved-lawn smell. The palate is quite steely with passionfruit and gooseberry flavours. These are followed by crisp acid on a long finish. The wine can be served well-chilled, and goes well with oysters steamed with ginger and soy.

Brown Brothers King Valley Verdelho

This is a Madeira variety that seems to be finding increasing favour with Australian producers. Some might argue the variety should have been left on the island in the Atlantic.

CURRENT RELEASE 1997 There are grapefruit and tropical aromas. The palate is substantial with rich lemon flavours and some tropical notes. The finish remains crisp in spite of the hearty alcohol. Serve well-chilled with a seafood paella.

Quality	▼▼▼⸱
Value	★★★⸱
Grapes	verdelho
Region	King Valley, Vic.
Cellar	▮ 2
Alc./Vol.	14.0%
RRP	$15.35

Brown Brothers Moscato

Hello, hello, this is a reduced alcohol wine with an alcoholic content of 6%. It's made from *muscat blanc à petits grains*. Why bother? It's a great apéritif, or after-dinner palate cleanser.

CURRENT RELEASE 1997 A sweet wine with strong muscat aromas, a lively palate and a gently fizzy texture. It needs to be served well-chilled to highlight the acid on the finish. Great with fresh fruit and yoghurt for breakfast.

Quality	▼▼▼⸱
Value	★★★⸱
Grapes	muscat blanc
Region	North East Vic.
Cellar	▮ 1
Alc./Vol.	6%
RRP	$13.60 (cellar door)

Brown Brothers Noble Riesling

When John Brown Senior first recognised noble rot in his Milawa vineyard in 1971 he chanced his arm and made a noble riesling. He started a trend that is now a significant part of the Australian market.

CURRENT RELEASE 1994 Lots of colour and that's just the start. The nose has rich honey and dried apricot aromas with a hint of toffee. The palate is rich and succulent with marmalade, toffee and honey flavours. Also present is a background of oak and zesty acid on the finish. It should be served well-chilled. Try it with a crème brûlée.

Quality	▼▼▼▼⸱
Value	★★★★
Grapes	riesling
Region	North East Vic.
Cellar	▮ 3
Alc./Vol.	10.0%
RRP	$21.75 (375 ml)

Brown Brothers Semillon

Quality	♀♀♀℔
Value	★★★ʳ
Grapes	semillon
Region	North East Vic.
Cellar	◊ 3
Alc./Vol.	13.5%
RRP	$15.50

The grapes for this wine were picked early and late, thus extending the flavour spectrum. Picking started in February and finished in late March.

CURRENT RELEASE 1996   There has been some wood treatment and this adds a smoky component to the citrus-dominant nose. The palate is rich and complex, with lemon as the major flavour. There's toasty oak and acid on the finish. It can be served well-chilled. Try with Moroccan chicken.

Browns of Padthaway Unwooded Chardonnay

Quality	♀♀♀♀
Value	★★★★
Grapes	chardonnay
Region	Padthaway, SA
Cellar	◊ 2
Alc./Vol.	13.0%
RRP	$14.00

Don't get confused with the brothers Brown at Milawa – there is no connection. This is an entirely different company.

CURRENT RELEASE 1996   This is an unwooded style that shows the full monty of the variety. A bit of wood could have been marvellous but we'll never know. The nose has peach and lychee aromas. The palate has a mouthfilling texture with peach and melon flavours. Clean crisp acid fills out the finish. It can be served well-chilled. Smoked trout won't disappoint as a match.

Campbells Chardonnay

Quality	♀♀♀
Value	★★★
Grapes	chardonnay
Region	Rutherglen, Vic.
Cellar	◊ 2
Alc./Vol.	14.1%
RRP	$14.25 ⑤

Why is it that whenever we see a bottle of Campbells' wine we think of soup? Such is the power of marketing. Maker Colin Campbell.

CURRENT RELEASE 1996   Youthful for its age, this has a medium–light yellow colour and suggestions of orange peel and apricot together with green herbs in its bouquet. It's slightly oily and the palate flavour is lime/citrus and a trifle phenolic. Good length. Would suit chicken cacciatore.

Campbells Trebbiano

Trebbiano is very much the poor relation these days. This one gets a leg up from snappy packaging: a clear label and a tall, clear bottle. Maker Colin Campbell.
CURRENT RELEASE 1997 Despite the packaging, it doesn't really transcend the humble stature of the grape. It's light in weight, and the profile is rather broad, closing with some astringency. The bouquet recalls wet straw, herbs and honey. A well-made plain dry white that goes with dim sum.

Quality	♟♟♟
Value	★★★
Grapes	trebbiano
Region	Rutherglen, Vic.
Cellar	♦ 2
Alc./Vol.	13.2%
RRP	$16.40

Canobolas-Smith Chardonnay

The Canobolas-Smith wines are all estate-grown and the vines are unirrigated, hand-pruned and hand-harvested. Maker Murray Smith.
Previous outstanding vintages: '94, '95
CURRENT RELEASE 1997 Superb chardonnay, showing all the restrained grapefruit, honey and mealy characters typical of the cool Orange district. It's at once fine and rich in the mouth; good fruit concentration is evident and the finish lingers long. It was fermented in new French oak but oak is not an obvious part of the flavour: it's complex and integrated. A good partner for Balmain bugs.

Quality	♟♟♟♟♟
Value	★★★★★
Grapes	chardonnay
Region	Orange, NSW
Cellar	♦ 6+
Alc./Vol.	14.5%
RRP	$22.00 (cellar door)

Capel Vale CV Sauvignon Blanc Chardonnay

CV is the bread-and-butter brand for Capel Vale's Peter Pratten. It occasionally throws up a bargain.
CURRENT RELEASE 1997 Smoky, toasty and cashew nut aromas blend with herbal elements. The flavour is pleasant and has some freshness. Light and uncomplicated, it has no great flavour dimension and will offend no one. Goes well with Chinese dumplings.

Quality	♟♟♟
Value	★★
Grapes	sauvignon blanc; chardonnay
Region	South West WA
Cellar	♦ 2
Alc./Vol.	13.0%
RRP	$16.30

Capel Vale Reserve Whispering Hill Riesling

Quality	?????
Value	★★★
Grapes	riesling
Region	Great Southern, WA
Cellar	➥ 1–5+
Alc./Vol.	13.5%
RRP	$25.00

This is the second release of the Whispering Hill label. It's Capel Vale's spread at Mount Barker. Maker Rob Bowen.

CURRENT RELEASE 1997   Very doughy young aromas, with soft floral and citrus notes beneath. The palate has some botrytis apricot, and there is some heat from volatility and alcohol. It has a trace of sweetness and the fruit needs time to fill out a little. Try it with a Thai salad or a *larb*.

Cape Mentelle Semillon Sauvignon Blanc

Quality	?????
Value	★★★
Grapes	semillon; sauvignon blanc
Region	Margaret River, WA
Cellar	🍷 3
Alc./Vol.	13.0%
RRP	$20.50

This blend has become all the rage in Margaret River and Mentelle's is one of the benchmarks. Maker John Durham.

CURRENT RELEASE 1997   This didn't blow the fuses quite like we expected, but it's a good wine. The trademark regional 'fruit-salad' note is there, with a certain Passiona (remember Passiona the passionfruit soft drink?) whiff, together with capsicum and crushed leaves. The flavour attacks strongly, and the profile is lean and narrow with a tangy finish. Serve with caesar salad.

Cassegrain Semillon

Quality	?????
Value	★★★★
Grapes	semillon
Region	Hastings Valley, NSW
Cellar	🍷 6+
Alc./Vol.	11.7%
RRP	$16.75

Semillon has proved itself one of the most successful varieties the Cassegrains have tried at damp Port Macquarie. 1997 was an incredibly wet harvest. Makers John Cassegrain and Glenn Goodall.

CURRENT RELEASE 1997   Opens with a green herbal nose and a hint of boiled potatoes, but comes into its own with airing. The palate is impressive. Intense, lively, focused and long, this is a traditional Hunter style transplanted to the Hastings. It should age superbly and goes well now with pan-fried flounder.

Castle Crossing Colombard Chardonnay

Yet another brand from the ubiquitous Alambie Wine Company. At least someone is still serving up decent wine at an affordable price.
CURRENT RELEASE 1997 This label's previous vintage pioneered the Kwik Kork, but it seems to have sunk without a trace. This is a decent, well-made drink. It smells of melon and cashew nut, is clean and fruity, and there are simple, soft, grapey flavours that flow easily over the palate. Try it with battered flathead.

Quality	♟♟♟
Value	★★★★
Grapes	colombard; chardonnay
Region	Murray Valley, Vic.
Cellar	🍶 1
Alc./Vol.	11.5%
RRP	$8.20 Ⓢ

Castle Rock Estate Chardonnay

This is a cool, high-altitude vineyard in the Porongurup Ranges near Albany. Maker is Gavin Berry at Plantagenet.
CURRENT RELEASE 1996 A fairly delicate style that's starting to hit its straps with some bottle-age. The colour is a bright medium yellow, and the nose smells of fruit, chiefly nectarine and apricot. The palate is lively with fresh acid and tingling grapefruit and lemon flavours. Just lacks a little persistence. Good drinking with lemon chicken.

Quality	♟♟♟♟
Value	★★★
Grapes	chardonnay
Region	Great Southern, WA
Cellar	🍶 4
Alc./Vol.	12.8%
RRP	$18.40

Castle Rock Estate Riesling

The Diletti family vineyard is in the high altitudes of the Porongurup Ranges near Albany in southern WA.
Previous outstanding vintages: '93, '94, '96
CURRENT RELEASE 1997 The riesling is the pick of the Castle Rock wines. It comes in a thrillingly racy, steely, dry style that can appear extremely delicate in youth but will mature gracefully with quite long ageing, building to an exotic, almost Germanic, overtone. There are lemon/lime aromas with an exotic mineral edge, and restrained palate flavours of great finesse and style, with a long lingering finish. Will show better in a year or two. Try it with oysters.

Quality	♟♟♟♟♟
Value	★★★★★
Grapes	riesling
Region	Lower Great Southern, WA
Cellar	🍶 10+
Alc./Vol.	12.0%
RRP	$15.00

Celtic Farm Riesling

Quality 🍷🍷🍷½
Value ★★★
Grapes riesling
Region Clare Valley, SA
Cellar 🍾 4
Alc./Vol. 12.0%
RRP $18.00

Great label! A mad cow for a couple of mad Celts. It's a fun diversion for wine industry fringe-dwellers Mark McKenzie and Gerry Taggert. By Celtic Farm they mean Australia's Scottish/Irish pioneer farming community.

CURRENT RELEASE 1997 Nice light yellow–green colour, and it has a low-key riesling bouquet: more a matter of wet straw and grassy aromas than flowers. The taste is soft and fairly light, and seems to lack a bit of acid bite. A good, clean, well-made riesling to serve with spring rolls.

Chain of Ponds Chardonnay

Quality 🍷🍷🍷🍷½
Value ★★★★
Grapes chardonnay
Region Adelaide Hills, SA
Cellar 🍾 4
Alc./Vol. 13.5%
RRP $28.00

The Amadio family have a vineyard on Kangaroo Island as well as this big spread at Gumeracha in the lower parts of the Adelaide Hills.

Previous outstanding vintages: '94, '96

CURRENT RELEASE 1997 A rich, complex style that is medium- to full-bodied and exhibits a strong malolactic character. Butterscotch, caramel and toasty oak scents mingle nicely. It's showing some forward development and the palate has a nice full finish and a long aftertaste. Serve with roast chicken.

Chain of Ponds Semillon

Quality 🍷🍷🍷🍷½
Value ★★★½
Grapes semillon
Region Adelaide Hills, SA
Cellar 🍾 4
Alc./Vol. 12.5%
RRP $19.70

The blurb tells us that 40 per cent of the wine underwent a malolactic fermentation in barrels. 'Malo' adds complexity and also softens the acidity in high-acid, cool-area whites.

Previous outstanding vintages: '96

CURRENT RELEASE 1997 A delicious wine built on oak rather than fruit. It has a toasty, nutty oak-influenced aroma that is quite complex. The palate is rich, full-bodied, smooth, beautifully poised and has a long, long follow-through. It makes a contrast to the delicate, unwooded styles of semillon. Food: roast chicken.

Chapel Hill Unwooded Chardonnay

This is a multi-region blend: Pam Dunsford believes shiraz is the only variety that stands by itself in McLaren Vale, great though the region is for blending material.
CURRENT RELEASE 1997   Heaps of fruit here: herbal and nectarine aromas, hints of melon and peach as well. Generous palate flavour too, and the finish is about fruit and alcohol warmth rather than acid, leaving a soft final impression. Try it with baked Kangaroo Island marron and lime.

Quality	♟♟♟♟
Value	★★★★
Grapes	chardonnay
Region	McLaren Vale, Padthaway & Barossa Valley, SA
Cellar	▮ 2
Alc./Vol.	13.0%
RRP	$16.40

Chapel Hill Verdelho

Chapel Hill planted nine hectares of verdelho at Kangarilla and harvested its first crop in 1997, *et voilà!* Maker Pam Dunsford.
CURRENT RELEASE 1997   Verdelho is a chameleon, and this is an aromatic style with honeysuckle and tropical fruit aromas. It's also one of the drier, more serious verdelhos around, and finishes with tongue-tingling natural acidity. The acid helps it cope well with food. Crab is a good bet.

Quality	♟♟♟♟
Value	★★★★
Grapes	verdelho
Region	McLaren Vale, SA
Cellar	▮ 2
Alc./Vol.	12.8%
RRP	$18.00

PENGUIN BEST WHITE BLEND/ OTHER VARIETY

Chateau Tahbilk Chardonnay

This National Trust-classified winery was established in 1860, and has 125 hectares of vineyards attached. Makers Neil Larson and Alister Purbrick.
CURRENT RELEASE 1996   This has a bouquet of shy lemony aromas with just a kiss of oak. In the mouth it has soft, oaky and sweet-fruit flavours without great distinction, but it's a very decent ready-drinking chardonnay at a friendly price. Try it with smoked trout.

Quality	♟♟♟♟
Value	★★★★
Grapes	chardonnay
Region	Goulburn Valley, Vic.
Cellar	▮ 2
Alc./Vol.	13.5%
RRP	$16.40 Ⓢ

Cloudy Bay Chardonnay

Quality	🍷🍷🍷🍷🍷
Value	★★★★½
Grapes	chardonnay
Region	Marlborough, NZ
Cellar	🍾 2
Alc./Vol.	14.0%
RRP	$29.50

Cloudy Bay winemaker Kevin Judd is a keen amateur photographer in his spare time. He's taken some great vineyard pictures.

Previous outstanding vintages: '90, '91, '92, '94, '95

CURRENT RELEASE 1996 Very much the usual Cloudy Bay gobsmacker. Pungent passionfruit, tropical and tea-leaf characters leap from the glass. Honey, malt and vanilla are in the background. A very pretty wine, delicious now but apparently lacking great strength for keeping. Who cares when it appeals so much now? Serve with duck and mango salad.

Cockfighter's Ghost Semillon

Quality	🍷🍷🍷½
Value	★★★½
Grapes	semillon
Region	Hunter Valley, NSW
Cellar	🍾 1–6+
Alc./Vol.	10.6%
RRP	$15.75

Cockfighter was a racehorse who got stuck in quicksand, and his ghost is reputed to haunt the Wollombi Brook. This brand is the second label of Poole's Rock, from the Broke sub-region. Maker Neil McGuigan.

CURRENT RELEASE 1997 There's a shock of sulfur at first, which will integrate in a few months and bodes well for ageing. There are also straw, dusty and lanolin scents. The palate is delicate and some greener herbal accents are added to the straw taste typical of Hunter semillon. This could cellar well. Food: oysters.

Coolangatta Estate Alexander Berry Chardonnay

Quality	🍷🍷🍷
Value	★★½
Grapes	chardonnay
Region	South Coast, NSW
Cellar	🍾 2
Alc./Vol.	12.8%
RRP	$23.50

Coolangatta Estate is a resort in the Shoalhaven area of NSW. It recently celebrated its tenth vintage, the twenty-fifth year of the resort and the centenary of the town of Berry (founded by Alexander B, of course) in one hit.

CURRENT RELEASE 1997 The pros at Tyrrell's have done a good job here. Although there are twinges of volatility and greenness in the wine it's a decent drink. A lean, medium-bodied, fruit-driven style of moderate complexity and length. A good partner for pumpkin risotto.

Cowra Estate Classic Bat Chardonnay

What has Victor Trumper got to do with chardonnay? Your guess is as good as ours. We'd have thought wine had graduated from swap-card status.

CURRENT RELEASE 1997   A clean, well-made, light and straightforward fruit-driven chardonnay with nectarine and herbal aromas, fairly basic flavour and negligible oak treatment. Drink with footie franks at a day–night match.

Quality	♈♈♈
Value	★★★
Grapes	chardonnay
Region	Cowra, NSW
Cellar	🍷 1
Alc./Vol.	13.5%
RRP	$15.75 Ⓢ

Crabtree Watervale Riesling

Robert Crabtree crushes 90 tonnes of grapes a year at his Watervale winery, and makes about 5000 cases of wine. He's one of the Clare's quieter achievers, and deserves to be better known.

CURRENT RELEASE 1997   A Jack Nicholson of a riesling – this is as good as it gets. Great intensity of aroma and palate: green-tinged lime juice, mineral, straw and lightly yeast-estery youthful aromas. The structure is taut, delicate and lean with a firm, dry finish. The purity and harmony of fruit have to be tasted to be believed. A great riesling, perfect with grilled whiting.

Quality	♈♈♈♈♈
Value	★★★★★
Grapes	riesling
Region	Clare Valley, SA
Cellar	🍷 10
Alc./Vol.	12.5%
RRP	$14.00

Craneford Riesling

Craneford has been in a rut for the last few years, but this won a trophy at the '97 Barossa Wine Show, a signal that this new owner means business.

CURRENT RELEASE 1997   A delicate, tightly wound style that is in very trad Eden Valley mode. The nose has mineral, straw and estery notes. The palate is as tight as a drum and fairly austere. The finish is dry and needs time for the flavours to evolve. Serve it with sashimi.

Quality	♈♈♈♈♊
Value	★★★★★
Grapes	riesling
Region	Eden Valley, SA
Cellar	🍷 8
Alc./Vol.	11.8%
RRP	$14.00

Cranswick Estate Vignette Unoaked Chardonnay

Quality	♟♟♟♟
Value	★★★★
Grapes	chardonnay
Region	Riverina, NSW
Cellar	▮ 2
Alc./Vol.	12.5%
RRP	$12.00 ⑤

Cranswick is one of the movers and shakers in the Griffith area, thanks to the energies of founder Graham Cranswick-Smith. Maker Ian Hongell.
CURRENT RELEASE 1997 There's an odd, sawdusty aroma and some herbal fruit characters in this very drinkable, simple chardonnay. Light-bodied, fruity, well-balanced: a top quaff. Serve with yabbies.

Cullen Sauvignon Blanc Semillon

Quality	♟♟♟♟♟
Value	★★★★ʳ
Grapes	sauvignon blanc 80%; semillon 20%
Region	Margaret River, WA
Cellar	▮ 8+
Alc./Vol.	13.0%
RRP	$28.30

The Cullens have done away with their former Reserve bottlings. We'd have to comment that all the wine is of Reserve standard, anyway. A percentage of this undergoes barrel fermentation. Maker Vanya Cullen.
CURRENT RELEASE 1997 A striking wine, cleverly modelled on the white Graves of Bordeaux. The colour is pale yellow and there's a tangy, grassy/nettle-like nose with hints of fresh green herbs. In the mouth it displays finesse and tight structure, with tremendous length. Intense dry flavours, concentration and power, yet refined. The oak is barely evident but contributes much in length. Serve with coq-au-vin cooked in white wine.

d'Arenberg The Dry Dam Riesling

Quality	♟♟♟♟
Value	★★★ʳ
Grapes	riesling
Region	McLaren Vale, SA
Cellar	▮ 2
Alc./Vol.	12.5%
RRP	$12.00

Rieslings from McLaren Vale are usually well-mannered but never stars. This one knows how to hold a knife and fork and can tell a fish knife from a steak knife.
CURRENT RELEASE 1997 There's a hint of kero on a citrus nose. The palate is medium-bodied with a zesty lemon flavour that is matched by a zing of acid. It can be served well-chilled. Try it with oysters mornay.

d'Arenberg The Dry Land Sauvignon Blanc

Behold, a pale wine from McLaren Vale. In contrast, the small-print blurb on the back label is very colourful.
CURRENT RELEASE 1997   The nose is a mixture of grass and tropical fruit aromas. The middle-weight palate continues the tropical theme with lemon flavours as an addition. The acid pulls the parcel together. The wine can be served well-chilled and goes well with scallops.

Quality	♀♀♀⟨
Value	★★★⟨
Grapes	sauvignon blanc
Region	McLaren Vale, SA
Cellar	▐ 2
Alc./Vol.	12.0%
RRP	$13.00

d'Arenberg The Other Side Chardonnay

Here's one for the late Jim Morrison of the Doors. 'Break on through to the other side'. In this case we don't get a psychedelic revelation, just a developing Aussie chardonnay.
CURRENT RELEASE 1996   Bottle-age is changing the characters here. The colour is developing more gold hues. The nose shows ripe melon and peach flavours, and the palate is also indicating some maturity. The peach and melon flavours have conjoined with the oak. It's a full-bodied style that needs a medium chill. Try it with smoked quail.

Quality	♀♀♀♀
Value	★★★★
Grapes	chardonnay
Region	McLaren Vale, SA
Cellar	▐ 3
Alc./Vol.	13.5%
RRP	$16.00

d'Arenberg White Ochre

This is a fighting brand for d'Arenberg. There is both red and white ochre (as in dirt) in the McLaren Vale district.
CURRENT RELEASE 1997   This is an odds-and-sorts style that was made for easy drinking. The nose is fruity, as is the palate, which has citrus flavours and sweetness. The finish has some subtle acid. It can be served well-chilled. Try it with a goat's cheese pizza.

Quality	♀♀♀
Value	★★★
Grapes	riesling 68%; crouchen 20%; chardonnay 12%
Region	McLaren Vale, SA
Cellar	▐
Alc./Vol.	13.0%
RRP	$10.00

Dalry Road Chardonnay

Quality	♥♥♥♡
Value	★★★r
Grapes	chardonnay
Region	Yarra Valley, Vic.
Cellar	▮ 2
Alc./Vol.	13.0%
RRP	$15.00

This is a second label from Eyton on Yarra. The labelling is distinctive but not to everybody's taste.
CURRENT RELEASE 1997   The nose hints at toasty oak, and there are also peach and citrus aromas. The medium-bodied palate offers citrus and melon flavours and the oak coats the tongue on a dry finish. It can be served with a medium chill. Try it with fish and chips.

Dalry Road Riesling Traminer

Quality	♥♥♥
Value	★★★
Grapes	riesling;
	gewürztraminer
Region	Yarra Valley, Vic.
Cellar	▮ 1
Alc./Vol.	12.0%
RRP	$13.00

The name comes from an old vineyard circa 1889. This is a fresh summer style that was made for drinking rather than thinking.
CURRENT RELEASE 1997   The nose is floral with lychee and lavender aromas. The palate has a hint of sweetness, and there are fresh citrus flavours. The acid on the finish contributes crispness. Serve well-chilled with tempura prawns.

Deakin Estate Alfred Chardonnay

Quality	♥♥♥♥
Value	★★★★
Grapes	chardonnay
Region	Mildura, Vic.
Cellar	▮ 2
Alc./Vol.	13.5%
RRP	$14.00

Deakin Estate is a tribute to the foresight of Alfred Deakin who, in the 1890s, helped establish a fruit-growing region along the fertile banks of the Murray River in North West Victoria.
CURRENT RELEASE 1997   The nose has strong peach and melon aromas and there is suggestion of a butter-scotch component. The medium-bodied palate offers a hint of barrel-fermentation characteristics in a slightly creamy texture. Peach is the major flavour and there is a persistent oak treatment on the finish. The wine can be served with a medium chill and is good with chicken Kiev.

Deakin Estate Sauvignon Blanc

Food and wine matching is all the rage. As an interesting concept the back label has an 1800 phone number for food suggestions.

CURRENT RELEASE 1997 The wine has a grassy herbal nose and the medium-weight palate has gooseberry fruit flavours and clean acid. It needs to be served well-chilled. Try it with Asian food.

Quality	🍷🍷🍷
Value	★★★
Grapes	sauvignon blanc
Region	Riverland, SA
Cellar	🍾
Alc./Vol.	12.5%
RRP	$10.00 (S)

De Bortoli Deen De Bortoli Vat 7 Chardonnay

Good-value wine with style above and beyond its humble origins. Maker Darren De Bortoli.

CURRENT RELEASE 1997 The colour is bright yellow with green tinges. The nose has a broad peach aroma and the full-bodied palate continues that theme. There's a firm finish and it should not be over-chilled. Try it with yabbies.

Quality	🍷🍷🍷🍷
Value	★★★★
Grapes	chardonnay
Region	Riverina, NSW
Cellar	🍾 3
Alc./Vol.	12.5%
RRP	$11.60 (S)

De Bortoli Montage

The label was inspired by an illustration by young Melbourne artist Paquita Maher. It depicts the Yarra Valley restaurant.

CURRENT RELEASE 1997 The style is fresh with some tropical flavours, stone fruit and gooseberries. These are backed up by crisp acid on a clean finish. It can be served well-chilled and is perfect with crab cakes.

Quality	🍷🍷🍷½
Value	★★★½
Grapes	chardonnay; semillon
Region	various, Vic.
Cellar	🍾 2
Alc./Vol.	12.0%
RRP	$9.50 (S)

De Bortoli Noble One

Quality	♟♟♟♟♟
Value	★★★★★
Grapes	semillon
Region	Riverina, NSW
Cellar	▮ 4
Alc./Vol.	11.0%
RRP	$25.00 (375 ml)

This is justly an Australian wine icon. It was the label that put Australian sweet (botrytis) styles on the global map.
Previous outstanding vintages: '82, '83, '84, '87, '90, '91, '92, '93, '94
CURRENT RELEASE 1995 The colour is a bright yellow–gold and the nose has botrytis and concentrated dried-fruit aromas. The palate floods the mouth with flavour. It's rich with honey, marmalade, toffee and citrus flavours. This is balanced by some crisp acid on a long finish. It needs to be served very well-chilled with a summer pudding.

De Bortoli Windy Peak Chardonnay

Quality	♟♟♟♟
Value	★★★★
Grapes	chardonnay
Region	South East Vic.
Cellar	▮ 2
Alc./Vol.	13.0%
RRP	$14.00

This is a very handsome drop at a reasonable price. The Windy Peak range is made to do battle in the middle price bracket. Maker David Slingsby-Smith.
CURRENT RELEASE 1997 The nose is typical chardonnay with peach and oak aromas. The palate is medium-bodied with a slightly creamy texture. Peach is the major flavour and there is a gentle oak influence on the finish. It can be served with a medium chill. Try it with tandoori chicken.

De Bortoli Windy Peak Rhine Riesling

Quality	♟♟♟♟
Value	★★★★
Grapes	riesling
Region	various, Vic.
Cellar	▮ 3
Alc./Vol.	12.0%
RRP	$14.00

It's a little-known fact that when it comes to wine production this marque is the sixth largest in Australia. For all the volume, the group can produce some classy wines.
CURRENT RELEASE 1996 This is a floral style that is starting to develop some bottle-age. The main theme is lime. There are citrus and lime aromas on the nose. The medium-bodied palate is a symphony in lime. The acid on the finish remains fresh and crisp. Give it a big chill and it will thrill with scallops in a lemon cream sauce.

De Bortoli Yarra Valley Chardonnay

This company has made a big commitment to chardonnay in the Yarra Valley. Their planting programme has meant a vast expansion of their vineyards.

CURRENT RELEASE 1997 There's no holding back with the wood here – it's like a full-blooded drive from Tiger Woods. The fruit can cope but it's a wood-driven wine. The nose has peach and toasty wood aromas. The palate has a creamy texture with peach and stone-fruit flavours. These are matched by spicy oak with a toasty character. It needs time and should be served lightly chilled. Try it with gyoza.

Quality	ΥΥΥΥ?
Value	★★★★
Grapes	chardonnay
Region	Yarra Valley, Vic.
Cellar	➾ 1–6
Alc./Vol.	13.0%
RRP	$25.60

de Gyffarde Sauvignon Blanc

Yet another new name to size up from the exploding Marlborough region of New Zealand. Kiwi sauvignon blanc is taking over the world!

CURRENT RELEASE 1997 Green aromas of varying kinds compete for attention here: nettle, cut capsicum and freshly shelled green peas, and the same aromas are found in the mouth. It's a crisp, punchy, intensely flavoured wine with a hint of sweetness and a long, long finish. Try it with asparagus quiche.

Quality	ΥΥΥΥ
Value	★★★★ʳ
Grapes	sauvignon blanc
Region	Marlborough, NZ
Cellar	▮ 2
Alc./Vol.	12.5%
RRP	$20.00

Devil's Lair Chardonnay

This is a bit of a bovver boy from the Margaret River region of WA. It has alcohol to burn with a strength of 14.5%.

CURRENT RELEASE 1996 The colour is bright yellow and the nose has strong fruit and oak aromas. The major flavour is peach and there are also melons and tropical fruits. The finish shows determined oak and a warmth of alcohol. It should be served near room temperature with pork spare ribs.

Quality	ΥΥΥΥ
Value	★★★
Grapes	chardonnay
Region	Margaret River, WA
Cellar	▮ 4
Alc./Vol.	14.5%
RRP	$36.90

Dromana Estate Chardonnay

Quality	com com com com com'
Value	★★★★⋆
Grapes	chardonnay
Region	Mornington Peninsula, Vic.
Cellar	🍾 4
Alc./Vol.	13.5%
RRP	$28.00

Dromana Estate was established in 1982 as a showpiece vineyard in what was then a new viticultural region. It remains a very advanced viticultural model. Maker Garry Crittenden.

CURRENT RELEASE 1997   The nose has peach and melon aromas plus some mellow wood smells. The palate is complex with peach, melon and cashew flavours. There is a creamy barrel-ferment character and a long, dry finish which adds balance. Try it with smoked cod.

Edenhope Chardonnay

Quality	com com com
Value	★★★⋆
Grapes	chardonnay
Region	Riverina, NSW
Cellar	🍾 1
Alc./Vol.	12.0%
RRP	$11.15

This is a second label from Steve Chatterton of St Peters fame. There's a town of that name in Victoria but there the connection ends.

CURRENT RELEASE 1997   Cheap and cheerful, plain and simple. This has a touch of sweetness, frisky balancing acid and an agreeable taste of herbal fruit. There's no oak to remark on. It's soft and easy on the gums. Try it with prosciutto and melon.

Elderton Chardonnay

Quality	com com com
Value	★★★
Grapes	chardonnay
Region	Barossa Valley, SA
Cellar	▬ 1–4
Alc./Vol.	13.5%
RRP	$15.75

Lorraine Ashmead heads up this Barossa winery, based on grapes from a single outstanding vineyard in the Nuriootpa township. Makers Peter Lehmann and friends, and Jim Irvine.

CURRENT RELEASE 1997   Tropical fruit aromas bounce from the glass, extreme to the point of lollipop/essence. Very delicate, somewhat wispy palate, and an abrupt finish. It may put on weight and become more vinous with time, in several months. A little confused at the time of tasting.

Evans & Tate Margaret River Chardonnay

Evans departed the scene years ago but the Tate family still owns this flourishing WA wine company. Maker Brian Fletcher.

CURRENT RELEASE 1996   Doesn't quite live up to the promise of the nose. The colour is bright with a green tinge; the nose pleasantly melony with lightly toasted wood. It lacks a bit of get-up-and-go with rather light fruit, and the soft palate could use more life. A decent drink, but expensive. Try it with WA marron.

Quality	▼▼▼▼
Value	★★★
Grapes	chardonnay
Region	Margaret River, WA
Cellar	◊ 3
Alc./Vol.	13.0%
RRP	$35.25

Evans & Tate Mount Barker Riesling

This is Evans & Tate's first riesling, so maybe they're punting on the much-vaunted resurgence. Maker Brian Fletcher.

CURRENT RELEASE 1997   The colour is pale and there are tropical, herbaceous and slightly sweaty Western Australian characters on the bouquet. There's acid at the beginning, a soft middle, and a kick of sweetness on the finish. Not exactly a classic riesling style, but a promising start. Try it with scallops.

Quality	▼▼▼
Value	★★★
Grapes	riesling
Region	Great Southern, WA
Cellar	◊ 4
Alc./Vol.	12.5%
RRP	$17.25

Evans & Tate Sauvignon Blanc

All the grapes for this wine came off E & T's new Lionel's vineyard at Jindong, a somewhat unproven sub-region that some critics reckon shouldn't be part of Margaret River.

CURRENT RELEASE 1997   Fresh but not grassy aromas of hand-cream, cashew and herbs. The flavours are ripe and quite piercing, and the light-bodied palate has frisky acidity and the merest trace of sweetness (which probably comes from alcohol as it only has 3 grams per litre of residual sugar). A good wine – take it to a vegetarian restaurant.

Quality	▼▼▼▼
Value	★★★
Grapes	sauvignon blanc
Region	Margaret River, WA
Cellar	◊ 1
Alc./Vol.	13.5%
RRP	$18.40

Evans & Tate Semillon

Quality	🍷🍷🍷½
Value	★★★
Grapes	semillon
Region	Margaret River, WA
Cellar	6+
Alc./Vol.	13.0%
RRP	$20.00

Part of this wine was barrel-fermented in French oak. It's one of the least grassy semillons from the Margaret River district. Maker Brian Fletcher.

CURRENT RELEASE 1997 This is a shy, delicate young thing. The colour is pale yellow and the aroma recalls lemons with a little nuttiness from very subtly handled wood. The flavour is lightly toasty and has a little richness conferred by the oak. It finishes nicely arid. A good food wine. Try it with lemon chicken.

Evans & Tate Two Vineyards Chardonnay

Quality	🍷🍷🍷½
Value	★★★
Grapes	chardonnay
Region	Margaret River, WA
Cellar	2
Alc./Vol.	13.0%
RRP	$19.00 (S)

E & T have moved their winemaking down south from the Swan Valley to Margaret River, a much more fashionable address these days.

CURRENT RELEASE 1997 Flowers and honeysuckle suggest themselves on a fairly shy bouquet. It's a reserved wine, lean and delicate with restrained oak, good liveliness and some persistence. A decent, but fairly expensive chardonnay. Try it with prawns dipped in hollandaise sauce.

Eyton Chardonnay

Quality	🍷🍷🍷½
Value	★★★
Grapes	chardonnay
Region	Yarra Valley, Vic.
Cellar	1
Alc./Vol.	13.7%
RRP	$19.50

Eyton on Yarra is one of the newer and more ambitious ventures in the Yarra Valley. The winemaker at present is Matt Aldridge, who earned his stripes at Rosemount and Killerby.

CURRENT RELEASE 1995 Developed characters have overtaken the primary fruit and the nose shows dusty and vanilla/caramel characters, which are echoed on the palate. It has good depth and life on the palate but it's not going upwards from here. So drink it down, perhaps with roast chicken.

CURRENT RELEASE 1996   Oak takes centre-stage here, giving cedary, toasty notes to the bouquet and some woody astringency to the finish. It's a fairly light-bodied wine, but the flavour lingers well. May be in better balance with a few more months' ageing. Try it with southern fried chicken.

Quality	♟♟♟
Value	★★★
Grapes	chardonnay
Region	Yarra Valley, Vic.
Cellar	▮ 3
Alc./Vol.	13.0%
RRP	$19.50

Fiddlers Creek Chardonnay

This is a fighting brand from the Remy group which is expanding its vineyard near Avoca.
CURRENT RELEASE 1997   The nose has a typical peach aroma with a hint of gunsmoke. The medium-bodied palate has peach and melon flavours. It shows a tight, compact nature. There is some toasty oak on a firm finish. Serve with a medium chill. It goes well with smoked cod.

Quality	♟♟♟?
Value	★★★≀
Grapes	chardonnay
Region	Pyrenees, Vic.
Cellar	▮ 3
Alc./Vol.	12.0%
RRP	$9.95

Fiddlers Creek Sauvignon Blanc

The creek was named after two musically inclined miners who were trying their luck in the Pyrenees district near Avoca.
CURRENT RELEASE 1997   The nose has tropical fruits and herbal aromas. The palate is medium-bodied and contains tropical flavours like passionfruit and pineapple, and there are notes of winter-green herbs. The finish has a slightly toasty quality and fresh acid. The wine can be served well-chilled with asparagus quiche.

Quality	♟♟♟♟
Value	★★★★
Grapes	sauvignon blanc
Region	Pyrenees, Vic.
Cellar	▮ 2
Alc./Vol.	12.5%
RRP	$9.95

Fiddlers Creek Semillon

This variety isn't really a signature of this region. However, it shows a lot of promise and it will be interesting to watch the progress with bottle-age.
CURRENT RELEASE 1997   The nose is toasty with some straw and smoky oak aromas. The medium-bodied palate has some gooseberry and loquat flavours, and there is a dusting of oak on the dry finish. A medium chill will be sufficient and smoked chicken salad is just the ticket.

Quality	♟♟♟?
Value	★★★≀
Grapes	semillon
Region	Pyrenees, Vic.
Cellar	▮ 4
Alc./Vol.	12.5%
RRP	$9.95

First Hunter Valley Semillon

Quality	♟♟♟♟♟
Value	★★★★★
Grapes	semillon
Region	Hunter Valley, NSW
Cellar	▯ 5+
Alc./Vol.	11.0%
RRP	$14.00

Drayton's, McWilliams and Tyrrell's pooled some fruit to make this blend, an attempt to promote Hunter semillon. It's supposed to be the first semillon of the vintage to be marketed, and went on sale on 30 March.

CURRENT RELEASE 1998   It's hard to imagine a better example of an up-front, early-drinking but fruit-driven Hunter semillon. There is a green tint in the colour and the nose is all freshly mown meadow hay. It's vibrant and zesty in the mouth, with a little bottling carbon dioxide, and has great intensity of fruit. Flavoursome and fine. Very cleverly done. Serve with calamari.

Flood Gully Chardonnay

Quality	♟♟♟
Value	★★★
Grapes	chardonnay
Region	Swan Valley, WA
Cellar	▯ 4
Alc./Vol.	13.0%
RRP	$14.00

This wine comes from a smallish winery in the Swan Valley, WA.

CURRENT RELEASE 1996   The nose has a toasty biscuit aroma. The palate is mouthfilling to the point of thickness and there are hints of honey with some peach flavours. The finish is assertive and long. Drink near room temperature, with pan-fried sardines.

Fox Creek Verdelho

Quality	♟♟♟♟
Value	★★★★
Grapes	verdelho
Region	McLaren Vale, SA
Cellar	▯ 3
Alc./Vol.	13.5
RRP	$16.00

Sometimes MS thinks this variety should be pruned with extreme prejudice; that is, at the roots. In the case of McLaren Vale, that thought should be revised.

CURRENT RELEASE 1997   The nose is rich with tropical fruit and lime aromas. The palate is full-bodied with lime, quince and mango flavours, and there is a creamy texture. The finish has soft acid. It can be served well-chilled. Serve it as a pre-dinner drink.

Garbin Estate Chenin Blanc

This low-profile winery at Toodyay Road, Middle Swan, was established in 1956.

CURRENT RELEASE 1997   This is a somewhat stripped wine, made in an old-fashioned European style. It has a certain lack of fruit and the bouquet is cosmetic – the classic 'ladies' handbag' character. The palate is light and lean, and doesn't challenge the senses. Try it with a very hot curry.

Quality	♟♟
Value	★★ℓ
Grapes	chenin blanc
Region	Swan Valley, WA
Cellar	▮ 1
Alc./Vol.	12.0%
RRP	$12.00

Geoff Merrill Chardonnay

Merrill celebrated the centenary of his Mount Hurtle winery in 1998. He still bases his wines on his McLaren Vale home-base, but blends freely from all over the map.

CURRENT RELEASE 1995   Delicious juicy, grapefruit aromas are typical of the grape variety. Cashew nut and creamy oak/barrel-ferment characters join in. The fresh, tangy palate is intense and long, and suits drinking in warmer summery weather. Serve with melon and prosciutto.

Quality	♟♟♟♟ℓ
Value	★★★★
Grapes	chardonnay
Region	McLaren Vale 42%; Coonawarra 30%; Goulburn Valley 16%; Mildura 12%
Cellar	▮ 2
Alc./Vol.	12.5%
RRP	$16.50

Geoff Merrill Reserve Chardonnay

Geoff Merrill celebrated his Mount Hurtle winery's cenFtenary in 1998. Of course he wasn't there at the beginning, but it's not as silly as it sounds. It was also his grandfather's hundredth year.

CURRENT RELEASE 1991   We wonder if Merrill is justified in ageing these wines so long. Does anyone really appreciate the trouble he goes to? It's deep golden in colour, and the very aged nose shows toast, vanilla and citrus peel. The palate is drying out and is dry, full-bodied and rather hefty. Definitely a food wine: try with a buttery crayfish dish.

Quality	♟♟♟ℓ
Value	★★★
Grapes	chardonnay
Region	McLaren Vale 67%; Coonawarra 33%, SA
Cellar	▮ 1
Alc./Vol.	12.5%
RRP	$28.00

Geographe White One Classic Dry White

Quality	♟♟♟
Value	★★★
Grapes	sauvignon blanc 50%; chardonnay 25%; verdelho 25%
Region	not stated
Cellar	▮ 1
Alc./Vol.	12.5%
RRP	$15.00

Ex-Virgin Hills winemaker Mark Sheppard is making some very different wines in his new venture. This one's straight out of left-field and recalls old-fashioned French or Italian winemaking.

CURRENT RELEASE 1997 A rather exotic style with a malty, somewhat stripped bouquet. Although a little lacking in fruit, it does have character. The palate is savoury with some toasty and floral inflexions. Should be a decent food style. Try with whitebait.

Glenguin Chardonnay

Quality	♟♟♟♟
Value	★★★
Grapes	chardonnay
Region	Hunter Valley, NSW
Cellar	▮ 3
Alc./Vol.	12.5%
RRP	$19.70

When the Tedders decided to plant vines they punted for Broke Fordwich, a Hunter Valley sub-region with more available land than Pokolbin. It's still building its reputation.

CURRENT RELEASE 1996 The straw-like nose is more Hunter-like than chardonnay, and it's starting to show some development. A light-bodied, soft, straightforward style with herbal fruit, gently played oak, and a soft dry finish. Suits vegetable terrines.

Glenguin Semillon

Quality	♟♟♟♟
Value	★★★⭑
Grapes	semillon
Region	Hunter Valley, NSW
Cellar	➥ 2–5+
Alc./Vol.	10.4%
RRP	$18.90

Glenguin is a relatively new brand from the Broke Fordwich sub-region of the Hunter Valley. Lord Robin Tedder (we're not kidding) is the head honcho.

CURRENT RELEASE 1997 Fine, fruit-driven, herbal semillon aroma. Lean, mean palate, with a fierce acid level. This is a traditionally styled Hunter semillon that is built to age. It's worth cellaring a few bottles. If you plan to drink it now, arrange to have it with fish in order to tame that tartness. Try pan-fried swordfish with lemon juice.

Glenguin Unwooded Chardonnay

It amazes us that so much ordinary unwooded chardonnay is being drunk when the same money can usually buy a much better riesling.
CURRENT RELEASE 1997   Hard to criticise this: it's a decent wine fully loaded with peach and pineapple fruit flavours, and it's soft and round in the mouth without great length. A good drink and typical of the style. Try it with chicken and mango salad.

Quality	▽▽▽?
Value	★★★
Grapes	chardonnay
Region	Hunter Valley, NSW
Cellar	2
Alc./Vol.	12.5%
RRP	$15.75

The Gorge Unwooded Chardonnay

This is a new label from the Hunter Valley and considering the wine is unwooded, at least the price reflects the obvious cost saving on oak.
CURRENT RELEASE 1997   The nose has strong lychee and honeydew melon aromas. The palate has a mouth-filling texture with lychee, peach and loquat flavours and the finish has a strong acid tingle. It can be served with a medium chill, and goes well with pasta carbonara.

Quality	▽▽▽▽
Value	★★★★
Grapes	chardonnay
Region	Hunter Valley, NSW
Cellar	2
Alc./Vol.	12.5%
RRP	$12.95

Goundrey Reserve Chardonnay

This firm, begun by Mike and Alison Goundrey, was bought by businessman Jack Bendat in 1994. The size of the company has been radically increased.
CURRENT RELEASE 1997   An unashamedly over-the-top style. The nose is dominated by heavy-toast oak, and smoky, toasty and caramelised characters abound. In the mouth it's a herculean wine, with strength and length aplenty. Unsubtle, but a good foil for its unwooded sister. Could possibly go with roast chicken.

Quality	▽▽▽▽
Value	★★★
Grapes	chardonnay
Region	Lower Great Southern, WA
Cellar	2
Alc./Vol.	14.0%
RRP	$26.25

Goundrey Reserve Riesling

Quality	⟡⟡⟡⟡⟡
Value	★★★★⟡
Grapes	riesling
Region	Lower Great Southern, WA
Cellar	🍷 6+
Alc./Vol.	12.5%
RRP	$19.70

The Mount Barker region is one of the best places in Australia to grow riesling. This wine was made by Brenden Smith, who has since departed the fold.

CURRENT RELEASE 1997   A delightful wine: slightly herbaceous, estery/bready aromas of a typical young riesling which is still yet to lose its fresh bloom of youth. Very fine, soft palate with flowery flavours and considerable finesse. Very drinkable now and will surely age superbly. Serve with trout and almonds.

Gramp's Chardonnay

Quality	⟡⟡⟡⟡
Value	★★★★
Grapes	chardonnay
Region	Barossa Valley, SA
Cellar	🍷 2
Alc./Vol.	13.0%
RRP	$14.45 Ⓢ

The Gramp family were the founders of Orlando, and although the family is no longer involved, the name is kept alive on this brand.

Previous outstanding vintages: '96

CURRENT RELEASE 1997   There's some forward development on this herbal-fruited chardonnay. It has a deft touch of sympathetic oak, and the palate has some delicacy and good balance. Keen value at the (often-discounted) price. Goes well with sweet-corn fritters.

Grant Burge Thorn Riesling

Quality	⟡⟡⟡⟡⟡
Value	★★★★★
Grapes	riesling
Region	Eden Valley, SA
Cellar	🍷 7
Alc./Vol.	13.5%
RRP	$14.75

Grant Burge names his wines after the vineyards or growers where the grapes come from. You get some funny ones, but then, they do give the wines distinction.

CURRENT RELEASE 1997   Burge's riesling style is full and rich, with relatively high alcohols. His are among the most consistent Eden Valley rieslings and this is Exhibit A. A big wine with masses of excellent riesling flavour, it's rich, fruity, dry on the finish and concludes with a slight grip. Could handle grilled scallops.

Greenstone Chardonnay

This is Portree Vineyard's cheaper, unwooded chardonnay. Aborigines used to quarry greenstone, a basalt flint stone, in the vicinity of the vineyard. Maker Ken Murchison.

CURRENT RELEASE 1997 A delicate but very intense, high-acid, cool-grown style in which the pure fruit is highlighted. There's no obvious wood or malolactic character to obscure the fresh apple, grapefruit and nectarine characters. Emphatic natural acidity makes it a great food wine. Try it with fish cakes.

Quality	🍷🍷🍷🍷½
Value	★★★★
Grapes	chardonnay
Region	Macedon, Vic.
Cellar	3
Alc./Vol.	13.0%
RRP	$17.00

Grosset Piccadilly Chardonnay

This Piccadilly is a valley in the Adelaide Hills, not a roundabout in a well-known English wine town. Maker Jeff Grosset.

Previous outstanding vintages: '90, '91, '92, '93, '94, '95, '96

CURRENT RELEASE 1997 This is an exercise in displaying the pristine quality of the Hills' chardonnay fruit. The oak is very much in the background and acts as a seasoning rather than the main event. Peach, nectarine and cashew aromas are classic chardonnay, and the fruit concentration is exemplary. Richness, textured mouth-feel, length and style make this is a great chardonnay. Try it with a smoked trout roulade.

Quality	🍷🍷🍷🍷🍷
Value	★★★★
Grapes	chardonnay
Region	Adelaide Hills, SA
Cellar	5
Alc./Vol.	13.5%
RRP	$34.50

Grosset Polish Hill Riesling

The Polish Hill and River were so named because migrants of Polish extraction were the early settlers. Maker Jeff Grosset.

Previous outstanding vintages: '82, '84, '86, '87, '88, '90, '92, '93, '94, '95, '96

CURRENT RELEASE 1997 A big, rich, strong wine which is atypical for this label and region. The nose still has doughy fresh esters and the palate has rich, ripe, stone-fruit flavours, seemingly with a trace of sweetness, but it may just be the ripeness. Stacks of flavour – this is no shrinking violet. Try it with snapper tails.

Quality	🍷🍷🍷🍷🍷
Value	★★★★★
Grapes	riesling
Region	Clare Valley, SA
Cellar	8+
Alc./Vol.	13.0%
RRP	$23.00

Grosset Watervale Riesling

Quality	♟♟♟♟♟
Value	★★★★★
Grapes	riesling
Region	Clare Valley, SA
Cellar	🍶 10+
Alc./Vol.	13.0%
RRP	$20.00

Jeffrey Grosset, an ex-Lindemans winemaker, set up his winery in an old butter factory in Auburn, the southernmost village in the Clare strip.
Previous outstanding vintages: '81, '85, '90, '91, '93, '94, '95, '96
CURRENT RELEASE 1997   Something of a role reversal: the Polish seems bigger than the Watervale in '97. This one's restrained, tight, high acid, lean and tangy. The flavours are slaty, minerally and citrusy, and the finish is very long and intense. Outstanding riesling. Cellar, or drink with asparagus quiche.

Grove Mill Chardonnay

Quality	♟♟♟♟
Value	★★★
Grapes	chardonnay
Region	Marlborough, NZ
Cellar	🍶 3
Alc./Vol.	13.0%
RRP	$19.35

This is a sizeable vineyard of 30 hectares, operated by dedicated and highly professional people. Winemaker David Pearce.
CURRENT RELEASE 1996   A typically aromatic fruit-salad Marlborough style with a little herbaceousness and perhaps some botrytis. The palate has an apricot flavour and an impression of sweetness, and the finish has some astringency. An enigmatic style. Goes well with rabbit terrine.

Grove Mill Sauvignon Blanc

Quality	♟♟♟♟?
Value	★★★★
Grapes	sauvignon blanc
Region	Marlborough, NZ
Cellar	🍶 2
Alc./Vol.	12.5%
RRP	$18.40

This winery, in Marlborough's Waihopai Valley, is one of the faster growing in the region and the white wines are consistently excellent.
CURRENT RELEASE 1997   The colour is paleish and there are herbal, citrus and light nettle-like aromas, showing good ripeness. It retains delicacy on the palate but the finish and length are exemplary. Fine acidity and freshness all round. Try it with freshly shucked oysters.

Hamilton Chardonnay

There seems to be a bottle battle raging at the moment. Can it be a flash wine in an ordinary stock standard bottle? Maker Ralph Fowler.
CURRENT RELEASE 1997 This is a typical regional style. The nose has peach and melon aromas. The palate is medium-bodied with a buttery texture. Peach is the major flavour and there are toasty oak characters on a dry finish. It should not be served too cold. Try it with a salmon mousse.

Quality	♥♥♥♥
Value	★★★⸀
Grapes	chardonnay
Region	McLaren Vale, SA
Cellar	▮ 3
Alc./Vol.	13.0%
RRP	$21.30

Hanging Rock Semillon Sauvignon Blanc

Behold, a pale white wine made in the Macedon district. Maker John Ellis is now sourcing grapes from cool locations similar to his Macedon district.
CURRENT RELEASE 1997 The nose is herbal with some tropical fruit notes and cut grass. The palate is full-flavoured with gooseberry and tropical fruit flavours. There is crisp acid on a lingering clean finish. It's a solid style that can be served well-chilled. Good with roast chook.

Quality	♥♥♥♥
Value	★★★★
Grapes	semillon; sauvignon blanc
Region	Macedon, Geelong, Vic.
Cellar	▮ 2
Alc./Vol.	12.0%
RRP	$17.00

Hanging Rock The Jim Jim Sauvignon Blanc

Some wine writers given to florid prose might describe this as a 'nervy' style. We'd prefer to say acid and crisp.
CURRENT RELEASE 1997 There is no doubt about the variety of this wine. It's loaded with varietal characters. The nose has strong cut-grass, herb and tropical aromas. The palate is very intense. The tropical elements are matched by gooseberry flavours. The finish is crisp and refreshing. It drinks well with a big chill.

Quality	♥♥♥♥
Value	★★★★
Grapes	sauvignon blanc
Region	Macedon, Vic.
Cellar	▮ 2
Alc./Vol.	11.5%
RRP	$22.00

Hanging Rock Victoria Riesling

Quality	🍷🍷🍷½
Value	★★★½
Grapes	riesling
Region	various, Vic.
Cellar	🍾 3
Alc./Vol.	11.5%
RRP	$14.00

These are the cold lands and getting grapes ripe can be difficult. You can never expect blockbusters from the Macedon region but do expect finesse.

CURRENT RELEASE 1997 The wine is delicate with some attractive lime aromas on the nose. The palate is lightweight with a delicate citrus flavour, and there is plenty of crisp acid on a lingering finish. It can be served well-chilled with raw sea perch.

Happs Marrime

Quality	🍷🍷🍷
Value	★★★
Grapes	semillon; chenin blanc; verdelho; viognier; marsanne; furmint
Region	Margaret River, WA
Cellar	🍾 1
Alc./Vol.	13.8%
RRP	$17.60

Pronounced Marri-imee. This is the name for the tall 300-year-old trees that shelter Happs' Karridale vineyard. The trees also flower at ripening time, distracting the birds.

CURRENT RELEASE 1997 The wine has an aromatic, flowery nose with a hint of oak. The palate has green-apple and herbal flavours and the finish is dried out by the wood. It can be served well-chilled. Try it with a kedgeree.

Hardys Eileen Hardy Chardonnay

Quality	🍷🍷🍷🍷🍷
Value	★★★★½
Grapes	chardonnay
Region	Padthaway, Adelaide Hills, SA; Canberra district, NSW
Cellar	🍾 5
Alc./Vol.	13.5%
RRP	$32.00

Lovely complex wine that needs time to develop in the bottle. Some of the fruit comes from Canberra where Hardys are investing in large plantings. It will become a substantial wine district.

Previous outstanding vintages: '86, '89, '90, '91, '94, '95

CURRENT RELEASE 1996 It has a very savoury nose with malt, vanilla and peach aromas. The palate is quite complex, with a buttery character and peach, melon and cashew flavours. These are married to some French oak on a long, dry finish. It goes well with turkey.

Hardys Hunter Ridge Chardonnay

This label would stop a clock. It graces (or should that be disgraces) BRL Hardy's presence in the Hunter Valley.

CURRENT RELEASE 1996 The nose has peach and apricot nectar aromas on a background of wood. The palate is medium-bodied with peach and tropical fruit flavours. There is some assertive oak, which controls the finish. It should be served with a medium chill. A chicken and mushroom pie works well.

Quality	🍷🍷🍷½
Value	★★★
Grapes	chardonnay
Region	Hunter Valley, NSW
Cellar	🍾 3
Alc./Vol.	13.5%
RRP	$14.95

Hardys Hunter Ridge Semillon

They won't get any medals for label design and it's got one of those artificial corks – in this case in a lurid bottle-green colour. It's enough to put you off.

CURRENT RELEASE 1996 There is evidence of some bottle-age which is starting to fill out the middle palate. The nose has damp straw and gooseberry aromas. The palate has a hint of honey and gooseberry flavours. The finish is dry and clean. It can be served well-chilled. Try it with nori king prawns.

Quality	🍷🍷🍷½
Value	★★★
Grapes	semillon
Region	Hunter Valley, NSW
Cellar	🍾 4
Alc./Vol.	11.5%
RRP	$14.95

Hardys Hunter Ridge Verdelho

You've got to pull the cork on this one, if for no other reason than to look at the ultramarine-coloured, branded synthetic cork.

CURRENT RELEASE 1996 The wine has typical tropical and passionfruit aromas. The medium-bodied palate offers simple tropical fruit flavours and there is some clean acid on a balanced finish. It can be served well-chilled and goes well with salmon patties.

Quality	🍷🍷🍷
Value	★★★½
Grapes	verdelho
Region	Hunter Valley, NSW
Cellar	🍾 2
Alc./Vol.	13.0%
RRP	$12.00 (S)

Hardys Nottage Hill Chardonnay

Quality	🍷🍷🍷
Value	★★★
Grapes	chardonnay
Region	various, SA
Cellar	🍾 1
Alc./Vol.	12.5%
RRP	$8.95 Ⓢ

Tom Nottage worked man and boy for 60 years in the Hardys Cellars. This label is dedicated to his memory.

CURRENT RELEASE 1997 The nose has overt peach aromas and the medium-bodied palate continues this theme. There are some toasty oak flavours on the dry finish. It can be served with a medium chill. It's fine with KFC.

Hardys Padthaway Noble Riesling

Quality	🍷🍷🍷🍷
Value	★★★★
Grapes	riesling
Region	Padthaway, SA
Cellar	🍾 2
Alc./Vol.	10.0%
RRP	$17.95

Noble-rot styles are gaining ground in the marketplace. Punters understand the various uses of these wines. If you are rich try poaching pears in this wine – yummy.

CURRENT RELEASE 1994 Really developed gold colour and a strong dried apricot nose are indicators of the maturity of this wine. The palate is rich with a honey texture and strong concentrated fruit flavours including dried apricot, nectarine and citrus. There is a distinct toffee flavour on the finish and the acid is crisp. It should be served well-chilled, and goes well with noble saffron pears with fresh cream.

Hardys Padthaway Unwooded Chardonnay

Quality	🍷🍷🍷½
Value	★★★½
Grapes	chardonnay
Region	Padthaway, SA
Cellar	🍾 2
Alc./Vol.	13.0%
RRP	$14.95

Do you see a boat race on the label or is that a fanciful interpretation from a bloke (MS) who hated watching the head of the river?

CURRENT RELEASE 1997 The nose has a mixture of grapefruit and melon aromas. The palate is intense with sweet melon flavours and tangy citrus. There is strong acid on the firm finish. It can be served well-chilled, and works with whitebait fritters.

Hardys Siegersdorf Chardonnay

This is a fighting brand that started life as a riesling and at the top of the Hardys' white wine tree. Wines like Eileen Hardy et al. have eclipsed it.

CURRENT RELEASE 1997 The nose has a smoky oak element as well as melon and peach aromas. The medium-bodied palate offers straightforward peach flavour, and there is some dusty oak on the dry finish. Don't over-chill, and try it with smoked chicken.

Quality	?????
Value	★★★⟨
Grapes	chardonnay
Region	various, SA
Cellar	2
Alc./Vol.	13.0%
RRP	$11.95 Ⓢ

Hardys Siegersdorf Rhine Riesling

This wine was started by James Irvine in 1969. It was named after a small hamlet in the Barossa Valley. Even the redoubtable Brian Croser had a turn at making this brand. Siegersdorf means 'victor's village'. These days the fruit source is not disclosed on the label.

CURRENT RELEASE 1997 This is a straightforward style with honest flavour. The nose has citrus aromas on a background of toast. The medium-bodied palate has clean lemon flavours and there is balancing acid on the finish. It can take the big chill. Try it with lightly curried scallops.

Quality	?????
Value	★★★⟨
Grapes	riesling
Region	not stated
Cellar	2
Alc./Vol.	12.0%
RRP	$12.30 Ⓢ

Hardys Sir James Chardonnay

Times must be slow for this wine – it hasn't changed vintage since the last *Guide*. The extra time in the bottle hasn't done it any harm.

CURRENT RELEASE 1996 Very cool dude, this is a fine wine with a citrus and peach nose. Toss in some nuts and toast for good measure. The palate has a slight buttery character and there are lively peach flavours. The finish shows some toasty oak. It can be served fairly cold. Try it with scallops.

Quality	?????
Value	★★★★
Grapes	chardonnay
Region	Padthaway, SA; Yarra Valley, Vic.; and others
Cellar	4
Alc./Vol.	13.5%
RRP	$14.95 Ⓢ

Hardys Stamps of Australia Riesling Traminer

Quality	♥♥♥
Value	★★★
Grapes	riesling; gewürztraminer
Region	South East Australia
Cellar	▮
Alc./Vol.	12.5%
RRP	$12.00 ⑤

Why not postage stamps? Everything else gets on the front labels of wine bottles. This is an affordable commercial range.

CURRENT RELEASE 1996 The nose is fruity and aromatic with some traminer perfume. The lightweight palate has a modicum of sweetness and lemon zest. The finish is clean and tidy. Give it a big chill and serve with KFC.

Harewood Estate Chardonnay

Quality	♥♥♥♥
Value	★★★★
Grapes	chardonnay
Region	Denmark, WA
Cellar	▮ 4
Alc./Vol.	13.0%
RRP	$22.00

This is a new label from Denmark in WA. The small vineyard was established in 1988 and produces around 400 cases per year. Maker John Wade (contract).

CURRENT RELEASE 1996 The nose has strong wood aromas plus peach and melon. The full-bodied palate has plenty of grunt in the food department. It has strong peach and melon flavours which are married to some very fresh toasty oak. It's rich enough to serve with pâté.

Haselgrove McLaren Vale Chardonnay

Quality	♥♥♥♥
Value	★★★★
Grapes	chardonnay
Region	McLaren Vale, SA
Cellar	▮ 3
Alc./Vol.	13.0%
RRP	$15.25

The winery seems to have taken a leap in quality. The latest releases have gained a consistency in quality.

CURRENT RELEASE 1997 This is a well-worked style that has been given the full treatment. The nose is nutty with oak and citrus. The palate is medium to full-bodied with a creamy texture and mouthfilling quality. The major flavour is peach, and the wood leaves a dry coating on the tongue. Don't over-chill, and try it with pork sausages.

Haselgrove McLaren Vale Reserve Botrytis Semillon

These days a portfolio isn't complete without a pocket rocket sticky (that is 375 ml) that has been influenced by noble rot. This is typical of the style.

CURRENT RELEASE 1997 There is an overwhelming aroma of honey on the nose and the background has dried apricot notes. The palate is nectar-like, with yellow-box honey flavours and dried fruits with orange peel. Fresh acid keeps the finish lively. It needs time. Try it well-chilled with fresh stone fruit.

Quality	🍷🍷🍷🍷
Value	★★★★
Grapes	semillon
Region	McLaren Vale, SA
Cellar	🍾 4
Alc./Vol.	11.0%
RRP	$16.00 (375 ml)

Hawkesbridge Sophie's Vineyard Chardonnay

This New Zealand vineyard belongs to Michael and Judy Veal and Sophie is a family member.

CURRENT RELEASE 1996 The nose has a strong peach aroma on a background of oak. The palate offers ripe peach flavours and nectarine. This is backed by some solid wood with a firm tannin finish. It should be served near room temperature. Try it with tripe in a black bean sauce.

Quality	🍷🍷🍷🍷
Value	★★★★
Grapes	chardonnay
Region	Marlborough, NZ
Cellar	🍾 3
Alc./Vol.	13.5%
RRP	$22.00

Hawkesbridge Willowbank Vineyard Sauvignon Blanc

The Willowbank vineyard is part of Hawkesbridge's 16-hectare estate. It was established in 1991.

CURRENT RELEASE 1996 A typical New Zealand style with lots of varietal character. The nose has tinned pea and strong tropical aromas. The palate continues the tropical fruit theme with mango and passionfruit flavours. There is crisp acid on the finish. It can be served well-chilled. Try it with a seafood risotto.

Quality	🍷🍷🍷🍷½
Value	★★★★½
Grapes	sauvignon blanc
Region	Marlborough, NZ
Cellar	🍾 2
Alc./Vol.	12.5%
RRP	$17.25

Hay Shed Hill Chardonnay

Quality	????
Value	★★★
Grapes	chardonnay
Region	Margaret River, WA
Cellar	▮ 4
Alc./Vol.	13.5%
RRP	$25.25

Why does this label remind MS of *American Gothic*? By rights it should feature birds because it's owned by a Perth ornithologist, Barry Morrison.
CURRENT RELEASE 1996 This boasts strong varietal characters including cling peaches on the nose and a concentrated peach flavour on the palate. It has a mouthfilling texture, dry gripping oak and impressive length. Don't over-chill, and serve with salmon patties.

Heggies Riesling

Quality	????
Value	★★★★
Grapes	riesling
Region	Eden Hills, SA
Cellar	▮ 3
Alc./Vol.	11.5%
RRP	$16.00

This is obviously a slow-moving line because bottle-age is starting to catch up with this riesling from the Eden Hills.
CURRENT RELEASE 1995 The colour is pale yellow and there are citrus and biscuit aromas on the nose. The palate has developed a full texture. Lime is the major flavour and this is balanced by some keen acid on the finish. It can be served with a full chill. Try it with a prawn cocktail.

Henschke Croft Chardonnay

Quality	?????
Value	★★★★
Grapes	chardonnay
Region	Lenswood, SA
Cellar	▮ 3
Alc./Vol.	13.5%
RRP	$34.00

MS once wrote that Stephen Henschke should stick to his day job and stick to making red wines. Perhaps MS should give up his day job.
CURRENT RELEASE 1997 There has been plenty of work put into this wine. It was picked late and fermented in Vosges oak. The nose has a creamy butterscotch aroma plus a suggestion of lychee nut. There is also a citrus background. The palate borders on buttery, with grapefruit and melon fruit flavours dominating. These make a seamless transition to an oak-driven finish. It should be lightly chilled. Serve it with chicken dumplings in a rich stock.

Henschke Green's Hill Riesling

This is an interesting contrast with the wine from Eden Valley. Green's Hill is a site on the Henschke Lenswood Vineyard, which is south of Mount Lofty.
CURRENT RELEASE 1997 The wine is very intense with concentrated citrus aromas that almost assume a distilled or essence character. The palate has strong lime flavours and there is crisp acid on a tingling finish. It's great with a big chill. Serve it with oysters natural.

Quality	🍷🍷🍷🍷½
Value	★★★★
Grapes	riesling
Region	Lenswood, SA
Cellar	5
Alc./Vol.	12.2%
RRP	$20.00

Henschke Joseph Hill Gewürztraminer

Joseph Hill isn't a place, it's a bloke. Joseph Hill Tyler was the first on the property where this vineyard is planted.
CURRENT RELEASE 1997 The bouquet of intense lychee and floral aromas gives you a real punch in the nose. The palate has a slightly oily texture with lychee and gooseberry flavours. Soft acid adds balance to the finish. It should be served well-chilled. Try it with an asparagus quiche.

Quality	🍷🍷🍷½
Value	★★★
Grapes	gewürztraminer
Region	Eden Valley, SA
Cellar	2
Alc./Vol.	13.5%
RRP	$19.00

Henschke Julius Eden Valley Riesling

Julius is a Henschke ancestor who carved out a reputation as a sculptor. This wine is dedicated to his memory.
CURRENT RELEASE 1997 An immaculate style typical of the region. Delicate but with plenty of flavour, the nose is very floral with rose-petal and citrus aromas. There is fresh lime flavour on the middle-bodied palate and crisp acid makes for a lively finish. It can be served well-chilled and is great with crab cakes.

Quality	🍷🍷🍷🍷½
Value	★★★½
Grapes	riesling
Region	Eden Valley, SA
Cellar	8+
Alc./Vol.	13.5%
RRP	$18.00

Hickinbotham Chardonnay

Quality	♥♥♥⟓
Value	★★★⟓
Grapes	chardonnay & aligoté
Region	Mornington Peninsula, Vic.
Cellar	▮ 3
Alc./Vol.	13.0%
RRP	$25.40

This wine comes from the Mornington Peninsula and is barrel-fermented. It includes some aligoté, which gives it an unusual flavour. Maker Andrew Hickinbotham.
CURRENT RELEASE 1996 The nose has peach, lychee and loquat aromas. The palate is mouthfilling to the point of being buttery. The major flavour is peach and the wood is united with the fruit. The finish is dry and slightly short. It should be served with a slight chill. Try it with smoked chicken salad.

Hickinbotham The Taminga

Quality	♥♥⟓
Value	★★⟓
Grapes	taminga
Region	not stated
Cellar	▮ 2
Alc./Vol.	12.5%
RRP	$15.00

This is an Australian grape variety developed by the CSIRO. It was meant for warm climates but this comes from the Hickinbotham stable on the Mornington Peninsula.
CURRENT RELEASE 1996 An aromatic style with lychee and gooseberry aromas. The palate is mouthfilling with spicy fruit characters; however, the finish is dry and slightly coarse. It needs to be served well-chilled. Take it on a picnic.

Highland Heritage Estate Mount Canobolas Chardonnay

Quality	♥♥♥♥⟓
Value	★★★★⟓
Grapes	chardonnay
Region	Orange, NSW
Cellar	▮ 4
Alc./Vol.	13.2%
RRP	$24.00

This is another label from the burgeoning Orange district. It was established in 1985 and produces around 3500 cases per annum. Maker John Hordern.
CURRENT RELEASE 1995 A full-flavoured complex style that is starting to show the benefit of bottle-age. The nose is an attractive mix of peach and wood aromas. The palate is mouthfilling, almost chewy, and this is backed up by some strong acid. It's here for the long haul. Try it with a pasta and chicken dish.

Highwood Sauvignon Blanc

The winery is located in Happy Valley and the fruit was grown in Padthaway. The proprietor is Rob Dundon.
CURRENT RELEASE 1997   The nose is herbal with some cut-grass aromas. The palate adds tropical fruit to a gooseberry flavour and there is plenty of crisp acid on a lingering finish. It can be served well-chilled. Try it with pasta and a rocket pesto.

Quality	♥♥♥↑
Value	★★★↑
Grapes	sauvignon blanc
Region	Padthaway
Cellar	🍾 2
Alc./Vol.	11.5%
RRP	$11.00

Hill of Hope Unwooded Chardonnay

This winery belongs to the Hope family, hence the name. It's located in the Broke Fordwich subregion of the Hunter Valley.
CURRENT RELEASE 1997   There is a strong varietal influence on the nose, lots of peach and nectarine. Ditto the palate, which is quite rich and adds a hint of citrus. Crisp acid fills the finish. It can be served well-chilled. Try it with scallops in a cream sauce.

Quality	♥♥♥↑
Value	★★★↑
Grapes	chardonnay
Region	Hunter Valley, NSW
Cellar	🍾 2
Alc./Vol.	12.2%
RRP	$15.00

Hill Smith Estate Sauvignon Blanc

The quiet achievers, the Hill Smith family, have always been at the cutting edge where vineyard development is concerned.
CURRENT RELEASE 1997   This wine from the Eden Hills is quite pale, yet power lurks beneath. The nose has herb and grass aromas plus a hint of tropical fruit. The palate is medium-bodied with an impressive depth of fruit. Gooseberry and tropical fruits are the major flavours and there are strong acids on a crisp finish. Try it with pipis in a black bean sauce.

Quality	♥♥♥♥
Value	★★★★
Grapes	sauvignon blanc
Region	Eden Valley, SA
Cellar	🍾 2
Alc./Vol.	12.0%
RRP	$16.00 Ⓢ

Hillstowe Buxton Chardonnay

Quality	❦❦❦❦
Value	★★★❦
Grapes	chardonnay
Region	McLaren Vale, SA
Cellar	▮ 3
Alc./Vol.	13.0%
RRP	$16.00

The founding date was 1980, and the credit goes to Chris Laurie and David Paxton. Paxton is no longer involved in the venture.

CURRENT RELEASE 1995   The wine is a deep green–yellow colour and the nose has overt peach aromas. The palate is very intense, with strong peach flavours that do battle with some slightly raw oak on a very assertive finish. It should be served lightly chilled. Try it with a vegetarian burger.

Hillstowe Buxton Sauvignon Blanc

Quality	❦❦❦❦
Value	★★★★
Grapes	sauvignon blanc
Region	Adelaide Hills, McLaren Vale, SA
Cellar	▮ 3
Alc./Vol.	12.5%
RRP	$16.00

The fruit comes from established locations. It has been made without wood treatment to develop the fruit flavours.

CURRENT RELEASE 1997   The nose is herbal with hints of the tropical fruit spectrum. The palate has an attractive level of sweetness and a strong passionfruit flavour. Crisp acid makes for a very refreshing finish. Big chill will thrill; serve it with spaghetti pesto.

Hillstowe Udys Mill Chardonnay

Quality	❦❦❦❦
Value	★★★★
Grapes	chardonnay
Region	Adelaide Hills
Cellar	▮ 4
Alc./Vol.	13.5%
RRP	$28.00

This is the cool-climate component of the Hillstowe range. Udys Mill is located at Carey Gully between Piccadilly and Lenswood.

CURRENT RELEASE 1995   The wine has a creamy nose with peach and melon aromas. The palate is complex with a creamy, almost buttery texture. Peach and melon are the obvious flavours. The wood on the finish is perfectly integrated. It can be served with a medium chill. Try it with chicken Kiev.

Hollick Sauvignon Blanc Semillon

Hollick has been restructured as far as the management is concerned. The product range is also expanding.

CURRENT RELEASE 1997 This is a civilised union of two varieties grown in the Coonawarra. The nose has a gooseberry and tropical fruit flavour. The palate is fresh with some tropical fruit flavours as well as gooseberry, and there is fresh crisp acid. It can take a big chill and still thrill. Drink now with a crayfish salad.

Quality	🍷🍷🍷🍷
Value	★★★★
Grapes	sauvignon blanc; semillon
Region	Coonawarra, SA
Cellar	🍾 2
Alc./Vol.	11.5%
RRP	$16.00

Horseshoe Vineyard Semillon

Bottle development has enhanced this wine from the Hunter Valley. The vineyard was established in 1986. Maker John Hordern.

CURRENT RELEASE 1994 The nose is nutty with hints of damp straw. It has a complex palate with gooseberry and nutty flavours, and the finish shows crisp acid. There is probably further development to be had, but it also drinks well now. Serve well-chilled with a seafood risotto.

Quality	🍷🍷🍷
Value	★★★
Grapes	semillon
Region	Hunter Valley, NSW
Cellar	🍾 2
Alc./Vol.	10.5%
RRP	$21.65

Horseshoe Vineyard Unwooded Semillon

There was a time when all Hunter semillons were unwooded. This is a typical early-picked style with a low alcohol content.

CURRENT RELEASE 1997 It captures the citrus end of the flavour spectrum. The nose has biscuit and citrus aromas. The palate is light- to medium-bodied with a strong citrus flavour (mostly lemon) and there is some crisp acid on a clean finish. It can be served well-chilled and there should be some beneficial development with bottle-age.

Quality	🍷🍷🍷½
Value	★★★½
Grapes	semillon
Region	Hunter Valley, SA
Cellar	🍾 4
Alc./Vol.	10.0%
RRP	$13.00

Houghton Rhine Riesling

Quality	♟♟♟♟
Value	★★★★↑
Grapes	riesling
Region	Frankland River, WA
Cellar	↑ 2
Alc./Vol.	11.5%
RRP	$11.95

Fresh as a spring morning, this is fine style at a decent price. Pity it's eclipsed by the white burgundy. Maker Paul Lapsley.

CURRENT RELEASE 1997   The nose is very floral with citrus and dried lavender aromas. The palate has a lime and lemon flavour which is attended by some crisp acid on a fresh finish. The wine can be served well-chilled.

Houghton Semillon Sauvignon Blanc

Quality	♟♟♟↑
Value	★★★★
Grapes	semillon; sauvignon blanc
Region	various, WA
Cellar	↑ 2
Alc./Vol.	12.5%
RRP	$12.95

Big on the tropical fruit and very crisp, it's a thoroughly modern sem/sav.

CURRENT RELEASE 1997   The nose has passionfruit and pineapple aromas. The palate is fresh with tropical fruit flavours, particularly pawpaw and passionfruit, and these are matched by some crisp acid on a pristine finish. Serve well-chilled with pan-fried calamari.

Houghton White Burgundy

Quality	♟♟♟↑
Value	★★★↑
Grapes	chenin blanc; muscadelle; semillon; chardonnay; verdelho; and others
Region	various, WA
Cellar	↑ 2
Alc./Vol.	13.0%
RRP	$11.95 Ⓢ

This wine was invented by the late Jack Mann in 1937 and it has been in continuous production since then. It's now in the top three white brands on the Australian market.

CURRENT RELEASE 1997   This is a party animal with a hint of cashew and herbs on the nose. The palate strikes a tropical chord and there are gooseberries in the background. The finish displays soft acid. It can be served well-chilled. Try it with fish and chips.

Houghton Wild Flower Ridge Chardonnay

This is a commercial line cashing in on the Western Australian preoccupation with wild flowers.
CURRENT RELEASE 1996 The nose has peach, loquat and vanilla aromas. The medium-bodied palate has peach flavours which are married to vanilla flavours from the wood. A medium chill is recommended. Cook up some salmon patties.

Quality	♥♥♥
Value	★★★
Grapes	chardonnay
Region	various, WA
Cellar	▮ 2
Alc./Vol.	13.5%
RRP	$13.50

Howard Family Semillon

Hunter semillon can be an elusive variety. When young, it's like a car left in park – neutral. According to the label Len Evans OBE gets into the act.
CURRENT RELEASE 1997 This is an example of a low-alcohol wine that could blossom with bottle-age. The nose has damp straw and gooseberry aromas. The light-weight palate has an austere gooseberry flavour and there is crisp acid on the finish. It can be served well-chilled. Try it with calamari.

Quality	♥♥♥
Value	★★★
Grapes	semillon
Region	Hunter Valley, NSW
Cellar	▮ 5
Alc./Vol.	11.0%
RRP	$18.00

Howard Park Chardonnay

It's the harmony and complexity that make this wine a winner. There is nothing out of place and the complexity is high. You'd expect nothing less from John Wade.
CURRENT RELEASE 1996 The nose has peach, lychee and cedar aromas. The palate is medium- to full-bodied and the flavour is layered. The soft textures are due to barrel fermentation and the finish is long and dry. The wood has youth on its side. Try it with roast turkey.

Quality	♥♥♥♥♥
Value	★★★★
Grapes	chardonnay
Region	Great Southern, WA
Cellar	▮ 6
Alc./Vol.	14.0%
RRP	$35.25

Howard Park Riesling

Quality	🍷🍷🍷🍷
Value	★★★★
Grapes	riesling
Region	Great Southern, WA
Cellar	🍾 5
Alc./Vol.	12.0%
RRP	$22.00

John and Wendy Wade are the proprietors of Howard Park. John Wade made his fame, if not fortune, by making the first John Riddoch for Wynns in Coonawarra.

CURRENT RELEASE 1996 This has a strongly aromatic nose. The palate is soft with a light lemon flavour and the acid on the finish is crisp. It needs more time to come together and should be served well-chilled. Serve with oysters natural.

Hugo Chardonnay

Quality	🍷🍷🍷🍷
Value	★★★★
Grapes	chardonnay
Region	McLaren Flat, SA
Cellar	🍾 4
Alc./Vol.	13.8%
RRP	$19.00

They are never afraid of flavour at this marque. Big and memorable seem to be the watchwords for these styles.

CURRENT RELEASE 1995 The nose is really pungent with a classic mixture of wood and varietal fruit flavours. The palate is rich and mouthfilling, with a straightforward peach flavour that is followed by some toasty oak and an emphatic finish.

Hugo Sauvignon Blanc

Quality	🍷🍷🍷
Value	★★★
Grapes	sauvignon blanc
Region	McLaren Flat, SA
Cellar	🍾 1
Alc./Vol.	12.0%
RRP	$17.00

The winery came into being in 1982 and these days produces around 6500 cases per annum.

CURRENT RELEASE 1997 This is a typical McLaren Vale style. The nose is herbal with some lantana and cut-grass aromas. The palate is medium-bodied with strong gooseberry and herb influences. The finish shows some clean acid. It can be served well-chilled. Enjoy with spaghetti pesto.

Hugo Unwooded Chardonnay

Looks like unwooded chardonnay is here to stay. To some (like MS) it's like a salad without a dressing. Maker John Hugo.
CURRENT RELEASE 1997 This wine smells like unwooded chardonnay. There is peach and melon on the nose. The palate continues the peach theme. It's medium-bodied and some soft acid is discernible on the finish. I can't help wondering what difference a touch of wood would have made. It can be served with a medium chill. Try it with sushi.

Quality	???
Value	★★★
Grapes	chardonnay
Region	McLaren Flat, SA
Cellar	2
Alc./Vol.	12.5%
RRP	$16.00

Hungerford Hill Griffith Botrytis Semillon

The grapes came from a very talented grower near Yenda. He supplies grapes to several makers.
CURRENT RELEASE 1993 This wine is ready to rock and roll. It has a deep gold colour and a strong botrytis nose of dried apricot and honey smells. The palate is thick and rich with a background of lemon, peels, dried fruit and marmalade. The acid on the finish is starting to soften and the wine is drying out. It needs a big chill. Serve it with soft blue cheese.

Quality	????
Value	★★★★
Grapes	semillon
Region	Griffith, NSW
Cellar	1
Alc./Vol.	11.0%
RRP	$12.50 (375 ml)

Hungerford Hill Young Semillon

What does a Young semillon taste like with bottle-age? Truth is, no-one knows but we're about to find out if folks can keep their hands off this wine.
CURRENT RELEASE 1995 The colour is pale straw and the nose offers damp straw and citrus aromas. The palate is medium-bodied with attractive citrus and gooseberry flavours, and the finish shows crisp acid. There has been no wood treatment. Serve well-chilled with prawn rice-paper rolls.

Quality	????
Value	★★★★
Grapes	semillon
Region	Young, NSW
Cellar	4
Alc./Vol.	11.5%
RRP	$16.50

Ingleburne Unwooded Semillon

Quality	♟♟♟
Value	★★★★
Grapes	semillon
Region	not stated
Cellar	▮ 1
Alc./Vol.	13.0%
RRP	$11.50 ⑤

This is another label for the Maglieri winery of McLaren Vale, which offers decent quaffing wines at very cheap prices. Good news for the consumer.

CURRENT RELEASE 1996   This surprised us: bottle-age can trick you into thinking there's some oak involvement. The nose has herbal, flinty, mineral and toasty developed nuances; the taste is soft and rich and somewhat broad. It's a plain dry white with generous flavour, and would be enhanced by a decent chill. Drink soon, with prawn wonton soup.

Innisfail Geelong Rhine Riesling

Quality	♟♟♟♟♟
Value	★★★★⚹
Grapes	riesling
Region	Geelong, Vic.
Cellar	▮ 4+
Alc./Vol.	12.5%
RRP	$12.00 (cellar door)

Innisfail's founder Ron Griffiths started planting the 15 acres he now has under vines in 1980. Gary Farr of Bannockburn, an old sailing mate, has helped him out occasionally.

CURRENT RELEASE 1997   A very fine, vibrant, pure riesling with bracing lime-juice aromas. The palate is fresh, zesty and tangy, with a steely structure and delicious balance. The finish is dry, with cleansing acidity. Serve with pan-fried whiting.

Jamiesons Run Chardonnay

Quality	♟♟♟♟
Value	★★★⚹
Grapes	chardonnay
Region	various
Cellar	▮ 2
Alc./Vol.	13.0%
RRP	$12.00 ⑤

Conversation with Mildara/Blass exec: 'Of course we had to change the label for the US, they didn't get it.' MS: 'What did you change?' Exec: 'We had to take the sheep off.' You figure that out. We can't; perhaps that's why we only write books.

CURRENT RELEASE 1997   The nose has a strong melon aroma and toasty wood smells. The palate is full-bodied with melon, tropical and stone-fruit flavours. There is a hint of butter on the creamy texture and the wood on the finish is soft. The wine goes well with smoked cod.

Jasper Hill Riesling

This maker is best known for his reds, but don't over-look the riesling: it's often a superb wine. Maker Ron Laughton.

CURRENT RELEASE 1997 Scintillating lime-juice and lemon-zest aromas which translate into an intensely fla-voured palate, bristling with sprightly acid. It winds up nicely arid on the finish. Has fruit concentration and length, and should cellar well. Good with Vietnamese dry noodles.

Quality	ᵀᵀᵀᵀₜ
Value	★★★ʳ
Grapes	riesling
Region	Heathcote, Vic.
Cellar	🍷 8+
Alc./Vol.	11.5%
RRP	$19.70

Jindalee Chardonnay

The headquarters of this label are in Geelong but the label states the grapes come from the 'Murray Darling'. Whatever . . .

CURRENT RELEASE 1997 The wine has a grapefruit and melon nose. The medium-bodied palate continues the grapefruit theme and there is subtle oak on the finish. It should be served with a medium chill. The wine goes well with spaghetti marinara.

Quality	ᵀᵀᵀₜ
Value	★★★ʳ
Grapes	chardonnay
Region	Riverland, SA
Cellar	🍷 2
Alc./Vol.	13.5%
RRP	$14.00

Katnook Estate Riesling

This company has followed a very sound policy of ageing its riesling for around 18 months before release. Maker Wayne Stehbens.

CURRENT RELEASE 1996 A very tasty drop of riesling, which is starting to show the benefits of bottle-age. The colour is still light/mid-yellow, and there are delicate toasty elements together with floral riesling aromas. In the mouth it's full, rich, smooth and slightly chunky, which is no criticism. A quite big but not fine or aro-matic riesling, and a beaut drink. Goes with prawn dumplings.

Quality	ᵀᵀᵀᵀₜ
Value	★★★★ʳ
Grapes	riesling
Region	Coonawarra, SA
Cellar	🍷 5
Alc./Vol.	12.0%
RRP	$16.50

Katnook Estate Sauvignon Blanc

Quality	♟♟♟♟♟
Value	★★★ᛕ
Grapes	sauvignon blanc
Region	Coonawarra, SA
Cellar	♟ 5
Alc./Vol.	13.5%
RRP	$26.00

This is one of the longest-standing sauvignons in Australia, and it has always commanded a premium price (it's probably the dearest in the entire country). Maker Wayne Stehbens.

Previous outstanding vintages: most of them

CURRENT RELEASE 1997 A powerful and cleverly made wine, which shows some cunningly concealed oak that adds to the richness and mouthfilling properties. Herbal, toasty, cedar and vanilla aromas greet the nose. Stacks of flavour which linger long on the afterpalate. Try it with smoked chicken and asparagus salad.

Kim Crawford Hawkes Bay Semillon

Quality	♟♟♟♟ᛕ
Value	★★★ᛕ
Grapes	semillon
Region	Hawkes Bay, NZ
Cellar	♟ 2+
Alc./Vol.	13.0%
RRP	$18.00

Kim Crawford, who is Coopers Creek's winemaker by day, claims this is made from a non-herbaceous clone of the semillon vine, imported to New Zealand from the Barossa Valley.

CURRENT RELEASE 1996 A clean, technically flawless wine with smart French oak combining with herbal semillon flavour. I'm not totally convinced about the compatibility of smoky, toasty oak with semillon fruit, but there's no doubting the high quality of the wine. Smooth, dry aftertaste; drinks well with a light chill.

Kim Crawford Marlborough Dry Riesling

Quality	♟♟♟♟ᛕ
Value	★★★★ᛕ
Grapes	riesling
Region	Marlborough, NZ
Cellar	♟ 5+
Alc./Vol.	13.0%
RRP	$18.00

The grapes were harvested on the fifteenth of May. That's very late, which may explain the hints of botrytis in the flavour.

CURRENT RELEASE 1997 A fragrant Germanic style, this shows classic lime/lemon riesling fruit plus a honeyed botrytis lift. The palate is deliciously tangy, with a crisp, tart acidity that more than balances the touch of sweetness. The result is a racy wine, fine and high-quality. Try it with Blenheim mussels and Bluff oysters.

Kim Crawford Tietjen Chardonnay

Tietjen is the name of the grapegrower, located at Gisborne, traditionally one of the best-regarded NZ regions for chardonnay.
CURRENT RELEASE 1997   The nose is a riot of vanilla, honey, apricot and toasty oak notes, and there seems to be some botrytis as well as plenty of oak involved in this complexity of aromas. The fairly lean and reserved fruit has been coupled with lots of artefact or winemaking characters. There's a hint of sweetness and moderate palate length. Try it with scallops.

Quality	♥♥♥♥
Value	★★★¼
Grapes	chardonnay
Region	Gisborne, NZ
Cellar	▯ 2
Alc./Vol.	13.5%
RRP	$26.30

Kingston Estate Chardonnay

Kingston Estate has quickly built a name for tremendous value from the Riverland in a straightforward, no-nonsense style. Maker Bill Moularadellis.
CURRENT RELEASE 1997   Exactly what's required in budget chardonnay. Nectarine and tropical aromas, light-bodied, easy on the oak (it's barely detectable) and a degree of delicacy. Uncomplicated and very gluggable. Goes well with a wide range of vegetarian foods.

Quality	♥♥♥½
Value	★★★★
Grapes	chardonnay
Region	Murray Valley, SA
Cellar	▯ 1
Alc./Vol.	13.0%
RRP	$11.50 Ⓢ

Kingston Estate Reserve Chardonnay

Bill Moularadellis reckons the Riverland is misunderstood and capable of much better wines than it presently produces. His new reserve range is an attempt to put his money where his mouth is.
CURRENT RELEASE 1996   A very pungent wine with passionfruit and glue-paste aromas which are a parody of the grape. It's fairly light in the mouth but has some fruit intensity. A good wine, for sure, but the style is confronting and some will find it a bit tutti-frutti. Scallops should provide a foil.

Quality	♥♥♥½
Value	★★★
Grapes	chardonnay
Region	Murray Valley, SA
Cellar	▯ 2
Alc./Vol.	13.0%
RRP	$25.00

Kingston Estate Semillon Sauvignon Blanc

Quality	♈♈♈
Value	★★★
Grapes	semillon; sauvignon blanc
Region	Murray Valley, SA
Cellar	♙ 1
Alc./Vol.	12.5%
RRP	$11.50 ⑤

Kingston Estate is the mouse that roared. It's grown like topsy and in 1998 crushed 20 000 tonnes of grapes.
CURRENT RELEASE 1997 Imagine a fistful of scrunched-up vine leaves; that's what this smells like. Green-picked fruit seems to have lent an aromatic pungency to it. The colour is a fairly advanced full yellow and the palate is light-bodied, simple and soft. It's a basic dry white that drinks well now. Serve with stuffed capsicums.

Knappstein Dry Style Gewürztraminer

Quality	♈♈♈♉
Value	★★★⟨
Grapes	gewürztraminer
Region	Clare Valley, SA
Cellar	♙ 2
Alc./Vol.	13.0%
RRP	$15.00

Most traminers and traminer riesling blends are somewhat sweet, hence the serious exponents put some words on the label to indicate a dry wine. Maker Andrew Hardy.
Previous outstanding vintages: '96
CURRENT RELEASE 1997 No doubting the grape variety here: the nose is very spicy with a decided muscat intensity. It brings to mind rose petals and lychees. The flavour is very delicate and it's a squeaky clean, well-made wine. Goes well with Vietnamese noodles.

Knappstein Hand Picked Riesling

Quality	♈♈♈♈♈
Value	★★★★★
Grapes	riesling
Region	Clare Valley, SA
Cellar	♙ 10
Alc./Vol.	12.5%
RRP	$16.00

You might think 'hand-picked' is hardly worth shouting about, but these days hand-picked grapes are getting to be a rarity. Maker Andrew Hardy.
CURRENT RELEASE 1997 A delicious riesling that reinforces the return to form of this marque. Doughy yeast esters plus citrus fruit to smell, and plenty of lively acid gives the palate freshness and verve. It has delicacy yet fine soft flavour, with lime-juice paramount. Excellent, long zesty aftertaste. Serve with onion quiche.

Knappstein Sauvignon Blanc Semillon

Knappstein wines have jumped ahead since Andrew Hardy was sent up to Clare by the owner, his previous employer Brian Croser of Petaluma.
CURRENT RELEASE 1997 This is halfway to a pina colada. It smells of pineapples and other tropical fruits, and in the mouth it builds gooseberry characters. The sauvignon blanc must have been nice and ripe because the greener grassy characters are pretty well absent. The palate is dry and subtle and has good flavour depth. Serve it with asparagus quiche.

Quality	ΥΥΥΥ
Value	★★★
Grapes	sauvignon blanc; semillon
Region	Clare Valley & Adelaide Hills, SA
Cellar	2
Alc./Vol.	13.0%
RRP	$20.00

Krondorf Rhine Riesling

Is Krondorf the last riesling producer in Australia using the Rhine prefix? It's very likely. Maker Nick Walker.
CURRENT RELEASE 1997 Riesling from the Barossa floor is never as fine as Eden Valley, but this is a well-made commercial style at the right price. The nose is open and up-front, with citrus and flowery aspects. The palate reveals plenty of fruit, a little sweetness and fairly broad structure. Goes well with swordfish.

Quality	ΥΥΥΥ
Value	★★★★⬩
Grapes	riesling
Region	Barossa Valley, SA
Cellar	3
Alc./Vol.	12.0%
RRP	$11.90 Ⓢ

Kumeu River Chardonnay

The Brajkovich family of North Auckland are leaders in the Kiwi wine industry, with their roots in the wartime wave of Dalmatian migrants to the north island. Maker Michael Brajkovich.
Previous outstanding vintages: '94
CURRENT RELEASE 1996 An exotically styled chardonnay far removed from the tutti-frutti epitome of the New World. It has more in common with Burgundy, with subtle wood and some nutty, malty and floral characters that suggest a fair degree of oxygen as well as grape solids in the juice. The profile is tight, restrained, and delicate with good length and a slight grip on the finish. Goes well with yabbies.

Quality	ΥΥΥΥ
Value	★★★
Grapes	chardonnay
Region	Auckland, NZ
Cellar	5
Alc./Vol.	13.0%
RRP	$42.65

Kumeu River Mate's Vineyard Chardonnay

Quality	♟♟♟♟
Value	★★★
Grapes	chardonnay
Region	Auckland, NZ
Cellar	➤ 1–5+
Alc./Vol.	13.5%
RRP	$48.40

The late Mate (pronounced Mattie) Brajkovich was a true gentleman and a high-profile member of the industry, serving on the Wine Institute board for many years. His son Michael is winemaker.

Previous outstanding vintages: '94

CURRENT RELEASE 1996   Finesse is the byword here. A delicate, restrained style which may appear to lack a bit in the fruit department while young, but it's a wine for drinking with food, not blind tastings. The colour is pale and the nose reveals lemony fruit and French oak of the highest quality. The palate has a fine nutty intensity, an arid finish and good length. It should grow in stature with some bottle-age. Serve with corn-fed chicken.

Kumeu River Sauvignon Semillon

Quality	♟♟♟♟
Value	★★★★
Grapes	sauvignon blanc; semillon
Region	Auckland, NZ
Cellar	▮ 4
Alc./Vol.	13.0%
RRP	$29.50

Mike Brajkovich uses the shortened European name for sauvignon blanc, and enlists every technique in the book in an effort to make this wine more complex. He succeeds.

CURRENT RELEASE 1996   A rich, powerful, well-structured dry white which has discreet herbal characters but avoids the mono-dimensional pungency of some Kiwi examples. A full, complex wine with cedary, toasty oak inflexions and a telltale twist of Kiwi boiled-potato character. Try it with chicken satays.

Lakes Folly Chardonnay

Quality	♟♟♟
Value	★★★
Grapes	chardonnay
Region	Hunter Valley, NSW
Cellar	▮ 3
Alc./Vol.	12.6%
RRP	$46.75

Somewhat old-fashioned in stylistic terms. Dr Max Lake was (along with Murray Tyrrell) a pioneer of the variety. Maker Stephen Lake.

CURRENT RELEASE 1995   The wine has a chewy quality. There are barrel-ferment odours on the nose along with peach and melon aromas. The palate is in the process of integrating; the fruit and new French oak have yet to make a full match. The finish is dry and assertive. Don't over-chill. It goes well with smoked chicken.

Leasingham Bin 7 Rhine Riesling

The bin number was made famous by Mick Knappstein and then nephew Tim took it to greater glory in the early seventies. Since then many wines have caught up with the standard, yet it remains a benchmark.
CURRENT RELEASE 1997   The nose is dominated by a crisp lime aroma. The palate is intense with a shock of fresh lime and there's tingling crisp acid on a long finish. It can be served well-chilled. Try it with oysters natural.

Quality	♟♟♟♟
Value	★★★★
Grapes	riesling
Region	Clare Valley, SA
Cellar	▮ 5
Alc./Vol.	12.0%
RRP	$13.95

Leasingham Bin 37 Chardonnay

They felled a forest in Kentucky to make this wine. It almost sings Yankee Doodle when you pull the cork.
CURRENT RELEASE 1996   The Yankee oak makes for a confectionery character on the nose, which also displays tropical fruit aromas. The palate has a sweet peach flavour and there's a touch of hardness on a firm finish. Don't over-chill, and serve it with scallops in a cream sauce.

Quality	♟♟♟
Value	★★★
Grapes	chardonnay
Region	Clare Valley, SA
Cellar	▮ 3
Alc./Vol.	13.5%
RRP	$13.95

Leasingham Classic Clare Rhine Riesling

This is the label that eclipsed the legendary Bin 7. For once, the 'classic' appellation applies, and the wine also shows the benefit of bottle-age.
CURRENT RELEASE 1995   There's a distinct whiff of kero on the nose and the palate is starting to develop an oily texture. The major flavour is lemon and there's a zest of lime. Clean acid marks the tingling finish. It can be served well-chilled. Try it with chilli calamari.

Quality	♟♟♟♟
Value	★★★
Grapes	riesling
Region	Clare Valley, SA
Cellar	▮ 3
Alc./Vol.	12.5%
RRP	$21.00

Leconfield Chardonnay

Quality	♟♟♟♟
Value	★★★★
Grapes	chardonnay
Region	Coonawarra, SA
Cellar	▮ 3
Alc./Vol.	13.2%
RRP	$17.00

This is yet another proxy red. As the old saying goes, 'every white wine would be a red wine if it could be'. That's particularly true in the Coonawarra.

CURRENT RELEASE 1997   The nose is a rich mixture of banana, peach, tropical fruit and oak aromas. The medium-bodied palate is heavy on peach flavours and there are tropical notes. The oak is compelling on the finish with a drying character and plenty of tannin. It should be served with a medium chill.

Leconfield Noble Riesling

Quality	♟♟♟♟
Value	★★★★
Grapes	riesling
Region	Coonawarra, SA
Cellar	▮ 4
Alc./Vol.	10.0%
RRP	$18.90 (375 ml)

Botrytis cinerea was artificially introduced into the district in the mid-seventies. It's been there ever since. Some say it's a blessing and red-wine makers call it a curse.

CURRENT RELEASE 1997   A young style that needs bottle-age to confirm the pedigree. It has a honeyed nose and there's also a powerful citrus aroma. The palate comes down to honey, citrus and apricot flavours backed by fresh acid on a clean and lingering finish. Serve well-chilled, with salmon gravlax.

Leconfield Old Vines Riesling

Quality	♟♟♟♟
Value	★★★★
Grapes	riesling
Region	Coonawarra, NSW
Cellar	▮ 5
Alc./Vol.	12.0%
RRP	$14.00

Coonawarra riesling doesn't seem to have a persona like the Clare or Eden Valley. The back label makes much of low-yielding old vines.

CURRENT RELEASE 1997   The wine has a soft citrus nose and the palate has a mouthfilling quality. There are citrus and lemon flavours which are matched by acid of medium intensity. It's a clean neat package that can be served well-chilled. Try it with barbecued prawns.

Leeuwin Estate Art Series Chardonnay

This may no longer be the dearest but it is still the greatest Australian chardonnay. It also ages better than any other. So Penfolds Yattarna, butt out! Makers Bob Cartwright and John Brocksopp.

Previous Outstanding Vintages: '80, '81, '82, '83, '85, '87, '89, '90, '92, '93

CURRENT RELEASE 1995 Sound the trumpets and bring on the conjurers and dancing girls, this is a great vintage of Leeuwin chardonnay. All the maker's hallmarks are there in abundance: tremendous fruit concentration, creamy cashew-nut, toasted hazelnut and honey flavours of great complexity and fantastic length on the palate. A magnificent wine to serve with BBQ lobster tails. Just compare it to a premier or grand cru Burgundy and you won't quibble about the price.

Quality	♟♟♟♟♟
Value	★★★★
Grapes	chardonnay
Region	Margaret River, WA
Cellar	➥ 6
Alc./Vol.	13.5%
RRP	$67.50

PENGUIN BEST
WHITE WINE
& BEST
CHARDONNAY

Le Grys Sauvignon Blanc

The label tells us that Le Grys, the name of one of the owners (Jennifer Joselin) dates back to 1066. Blood's thicker than wine . . .

CURRENT RELEASE 1997 This is a vibrant sauvignon with bell-clear varietal and regional identity. There are intense capsicum and lantana characters on the nose, and the palate has delicacy, softness and life. There's a touch of the pussycat about it, which doesn't detract. Try it with lamb's brains.

Quality	♟♟♟♟♟
Value	★★★★
Grapes	sauvignon blanc
Region	Marlborough, NZ
Cellar	▮ 1
Alc./Vol.	12.5%
RRP	$19.00

Leydens Vale Chardonnay

The label comes from Blue Pyrenees estate and is named after one of the first land-holders in the Avoca district.

CURRENT RELEASE 1997 The nose has distinctive fig, melon and peach aromas. The palate is medium- to full-bodied with rich peach flavours. The wood is bordering on the stroppy side – it's fresh and assertive, but time in the bottle will remedy this. It should be served with a light chill. It can handle roast turkey.

Quality	♟♟♟♟
Value	★★★★
Grapes	chardonnay
Region	Pyrenees, Vic.
Cellar	▮ 3
Alc./Vol.	13.0%
RRP	$18.00

Leydens Vale Noble Semillon

Quality	ҮҮҮҮ
Value	★★★★
Grapes	semillon
Region	Pyrenees, Vic.
Cellar	🍷 4
Alc./Vol.	12.0%
RRP	$15.00 (375 ml)

The label offers a great depiction of noble rot-affected grapes. In the crusher the juice often looks like liquid cow manure but miracles happen and golden nectar results.

CURRENT RELEASE 1996 The nose has some musty botrytis aromas plus dried apricot and peel notes. The palate is medium-bodied and complex with lots of lime, lemon and apricot flavours. The finish offers plenty of acid. It needs a big chill and has refreshing qualities. Try it with smoked salmon.

Leydens Vale Riesling

Quality	ҮҮҮҮ
Value	★★★★
Grapes	riesling
Region	Pyrenees, Vic.
Cellar	🍷 2
Alc./Vol.	12.0%
RRP	$15.00

Aged Pyrenees riesling, now there's a thought. No sooner thought than done. The wine has developed well.

CURRENT RELEASE 1995 The nose has biscuit and lime aromas with a wisp of kero. The palate is rich with strong lime flavours and there's plenty of acid on the finish. It can take the big chill and is great with beer-battered flathead.

Leydens Vale Sauvignon Blanc

Quality	ҮҮҮҮ
Value	★★★★
Grapes	sauvignon blanc
Region	Pyrenees, Vic.
Cellar	🍷 2
Alc./Vol.	13.0%
RRP	$15.00

The label gives you a lesson in viticulture with an authentic rendition of the variety and the leaf formation.

CURRENT RELEASE 1997 This is a big wine with a powerful grassy nose. The palate has sweetness and rich tropical fruit flavours. Passionfruit and pineapple are dominant, and there's plenty of acid on an assertive finish. The wine can be served well-chilled and it's great with black-lip mussels poached in a drop of the same.

Lindemans Bin 65 Chardonnay

This is the sixth biggest-selling chardonnay in the US, never mind anywhere else. They made 1.5 million cases of the '98, an amazing achievement. No fewer than 19 winegrowing areas are represented in the blend. Maker: Phillip John and team.

CURRENT RELEASE 1997 This is a fresh young chardonnay made to drink well now. It's straightforward in terms of structure, with peach and melon flavours dominating the nose and palate. The wine has a light to medium body and the finish is clean. You can serve it fairly well-chilled with fish and chips.

Quality	♈♈♈♈
Value	★★★★
Grapes	chardonnay
Region	various, Vic.
Cellar	🍾 1 year
Alc./Vol.	13.0%
RRP	$9.70 Ⓢ

CURRENT RELEASE 1998 Just a few weeks old when tasted, but already in its prime! A full buttercup yellow, it has a voluminous bouquet of ripe peach, cashew and buttered toast which leaps from the glass. It tastes rich and fruity, but also incredibly soft and smooth – almost unctuous. It fills the mouth with flavour and has no sharp edges. It isn't sweet, nor does it show youthfully aggressive acid. In short, it's a winemaking triumph to make a white wine taste so good so young. Food: spicy chicken wings.

Quality	♈♈♈♈
Value	★★★★★
Grapes	chardonnay
Region	various
Cellar	🍾 2
Alc./Vol.	13.5%
RRP	$9.70 Ⓢ

PENGUIN WINE OF THE YEAR AND BEST BARGAIN WHITE

Lindemans Bin 77 Semillon Chardonnay

Yet another variation on a theme, this range seems to be expanding and the price is right.

CURRENT RELEASE 1997 Straight down the middle in terms of style. Peach and gooseberry on the nose, touch of sweetness on the palate, and peach flavours. The finish is dry but a tad short. It can be served well-chilled. Try it with stir-fried rice.

Quality	♈♈♈
Value	★★★
Grapes	semillon; chardonnay
Region	various, SA
Cellar	🍾 1
Alc./Vol.	12.5%
RRP	$10.00 Ⓢ

Lindemans Classic Dry White

Quality	♥♥♥
Value	★★★
Grapes	semillon; verdelho; sauvignon blanc; chardonnay
Region	not stated
Cellar	▮ 2
Alc./Vol.	12.5%
RRP	$10.80

It's hard to understand what makes a blend of semillon, verdelho, sauvignon blanc and chardonnay a classic dry white. It sounds more like a bucket of offcuts.

CURRENT RELEASE 1997   A useful white. The nose is herbal with gooseberry aromas. The medium-bodied palate has some complexity by dint of the blend. It's followed by a refreshing finish. It can be served with a medium chill. Try it with a ham salad.

Lindemans Limestone Coast Chardonnay

Quality	♥♥♥
Value	★★★
Grapes	chardonnay
Region	Limestone Coast, SA
Cellar	▮ 3
Alc./Vol.	13.0%
RRP	$11.30

The Limestone Coast is a broad regional description taking in Bordertown, Padthaway and Coonawarra.

CURRENT RELEASE 1997   This is the first release under this banner. The nose is peachy with some hint of melon and smoky wood. The palate is medium-bodied with peach and melon flavours, and the vanillan oak is dominant on the finish. Don't over-chill, and serve it with crayfish.

Lindemans Padthaway Vineyard Chardonnay

Quality	♥♥♥♥
Value	★★★★
Grapes	chardonnay
Region	Padthaway, SA
Cellar	▮ 3
Alc./Vol.	13.5%
RRP	$16.00

The Padthaway vineyard has become a presence in the marketplace. It's always a rich and affordable style that never lacks flavour.

CURRENT RELEASE 1997   As usual, this example doesn't disappoint. The wood tends to get in the way at the moment, adding a strong smoky element to the nose. There's underlying peach aroma. The wood intrudes on the palate and there are peach and melon fruit components. Naturally oak dominates the finish with a nutty smoky texture. It should not be over-chilled, and goes well with smoked chicken.

Lowe Mudgee Chardonnay

Ex-Rothbury winemaker David Lowe is widely travelled and experienced. He and his wife Jane have settled back in his home area of Mudgee to develop their own brand. The packaging is very smart.
CURRENT RELEASE 1997 Made from 20-year-old Mudgee vines owned by the Lowe family. It's a lightly wooded, delicate style: there are herbal, lemon and lanolin aromas and a touch of grapefruit in the mouth. It's fruit-driven and pleasingly dry, but not especially complex. A refreshing drink now, although a year or two's age will probably do no harm.

Quality	♥♥♥♥
Value	★★★⭒
Grapes	chardonnay
Region	Mudgee, NSW
Cellar	↓ 3+
Alc./Vol.	13.0%
RRP	$20.50

Maglieri Chardonnay

This company has been excelling with its gutsy reds, but the whites are somewhat less inspiring. Maker John Loxton.
CURRENT RELEASE 1996 The oak character is somewhat raw, reflecting the fact that it was matured in wood but not barrel-fermented. There's an assertive vanilla milkshake character and it's soft and light on the palate. A decent drink that won't set the world aflame.

Quality	♥♥⭒
Value	★★★
Grapes	chardonnay
Region	McLaren Vale, SA
Cellar	↓ 1
Alc./Vol.	13.5%
RRP	$14.20

Maglieri Scenario Soft Press

Buzzwords like 'soft press' are all the rage in the ultra-trendy modern wine biz. The see-through bottle magnifies the back of the label, which features a Rubenesque nude. Naughty, naughty!
CURRENT RELEASE 1997 This has an appropriate light yellow hue and the nose is decidedly spicy. In the mouth it's light and straightforward with grassy and spicy flavours, a little sweetness, and a soft dry finish. A decent drink and the bottle's a conversation piece! Try with seafood and salad.

Quality	♥♥♥
Value	★★★⭒
Grapes	semillon; sauvignon blanc; chenin blanc
Region	McLaren Vale, SA
Cellar	↓ 1
Alc./Vol.	12.0%
RRP	$13.30

Main Ridge Estate Chardonnay

Quality	♥♥♥
Value	★★ʳ
Grapes	chardonnay
Region	Mornington Peninsula, Vic.
Cellar	↓ 2
Alc./Vol.	13.0%
RRP	$33.00 (cellar door)

Nat White lays claim to being one of the pioneers of the Mornington Peninsula wine industry. The vineyard is high on the red soil ridge.

CURRENT RELEASE 1996   '96 was what they term a difficult vintage on the peninsula, meaning that there was rain, rot and a lot of botrytis in the whites. This has some apricot and marmalade botrytis characters plus a certain asparagus character from the cold year. The palate has some hardness and green acid. Best served with food to combat the acid. Try with a gratin of asparagus.

Marienberg Reserve Chardonnay

Quality	♥♥♥♥
Value	★★★★
Grapes	chardonnay
Region	McLaren Vale, SA
Cellar	↓ 3
Alc./Vol.	13.7%
RRP	$16.40

Marienberg was founded by the winemaker Ursula Marie Pridham, whose label used to feature a medallion with her own head in profile. These days Marienberg is one of several brands owned by Hill International.

CURRENT RELEASE 1997   The nose is slightly volcanic but when the sulfur breathes off it has peach and melon fruit aromas with a well-judged nutty oak influence. Could benefit from six months' cellaring. The balance and style of the wine are good and the flavour lingers well. Suits serving with yabbies.

Massoni Red Hill Chardonnay

Quality	♥♥♥♥ʳ
Value	★★★ʳ
Grapes	chardonnay
Region	Mornington Peninsula, Vic.
Cellar	↓ 3
Alc./Vol.	13.5%
RRP	$33.00

Red Hill is a stretch of volcanic red soil on the hilltops of the Mornington Peninsula. It takes smart viticulture to produce good results. And good vintages like '97.

CURRENT RELEASE 1997   Very much a cool-climate chardonnay. This has high acidity as well as an obvious malolactic character, which gives a butterscotch note. It also has good fruit character and complexity. The mouth-feel has viscosity and roundness and the finish is persistent. Goes well with crayfish.

McLarens On The Lake Chardonnay

Great label. It's a duck waddling about with a red gingham napkin around its neck. Is it about to *have* lunch or *be* lunch?

CURRENT RELEASE 1997   Very good basic chardonnay, smelling of peaches and nuts. It's mostly about varietal fruit with just a smidgin of cleverly applied oak. The palate has some real richness and depth, more than we'd expect to find at the price. Drink it with chicken à l'orange.

Quality	♛♛♛♛
Value	★★★★⊦
Grapes	chardonnay
Region	not stated
Cellar	▮ 2
Alc./Vol.	13.0%
RRP	$12.80 Ⓢ

McLarens On The Lake Colombard Semillon Chardonnay

Phew, what a mouthful! Why not a simple name such as Andy's Answer? Winemaker Andrew Garrett (yes, the real one) sold his first two companies and his name to Mildara Blass. This is his third incarnation.

CURRENT RELEASE 1997   This has modest aspirations, and achieves them. The colour is mid-yellow, the nose has spicy, earthy and slightly muscat-like aromatics, and the palate is very light and basic. The acid carries the finish and doesn't challenge the senses. Quaff with fish and chips.

Quality	♛♛⸘
Value	★★★
Grapes	colombard; semillon;
	chardonnay
Region	not stated
Cellar	▮ 1
Alc./Vol.	10.5%
RRP	$11.20 Ⓢ

McWilliams Hanwood Chardonnay

The McWilliams complex is just outside Griffith at the village of Hanwood. The tasting room is the biggest barrel you're ever likely to clap eyes on.

CURRENT RELEASE 1996   Remarkably fresh for a '96! We assume it's been in tank for most of the last two years. Fresh, simple, herbal aroma, with a hint of greenness. Light-bodied and straightforward with softness for drinkability. Certainly not complex, but good value for money. Try it with wonton soup and a coriander garnish. ▸

Quality	♛♛♛
Value	★★★⊦
Grapes	chardonnay
Region	Riverina, NSW
Cellar	▮ 1
Alc./Vol.	13.0%
RRP	$10.20 Ⓢ

Quality	♟♟♟♗
Value	★★★★⸸
Grapes	chardonnay
Region	Riverina, NSW
Cellar	▬ 2
Alc./Vol.	14.0%
RRP	$10.20 ⑤

CURRENT RELEASE 1997 A triple-trophy winner at the Griffith Show, and while it's terrific value and a very high-quality cheapie, it's still a cheapie. Cashew and herbal chardonnay aromas; clean, fresh and simple. No obvious oak, and fairly short on the finish, but there's pristine chardonnay flavour and we'd be happy to serve it at our table. Serve with scampi.

McWilliams Mount Pleasant Chardonnay

Quality	♟♟♟
Value	★★★
Grapes	chardonnay
Region	Hunter Valley, NSW
Cellar	▬ 2
Alc./Vol.	13.5%
RRP	$14.00 ⑤

The capsules have Phil Ryan's signature on them, but nowhere is it explained who he is. (He's the winemaker.) CURRENT RELEASE 1996 A straightforward fruit-driven wine that recalls more of a regional Hunter dry white than a varietal chardonnay. It has a full yellow colour. The nose is of straw or dry grass with a background of fresh herbs, and the taste is dry and almost austere. A lean and fairly low-key wine, which teams well with chicken schnitzel.

McWilliams Mount Pleasant Elizabeth

Quality	♟♟♟♟♗
Value	★★★★★
Grapes	semillon
Region	Hunter Valley, NSW
Cellar	▬ 6
Alc./Vol.	10.0%
RRP	$14.75 ⑤

There's a debate raging about whether this wine is damaging the reputation of fine aged Hunter semillon by being so inexpensive. The thrust is that great wine shouldn't be cheap. Our attitude is make hay while the sun shines.

Previous outstanding vintages: '82, '83, '86, '87, '89, '91

CURRENT RELEASE 1993 **An impressive Elizabeth, still youthful and filled with fresh herbal (basil and parsley) aromas and a little toasty development. The palate has a tart, lemony beginning and follows a lean profile that finishes dry and citrusy. It's lean now and will flesh out with further age. The price sometimes dips as low as $12 and is great value. Serve with crab cakes.**

Milburn Park Chardonnay

This won a trophy at the '96 Melbourne Wine Show. Dare we suggest that this type of Murray Valley white is best shown (and drunk) as young as possible?
CURRENT RELEASE 1996   Deep golden colour, very developed bouquet, toasty and liqueury smelling – it's more like tokay than chardonnay! Big, blowzy developed flavour with no subtlety. A thick, syrupy palate with the incongruous flavours of green/herbal fruit and major age development. A good ad for drinking young.

Quality	♟♟♟
Value	★★★
Grapes	chardonnay
Region	Murray Valley, Vic.
Cellar	▮
Alc./Vol.	13.0%
RRP	$13.00 Ⓢ

Milburn Park Reserve Chardonnay

Milburn Park is one of the many labels of the Alambie Wine Co. It has a big winery at Irymple, near Mildura. Maker Bob Shields.
CURRENT RELEASE 1997   This is a lightweight with happily subtle wood and an interesting melange of tea-leaf, grape juice, herbal and straw aromas. It has a straightforward fruit-accented palate and is well-balanced. It drinks well now with seafood pizza.

Quality	♟♟♟
Value	★★★
Grapes	chardonnay
Region	Murray Valley, Vic.
Cellar	▮ 2
Alc./Vol.	13.5%
RRP	$13.15 Ⓢ

Mildara Blass Half Mile Creek Chardonnay

Mildara reveals a case of the Banrocks here. The back label is crammed with new-age bullshit and if you fall for it, you'll fall for anything.
CURRENT RELEASE 1997   A very decent wine that even tastes like Banrock Station. Peachy, cashew nut chardonnay aromas, plenty of fruit flavour, negligible wood involvement, and a tickle of volatility – but only pedantic wine scribes notice such things. Some richness and oodles of appeal at the price. Serve with KFC.

Quality	♟♟♟
Value	★★★
Grapes	chardonnay
Region	Cowra, NSW
Cellar	▮ 1
Alc./Vol.	13.0%
RRP	$12.50 Ⓢ

Mildara Blass Half Mile Creek Verdelho

Quality	♆♆♆♆
Value	★★★★
Grapes	verdelho
Region	Hunter Valley, NSW
Cellar	▲ 2
Alc./Vol.	12.0%
RRP	$12.50 Ⓢ

Does Half Mile Creek run all the way from the Hunter (verdelho) to Cowra (chardonnay)? And why haven't they gone metric? Oh, we do like to make fun of the image-makers.

CURRENT RELEASE 1997   This is a nicely turned-out verdelho. It has an attractive green–yellow colour, some richness in its herbal/straw and lemony aromas, and an enticingly zesty taste. There are delicate spicy flavours and a twist of sweetness that dries nicely on the aftertaste. Very more-ish. Serve with fish balls.

Miranda Christy's Land Semillon Sauvignon Blanc

Quality	♆♆♆
Value	★★★⋆
Grapes	semillon; sauvignon blanc
Region	Riverina, NSW
Cellar	▲
Alc./Vol.	11.0%
RRP	$6.00

Interesting that even at the bottom end of the bottled-wine market they're starting to dream up brand-names for basic quaffing wines.

CURRENT RELEASE 1996   This is a simple white wine that offers very good value at a humble price. It has some nettle and green-stalk aromas and the acidity is prominent and tastes 'corrected'; that is, it's come out of a bag rather than the grape itself. The palate is light, fruity and short, which is quite acceptable if you have it with food. Try it with vegetarian lasagna.

Miranda Golden Botrytis

Quality	♆♆♆♆♆
Value	★★★★★
Grapes	semillon; riesling
Region	Riverina, NSW; King Valley, Vic.
Cellar	▲ 3
Alc./Vol.	11.0%
RRP	$14.00 (375 ml) Ⓢ

This is a dual-trophy, six-time gold medal winner and a great wine to boot, but the makers had to drop the price to sell it because they made too much.

CURRENT RELEASE 1995   Golden it is. And the nose smells like liquid gold: honey, toffee, butterscotch and lots of other things. It's very sweet and luscious with great flavour and harmony. The texture is very viscous and gives new meaning to the word rich. A beautiful wine to have with caramelised tarte tatin.

PENGUIN BEST SWEET WINE

Miranda Grey Series Chardonnay

Miranda is one of several larger companies to get interested in King Valley grapes, to the extent that it now
has a fully fledged winery there.
CURRENT RELEASE 1996   Intriguing stuff: the nose has
guava/tropical fruit, a tea-leafy herbal scent typical of
Miranda's King Valley whites, and some buttery overtones. The oak is gently handled and adds an aromatic
component. A most entertaining drink, but cellaring is
not recommended.

Quality	♟♟♟♟
Value	★★★★ｋ
Grapes	chardonnay
Region	Barossa Valley, SA; King Valley, Vic.
Cellar	▮ 1
Alc./Vol.	13.5%
RRP	$14.00 Ⓢ

Miranda Mirrool Creek Chardonnay

Mirrool Creek is a real creek in the Riverina. The wine
has a money-back guarantee if you're unhappy with the
quality. We don't believe you would be.
CURRENT RELEASE 1997   This is a rising star in the
quaffing chardonnay category, and could give Lindemans
Bin 65 a shake. It has a full yellow colour and a soft,
rich, peach and cashew aroma that is dinky-di chardonnay. It's full of flavour, has surprisingly good weight and
a satisfying finish. Try it with stirfried chicken.

Quality	♟♟♟ｌ
Value	★★★★
Grapes	chardonnay
Region	Riverina, NSW
Cellar	▮ 1
Alc./Vol.	13.5%
RRP	$9.20 Ⓢ

Miranda Show Reserve Eden Valley Chardonnay

This is the top of the tree for Miranda, a company with
a thousand and one labels.
CURRENT RELEASE 1995   Golden colour and plenty of
development here. A big solid lump of a wine, with bags
of full-frontal oaky chardonnay flavour that is starting to
fatten out a bit. It's a complex style, with smoke and
toast aromas over peach and herbal fruit. Not a wine of
finesse, but many will love its buxom heartiness. Serve
with roast chicken.

Quality	♟♟♟♟ｌ
Value	★★★ｋ
Grapes	chardonnay
Region	Eden Valley, SA
Cellar	▮ 2
Alc./Vol.	13.5%
RRP	$24.50 Ⓢ

Mitchell The Growers Semillon

Quality 🍷🍷🍷
Value ★★★
Grapes semillon; sauvignon blanc
Region Clare Valley, SA
Cellar 🍾 4
Alc./Vol. 13.0%
RRP $14.00

The Mitchells believe in Clare semillon, but they don't even try to make chardonnay, which tells you what they think of that variety in their area.

CURRENT RELEASE 1997 This is very lightly oaked with French wood, and has a lightly nutty overtone to the straw-like, herbal varietal fruit. It has a big presence in the mouth, with strong flavour and a little hardness on the finish. It's better with food: try pasta with pesto.

Mitchell Watervale Riesling

Quality 🍷🍷🍷🍷🍷
Value ★★★★★
Grapes riesling
Region Clare Valley, SA
Cellar 🍾 9
Alc./Vol. 11.5%
RRP $14.75

The 1997 harvest brought an embarrassment of riches for the riesling makers of Clare. Despite a heatwave in February, they made great wines. Maker Andrew Mitchell.

Previous outstanding vintages: '86, '88, '91, '92, '93, '94, '95

CURRENT RELEASE 1997 This one's come up superbly with a little bottle-age. It started off looking reserved, then blossomed in the bottle. It has impressive intensity and volume of citrus flavour. There's richness, concentration and length, and the promise of a big future. Food: trout and almonds.

Mitchelton Blackwood Park Riesling

Quality 🍷🍷🍷🍷
Value ★★★★
Grapes riesling
Region Goulburn Valley, Vic.
Cellar 🍾 4
Alc./Vol. 12.5%
RRP $14.00 (S)

Mitchelton is part of the Petaluma group. Don Lewis has been winemaker since the earliest days, and his name is highly regarded in the wine biz.

Previous outstanding vintages: '85, '90, '91, '92, '94, '95, '96

CURRENT RELEASE 1997 Doesn't seem to show quite the botrytis lift that is typical of previous vintages. The nose is shy, spicy, ethereal, with some nettles and minerals. It's a lighter wine, with delicacy and fresh acid on the finish. Goes well with scallops *en brochette*.

Mitchelton Chardonnay

This wine gets the full treatment: barrel-fermentation malolactic, various oaks, lees-stirring and skin contact in an effort to imbue it with maximum complexity. Makers Don Lewis and Alan George.

CURRENT RELEASE 1996 Botrytis characteristics are evident in this wine, a fairly common event in '96 southern Victorian whites. There are aromas of apricot and fig jam, together with toasty oak and nutty elements. In the mouth, it's lean and dry, finishing with savoury flavours. Could go well with chicken schnitzel.

Quality	♟♟♟♟
Value	★★★
Grapes	chardonnay
Region	various, Vic.
Cellar	▮ 2
Alc./Vol.	13.5%
RRP	$23.80 ⑤

Mitchelton Marsanne

Another new label; this time it looks as though the Mitchelton III white blend is reborn. It's barrel-fermented and is like a junior version of the Reserve Marsanne.

CURRENT RELEASE 1996   Toasty, cedary oak characters flood the bouquet and palate, making for a rich, opulent, slightly broad style of dry white with good complexity and mouth-feel. It really fills the mouth and goes well with honey prawns and noodles.

Quality	♟♟♟♟
Value	★★★★
Grapes	marsanne 85%; plus viognier and roussanne
Region	Goulburn Valley, Vic.
Cellar	▮ 4
Alc./Vol.	13.0%
RRP	$15.60

Mitchelton Reserve Marsanne

This is a serious heavyweight dry white, made in an extreme style that is as different from neighbour Chateau Tahbilk's as imaginable. Maker Don Lewis.

Previous outstanding vintages: '80, '82, '84, '86, '88, '90
CURRENT RELEASE 1994 Deep yellow colour and a very developed, complex nose of butterscotch, pineapple and asparagus aromas. The palate is soft and broad and has filled right out. Oak and bottle-age tend to domi nate. A big mouthful of white wine. Try it with stuffed roast chicken.

Quality	♟♟♟♟
Value	★★★
Grapes	marsanne
Region	Goulburn Valley, Vic.
Cellar	▮ 4
Alc./Vol.	13.0%
RRP	$23.80

Monichino Chardonnay

Quality	♥♥♥♥
Value	★★★★⅜
Grapes	chardonnay
Region	Goulburn Valley, Vic.
Cellar	▮ 2
Alc./Vol.	13.8%
RRP	$14.75

This is a discovery! A little-known producer in the northern Goulburn Valley producing wines of real merit across the board – at prices that loosen the wallet. Maker Carlo Monichino.

CURRENT RELEASE 1996   This is a nicely balanced chardonnay with clean, peachy, ripe fruit flavours and a little toasty oak that's nicely understated. Rich fruit on the palate is backed by toasty oak and a semblance of sweetness, due to fairly high alcohol. Ageing gracefully, too. Try it with roast chicken.

Montana Reserve Marlborough Chardonnay

Quality	♥♥♥⅜
Value	★★★
Grapes	chardonnay
Region	Marlborough, NZ
Cellar	▮ 2
Alc./Vol.	13.0%
RRP	$28.70

This is part of a new range of Montana's, and comes in a special heavy-glass bottle with a thick lip.

CURRENT RELEASE 1996   The butterscotch-like malolactic characters are typical of New Zealand, and tend to dominate this wine. In the mouth, it's very soft with a hint of sweetness but lacks a bit of focus. It has plenty of flavour and the buttery character appeals to many people.

Montara Grampians Chardonnay

Quality	♥♥♥⅜
Value	★★★
Grapes	chardonnay
Region	Grampians, Vic.
Cellar	▮ 4
Alc./Vol.	13.0%
RRP	$20.00

The Montara vineyard is almost in the township of Ararat, on the lower slopes of Mount Chalambar. Maker Mike McRae.

CURRENT RELEASE 1996   This one has an aroma of restrained passionfruit, with touches of honey and vanilla. A subtle wine, it has honey and marmalade characters in the mouth and a trace of sweetness. The finish is a trifle short, but it could be a pleasant drink with chicken stuffed with apricots.

Moondah Brook Chardonnay

Moondah started off being a single vineyard wine from the patch of the same name, at Gingin, north of Perth, but is now a blend of WA regions. Maker Paul Lapsley. CURRENT RELEASE 1996 Wow, this is rich stuff indeed. Toasty oak gives extra authority and a certain rubbery character to the developed bouquet. It's big and powerful with some astringency on the finish due to the alcohol and oak, and you'd be pedantic to want more flavour than this from a chardonnay. Needs rich food, such as veal sweetbreads.

Quality	♥♥♥♥
Value	★★★★
Grapes	chardonnay
Region	various, WA
Cellar	🍾 2
Alc./Vol.	13.5%
RRP	$15.60 Ⓢ

CURRENT RELEASE 1997   A terrific wine, and a bargain at $16! The colour is bright lemon yellow. The nose is pungent with fine grapefruit, peach and passionfruit aromas. The oak is less evident than earlier vintages. There's a creamy, sur-lie character and while it's a lighter-weight style, it has great finesse, crispness and elegance. A beaut drink with barbecued scallops.

Quality	♥♥♥♥♥
Value	★★★★★
Grapes	chardonnay
Region	various, WA
Cellar	🍾 4+
Alc./Vol.	13.5%
RRP	$15.95 Ⓢ

Moondah Brook Chenin Blanc

Chenin blanc has more street cred in WA than most places, thanks to its long and glorious history as the major grape in Houghton's White Burgundy. Maker Paul Lapsley.
CURRENT RELEASE 1996   Moondah chenin is always released with some bottle-age, and this is an impressive model that is ageing gracefully. It has a clean, fresh bouquet of chalky, mineral and apple aromas, and the palate is fresh and delicate for its age. It's fruit-driven, soft, round and finishes dry, which is itself unusual for the Australian chenin. Serve it with niçoise salad.

Quality	♥♥♥♥
Value	★★★★
Grapes	chenin blanc
Region	Darling Ranges, WA
Cellar	🍾 2
Alc./Vol.	13.0%
RRP	$16.00 Ⓢ

Moondah Brook Maritime WA Dry White

Quality	♟♟♟
Value	★★★
Grapes	verdelho; sauvignon blanc; and others
Region	Darling Ranges; Great Southern, WA
Cellar	▮ 1
Alc./Vol.	12.5%
RRP	$12.50 ⑤

Is there a revival of non-vintage table wines going on out there? This new 'concept' wine has a blue synthetic cork, which helps retain its fruit freshness.

CURRENT RELEASE *non-vintage* Nice and fresh, with gooseberry and sweaty herbaceous WA characters leaping out of the glass. (Why do all Houghton/Moondah wines smell like this?) It's a very nice drink, with bags of fruit, although the structure is a tad flimsy, which goes with the grassiness. A very decent quaff while young, and good value. Food: salads.

Moorebank Charlton Chardonnay

Quality	♟♟♟
Value	★★★
Grapes	chardonnay
Region	Hunter Valley, NSW
Cellar	▮ 1
Alc./Vol.	12.5%
RRP	$24.50 (500 ml)

The back label of this snappily packaged wine makes an ambitious cellaring statement. We find it's already as mature as we'd like to drink it.

CURRENT RELEASE 1996 An unsubtle wine showing forward development, this chardonnay is full yellow in colour and the bouquet is all about developed apricot and marmalade scents. The toasty and citrus peel flavours translate onto the palate, where they are somewhat blowzy, with a phenolic grip to finish. Serve with egg-and-bacon pie.

Moorebank Dry Style Gewürztraminer

Quality	♟♟♟
Value	★★
Grapes	gewürztraminer
Region	Hunter Valley, NSW
Cellar	▮ 1
Alc./Vol.	11.0%
RRP	$19.50 (500 ml)

Where's the best place in Australia to grow traminer? Probably somewhere a lot cooler than the Hunter Valley, but we give them points for trying. It has very snazzy packaging.

CURRENT RELEASE 1997 An unusual style that smacks of apricot jam and pineapple, which may reflect some botrytis in the grapes. The taste is very light and there's a trace of sweetness together with some astringency on the finish. The overall impression is dry and very laid-back. Try it with sesame prawns.

Moorebank Late Harvest Gewürztraminer

This is probably a better use for traminer in the Hunter than a dry wine. Proprietors are Debra Moore and Ian Burgess.
CURRENT RELEASE 1996 Lots happening here. There are apricot and spiced honey late-picked notes under lanolin and slightly sulfury elements. It's very sweet in a juicy sort of way, without real richness, and there's an appley note and plenty of acid on the finish. Should go well with fruit salad.

Quality	ՄՄՄՅ
Value	★★ր
Grapes	gewürztraminer
Region	Hunter Valley, NSW
Cellar	🍷 2
Alc./Vol.	11.0%
RRP	$24.50 (500 ml)

Moorebank Summar Semillon

Nothing to do with that well-known semillon-drinking season. Summar is the name of the proprietor's daughter.
CURRENT RELEASE 1996 There's a lot of lanolin in the bouquet, to the point of a slight shearing-shed aroma. The wine is very delicate and seems to be ageing slowly. A passionfruit/tropical character is added on the palate. Could improve with age, but drinks well now with delicate fish dishes.

Quality	ՄՄՄ
Value	★★★
Grapes	semillon
Region	Hunter Valley, NSW
Cellar	🍷 5
Alc./Vol.	10.5%
RRP	$19.50 (500 ml)

Moorilla Estate Chardonnay

This is a 100% barrel-fermented style sourced from the West Tamar. Moorilla is now owned by a syndicate of Tasmanian investors. Maker Alain Rousseau.
CURRENT RELEASE 1996 This is a product of a less-than-satisfactory season. It has an odd combination of herbaceous and botrytis-affected flavours, as well as searing acidity. It smells of honey, bracken, apricot and vanilla, and while it's not very chardish, it's a good drink, especially with the right sort of food to meet that acid. Try it with a creamy scallop dish.

Quality	ՄՄՄՅ
Value	★★ր
Grapes	chardonnay
Region	Tamar Valley, Tas.
Cellar	🍷 2
Alc./Vol.	12.7%
RRP	$26.60

Moorilla Estate Gewürztraminer

Quality	ΨΨΨΨ𝗍
Value	★★★𝗍
Grapes	gewürztraminer
Region	Tasmania
Cellar	🍶 5
Alc./Vol.	12.0%
RRP	$27.00

On paper, Tassie is a very suitable place for traminer, and the proof is in the pudding – this year, and indeed most years. Maker Alain Rousseau.

CURRENT RELEASE 1997 A discreetly spicy gewürz, with a youthful light yellow colour and an unmistakable lychee, rose-petal aroma. It's a fine wine, perhaps lighter than in warmer, drier years, but with good intensity and length, and the balance is very pleasing. Try it with a cold duck and lychee green salad.

Morris Semillon

Quality	ΨΨΨΨ𝗍
Value	★★★★𝗍
Grapes	semillon
Region	not stated
Cellar	🍶 3
Alc./Vol.	13.0%
RRP	$13.60 ⑤

The Morris white wines are made by parent company Orlando. Where the grapes come from is not always clear.

CURRENT RELEASE 1996 This is developing a toasty, dry-straw, aged-semillon bouquet but is still very lively and fresh. A very attractive style with a hint of wood-maturation. There are lanolin, lemon, toast and straw flavours in the mouth and it finishes dry. Most impressive in the Top 100 judging, where it teamed well with lime-marinated fish.

Morton Estate Hawkes Bay Chardonnay

Quality	ΨΨΨ𝗍
Value	★★★
Grapes	chardonnay
Region	Hawkes Bay, NZ
Cellar	🍶 2
Alc./Vol.	13.0%
RRP	$20.70

This well-established winery has changed hands and long-time winemaker John Hancock has left to start his own venture. Maker Steve Bird.

CURRENT RELEASE 1996 Terrifically complex wine very much in the tradition of the marque, with solid butterscotch, sur-lie characters. A fair botrytis influence is suspected. Lots of honey on the nose and palate, although it lacks a little fruit in the mouth and the finish carries some bitter phenolics. A confronting style! Try it with barbecued crayfish.

Mountadam Chardonnay

Somebody with a penchant for purple prose is penning the Mountadam back labels: 'when the corkscrew performs its pretty pirouette'. Indeed!
CURRENT RELEASE 1996 Adam Wynn sure is making 'em big these days. Smoky, toasty, apricot, light asparagus aromas, and the same flavours come through into the mouth, where it's big and slightly clumsy with some oaky grip and a little alcohol warmth to close. Strong flavours; not a wine of subtlety. Serve with lobster.

Quality	▼▼▼▼
Value	★★★ꜩ
Grapes	chardonnay
Region	High Eden Ridge, SA
Cellar	▮ 3
Alc./Vol.	14.5%
RRP	$33.00

Mount Avoca Classic Dry White

Trebbiano, the ubiquitous white grape of Italy, is the basis of this wine. It was the big hope of the Pyrenees district in its formative years.
CURRENT RELEASE 1997 This is a nice drink: it has real delicacy and you can drink more than one glass without it palling. Light yellow hue; fresh, lightly floral nose; slightly cashewy flavour enlivened by frisky acidity. Goes well with salads.

Quality	▼▼▼▼
Value	★★★★
Grapes	trebbiano 56%; semillon 28%; sauvignon blanc 16%
Region	Pyrenees, Vic.
Cellar	▮ 2
Alc./Vol.	12.5%
RRP	$14.80

Mount Helen Chardonnay

The old Tisdall name has finally bowed out – this Mildara Blass brand is just called Mount Helen. Maker Toni Stockhausen.
CURRENT RELEASE 1997 A strongly oaked wine, and consequently rich and weighty on the palate with a drying finish. The oak seems high quality but is a trifle overdone. The palate is full and broad with plenty of flavour but without a great deal of finesse. Pair it with barbecued chicken.

Quality	▼▼▼ꜩ
Value	★★★
Grapes	chardonnay
Region	Strathbogie Ranges, Vic.
Cellar	▮ 3
Alc./Vol.	13.5%
RRP	$22.20

Mount Horrocks Chardonnay

Quality	♟♟♟♟
Value	★★★★
Grapes	chardonnay
Region	Clare Valley, SA
Cellar	🍷 2
Alc./Vol.	13.0%
RRP	$17.25

This 'mountain' was named after the early settler, John Horrocks, who pitched camp in the Clare Valley in the 1840s. Maker Stephanie Toole.

CURRENT RELEASE 1997 A delicious fruit-driven chardonnay, which has no evidence of oak maturation. In this case, it's 'no wood is good'. Aromas of peach and cashew are enticing; the palate is smooth and fruity with a proliferation of peachy fruit. Very drinkable and takes a chill well. Try it with chicken and mushroom risotto.

Mount Horrocks Semillon

Quality	♟♟♟
Value	★★★
Grapes	semillon
Region	Clare Valley, SA
Cellar	🍷 5
Alc./Vol.	13.0%
RRP	$18.00

This is an attempt to do something more with semillon, to make it into a complex wine as a youngster, without waiting for bottle-age to work its magic. Maker Stephanie Toole.

CURRENT RELEASE 1997 Fermentation and maturation in French oak have added some subtle oak inflexions, but the dominant characters are of herbs and melony fruit. It's a soft, more open-knit, fuller style of semillon that finishes pleasingly dry. Just the shot for vegetarian lasagne.

Mount Horrocks Watervale Riesling

Quality	♟♟♟♟♟
Value	★★★★★
Grapes	riesling
Region	Clare Valley, SA
Cellar	🍷 6
Alc./Vol.	13.0%
RRP	$18.00

Mount Horrocks is Stephanie Toole's baby but with partner Jeff Grosset looking over her shoulder, how could she not make brilliant riesling?

CURRENT RELEASE 1997 A fabulous young riesling that smells of peach blossom, limes and flowers. There's a touch of sweetness on the forepalate which then fills out with generous, soft, ripe blossomy riesling flavour. It has great richness and length. Serve it with smoked salmon blinis.

Mount Langi Ghiran Chardonnay

This is a very exciting vineyard but unfortunately the whites tend to be eclipsed by the exceptional reds. The whites also deserve their place in the sun. Maker Trevor Mast.

CURRENT RELEASE 1997 Quite a refined style that sits at the citrus end of the chardonnay spectrum. The nose has lemon and grapefruit aromas on a creamy background. The medium-bodied palate has a creamy texture and an intense grapefruit flavour. The wood on the finish adds a savoury garnish. Don't over-chill, and serve it with smoked salmon.

Quality	?????
Value	★★★★
Grapes	chardonnay
Region	Western District, Vic.
Cellar	2
Alc./Vol.	13.0%
RRP	$19.95

Mount Mary Chardonnay

Mount Mary chardonnays are built for ageing, and John Middleton doesn't mind one iota if some think they lack fruit. He doesn't like 'fruity' wines.
Previous outstanding vintages: '92, '93, '94, '95
CURRENT RELEASE 1996 Restrained cashew, melon-like fruit aromas with very discreet oak. In the mouth it's delicate and dry, with understated – even austere – fruit, but great length and latent power. Excellent ageing potential. Cellar, then serve with crayfish.

Quality	?????
Value	★★★★
Grapes	chardonnay
Region	Yarra Valley, Vic.
Cellar	3–8+
Alc./Vol.	12.5%
RRP	$30.24 (cellar door)

Mount Mary Triolet

According to Dr John Middleton, who also plays the piano, a triolet is a trio of musical notes. It's one of only two or three Australian wines made from all three Bordeaux white varieties.
Previous outstanding vintages: '93
CURRENT RELEASE 1996 An unusual style, aged in old oak so it's not woody at all. The aromas recall sage bush, bracken and dry twigs. The palate is lean and tightly structured with bright flavours, frisky acid, and no greenness. Should develop like a good Graves. Try it with abalone.

Quality	????
Value	★★★
Grapes	sauvignon blanc 75%; semillon 22%; muscadelle 3%
Region	Yarra Valley, Vic.
Cellar	6+
Alc./Vol.	12.5%
RRP	$30.24 (cellar door)

Murrindindi Chardonnay

Quality	▼▼▼▼?
Value	★★★★
Grapes	chardonnay
Region	Yea, Vic.
Cellar	▲ 4
Alc./Vol.	13.0%
RRP	$23.80

The Cuthbertson family's vineyard is at Yea, just outside the Yarra Valley's boundary. It's been producing fine chardonnay for several years.
Previous outstanding vintages: '94, '95, '96
CURRENT RELEASE 1997 Strong malolactic influence shows here, with buttery and honeyed aromas and a rich, unctuous mouth-feel. There are herbal and candy notes and some Cognac-like oak. An excellent drink now with sesame prawns.

Nautilus Chardonnay

Quality	▼▼▼▼
Value	★★★★
Grapes	chardonnay
Region	Marlborough, NZ
Cellar	▲ 4
Alc./Vol.	13.0%
RRP	$21.00

This is a very sophisticated wine from Marlborough in New Zealand. It's part of the Hill Smith group.
CURRENT RELEASE 1996 The nose has peach and tropical fruit aromas. The medium-bodied palate has peach and pineapple flavours and there's some tinder-dry oak on a long finish. The wine should be served with a medium chill. Try it with raw tuna.

Nautilus Sauvignon Blanc

Quality	▼▼▼▼
Value	★★★★
Grapes	sauvignon blanc
Region	Marlborough, NZ
Cellar	▲ 3
Alc./Vol.	12.0%
RRP	$21.00

Very classy wine that has refinement but not at the expense of flavour. It's a wine from the textbooks.
CURRENT RELEASE 1996 The nose has gooseberry and tropical fruit elements. The palate is medium-weight with fresh gooseberry and herbal flavours. These are balanced by some crisp acid on a well-integrated finish. It can be served well-chilled and it goes well with spaghetti pesto.

Nepenthe Chardonnay

This one from the Adelaide Hills has all the bells and whistles including lees contact and barrel fermentation. This outfit runs on a no-expense-spared basis. Maker Peter Leske.

CURRENT RELEASE 1997 The nose has some caramel and oak toast as well as peach and melon aromas. The palate is full-bodied with a creamy texture. There are peach and nectarine flavours which are backed up by some toasty oak. It's great with chargrilled tuna.

Quality	?????
Value	****
Grapes	chardonnay
Region	Adelaide Hills, SA
Cellar	4
Alc./Vol.	14.0%
RRP	$25.00

Nepenthe Sauvignon Blanc

The name means a substance or a drug that banishes sorrow. Amen to that!

CURRENT RELEASE 1997 A pale sauvignon blanc from the Hills in a very fresh style. It has a fresh gooseberry nose with plenty of herbal notes. The palate is intense with tropical fruit and gooseberry flavours, and there's crisp acid on a fresh finish. A big chill doesn't hurt. Serve it with goat's cheese.

Quality	?????
Value	****
Grapes	sauvignon blanc
Region	Adelaide Hills, SA
Cellar	2
Alc./Vol.	11.0%
RRP	$17.00

Nepenthe Semillon

The use of this variety in these parts is somewhat unusual. It seems the winemaker has aimed for a real flavour statement.

CURRENT RELEASE 1997 A big bold style that makes much of obvious wood. The colour is a bright green–gold and the nose has toasty oak and gooseberry. There's a whiff of custard powder. The palate is creamy and there are strong gooseberry flavours which are followed by some powdery sensations from the wood treatment. It should not be served too cold and is great with smoked cod.

Quality	?????
Value	****
Grapes	semillon
Region	Adelaide Hills, SA
Cellar	4
Alc./Vol.	13.0%
RRP	$19.00

Neudorf Moutere Chardonnay

Quality	ŸŸŸŸŸ
Value	★★★★
Grapes	chardonnay
Region	Nelson, NZ
Cellar	🍶 5
Alc./Vol.	13.0%
RRP	$49.00

Tim and Judy Finn produce one of the classic New Zealand chardonnays from their 5.5-hectare vineyard at Moutere, near Nelson.
Previous outstanding vintages: '91, '93
CURRENT RELEASE 1996 With a fancy Burgundy bottle and fancy price, you'd expect something special. And it is. An immensely complex style of great power and singular character. The structure is taut and bodes well for ageing. The flavours are of toast, grilled nuts, white peach and honey, but like all fine wine, it's much more than words can describe. Just try it!

Normans Bin C 207 Chardonnay

Quality	ŸŸŸŸ
Value	★★★★⬩
Grapes	chardonnay
Region	Clarendon, SA
Cellar	🍶 3
Alc./Vol.	14.0%
RRP	$14.00

This is the mid-range label from Normans and it represents great value for money.
CURRENT RELEASE 1996 The wine is a hulking drop with plenty of intense fruit, alcohol and oak. There are peach aromas on the nose and the palate is very peachy with a mouthfilling texture. The American oak on the finish is quite strong, adding vanilla and toast. It can be served with a slight chill. Try it with pork chops in a peach sauce.

Quality	ŸŸŸŸ
Value	★★★★⬩
Grapes	chardonnay
Region	Clarendon, SA
Cellar	🍶 3
Alc./Vol.	14.0%
RRP	$14.00

CURRENT RELEASE 1997 They like building them big: lashings of oak wrestling with an equal weight of flavours. The nose is toasty with a hint of vanilla and peach. The palate is mouthfilling with rich peach and melon flavours that flood the palate. These are matched by toasty oak on a dry finish. It should be served at room temperature during winter.

Normans Family Reserve Riesling

This is a commercial style that is starting to show evidence of bottle-age. It drinks well. Maker Brian Light.

CURRENT RELEASE 1995 The nose is an interesting mix of kero, lime and other citrus aromas. The palate has a shock of lime, and there's a round texture. Acid still keeps the finish fresh. It can take a big chill and goes well with yabbies.

Quality	🍷🍷🍷
Value	★★★
Grapes	riesling
Region	Clarendon, SA
Cellar	🍾 2
Alc./Vol.	12.5%
RRP	$9.90

Normans Unwooded Chardonnay

Here's a wine that stepped out without its trousers. What would it have been like with wood?

CURRENT RELEASE 1997 The nose is toasty with underlying peach. There are tropical fruit flavours, apple and spices on the palate and the finish has fresh acid. Give it the kickstart of a big chill. The wine goes well with stirfried chicken and noodles.

Quality	🍷🍷🍷
Value	★★★
Grapes	chardonnay
Region	not stated
Cellar	🍾
Alc./Vol.	13.5%
RRP	$11.00

Normans Verdelho Bin C208

Yet another bloody verdelho, goes MS, but this one is actually quite nice. Originally the grape variety came from Portugal and it seems to produce good fruit in this location.

CURRENT RELEASE 1997 The emphasis is on tropical fruit; the nose has pineapple and passionfruit aromas. The medium-bodied palate has passionfruit and the aforementioned pineapple plus a hint of melon. The finish is dry and crisp. It can be served well-chilled. Try it with pasta with a rocket pesto.

Quality	🍷🍷🍷🍷
Value	★★★★
Grapes	verdelho
Region	McLaren Vale, SA
Cellar	🍾 4
Alc./Vol.	11.0%
RRP	$13.00

Notley Gorge Vineyard Chardonnay

Quality	♟♟♟
Value	★★★
Grapes	chardonnay
Region	Tamar Valley, Tas.
Cellar	♟ 3
Alc./Vol.	11.5%
RRP	$19.00

The vineyard was planted in 1983 and the annual production is around 3200 cases per year. Maker Andrew Hood (contract).
CURRENT RELEASE 1996 There's a strong lychee aroma on the nose and obvious oak. The palate is light with melon and citrus flavours. The oak and acid are quite concentrated and tend to dominate the fruit. For best results drink near room temperature. Try it with pan-fried calamari.

Oakland Semillon Sauvignon Blanc

Quality	♟♟♟
Value	★★★ʳ
Grapes	semillon; sauvignon blanc
Region	Barossa Valley, SA
Cellar	♟
Alc./Vol.	12.5%
RRP	$12.30 ⑤

Oakland is a secondary label for Grant Burge. It's pitched at the fighting varietal market.
CURRENT RELEASE 1997   Shy, subdued aromas have a dry-herb, straw-like character and there's good flavour intensity with lively acidity, giving it a slight tartness and finishing a trifle hard. The fruit is showing signs of developing quickly and will be best drunk as young as possible. Serve with salads.

Olssen Riesling

Quality	♟♟♟ʔ
Value	★★★ʳ
Grapes	riesling
Region	Clare Valley, SA
Cellar	♟ 5
Alc./Vol.	13.0%
RRP	$14.00

Olssen is a very small Clare Valley winery that sources its fruit from Watervale.
CURRENT RELEASE 1997   This is a good riesling from an outstanding vintage. Bread-doughy fermentation esters are still noticeable, together with lime zest and other citrus smells. It has lively acidity, a juicy middle, a well-balanced, dry-finishing palate and good length. The only downside is a twinge of volatility. Drinks well with John Dory meunière.

Orlando Jacob's Creek Riesling

Jacob's Creek was named after an early settler, William Jacob. It's not just a brand name: it really exists.
CURRENT RELEASE 1997 A respectable, well-made but ultimately simple riesling that only lacks intensity. The subdued aromas are of slate and minerals, and it seems a trifle dilute. Excellent value nonetheless, and deserves to win many friends. Serve with tofu.

Quality	♟♟♟
Value	★★★★
Grapes	riesling
Region	not stated
Cellar	▮ 1
Alc./Vol.	12.0%
RRP	$10.00 Ⓢ

Orlando Russet Ridge Chardonnay

This is a new label. These days, wines come in families and there seems to be a baby boom in progress. Even a sparkling Jacobs Creek is in the wings, we're told.
CURRENT RELEASE 1997 A rather clumsy, if flavoursome, white wine which has a slightly wood-dominant bouquet giving it vanilla and toasty aromas. The oak reappears on the finish and leaves a woody aftertaste. Best not to chill it, and serve with smoked cod.

Quality	♟♟♟
Value	★★▸
Grapes	chardonnay
Region	Coonawarra, SA
Cellar	▮ 1
Alc./Vol.	13.5%
RRP	$16.40 Ⓢ

Orlando Steingarten Riesling

The 'garden of stones' was planted by the Gramps high above the Barossa Valley floor to try to approximate the vineyards of the Rhine. Not all the grapes come from that vineyard these days.
CURRENT RELEASE 1997 A delicate, seamless wine that has abundant fruit but also great subtlety. The nose is shy, slightly doughy or estery, and the palate has a fluency of flavour that is tremendously charming. It's just a baby, and will do much with time. Serve with grilled whiting.

Quality	♟♟♟♟♟
Value	★★★★★
Grapes	riesling
Region	Eden Valley, SA
Cellar	▮ 10
Alc./Vol.	12.5%
RRP	$20.50

Orlando St Helga Riesling

What more evocative name could there be for a coy Barossa *fräulein* than Helga?
CURRENT RELEASE 1997 A fine, highly aromatic riesling that is St Helga at its pinnacle. This wine has it all: depth of fruit, finesse, delicacy and length. It has a nose like a bunch of flowers and the palate flavour is pristine. Goes well with crab.

Quality	♟♟♟♟♟
Value	★★★★★
Grapes	riesling
Region	Eden Valley, SA
Cellar	▮ 8+
Alc./Vol.	12.5%
RRP	$14.00 Ⓢ

Orlando St Hilary Chardonnay

Quality	▼▼▼▼?
Value	★★★★★
Grapes	chardonnay
Region	Padthaway, SA
Cellar	▮ 4
Alc./Vol.	13.0%
RRP	$15.75

Orlando should be able to sell plenty of this into the White House, political egos being what they are. Makers Bernie Hickin and team.

CURRENT RELEASE 1997   This is a fine, reserved wine – a turnaround for St Hilary from the woody wines of the past. The bouquet has subdued cashew and melon aromas and the palate begins with lemony flavours and vibrant, fresh acid. It tastes delicate yet intense, with lemon-lime flavours and jumpy acidity. Should go with ocean trout sashimi.

Pegasus Bay Chardonnay

Quality	▼▼▼▼
Value	★★★★
Grapes	chardonnay
Region	Canterbury, NZ
Cellar	▮ 3
Alc./Vol.	14.0%
RRP	$22.00

Established in 1992, this is a serious 20-hectare vineyard with a striking winery and restaurant. Production is at around 15 000 cases per annum.

CURRENT RELEASE 1996   The wine has obviously been given the treatment and the grapes were very ripe. The nose has strong peach and nectarine aromas. The palate is mouthfilling and rich with developed fruit flavours. There are several flavours, including lychee and grapefruit. The wood on the finish is very well integrated, and adds to the length of the wine. It should not be too cold. Try it with pan-fried quail.

Penfolds Barossa Valley Semillon Chardonnay

Quality	▼▼▼?
Value	★★★✦
Grapes	semillon;
	chardonnay
Region	Barossa Valley, SA
Cellar	▮ 2
Alc./Vol.	13.0%
RRP	$18.00

This is a soft, full-bodied style that was made for early and affordable drinking.

CURRENT RELEASE 1997   The nose has hay and gooseberry aromas. The palate is mouthfilling with peach and gooseberry flavours, and the finish shows some soft acid. It's probably destined to be over-chilled in pub fridges and ice buckets. Never mind, it will serve well-chilled. Try it with salmon patties.

Penfolds Old Vine Semillon

Want to know more? Go to *http://www.penfolds. com.au* to find out about old vines and all that jazz.

Previous outstanding vintages: '95

CURRENT RELEASE 1996 The colour is a very healthy lemon yellow and the nose has toasty elements plus citrus and gooseberry. The palate is rich with ripe sem-_illon flavours and a creamy texture, thanks to barrel fermentation. The finish continues the creamy oak theme. The wine can be served near room temperature. Try it with a warm chicken salad.

Quality	🍷🍷🍷🍷
Value	★★★★
Grapes	semillon
Region	Barossa Valley, SA
Cellar	4
Alc./Vol.	12.0%
RRP	$18.00 (S)

Penfolds Reserve Bin 94A Chardonnay

This is a one-off, proof positive that Penfolds can make a good white wine. It hasn't happened since the great Hunter semillon under the 6K banner in the 1970s.

CURRENT RELEASE 1994 The wine has a bright green–gold colour and the nose has strong wood and loquat aromas. The palate is rich and creamy with a developed peach-fruit flavour. It's mouthfilling and this is balanced by some well-integrated oak. A beautifully balanced package. The wine should be lightly chilled. Try it with kassler and lentils.

Quality	🍷🍷🍷🍷½
Value	★★★½
Grapes	chardonnay
Region	not stated
Cellar	4
Alc./Vol.	13.5%
RRP	$45.00

Penfolds The Valleys Chardonnay

The Valleys are Clare and Eden, and this wine has been given the works as far as the making process is concerned. Barrel ferment, malolactic fermentation, lees contact and so on. It's part of the Penfolds push for an outstanding white.

CURRENT RELEASE 1997 The result of the wine-making is a smooth, seamless wine with a peaches and cream nose. The palate has peach and melon flavours which meld into a long dry finish. It can be served with a medium chill with pâté.

Quality	🍷🍷🍷🍷
Value	★★★★
Grapes	chardonnay
Region	Clare & Eden Valleys, SA
Cellar	3
Alc./Vol.	13.5%
RRP	$15.25

Penfolds Trial Bin Chardonnay

Quality	ŶŶŶŶĬ
Value	★★★★
Grapes	chardonnay
Region	Adelaide Hills, SA
Cellar	▮ 3
Alc./Vol.	13.0%
RRP	$32.00

Try it again, Sam. Let's hope they keep trying; it might not be white Grange but it's no trial to drink.
Previous outstanding vintages: '95
CURRENT RELEASE 1996   A very polished wine. The nose has melon and creamy wood aromas. The palate is mouthfilling with peach and melon flavours. The wood fits perfectly, adding length to the finish. It should be served with a light chill and fillet of pork in a mango sauce.

Penfolds Yattarna Chardonnay

Quality	ŶŶŶŶŶ
Value	★★
Grapes	chardonnay
Region	Adelaide Hills;
	McLaren Vale, SA
Cellar	▮ 3
Alc./Vol.	13.0%
RRP	$75.00–$150

This is recorded for posterity because most folks will never get to try it. It's touted as 'White Grange' by the press, something not discouraged by the makers. There was a feeding frenzy at bottle shops – only some 1180 cases were released.
CURRENT RELEASE 1995   As you would expect, it's a very refined style and although somewhat restrained, it has great complexity. The wood treatment is magnificent and there are malo and barrel characters right through the score. The nose is a mixture of cashew, barrel, citrus and melon aromas. The medium- to full-bodied palate has layers of flavour and a creamy texture. There are peach, melon, fig, cashew and toasty oak flavours. The finish sets it apart: it's ultra-long and very impressive. Don't over-chill, and serve it with stuffed goose.

Penley Estate Chardonnay

Quality	ŶŶŶĬ
Value	★★★
Grapes	chardonnay
Region	Coonawarra, SA
Cellar	▮ 3
Alc./Vol.	12.5%
RRP	$20.00

Coonawarra chardonnay is a bit of a bridesmaid and probably will be ever thus. Face it, the area is all about red wine.
CURRENT RELEASE 1996   This is an overt chardonnay where the variety is concerned, with direct wood and peach aromas. The palate is a simple medley of peach fruit and dusty wood. The oak is a little on the raw side. Don't over-chill, and serve it with smoked cod.

Petaluma Chardonnay

This would have to be one of the top contenders for the best chardonnay made in Australia. It won the Gold Penguin for the best wine in last year's *Guide*. It's great to revisit the label, which is as impressive as ever. Maker Brian Croser.

Previous outstanding vintages: '90, '91, '92, '93, '94, '95, '96

CURRENT RELEASE 1997   This youngster is just setting out on a long journey to maturity, and shows lots of promise. The nose is a mixture of classy oak and peach, melon, fig and cashew aromas. The palate is on the point of being flinty with some attractive grapefruit and stone-fruit flavours that tango with barrel-ferment flavours. The finish is dry and lengthy, and its complex structure sets it apart. It's like a long-tail Porsche 917 at the breaking point on Muslane straight at Le Mans. That's racy for you. Try it with crayfish.

Quality	ΤΤΤΤΤ
Value	★★★★⯪
Grapes	chardonnay
Region	Adelaide Hills, SA
Cellar	▮ 8
Alc./Vol.	13.8%
RRP	$40.00

Petaluma Riesling

This has long been a benchmark style and one of the jewels in the crown of the Clare Valley. Trivia buffs will enjoy the knowledge that Petaluma is also a town in California where they hold the world arm-wrestling championships.

Previous outstanding vintages: '80, '85, '86, '88, '90, '92, '93, '94, '95, '96

CURRENT RELEASE 1997   This wine has the usual citrus and lime aromas. The palate tends to be rounder than usual and the lime has a subdued edge. Lemon tends to be the major flavour and the acid is reviving and crisp. It can be served well-chilled and goes admirably with an Asian chicken salad on crystal noodles.

Quality	ΤΤΤΤ
Value	★★★
Grapes	riesling
Region	Clare Valley, SA
Cellar	▮ 4
Alc./Vol.	12.7%
RRP	$22.00

Peter Lehmann Chardonnay

Quality	♥♥♥↺
Value	★★★↺
Grapes	chardonnay
Region	Barossa Valley, SA
Cellar	↧ 2
Alc./Vol.	13.5%
RRP	$13.95

Barossa chardonnay can develop a weight problem and become broad in the beam, and being cloaked in excessive American oak doesn't help.

CURRENT RELEASE 1997   This wine is almost portly but retains a semblance of style. The nose has ripe peach aromas. The palate is a mixture of peach and melon flavours and there's some American oak adding vanilla on the finish. It can be served well-chilled. Try it with Singapore flounder.

Peter Lehmann Riesling

Quality	♥♥♥♥
Value	★★★★
Grapes	riesling
Region	Eden Valley, SA
Cellar	↧ 4
Alc./Vol.	12.5%
RRP	$11.50

What's a Barossa good ol' boy doing messing with fruit from the Eden Valley? It happens, and it's good that it does.

CURRENT RELEASE 1997   The wine has a typically tropical aroma, redolent of citrus. The palate comes with a zesty fresh shock of lime flavours and the acid adds a tingling zing. It drinks well with the full chill, and is great with open-shell scallops.

Pewsey Vale Riesling

Quality	♥♥♥♥
Value	★★★★
Grapes	riesling
Region	Eden Valley, SA
Cellar	↧ 4
Alc./Vol.	12.5%
RRP	$12.80 Ⓢ

The first Hill Smith company is celebrating 150 years of winemaking. What that's doing on the front label of this wine is a moot point. Pewsey Vale vineyard was planted in 1961.

CURRENT RELEASE 1997   The wine is one of the better examples of the style. The nose has fresh lemon and lime aromas. Ditto the palate, which is quite intense with zesty flavours. There's plenty of acid on the finish. It can be served well-chilled. Try it with a yabby-and-prawn terrine.

Phantom's Lake Chardonnay

More flash than dash – what's with this trend of putting wine in funny bottles and a cute story on the back label? This one comes from the Mildara Blass stable.

CURRENT RELEASE 1996   A soft style with good varietal integrity. The nose is slightly sappy with hints of peach and tropical fruits. The medium-bodied palate has citrus and peach flavours which are backed by some subtle oak on a dry finish. It can take a medium chill. Serve it with chicken-and-chives sausages.

Quality	♟♟♟?
Value	★★★
Grapes	chardonnay
Region	Glenrowan, Vic.; Barossa Valley, Langhorne Creek, SA
Cellar	▮ 3
Alc./Vol.	13.0%
RRP	$14.50

Phillip Island Sauvignon Blanc

The vineyard is the first on the island and is totally netted to protect the vines against birds and wind. Maker David Lance.

CURRENT RELEASE 1997   This wine shows a good deal of restraint. The nose has herb and grassy aromas with some tropical fruit flavours. The palate is medium-bodied with herb and tropical fruit flavours, followed by crisp acid. It can be served well-chilled. Try it with mussels poached in white wine.

Quality	♟♟♟♟
Value	★★★★
Grapes	sauvignon blanc
Region	Phillip Island, Vic.
Cellar	▮ 2
Alc./Vol.	12.5%
RRP	$17.50

Pierro Chardonnay

Mike Peterkin's is usually one of the best chardonnays in Margaret River. It has the full Burgundy treatment as he tries to invest it with maximum complexity.

Previous outstanding vintages: '86, '90, '92, '94, '95

CURRENT RELEASE 1996   Looking a trifle spotty and argumentative in its adolescence, this wine is perhaps in need of more time in the cellar. The nose shows plenty of oak with a toasted-nut, mealy, vanillan intensity and the palate has butterscotch, vanilla and caramel flavours. It winds up with heat from the alcohol and some oak astringency. Cellar, then serve with crayfish.

Quality	♟♟♟♟?
Value	★★★
Grapes	chardonnay
Region	Margaret River, WA
Cellar	➬ 1–5
Alc./Vol.	14.5%
RRP	$49.20

Pierro Semillon Sauvignon Blanc LTC

Quality	♥♥♥♥◕
Value	★★★◕
Grapes	semillon; sauvignon blanc; chardonnay
Region	Margaret River, WA
Cellar	◑ 3
Alc./Vol.	13.0%
RRP	$21.80

The LTC stands for Les Trois Cuvées, its original name. The third variety is a smidgin of chardonnay. Maker Mike Peterkin.

CURRENT RELEASE 1997   This is a white for drinking, not tasting. It lacks some of the lifted aromatics of other examples from the region, but has excellent ripe fruit character in the straw, lemon and tropical fruit range. It is properly dry with good structure and length. Has the strength to partner grilled snapper with beurre blanc.

Pikes Reserve Riesling

Quality	♥♥♥♥♥
Value	★★★★◕
Grapes	riesling
Region	Clare Valley, SA
Cellar	◑ 8
Alc./Vol.	13.0%
RRP	$21.30

From the oldest and best part of the Pike riesling vineyards at Polish Hill River. Maker Neil Pike.

CURRENT RELEASE 1997   This is a graceful, understated style of riesling; intense but subtle. There are lime/lemon flavours and the palate is smooth and nothing is out of place. Beautifully balanced and harmonious, it can only get better with cellaring. Try it with lemon sole.

Pitchfork White

Quality	♥♥♥◕
Value	★★★◕
Grapes	not stated
Region	Margaret River, WA
Cellar	◑ 2
Alc./Vol.	13.5%
RRP	$15.60

Why does the name sound uncomfortable? The back label talks about 'fruit grunt'. Full marks from a rev head. (MS is guilty.)

CURRENT RELEASE 1997   The wine has a strong tropical aroma. The palate is medium-bodied with a continuation of the tropical fruit flavour that includes passionfruit and citrus. The finish has crisp acid and lingers long. It's not bad with marron.

Plunkett Blackwood Ridge Gewürztraminer

Quality	♥♥♥◕
Value	★★★◕
Grapes	gewürztraminer
Region	Strathbogie, Vic.
Cellar	◑ 2
Alc./Vol.	12.1%
RRP	$16.00

Well-made style from the Strathbogie Ranges in central Victoria that captures the pungency of the grape variety.

CURRENT RELEASE 1997   The nose is very floral with violet and crushed flower aromas. The palate has lychee and gooseberry flavours and these are balanced by some clean acid on a long finish. It should be served well-chilled and goes well with quiche.

Plunkett Blackwood Ridge Unwooded Chardonnay

Fast out of the blocks from the Strathbogie Ranges in Victoria. There's plenty of flavour.

CURRENT RELEASE 1997 The nose has strong tropical fruit aromas on the nose. The palate is quite rich with a strong passionfruit aroma and underlying peach. Clean acid makes for a long finish. It can be served well-chilled with a lightly curried chicken casserole.

Quality	♟♟♟♟
Value	★★★★
Grapes	chardonnay
Region	Strathbogie, Vic.
Cellar	▮ 2
Alc./Vol.	13.6%
RRP	$16.00

Plunkett Strathbogie Ranges Chardonnay

Plunkett was established in 1980 and the cellar door was shifted down the hill to a convenient location beside the Hume Freeway.

CURRENT RELEASE 1995 A bit of bottle-age doesn't hurt this wine. You can pick it up in the deepening of the colour. The nose has strong peach and melon aromas with a hint of lychee. The palate offers a creamy, almost buttery texture with the peach flavour dominant; the wood adds to a stout finish. It drinks well near room temperature. Serve it with pâté.

Quality	♟♟♟♟
Value	★★★★
Grapes	chardonnay
Region	Strathbogie, Vic.
Cellar	▮ 4
Alc./Vol.	14.2%
RRP	$19.00

CURRENT RELEASE 1996 This is a powerful wine with some intense tropical characters. The nose has lychee and pineapple with a hint of clove. The intense palate has rich lime and peach flavours, and there's some assertive oak on a dry finish. Don't over-chill. The wine goes well with turkey.

Quality	♟♟♟♟
Value	★★★★
Grapes	chardonnay
Region	Strathbogie, Vic.
Cellar	▮ 4
Alc./Vol.	13.7%
RRP	$21.00

Plunkett Strathbogie Ranges Riesling

There seemed to be a long and sometimes painful refinement in the label department. Now the packaging is understated and quite elegant.

CURRENT RELEASE 1997 The nose has lychee, yeast and citrus aromas and the colour is a vivid pale lemon yellow. The palate is rich and tangy with strong citrus flavours and a hint of honey. The finish has crisp acid. It can be served well-chilled. Try it with oysters.

Quality	♟♟♟♟
Value	★★★★
Grapes	riesling
Region	Strathbogie, Vic.
Cellar	▮ 4
Alc./Vol.	12.7%
RRP	$18.00

Poole's Rock Chardonnay

Quality	♥♥♥♡
Value	★★★☆
Grapes	chardonnay
Region	Hunter Valley, NSW
Cellar	▮ 2
Alc./Vol.	12.5%
RRP	$20.00

The vineyard was established in 1988 by businessman David Cark. The first vintage was released in 1990.
CURRENT RELEASE 1997   This wine shows an austerity of style. The nose is dominated by oak, with some yeast and citrus aromas. The palate is medium-bodied with grapefruit flavour and a toasty oak character. The finish has some strict oak that calls the tune; it's a bit B&D. Don't over-chill. It goes well with conch in a ginger and garlic sauce.

Port Phillip Estate Chardonnay

Quality	♥♥♥♥♡
Value	★★★★☆
Grapes	chardonnay
Region	Mornington Peninsula, Vic.
Cellar	▮ 4
Alc./Vol.	13.5%
RRP	$22.00

The back label says it all: 'Port Phillip Estate was established in 1987 in the rich red loam soils of Red Hill on the Mornington Peninsula.' It's the golden handcuffs for Diana and Jeffrey Sher QC. Maker Lindsay McCall.
CURRENT RELEASE 1997   The wine is very much oak driven with strong vanilla and coconut influences. The nose has grapefruit, peach and lemon aromas and toasty wood smells. The palate is full-bodied with some attractive peach and grapefruit flavours and a creamy texture. The finish is dominated by wood. Don't over-chill. Serve with a seafood risotto.

Portree Vineyard Chardonnay

Quality	♥♥♥♥♡
Value	★★★★☆
Grapes	chardonnay
Region	Macedon, Vic.
Cellar	▮ 5
Alc./Vol.	12.6%
RRP	$21.00

This is a very impressive wine from the cool regions of Macedon, Victoria. It doesn't want for flavour or finesse. The vineyard was established in 1983 and produces around 1200 cases per year.
CURRENT RELEASE 1996   The colour is a bright yellow tinged with gold. The nose has strong peach aromas laced with wood. The medium-bodied palate has intense peach and melon flavours and this is combined with some attractive wood on a long, dry, flinty finish. The wine will develop well with cellaring. If drinking now it's at its best near room temperature. A crayfish tail will tell the tale.

Preece Chardonnay

Colin Preece was a titan of the Australian wine industry. He made the first wines at Mitchelton after retiring from a distinguished career at Seppelt, Great Western. CURRENT RELEASE 1997 This wine has a pale straw colour and the nose offers grapefruit and gentle oak aromas. The palate is medium-bodied with citrus and stone-fruit flavours. These are followed by some soft acid on a gentle finish. The wine can be served well-chilled. It goes well with a chicken stirfry.

Quality	???
Value	★★★⋆
Grapes	chardonnay
Region	various, Vic.
Cellar	▮ 2
Alc./Vol.	13.5%
RRP	$14.50 Ⓢ

Prentice Chenin Blanc

This is a slightly out-of-fashion chenin blanc, right, so cop this back label: 'My dreams they dress in blue, sipping sin on balmy evenings, and when the cocktail hour is through . . .' What would the maker say about chardonnay? Stop it or you'll need a seeing-eye dog. CURRENT RELEASE 1996 There's a whisper of passion-fruit in the aromatic, fruit-salady nose. The palate is lightweight and straight up and down, with herbaceous fruity notes and a delicate structure. It's soft and slips down easily. Try serving it with caesar salad.

Quality	???
Value	★★★
Grapes	chenin blanc
Region	not stated
Cellar	▮ 1
Alc./Vol.	12.0%
RRP	$16.00

CURRENT RELEASE 1997 The wine has a pleasant spicy granny smith apple aroma. The palate offers an obvious level of sweetness which is balanced by some tart acid that lingers on the finish. It can be served well-chilled with roast pork.

Quality	???
Value	★★★⋆
Grapes	chenin blanc
Region	not stated
Cellar	▮ 1
Alc./Vol.	12.5%
RRP	$16.50

Primo Estate Colombard

The Grilli family have always been keepers of the faith where this variety is concerned. It has paid dividends because it's an ever-reliable style. Maker Joe Grilli. CURRENT RELEASE 1997 The nose has strong passion-fruit and pineapple aromas. The palate is medium-bodied with tropical fruit flavour, and there's plenty of crisp acid on a tingling finish. Use it as a pre-dinner drink.

Quality	???
Value	★★★⋆
Grapes	colombard
Region	Adelaide Plains, SA
Cellar	▮ 1
Alc./Vol.	12.0%
RRP	$12.00 Ⓢ

Quelltaler Carlsfield Vineyard Riesling

Quality	ΨΨΨΨΨ
Value	★★★★★
Grapes	riesling
Region	Clare Valley, SA
Cellar	🍷 10
Alc./Vol.	11.5%
RRP	$14.80 Ⓢ

Quelltaler winemaker Dave O'Leary has got into the spirit of the riesling revival and launched three individual vineyard '97 rieslings called The Clare Essentials. Bravo! This is one of the most prized Quelltaler vineyards, named after co-founder Carl Sobels.

CURRENT RELEASE 1997   Classy wine indeed, a model example of richness and finesse in the same bottle. The nose has flinty, mineral notes plus citrus fruits. It really comes into its own when it's allowed to breathe and warm up. Don't over-chill, and serve with steamed dim sum.

Quelltaler Polish Hill River Vineyard Riesling

Quality	ΨΨΨΨ
Value	★★★★
Grapes	riesling
Region	Clare Valley, SA
Cellar	🍷 7+
Alc./Vol.	11.5%
RRP	$14.80 Ⓢ

The Polish sub-region is slightly cooler and higher than Watervale, where the winery and main vineyards are located.

CURRENT RELEASE 1997   This is perhaps the least engaging of the three in its youth, showing earthy, mineral characters and less of the lifted aromatics. It's big and slightly broad in the mouth, with lots of lemony flavour and some richness. Needs time, then serve with fish pie.

Quelltaler Prospect Vineyard Riesling

Quality	ΨΨΨΨ⸮
Value	★★★★⸓
Grapes	riesling
Region	Clare Valley, SA
Cellar	🍷 7+
Alc./Vol.	11.5%
RRP	$14.80 Ⓢ

This is the third wine of The Clare Essentials trio, and it comes from sandy red loam soils over limestone. Maker David O'Leary.

CURRENT RELEASE 1997   The nose is classic Clare lime–citrus and flowers. It's a rich wine with plenty of fruit and flavour and finishes with fresh acidity. Has the strength to age, too. Goes well now with pan-fried flathead.

Redgate OFS Semillon

What does OFS stand for, we hear you ask? According to winemaker Andrew Forsell, 'out f---ing standing', and he might be right.

CURRENT RELEASE 1997   A very complex wine that has had the treatment. The nose has barrel-ferment aromas as well as citrus character. The full-bodied palate is broad with rich lemon and buttery characters. It's mouthfilling and the finish has creamy oak textures. How it will age is an interesting question. At the moment it goes well with a warm salad of goat's cheese.

Quality	♥♥♥♥?
Value	★★★★⊦
Grapes	semillon
Region	Margaret River, WA
Cellar	🍷 4
Alc./Vol.	13.0%
RRP	$18.00

Redgate Reserve Sauvignon Blanc

Redgate was established in 1977 and there are 20 hectares under vines. The annual production is around 8000 cases per vintage.

CURRENT RELEASE 1997   This is so tropical it should be wearing a grass skirt and lei. Actually, scratch the skirt because there's no cut-grass character. The nose has pineapple, mango and passionfruit aromas. The rich palate continues the tropical theme and there's a zest of fresh acid on a solid finish which shows a touch of oak. In spite of the relatively high level of alcohol, there's a pleasing crisp element. Serve it with mussels poached in white wine.

Quality	♥♥♥♥
Value	★★★★
Grapes	sauvignon blanc
Region	Margaret River, WA
Cellar	🍷 3
Alc./Vol.	14.0%
RRP	$18.00

Red Hill Estate Chardonnay

This is a large estate by Mornington Peninsula standards; it also makes a fine sparkling wine.

CURRENT RELEASE 1996   This wine was given the full treatment but it remains flinty. Instead of weight watchers it needs ignorers. It has a grapefruit and melon nose with evidence of wood. The medium-bodied palate has citrus, melon and a hint of nuts; there's a vanillin lift on the steely finish. Very much in the chablis style. Try it with crayfish. ►

Quality	♥♥♥?
Value	★★★⊦
Grapes	chardonnay
Region	Mornington Peninsula, Vic.
Cellar	🍷 5
Alc./Vol.	12.6%
RRP	$22.00

Quality	????
Value	★★★★
Grapes	chardonnay
Region	Mornington Peninsula, Vic.
Cellar	▮ 4
Alc./Vol.	13.9%
RRP	$22.00

CURRENT RELEASE 1997   This was a year when the fruit was fully ripe. The nose is bursting with peach, melon and tropical fruit aromas. The palate has a mouthfilling texture with melon, peach and fig flavours at the fore. There are also toast and vanilla, thanks to the oak. The finish is dry and long, and it needs a medium chill to show off. It works with satay chicken.

Ribbon Vale Estate Sauvignon Blanc

Quality	????
Value	★★★
Grapes	sauvignon blanc
Region	Margaret River, WA
Cellar	▮ 2
Alc./Vol.	13.0%
RRP	$18.95

The owl and the pussycat went to sea in a beautiful pea-green boat. That's what springs to mind when the cork is pulled. Maker Mike Davies.
CURRENT RELEASE 1997   The nose is pungent with herbal and canned pea smells. The palate is medium-bodied with gooseberry and tropical fruit flavours. The finish shows some clean acid. It can be served well-chilled. Try it with mussels poached in white wine.

Ribbon Vale Estate Semillon Sauvignon Blanc

Quality	????
Value	★★★
Grapes	semillon; sauvignon blanc
Region	Margaret River, WA
Cellar	▮ 1
Alc./Vol.	13.0%
RRP	$18.10

The vineyard and winery were established in 1977, and annual production is in the order of 4000 cases per annum.
CURRENT RELEASE 1997   This is a pleasant, easy-drinking style. The nose is a mixture of herbs and new-mown grass. The medium-bodied palate has citrus and gooseberry fruit flavours. There's crisp acid on the finish and the wine can take a big chill. Try it with a leafy green salad.

Richard Hamilton Chardonnay

This McLaren Vale chardonnay shows evidence of new oak. Dr Richard Hamilton is celebrating 25 years in the wine business. Maker Ralph Fowler.

CURRENT RELEASE 1996   The nose is a mixture of peach and pencil shavings. The palate is firm with sweet varietal fruit flavours. There's some sappy quality to the finish, thanks to a sting of new oak. It needs time in the bottle to tame the oak. Don't over-chill, and try it with smoked cod.

Quality	♥♥♥⁍
Value	★★★⊦
Grapes	chardonnay
Region	McLaren Vale, SA
Cellar	▮ 4
Alc./Vol.	13.5%
RRP	$21.30

Riddoch Chardonnay

Yet another in the fighting brand range. This is very good value for money and shows reasonable complexity plus style.

CURRENT RELEASE 1996   A tidy package that shows some deft wood handling. The nose has savoury toasty oak and peach aromas. The medium-bodied palate offers peach and nectarine flavours which are wedded to some toasty oak on a lingering finish. Too much cold brings out too much oak. Try it with ocean trout.

Quality	♥♥♥♥
Value	★★★★
Grapes	chardonnay
Region	Coonawarra, SA
Cellar	▮ 3
Alc./Vol.	13.5%
RRP	$16.00 Ⓢ

R L Buller and Son Chardonnay

This is a very respectable style from Beverford near Swan Hill in Victoria. Maker Richard Buller Jr.

CURRENT RELEASE 1996   A typical melon and peach-scented nose. The palate is medium-bodied with clean, fresh peach flavours. Discreet wood treatment adds balance and dries the finish. It drinks well with a medium chill. Try it with pan-fried veal.

Quality	♥♥♥♥
Value	★★★★
Grapes	chardonnay
Region	Swan Hill, Vic.
Cellar	▮ 3
Alc./Vol.	13.8%
RRP	$17.00

R L Buller Victoria Classic White

Quality	ŦŦŦ
Value	★★★
Grapes	not stated
Region	Swan Hill, Vic.
Cellar	▮ 1
Alc./Vol.	12.9%
RRP	$14.50

There's no indication of the varieties used in this white blend from the Swan Hill district. MS suspects there's a chenin blanc component in the blend.

CURRENT RELEASE 1996 A crisp dry white with a fruity nose. The medium-bodied palate has some crisp green-apple flavours and these are matched by some clean acid on a dry finish. It can be served well-chilled at a barbecue.

Rosemount Giant's Creek Chardonnay

Quality	ŦŦŦŦ
Value	★★★★
Grapes	chardonnay
Region	Hunter Valley, NSW
Cellar	▮ 4
Alc./Vol.	14.0%
RRP	$19.70

This wine is hastening slowly towards bottle-age. (Pardon the oxymoron, folks.)

CURRENT RELEASE 1995 A rather reserved and steely style that seems to cloak the relatively high alcohol (14.0%). The nose has wood and citrus aromas, and melon and grapefruit flavours. These are supported by some French oak and the finish is dry and flinty. It should be served near room temperature with whitebait fritters.

Rosemount Orange Vineyard Chardonnay

Quality	ŦŦŦŦꝰ
Value	★★★★
Grapes	chardonnay
Region	Orange, NSW
Cellar	▮ 5
Alc./Vol.	14.0%
RRP	$21.30

This is a very exciting style. Given the quality of the early releases, Orange should be a region to be reckoned with. Maker Phil Shaw.

CURRENT RELEASE 1996 The nose is a mixture of stone-fruit and oak aromas. The palate has a flinty element but peach dominates the flavour spectrum. The finish is dominated by coconut, oak and a wood tannin grip. It needs only a medium chill. Try it with a hearty fish soup.

Rosemount Roxburgh Chardonnay

The good, the bold and the buxom. This is always a no-holds-barred style which is lots of fun.

Previous outstanding vintages: '84, '87, '90, '92, '93, '94

CURRENT RELEASE 1995 The colour is a bright yellow–gold and the nose has strong peach and nectarine aromas. The palate is full-bodied and mouthfilling. The major flavours are peach and melon with a hint of fig. The wood always makes its presence felt with a coconut flavour. It's best when served with a medium chill. Try it with pan-fried tuna.

Quality	▼▼▼▼▼
Value	★★★★
Grapes	chardonnay
Region	Hunter Valley, NSW
Cellar	▮ 5
Alc./Vol.	14.0%
RRP	$45.00

Rosemount Sauvignon Blanc

Yet another wine in the popular diamond-label series. These are fighting brands, so shop around for the best price.

CURRENT RELEASE 1997 The wine has a leafy aroma and a hint of smoke. The medium to lightweight palate is gooseberry flavoured and there's a slight coarseness on the finish. It should be served well-chilled. Take it to a picnic.

Quality	▼▼▼
Value	★★★
Grapes	sauvignon blanc
Region	not stated
Cellar	▮ 1
Alc./Vol.	12.5%
RRP	$12.00 Ⓢ

Rosemount Semillon

This is the commercial spear-carrier for Rosemount. It fights on the bar, in the bottle shops and on bistro tables.

CURRENT RELEASE 1997 This is a pleasant commercial style with some damp straw aromas on the nose. The palate has a fresh lemon flavour and the finish offers crisp acid and mouth-cleansing properties. It can be served with a medium chill. It goes well with flounder.

Quality	▼▼▼▼
Value	★★★★
Grapes	semillon
Region	Hunter Valley, NSW
Cellar	▮ 2
Alc./Vol.	12.5%
RRP	$16.00

Rosemount Semillon Chardonnay

Quality	�♥♥
Value	★★★
Grapes	semillon;
	chardonnay
Region	Hunter Valley,
	NSW
Cellar	▮ 1
Alc./Vol.	12.0%
RRP	$12.00 Ⓢ

Another variation on a theme of the diamond label. It's designed for drive-in bottle shops when folks are looking for a cheap non-think bottle.

CURRENT RELEASE 1997 The nose has strong toast and damp straw aromas. The palate is middleweight with a light fruit flavour. Peaches dominate, and the wood is dry and toasty. The wine can be served well-chilled. It's good with fish and chips.

Rosemount Show Reserve Semillon

Quality	♥♥♥♥♥
Value	★★★★★
Grapes	semillon
Region	Hunter Valley,
	NSW
Cellar	▮ 5
Alc./Vol.	12.5%
RRP	$25.40

This is the show reserve from the Hunter Valley. It's a pretty classy wine with well-structured oak. Not to be confused with the commercial diamond label.

CURRENT RELEASE 1995 It has a strong straw aroma on the nose with hints of gooseberry jam. The palate is medium-bodied with attractive gooseberry and quince flavours. The wood fits like a glove and adds to the complexity. The finish is long with a satisfying grip. It can be served with a medium chill with stirfried pork.

Rossetto Promenade

Quality	♥♥♥♥
Value	★★★★
Grapes	semillon
Region	Murrumbidgee
	Irrigation Area,
	NSW
Cellar	▮ 3
Alc./Vol.	12.5%
RRP	$14.50

As the name suggests, this is a gentle stroll rather than a walk on the wild side. Rossetto was established in 1930 and makes around 850 000 cases per annum. Maker Eddy Rossi.

CURRENT RELEASE 1997 Mouth-feel is the key to this wine, which shows a thick, creamy texture thanks to barrel fermentation. The nose has a gentle wood aroma and a suggestion of honey. There are honey and citrus flavours on the full-bodied palate. Oak makes for a dry finish that coats the mouth with tannin. Don't over-chill, and serve with roast pork and apple sauce.

Rothbury Estate Brokenback Chardonnay

This is the top of the Rothbury white-wine tree and gets the Rolls Royce wood treatment and very careful handling. The wine takes its name from a range of hills that provides a backdrop to the Hunter Valley.
CURRENT RELEASE 1997 The nose offers a mixture of vanilla, melon and fig. The palate is heavy-metal peach with fig and melon elements, and the wood treatment adds a toasty vanilla character. The dryness is appealing and it goes well with straight roast chook and plenty of stuffing.

Quality	▛▛▛▛
Value	★★★★
Grapes	chardonnay
Region	Hunter Valley, NSW
Cellar	▮ 4
Alc./Vol.	13.0%
RRP	$18.50

Rothbury Estate Brokenback Semillon

The Rothbury Estate take-over was naturally a bitter disappointment to Len Evans. The new management has pledged plenty of funds for an upgrade of the winery and facilities. Maker Adam Eggins.
CURRENT RELEASE 1997 Sometimes young Hunter semillons can be shy and lean, but not in this case. The nose has lanolin, gooseberry and herb aromas. The palate is medium-bodied with plenty of citrus and a whisper of a tropical fruit cocktail. The acid on the finish is high and clean. The wine can be served well-chilled, and goes with spaghetti pesto.

Quality	▛▛▛▛
Value	★★★★
Grapes	semillon
Region	Hunter Valley, NSW
Cellar	▮ 8
Alc./Vol.	11.0%
RRP	$18.50

Rothbury Estate Cowra Chardonnay

New livery for the regenerating Rothbury which is under the Mildara Blass–cum–Fosters Brewing umbrella.
CURRENT RELEASE 1997 The wine is quite rich with a deep yellow–gold colour. The nose has honey, peach nectar and vanilla aromas. The palate is all about peach and there's a sweet mouthfilling quality which is balanced by the oak. It needs a medium chill. Try it with Singapore deep-fried flounder.

Quality	▛▛▛▛
Value	★★★★
Grapes	chardonnay
Region	Cowra, NSW
Cellar	▮ 2
Alc./Vol.	13.5%
RRP	$13.30

Rothbury Estate Verdelho

Quality	♈♈♈♈
Value	★★★★
Grapes	verdelho
Region	Upper Hunter Valley, NSW
Cellar	▮ 2
Alc./Vol.	12.0%
RRP	$15.00

This variety has a long history in the Hunter Valley. It usually makes some worthy rather than remarkable wines.

CURRENT RELEASE 1997   Very tropical in character, the nose opens with pineapple and passionfruit aromas. The palate is a mixture of stone fruits, pineapple and passionfruit, and these are matched by some crisp acid on a very fresh finish. It can be served with a high degree of chilling. Satay prawns work well.

Ryecroft Unoaked Chardonnay

Quality	♈♈♈
Value	★★★
Grapes	chardonnay
Region	McLaren Vale, SA
Cellar	▮
Alc./Vol.	13.0%
RRP	$12.00

Jim Ingoldby made Ryecroft famous in the sixties. Since then it has had several changes of ownership. Today it's a second label for the Rosemount group.

CURRENT RELEASE 1998   Strange wine – the nose is regulation peach with a hint of melon; the palate is sweet to the point of being unctuous. It seems to have a high level of sugar and the citrus flavours battle to combat the sweetness. The finish is soft. Give it a super chill and try it with chilli calamari.

Salisbury Chardonnay

Quality	♈♈♈♈
Value	★★★★★
Grapes	chardonnay
Region	Murray Valley, Vic.
Cellar	▮ 2
Alc./Vol.	13.0%
RRP	$10.00 ⑤

This is a reliable brand for consistently drinkable everyday wines at the right price. You're better off punting on Salisbury than many a cool-climate boutique.

CURRENT RELEASE 1997   Ten-dollar chardonnay simply doesn't get any better than this. It's mid-yellow in colour and smells peachy and buttery: fresh, clean and inviting. In the mouth it's soft, clean and flavoursome, with butterscotch and peach flavours that are beautifully balanced and just so drinkable. Pour it into a Mornington Peninsula bottle and watch people fall about. Serve with chicken kebabs.

Salisbury Chardonnay Semillon

The folk at Salisbury/Alambie Wine Co. use technology to great effect in the vineyard, where they get the best out of the warm, sunny fertile conditions of the Riverland. Maker Bob Shields.
CURRENT RELEASE 1997 Fennel-like herbal semillon aromas combine with a suggestion of peach from the chardonnay. The overall package is soft without being sweet, fruity, simple and quaffable. Light-bodied and slips down easily. Serve it with Murray cod.

Quality	♟♟♟
Value	★★★★
Grapes	chardonnay; semillon
Region	Murray Valley, Vic.
Cellar	▮ 1
Alc./Vol.	12.5%
RRP	$10.00 Ⓢ

Saltram Mamre Brook Chardonnay

The founder, William Salter, was a religious man and the name Mamre is a biblical reference. Saltram is where Peter Lehmann worked for much of his life. Today it's part of the Mildara group. Maker Nige Dolan.
CURRENT RELEASE 1997 Here's a chardonnay with some subtlety and attractive fruit highlights. Delicate melon and nectarine aromas; fine, well-harmonised palate flavours with understated oak, and good acidity which maintains life and freshness. A stylish wine that could take some age gracefully. Serve with oven-roasted scampi.

Quality	♟♟♟♟?
Value	★★★★⸜
Grapes	chardonnay
Region	Barossa Valley, SA
Cellar	▮ 4
Alc./Vol.	13.5%
RRP	$18.90

Sandalford Verdelho

Verdelho is something of a speciality in the West. Blame it on Jack Mann of Houghton, who had a vine in his backyard from which all the vines in WA are supposed to be descended.
CURRENT RELEASE 1997 The colour is a promising light green–yellow, and the nose is fresh with straightforward appley hints. It has a fairly sweet entry and then some heat – from alcohol and a little volatility – intrudes. Chill it well, and serve with prawns in honey and sesame seeds.

Quality	♟♟♟
Value	★★★
Grapes	verdelho
Region	Margaret River, WA
Cellar	▮ 1
Alc./Vol.	13.5%
RRP	$18.90

Sarantos Soft Press Chardonnay

Quality	♟♟♟♟
Value	★★★★
Grapes	chardonnay
Region	Riverland, SA
Cellar	▮ 1
Alc./Vol.	13.5%
RRP	$14.00 Ⓢ

Sarantos Moularadellis, aka Steve, migrated to Australia from Athens in 1955. With his wife Nina and sons he has built this company into the go-ahead show it is today.

CURRENT RELEASE 1996 A newie from Kingston Estate, with packaging that would make Liberace blush. The wine is excellent value: full and rich in the mouth, with some straw/hay and toasty development on the nose. It's a real mouthful: warm and resonant, with some butteriness and a trace of astringency from alcohol. Drinks well with chicken and cashew nuts.

Scribbly Gum Semillon

Quality	♟♟♟
Value	★★★⊦
Grapes	semillon
Region	Hunter Valley, NSW
Cellar	▮ 2
Alc./Vol.	13.0%
RRP	$9.90

The name derives from the habit some grubs have of digging their tracks in the trunks of some gum trees. This is a budget brand of the Saddlers Creek winery.

CURRENT RELEASE 1996 Simple, fresh lemony grape aromas, with a hint of typical Hunter semillon lanolin. It's very light-bodied, to the point of being flimsy. A clean, well-made semillon and fair value at the price. Drink it with sushi.

Seaview Chardonnay

Quality	♟♟♟♟
Value	★★★★★
Grapes	chardonnay
Region	McLaren Vale, SA
Cellar	▮ 1
Alc./Vol.	12.5%
RRP	$11.50 Ⓢ

Mike 'Foxy' Farmilo, who used to make the Seaview wines, has left to start a new contract winemaking venture in McLaren Vale called Boar's Rock.

CURRENT RELEASE 1997 This is great value, especially when it dips as low as $8.99 on special. Shy cashew nut aromas introduce a gently wooded chardonnay. It has richness but is well-controlled and lacks the heaviness of some McLaren Vale chardonnays. A fresh, modern, fruit-driven wine that's very drinkable now, but is probably not for keeping.

Seppelt Corella Ridge Chardonnay

No sooner had we got used to the stylish, Barrie Tucker–designed Victorian portfolio labels than they change them. Design elements remain, but the new deep-etched look is clumsy and unattractive.

CURRENT RELEASE 1996 A complex wine that shows off the winemaker's box of tricks, but too woody for our tastes. Toasty oak, butterscotch, peach and some aged character is creeping in. The oak provides power and length but also makes the finish very hard. Lots of appeal, nevertheless. Serve with pumpkin risotto.

Quality	▼▼▼▼
Value	★★★⋆
Grapes	chardonnay
Region	various, Vic.
Cellar	▮ 1
Alc./Vol.	13.5%
RRP	$14.00 Ⓢ

Seppelt Drumborg Riesling

This vineyard was first planted by Karl Seppelt in 1964. The label declares the '97 a great vintage. Maker Ian McKenzie and team.

CURRENT RELEASE 1997 All the signs scream 'cool climate'. Green-pea herbaceous aromas bear more than a passing resemblance to sauvignon blanc. It tastes terrific: high-quality citrusy fruit and zesty acid are skilfully balanced with a hint of sweetness. It has a tight cool-grown structure that bodes well for ageing, and the finish lingers on and on. Best if cellared a couple of years, then drink with Alsatian onion tart.

Quality	▼▼▼▼▼
Value	★★★★
Grapes	riesling
Region	Drumborg, Vic.
Cellar	➡ 1–7+
Alc./Vol.	12.5%
RRP	$23.30 Ⓢ

Seppelt Moyston Unoaked Chardonnay

Moyston is a little town in the hills not far from Great Western, best known for its World Rabbit Skinning Championship. This is one of the baselines of Southcorp's portfolio, which has no fewer than 45 chardonnays!

CURRENT RELEASE 1997 Basic summery QDW (quaffing dry white) here. It has a pale yellow colour; a light, simple melon aroma without wood complexity; and the taste is wispy and very rudimentary. Use it to wash down fish and chips.

Quality	▼▼▼
Value	★★★
Grapes	chardonnay
Region	not stated
Cellar	▮ 1
Alc./Vol.	13.0%
RRP	$8.90 Ⓢ

Seresin Chardonnay

Quality	♟♟♟♟
Value	★★★ᵧ
Grapes	chardonnay
Region	Marlborough, NZ
Cellar	▬ 4+
Alc./Vol.	13.5%
RRP	$24.00

Seresin is a very small, very new winery at Blenheim in the Marlborough district. It has quickly become one of the rising stars of Kiwi land.

CURRENT RELEASE 1996   A fine, restrained chardonnay with a lot of style. The tight structure gives an impression of austerity. It has very good fruit intensity despite its subtlety. A stayer that could be cellared. Try it with shellfish.

Seresin Sauvignon Blanc

Quality	♟♟♟
Value	★★★
Grapes	sauvignon blanc
Region	Marlborough, NZ
Cellar	▬ 2
Alc./Vol.	13.0%
RRP	$21.00

Will there be any end to the flow of sauvignon blancs from this area? The winemaker has cut this wine with 7% semillon and given 14% of the total a barrel fermentation.

CURRENT RELEASE 1997   The colour is a light lemon yellow and there are lemon, lime and other citrus aromas. It's a delicate wine with straightforward but well-balanced sauvignon varietal flavours. Our bottle may have had a marginal cork taint, in which case it's an even better wine than we rated it. Try it with niçoise salad.

Seville Estate Chardonnay

Quality	♟♟♟♟♟
Value	★★★★ᵧ
Grapes	chardonnay
Region	Yarra Valley, Vic.
Cellar	▬ 5+
Alc./Vol.	13.5%
RRP	$27.50

In 1997, Brokenwood purchased this vineyard/winery from the founders, Peter and Margaret McMahon. It's in good hands. Maker Alastair Butt.

CURRENT RELEASE 1997   A classy chardonnay and an exercise in finesse. Creamy barrel ferment and melon fruit characters are well integrated and the fruit is to the fore. Lovely finesse, beaut balance and admirable length. As good as it is right now, cellaring could richly reward. Food: try agedashi tofu.

Sharefarmers Chardonnay Sauvignon Blanc

This is a rare blend of grape varieties, but why not? It makes for a nice change, and the sauvignon adds an aromatic lift. Maker Brian Croser and team.

CURRENT RELEASE 1997 The colour is pale yellow and it smells high-toned, with an almost sweaty passionfruit/herbaceous element, no doubt contributed by the sauvignon blanc. There are lemony aromas too, and these reappear in the mouth, where it's delicate, tangy and very alive. An individual style which reminds little of chardonnay and would suit many seafood dishes, especially a lemony baby octopus salad.

Quality	♟♟♟♟
Value	★★★⭑
Grapes	chardonnay 67%, sauvignon blanc 33%
Region	Coonawarra, SA
Cellar	▮ 2
Alc./Vol.	13.0%
RRP	$18.00

Shaw & Smith Reserve Chardonnay

This company, run by cousins Mike Hill Smith and Martin Shaw, now churns out 25 000 cases a year.
Previous outstanding vintages: '92, '94, '95
CURRENT RELEASE 1996 One of the richer Adelaide Hills chardonnays, this has a full yellow colour and is starting to show some bottle development. There are also nutty oak, grapefruit and tropical fruit characters typical of the region. It has power, concentration and length. Serve with Woodside Charleston brie.

Quality	♟♟♟♟⭷
Value	★★★★
Grapes	chardonnay
Region	Adelaide Hills, SA
Cellar	▮ 3+
Alc./Vol.	13.0%
RRP	$28.70

Shaw & Smith Sauvignon Blanc

Very few Australian producers do a pure sauvignon blanc well. Shaw & Smith does. Otherwise, you'd be well advised to punt on one of the many New Zealand versions.
Previous outstanding vintages: all of them
CURRENT RELEASE 1997 A lovely wine, smelling fragrantly of tropical fruits and gooseberry with minor herbal pungency. It speaks of ripe grapes, with soft, well-balanced flavour of medium intensity. Perhaps lacking just a little of the vivaciousness we look for in this variety. Soft enough to drink on its own, but would team well with dim sum.

Quality	♟♟♟♟⭷
Value	★★★★
Grapes	sauvignon blanc
Region	Adelaide Hills, SA
Cellar	▮ 2
Alc./Vol.	13.0%
RRP	$19.35

Skillogalee Riesling

Quality	▼▼▼
Value	★★★
Grapes	riesling
Region	Clare Valley, SA
Cellar	➥ 2–6+
Alc./Vol.	13.0%
RRP	$17.00

What a great name for a winery! Beats the usual innocuous Bellevue Heights or Windbag Ridge. Maker Dave Palmer.

CURRENT RELEASE 1997   One of the more restrained '97 Clares we've seen. It's a backward style with a light colour and grass/straw and lemony riesling aromas. It tastes quite delicate and austere, with a dry finish and seems relatively undeveloped. Give it time, then serve with oysters.

Somerset Crossing Chardonnay

Quality	▼▼▼▼
Value	★★★
Grapes	chardonnay
Region	Goulburn Valley, Vic.
Cellar	▮ 2
Alc./Vol.	13.2%
RRP	$18.00

An estate-grown wine from vines planted on the fertile alluvial banks of the Goulburn River in 1969. The winery is in Seymour and has a restaurant attached.

CURRENT RELEASE 1996   A pleasant surprise, considering some distinctly left-field wines we've seen from this maker. It's retaining its freshness well, and has a shy, slightly sweaty nose and attractive ripe fig/melon flavours. It's dry in the mouth and has some delicacy and length, finishing with a slight grip. Try it with pan-fried perch.

Somerton Semillon Chardonnay

Quality	▼▼
Value	★★★
Grapes	semillon; chardonnay
Region	Riverina, NSW
Cellar	▮ 1
Alc./Vol.	12.5%
RRP	$6.50 Ⓢ

Coloured wine labels sell! This is Miranda's entry in the colour and movement stakes.

CURRENT RELEASE 1997   This tastes good as a youngster because it's very estery. Passionfruit and tea-leaf aromas predominate, and it's very light in the mouth with a slight sweet/sour tartness. Very basic quaffing white at an appealing price. Try it with vegetables.

Sorrenberg Chardonnay

This is a small vineyard at Beechworth, which isn't exactly a big viticultural region, being just outside the King Valley. Maker Barry Morey.

CURRENT RELEASE 1996   With its Burgundy-inspired label, this place is obviously run by a Francophile, especially when you taste the wine. It has a slightly feral character; hot-solids fermentation is suspected, and the malolactic character is prominent. All that means is that the fruit is secondary to winemaking characters. It's lean and tight and could age well. Food: snails in parsley garlic butter.

Quality	♥♥♥◊
Value	★★★
Grapes	chardonnay
Region	Beechworth, Vic.
Cellar	▯ 4+
Alc./Vol.	13.0%
RRP	$25.00 (cellar door)

Stanley Brothers Chardonnay Pristine

This small, Barossa family operation is in the former Kroemer Estate winery by the main road in Tanunda. Winemaker is the experienced Lindsay Stanley.

CURRENT RELEASE 1997   If pristine means it's unencumbered by oak and the emphasis is intentionally on fruit, this succeeds. Pronounced fruity aromas of pear juice, simple and grapey. It's slightly flat and lacks a bit of zip, but it's a clean, fruity, well-made drop. Take it to a vegetarian restaurant.

Quality	♥♥♥
Value	★★★
Grapes	chardonnay
Region	Barossa Valley, SA
Cellar	▯ 2
Alc./Vol.	12.0%
RRP	$16.50

St Hallett Riesling

This was a trophy-winner at the '97 Barossa Wine Show. Like all of the Barossa's best rieslings, it hails from the high country. Maker Cathy Spratt.

CURRENT RELEASE 1997   This is developing nicely and slowly. The nose has shy herbal elements. In the mouth it offers good, refined fruit on a tightly structured framework, with a gentle touch of sweetness. Promises to age well, too. Serve with crab cakes.

Quality	♥♥♥♥◊
Value	★★★★
Grapes	riesling
Region	Eden Valley, SA
Cellar	▯ 6+
Alc./Vol.	12.5%
RRP	$19.70

St Huberts Roussanne

Quality	♟♟♟?
Value	★★★
Grapes	roussanne
Region	Yarra Valley, Vic.
Cellar	▮ 2
Alc./Vol.	12.0%
RRP	$21.00 ⓢ

This is one of the very few roussannes in Australia. Gay sybarites who believe variety is the spice of life will approve.

CURRENT RELEASE 1997 This is different! A delicate dry white, it has flowery/estery aromas with a hint of sandalwood and you know straightaway it's not familiar fodder. The structure is lean and tight, with a dry, slightly austere finish. Something to fool your friends with. Try it with antipasto.

St Matthias Chardonnay

Quality	♟♟?
Value	★★★
Grapes	chardonnay
Region	Tamar Valley, Tas.
Cellar	▮ 2
Alc./Vol.	12.0%
RRP	$15.00

This is the second label of Moorilla Estate, established by the Alcorso family at Berriedale in 1958. The restaurant at Moorilla is worth a detour. There are also cellar-door sales at St Matthias, which is on the Tamar.

CURRENT RELEASE 1996 Beware: fearsome acid here! There's some evidence of botrytis in this lean, straight-forward wine and the flavours are of honey and herbs. The oak is very restrained and there's a trace of hardness on the finish. Needs food: try it with Tassie oysters.

Stonier's Reserve Chardonnay

Quality	♟♟♟♟♟
Value	★★★★℘
Grapes	chardonnay
Region	Mornington Peninsula, Vic.
Cellar	▮ 4
Alc./Vol.	13.5%
RRP	$36.00

Just before press time, Petaluma bought a half share of this leading Mornington winery. Petaluma's Brian Croser knows a good thing when he sees one. Maker Tod Dexter.

Previous outstanding vintages: '91, '93, '95

CURRENT RELEASE 1996 Delicious chardonnay! It's a full yellow colour and has aromas of fig, melon and some milky/creamy malo complexity. The oak is there but supportive rather than domineering. The tightly struc-tured palate adds vanilla and butterscotch nuances. The aftertaste lingers on and on. Serve it with barbecued prawns.

St Peters Reserve Chardonnay

St Peter has always been closely associated with wine, not least the Bordeaux icon, Petrus. This is a pretender from the Riverina.

CURRENT RELEASE 1996   Lots of oak, a big malolactic butterscotch character, and a full-bodied, rich flavour are the hallmarks of this wine. It's quite developed and has a mature peachy, toasty flavour. Lacks a little in focus but a generous mouthful. Try it with chicken schnitzel.

Quality	♟♟♟♟
Value	★★★★
Grapes	chardonnay
Region	Hunter Valley & Riverina, NSW
Cellar	▯ 2
Alc./Vol.	13.5%
RRP	$16.00

Tait Wines Chardonnay

This is a new label from the Barossa Valley. The Tait family have been in the coopering business near Lyndoch for over 100 years. Maker David Tait.

CURRENT RELEASE 1997   The nose has melon and peach aromas. The palate is medium- to full-bodied with some mouthfilling textures. Melon and tropical fruit flavours are the main components. The wood is subtle but adds balance. It should be served with a light chill. Try it with veal in a light cream sauce.

Quality	♟♟♟♟
Value	★★★★
Grapes	chardonnay
Region	Barossa Valley, SA
Cellar	▯ 3
Alc./Vol.	14.0%
RRP	$18.50

Tarra Warra Chardonnay

Tarra Warra is a very impressive project that brooks no compromise as far as winemaking is concerned.

CURRENT RELEASE 1996   A great double act between fruit and oak. The nose has peachy aromas plus cashew and savoury oak aromas. The palate is complex with peach, melon and nectarine flavours, and these are married to some attractive oak on a long finish. It doesn't need a big chill. It goes well with a warm salad of turkey breast.

Quality	♟♟♟♟♟
Value	★★★★⊦
Grapes	chardonnay
Region	Yarra Valley, Vic.
Cellar	▯ 6
Alc./Vol.	13.0%
RRP	$35.00

Tatachilla Chardonnay

Quality	🍷🍷🍷🍷
Value	★★★★
Grapes	chardonnay
Region	Clarendon, SA
Cellar	🍾 4
Alc./Vol.	13.5%
RRP	$16.00

They are really trying hard at Tatachilla to rekindle an old flame which first burned in the Southern Vales district in 1901. Maker Michael Fragos.

CURRENT RELEASE 1997 The wine has obvious barrel-ferment characters. Peach and melon dominate the nose. The medium-bodied palate has a creamy texture and plenty of flavour which is dominated by citrus and grapefruit. The wood on the finish is well integrated. It can be served with a medium chill. Try it with flathead in beer batter.

Terrace Vale Gewürztraminer

Quality	🍷🍷🍷½
Value	★★★½
Grapes	gewürztraminer
Region	Hunter Valley, NSW
Cellar	🍾 2
Alc./Vol.	12.5%
RRP	$16.00

Terrace Vale was first planted in 1971 and the annual production averages 9500 cases. Maker Alain Le Prince.

CURRENT RELEASE 1996 Yup, it's gewürtz all right! Very pungent nose, full of flowers and exotic spices. The palate is rich with lychee, lemon and spices, and there's plenty of acid to keep things lively. It ain't supposed to work in the Hunter but this one does. The variety is very difficult to handle in the heat. It needs a big chill and goes well with egg-and-bacon tart.

Terrace Vale T Chardonnay

Quality	🍷🍷🍷½
Value	★★★½
Grapes	chardonnay
Region	Hunter Valley, NSW
Cellar	🍾 2
Alc./Vol.	13.0%
RRP	$16.50

This is a very bold Hunter Valley label. I looked hard but couldn't find a vintage on this bottle. (I finally found the vintage on third glance.) I won't spoil the mystery, have a look for yourself.

CURRENT RELEASE 1997 The nose is slightly flinty with a hint of citrus. The palate has grapefruit and nectarine flavours, and the finish is clean and fresh. It can be served with plenty of chill; try it with pasta and a white sauce.

Terrace Vale T Semillon

This is a typical Hunter style; well made and capturing the essence of the variety.

CURRENT RELEASE 1997   The nose is smoky and the palate packs lemon and other citrus flavours. It's medium-bodied but quite intense in terms of flavour. The finish is dry and lingering; the alcohol demure. It can be served well-chilled. Serve as a pre-dinner drink.

Quality	♟♟♟
Value	★★★
Grapes	semillon
Region	Hunter Valley, NSW
Cellar	🍾 4
Alc./Vol.	11.5%
RRP	$16.50

T'Gallant Celia's White Pinot

Why do this to pinot noir? It's a brave try at a different style, but we can't help wondering what this would have been like if it was a red wine.

CURRENT RELEASE 1996   There's a champagne-based element to the nose which smells slightly like strawberries. The palate is rich and mouthfilling with a slightly oily texture and a hint of cherry pip. The finish is soft and there's a warmth of alcohol, a hearty 14.1%. It can be served well-chilled with an antipasto platter.

Quality	♟♟♟♟
Value	★★★
Grapes	pinot noir
Region	Mornington Peninsula, Vic.
Cellar	🍾 2
Alc./Vol.	14.1%
RRP	$23.80

CURRENT RELEASE 1997   There's a slight hint of onion skin in the colour and the nose has meaty elements. It has a full-bodied palate which tastes a little like a flat sparkling-wine base. There are faint strawberry flavours and the finish shows a slightly coarse character. It should be served well-chilled and would go well with pipis in a black bean sauce.

Quality	♟♟♟♟
Value	★★★
Grapes	pinot noir
Region	Mornington Peninsula, Vic.
Cellar	🍾 1
Alc./Vol.	14.1%
RRP	$23.80

T'Gallant Chardonnay

Quality	♥♥♥♥c
Value	★★★★
Grapes	chardonnay
Region	Mornington Peninsula, Vic.
Cellar	▮ 2
Alc./Vol.	13.8%
RRP	$22.40

Yet another new and radical label. We can expect the winemakers to be wearing designer gumboots if this success keeps up.

CURRENT RELEASE 1997   Probably one of the most convincing unoaked chardonnays on the market because it shows structure. The nose has grapefruit and peach aromas. There's a strong melon component in the palate's flavour spectrum and citrus also makes a contribution. The acid on the finish is clean and lingering. It can be served well-chilled. Try it with pan-fried flounder.

T'Gallant Holystone

Quality	♥♥♥c
Value	★★★c
Grapes	pinot noir; chardonnay
Region	Mornington Peninsula, Vic.
Cellar	▮ 2
Alc./Vol.	13.3%
RRP	$17.25

At the risk of being stoned to death by the editor, it's impossible not to make a politically incorrect observation. This wine's presentation makes it a girl's style.

CURRENT RELEASE 1996   The colour is party-frock or rose-petal pink. The nose smells like a champagne base. The palate has meaty pinot characters and some citrus tones. There's plenty of acid on the finish. It can be served well-chilled. Try it with fish cakes.

T'Gallant Lot 2 New Address Chardonnay

Quality	♥♥♥
Value	★★★
Grapes	chardonnay
Region	Mornington Peninsula, Vic.
Cellar	▮ 1
Alc./Vol.	13.9%
RRP	$22.40

Very new-age presentation for this unwooded style from the Mornington Peninsula.

CURRENT RELEASE 1996   The nose is sappy with little varietal aroma. The palate is full-bodied and smooth-textured. There are hints of melon and quince, and the flavour has a slightly coarse feel. You could be forgiven for believing this has been in oak. It should be served well-chilled. Try it with Singapore noodles.

T'Gallant Pinot Grigio

Confused? What's the difference between pinot grigio and pinot gris? It's a murky area. What about pinot bianco, tokay d'Alsace or pinot blanc? Stop worrying and drink up.

CURRENT RELEASE 1998   This is an interesting wine – it's as if there's some secret flavour that you know is there but is difficult to describe. The nose has perfumed aromatics and the palate offers rich tropical and gooseberry flavours. There's clean acid on the finish. It needs a big chill. Try it with spaghetti marinara.

Quality	♈♈♈♈
Value	★★★
Grapes	pinot grigio
Region	Mornington Peninsula, Vic.
Cellar	♦ 2
Alc./Vol.	14.0%
RRP	$27.00

T'Gallant Tribute

This wine was released as a tribute to Madeleine McCabe. In 1989 she pioneered the then-untested variety, pinot gris, on the deep red soils of the Mornington Peninsula.

CURRENT RELEASE 1997   This is a pungent style with a typical varietal signature. The exotic nose has tropical fruits like guava, custard apple and pineapple. The full-bodied palate is rich with a mixture of tropical flavours. The wine is unoaked but there's an impression of tannin and the alcohol is hardly bashful. It can be served well-chilled. Try it with Italian-style tripe.

Quality	♈♈♈♈♈
Value	★★★★
Grapes	pinot gris
Region	Mornington Peninsula, Vic.
Cellar	♦ 3
Alc./Vol.	14.7%
RRP	$27.00

Tim Adams Riesling

This is the way to enjoy Clare Valley riesling, while it's young and frisky. Clare is God's own country for riesling. Maker Tim Adams.

CURRENT RELEASE 1997   The nose is fresh with strong lime aromas. The palate is medium-bodied and continues the lime theme, and there's strong acid on a long lingering finish. It can be served well-chilled. Take it to your favourite Japanese restaurant.

Quality	♈♈♈♈
Value	★★★★
Grapes	riesling
Region	Clare Valley, SA
Cellar	♦ 5
Alc./Vol.	12.0%
RRP	13.75

Tim Adams Semillon

Quality	♈♈♈♈
Value	★★★★
Grapes	semillon
Region	Clare Valley, SA
Cellar	▯ 4
Alc./Vol.	13.0%
RRP	$17.25

This is a big chewy style from the Clare Valley. It was made to maximise flavour.
CURRENT RELEASE 1996   The nose is dominated by citrus and there's a touch of lanolin. The palate is a mixture of lemon and lime with a slight buttery character, and there's some assertive oak on a dry and lingering finish. It should be served with a medium chill. Team it with crab soufflé.

Tim Gramp Watervale Riesling

Quality	♈♈♈♈♈
Value	★★★★★
Grapes	riesling
Region	Clare Valley, SA
Cellar	▯ 5
Alc./Vol.	12.0%
RRP	$13.50

Are we looking at the stairway to heaven on the front label? Or the stairway to infinity? Who knows?
CURRENT RELEASE 1997   The wine is pretty heavenly. There are strong lime and citrus aromas on the nose. The palate has profound lime flavours and there's some very zesty acid on a crisp, fresh finish. It needs to be well-chilled. Lightly curried scallops would go well.

Tisdall Chardonnay Semillon

Quality	♈♈♈♈
Value	★★★★
Grapes	chardonnay;
	semillon
Region	not stated
Cellar	▯ 2
Alc./Vol.	13.5%
RRP	$10.00

Whatever happened to Dr Peter Tisdall, the GP who founded this winery before it became part of the Mildara/Blass/Foster's conglomerate? Recent rumour has it he's starting another wine venture.
CURRENT RELEASE 1997   A good bargain-style wine that drinks well. It has a peachy nose, and peach is the major flavour on the palate. There's also some gooseberry from the semillon. It's slightly buttery in texture and the finish is dry. Good with straight roast chook and stuffing.

Tollana Botrytis Riesling

The grapes were grown at Coonawarra, and the style is much neglected in the marketplace. It will probably never find its place in the sun, so keep mum and enjoy the rewards.

CURRENT RELEASE 1995 There's abundant evidence of botrytis on the nose plus intense honey aromas. The palate is intense with clean honeyed fruit, dried apricot and marmalade. Fresh acid and a hint of pectin make for a clean finish. It should be served very cold with a summer pudding.

Quality	♟♟♟♟
Value	★★★★
Grapes	riesling
Region	Coonawarra, SA
Cellar	▌ 2
Alc./Vol.	12.0%
RRP	$13.20 (375 ml)

Tollana Chardonnay

Tollana started life as part of a distilling group and wine was a new addition. These days it is part of the Southcorp Group. Maker Neville Falkenberg.

CURRENT RELEASE 1996 The nose has peach and tropical fruit aromas plus a touch of spicy oak. The medium-bodied palate has rich peach flavours and a touch of citrus. The wood adds to the structure. The finish is dry and mouth-cleansing. It should be served after a light chill and goes well with a smoked chicken risotto.

Quality	♟♟♟♟
Value	★★★★
Grapes	chardonnay
Region	Eden Valley, SA
Cellar	▌ 4
Alc./Vol.	13.0%
RRP	$14.10

Tollana Riesling

This is a much underestimated and somewhat under-promoted label. The current release is two years old and a real bargain.

CURRENT RELEASE 1995 The colour is a bright yellow–gold and the nose has citrus and kero aromas. The palate is showing some bottle development with a slightly oily texture and a solid lemon flavour. The finish has plenty of crisp refreshing acid. It can take the big chill. Serve with a plate of oysters natural.

Quality	♟♟♟♟
Value	★★★★⊢
Grapes	riesling
Region	Eden Valley, SA
Cellar	▌ 3
Alc./Vol.	11.5%
RRP	$11.30

Tollana Sauvignon Blanc

Quality	🍷🍷🍷½
Value	★★★½
Grapes	sauvignon blanc
Region	Eden Valley, Adelaide Hills, SA
Cellar	🍾 2
Alc./Vol.	12.5%
RRP	$12.25

It's unusual to have a current-release sauvignon blanc with a few years on the clock. The variety is usually drunk young and fresh.

CURRENT RELEASE 1994 The nose has a strident passionfruit aroma and the palate continues this tropical theme. There's pineapple and passionfruit with a hint of herbs on the palate. The acid on the finish remains fresh and proves that the wine has stood the test of time. It can be served well-chilled with smoked trout.

Trentham Estate Chardonnay

Quality	🍷🍷🍷🍷
Value	★★★★
Grapes	chardonnay
Region	Mildura, Vic.
Cellar	🍾 3
Alc./Vol.	13.5%
RRP	$14.00

This is a very useful style that doesn't break the bank. This estate usually doesn't put a foot wrong when it comes to making very drinkable wines. Maker Tony Murphy.

CURRENT RELEASE 1997 The nose is a mixture of oak and varietal aromas. The palate comes down on the peach side of the chardonnay spectrum and the oak adds a caramel note. The finish is balanced and dry. Don't over-chill, and serve with a seafood paella.

Trentham Estate Riesling

Quality	🍷🍷🍷🍷
Value	★★★★
Grapes	riesling
Region	Mildura, Vic.
Cellar	🍾 2
Alc./Vol.	11.5%
RRP	$9.90

This is a charming surprise from Mildura; there are fine aromatics and strong varietal character. This isn't supposed to be possible in this region.

CURRENT RELEASE 1997 The nose has strong lime-essence aromas. The palate is a mix of lime and other citrus flavours and there's crisp acid on a clean finish. Chill to thrill and serve with deep-fried calamari.

Tuck's Ridge Chardonnay

This variety seems right for the district. Tuck's Ridge has planted wisely, with pinot noir, pinot meunier, riesling and semillon in the vineyard under the care of Shane Strange.

CURRENT RELEASE 1996 A well-made wine that has been finessed in terms of wood treatment. The nose has citrus and butterscotch aromas. The medium-bodied palate has a creamy/buttery texture and there are pronounced grapefruit and melon flavours. The finish is dry and dominated by French oak. It doesn't need to be served super cold. It goes well with chicken pie.

Quality	♀♀♀♀
Value	★★★
Grapes	chardonnay
Region	Mornington Peninsula, Vic.
Cellar	▲ 4
Alc./Vol.	12.4%
RRP	$20.50

Turkey Flat Semillon

Turkey Flat is a Barossa vineyard that seems to know its worth. Fame is a heady tonic and Turkey Flat has enjoyed its share.

CURRENT RELEASE 1995 This is a rich, generous Barossa style that shows the benefit of bottle-age. It has a strong gooseberry nose with a background of damp straw. The palate is mouthfilling with rich developed gooseberry flavours, and the oak on the finish adds to the structure. It can be drunk with a medium chill with chicken and veal risotto.

Quality	♀♀♀♀
Value	★★★★
Grapes	semillon
Region	Barossa Valley, SA
Cellar	▲ 3
Alc./Vol.	12.5%
RRP	$20.50

Turramurra Estate Chardonnay

Here's a new label from the Mornington Peninsula. It's right down the regional track, bless all those who sail under the banner.

CURRENT RELEASE 1996 The nose is profound, with strong peach and melon aromas. The full-bodied palate has a mouthfilling texture. Peach is the major flavour and oak is never far away, adding a nutty flavour to the palate. The finish is long and dry. The alcohol is hefty and it can handle kassler with lentils. Too much chilling will kill the flavour.

Quality	♀♀♀♀ℓ
Value	★★★ʳ
Grapes	chardonnay
Region	Mornington Peninsula, Vic.
Cellar	▲ 4
Alc./Vol.	14.3%
RRP	$28.00

Turramurra Estate Sauvignon Blanc

Quality	♟♟♟
Value	★★★
Grapes	sauvignon blanc
Region	Mornington Peninsula, Vic.
Cellar	2
Alc./Vol.	12.3%
RRP	$24.60

This Mornington Peninsula–style comes down on the tropical end of the sauvignon blanc spectrum.

CURRENT RELEASE 1996   The nose has pineapple and passionfruit aromas. The palate is medium-bodied and the major flavour is gooseberry with hints of pineapple. There's plenty of crisp acid on a lingering finish. It can take a fair amount of chilling. It's great with crayfish, so drink up.

Tyrrell's Lost Block Semillon

Quality	♟♟♟♟
Value	★★★★
Grapes	semillon
Region	Hunter Valley, NSW
Cellar	10
Alc./Vol.	10.4%
RRP	$17.60

Don't do your block; pick them early and let them develop in the bottle. That's the way of Hunter semillon, and this is no exception.

CURRENT RELEASE 1997   The nose is toasty with some damp straw aromas. The palate has keen citrus flavours with a hint of gooseberry and there's plenty of fresh acid on the finish. It will take years to develop and the wine can be served well-chilled with crayfish.

Tyrrell's Moon Mountain Chardonnay

Quality	♟♟♟♟
Value	★★★★
Grapes	chardonnay
Region	Hunter Valley, NSW
Cellar	3
Alc./Vol.	12.5%
RRP	$21.30

Obviously Moon Mountain is an individual vineyard in the Tyrrell empire. It's one of the original Hunter Valley plantings.

CURRENT RELEASE 1997   The wine shows some early bottle development – some might think there are signs of premature age. The colour is a bright green–gold and the nose has a loquat, citrus aroma. The palate offers tropical fruits and citrus flavours and a mouthfilling barrel-ferment texture. The finish is dry and protracted. It goes well with pipis in a black bean sauce.

Tyrrell's Old Winery Semillon

The Old Winery label is in the middle of the Tyrrell pecking order. It's above the Long Flat range but below the individual vineyard and winemaker's selection.
CURRENT RELEASE 1996 The nose is smoky with a hint of sap and damp straw. The palate has gooseberry and lemon flavours and the finish is dry. It can tolerate a medium chill. Try it with fried chicken.

Quality	▼▼▼▼
Value	★★★★
Grapes	semillon
Region	Hunter Valley, NSW
Cellar	▌ 2
Alc./Vol.	12.0%
RRP	$15.60 Ⓢ

Tyrrell's Old Winery Semillon Sauvignon Blanc

Interesting that Tyrrell's have committed to synthetic corks for this range. We'd better get used to them but it will be interesting to see if they use them for the top of the range.
CURRENT RELEASE 1997 The nose is herbal with some damp straw aromas. The palate has an attractive touch of sweetness with gooseberry and herb flavours and the finish offers balance and dry sensations. Serve it well-chilled with fish and chips.

Quality	▼▼▼
Value	★★★
Grapes	semillon; sauvignon blanc
Region	Hunter Valley, NSW; McLaren Vale, SA
Cellar	▌
Alc./Vol.	12.5%
RRP	$15.60 Ⓢ

Tyrrell's Shee Oak Chardonnay

Although it's *sotto voce* on the label, this is an unoaked style from the Hunter Valley.
CURRENT RELEASE 1997 It has an interesting nose with a perfumed soap character. The palate is a mixture of stone-fruit flavours and citrus. There's clean acid on the finish. Since oak is absent, a reasonable chill won't hurt. Try it with a fish pie.

Quality	▼▼▼
Value	★★★
Grapes	chardonnay
Region	Hunter Valley, NSW
Cellar	▌ 2
Alc./Vol.	12.6%
RRP	$17.60

Tyrrell's Vat 1 Semillon

Quality	♥♥♥♥¢
Value	★★★★⋆
Grapes	semillon
Region	Hunter River, NSW
Cellar	🍶 5
Alc./Vol.	10.5%
RRP	$32.00

Numero uno this was in Tyrrell's arsenal until that uppity Vat 47 came along. We live in the age of chardonnay, goddamnit. About 80% of Vat 1 is released as a mature wine these days.

Previous outstanding vintages: '65, '77, '79, '83, '84, '85, '86, '87, '90, '91, '92, '93, '94, '95

CURRENT RELEASE 1993 The back label mentions a 'velvet soap character' which I can't find, but it does have rich mouth-feel. The nose has damp straw aromas and the palate has developed some complexity due to bottle-age. There are gooseberry and lemon flavours which are followed by some soft acid on a clean and lingering finish. It can be given a medium chill. *And be patient!*

Vavasour Single Vineyard Sauvignon Blanc

Quality	♥♥♥♥¢
Value	★★★
Grapes	sauvignon blanc
Region	Marlborough, NZ
Cellar	🍶 3
Alc./Vol.	13.5%
RRP	$31.20

Vavasour is in the Awatere Valley, a distinct sub-region of Marlborough, separate from the Wairau Valley, home to most of the vineyards. Made by the very talented Glenn Thomas.

CURRENT RELEASE 1996 A very pungent wine that is typical of Marlborough, with its over-the-top asparagus/capsicum vegetal perfume. Very good palate flavour, and the structure redeems the wine: good depth, roundness, ripe flavour and length. A fine drink with asparagus gratin.

Wandin Valley Estate WVE Reserve Chardonnay

Quality	♥♥♥
Value	★★⋆
Grapes	chardonnay
Region	Hunter Valley, NSW
Cellar	🍶 2
Alc./Vol.	12.5%
RRP	$24.35

This is TV producer James and Philippa Davern's country practice. It's in the Lovedale sub-region of the Hunter. Maker Geoff Broadfield.

CURRENT RELEASE 1997 The nose is shy with basil and parsley hints, and the wine is sensitively oaked. It's fairly light-bodied – thanks no doubt to the light year – and while it lacks a little concentration, it's nicely balanced. Try it with snapper quenelles.

Waterwheel Bendigo Chardonnay

Waterwheel is at Bridgewater, some distance north of
Bendigo, and the winery is beside the Loddon River. Its
wines are some of the best value around.
CURRENT RELEASE 1997 This is a boots-and-all style
from Peter Cumming. There are honey and butterscotch
and vanilla oak aromas. The palate is rich and viscous
with some alcohol warmth plus drink-now softness. A
chewy wine with density and malolactic characters. Goes
well with chargrilled crayfish.

Quality	🍷🍷🍷🍷
Value	★★★★
Grapes	chardonnay
Region	Bendigo, Vic.
Cellar	🍷 2
Alc./Vol.	13.5%
RRP	$15.00

Westend 3 Bridges Golden Mist

This is a botrytis-style wine packaged in the now-
fashionable tall half-bottle that was probably initially
designed for olive oil. Maker William Calabria and
James Ceccato.
CURRENT RELEASE 1996 The nose smells of honeysuckle and nectar. There's also some pronounced botrytis
aroma. The palate is sweet with a mouthfilling texture.
There are citrus, marmalade and toffee flavours, and
some clean acid on a balanced finish. The wine should
be served well-chilled. Try it with an apricot tart.

Quality	🍷🍷🍷🍷🍷
Value	★★★★
Grapes	semillon
Region	Griffith, NSW
Cellar	🍷 3
Alc./Vol.	10.5%
RRP	$19.70 (375 ml)

Wilderness Estate Unwooded Chardonnay

This is the renamed and reborn Lesnick's of Wilderness
Road, Pokolbin, in the Lower Hunter. Maker is the
experienced John Baruzzi.
CURRENT RELEASE 1997 There's a certain greenness in
this wine and a possible lack of ripeness, which fits with
the searingly high acidity. There are some toasty developed flavours on the palate and a modest helping of fruit
flavour. A Chablis style. It will be interesting to see if
some bottle-age improves it. Serve with fish balls.

Quality	🍷🍷🍷
Value	★★★
Grapes	chardonnay
Region	Hunter Valley, NSW
Cellar	🍷 3
Alc./Vol.	13.0%
RRP	$17.65

Willow Creek Unoaked Chardonnay

Quality	♛♛♛♛
Value	★★
Grapes	chardonnay
Region	Mornington Peninsula, Vic.
Cellar	▮ 2
Alc./Vol.	13.5%
RRP	$18.50

You'd think the absence of wood would be reflected in the price. In this case, perhaps the region is the reason for the loading.

CURRENT RELEASE 1997 The nose has a citrus component and hints of melon. The medium-bodied palate is dominated by a grapefruit flavour. There's strong acid on a lively finish. The wine can be served well-chilled. It goes well with roast chook and baked spuds.

The Willows Semillon

Quality	♛♛♛♛
Value	★★★★
Grapes	semillon
Region	Barossa Valley, SA
Cellar	▮ 3
Alc./Vol.	13.0%
RRP	$14.75

This vineyard belongs to the Scholz family. It was established in 1989 and the maker, Peter Scholz, also makes wine for Peter Lehmann.

CURRENT RELEASE 1996 This is a full-on Mother Barossa style with a slight hint of lanolin and gooseberry aromas. The palate is full-bodied and rich, with a mouthfilling buttery texture. There's a strong citrus flavour and this is balanced by gooseberry. There's a lift of American oak. It needs a medium chill and roast chook.

Will Taylor Clare Valley Riesling

Quality	♛♛♛♛♛
Value	★★★★
Grapes	riesling
Region	Clare Valley, SA
Cellar	▮ 5
Alc./Vol.	13.4%
RRP	$20.00

Will Taylor is a canny Adelaide legal eagle who specialises in wine-industry matters. He doesn't have a winery or vineyards, but selects parcels of wine from various appropriate regions.

CURRENT RELEASE 1997 A high-ripeness Clare riesling with a tremendously intense flowery, bread-doughy aroma and great richness and concentration on the palate. A very impressive debut. It will be interesting to see how it ages. Serve with pan-fried whiting and beurre blanc.

The Wilson Vineyard Chardonnay

The grapes were grown at Polish Hill River and the wine has been lightly oaked (a proportion spent weeks in new oak) so the emphasis is on fruit.
CURRENT RELEASE 1997 The nose is dominated by peach aromas. The palate is full-bodied and although the oak is light, it makes its presence apparent. Any longer in the wood and the fruit would have lost the plot. Don't over-chill, and serve with tandoori chicken.

Quality	♈♈♈♈
Value	★★★★
Grapes	chardonnay
Region	Clare Valley, SA
Cellar	🍾 4
Alc./Vol.	13.0%
RRP	$15.50

The Wilson Vineyard Gallery Series Riesling

This estate is owned by Dr Wilson, one of the industry characters. He established the vineyard in 1974.
CURRENT RELEASE 1997 The nose has a strong lime aroma and there's a suggestion of sweetness on the palate. Citrus is the major flavour and there's plenty of acid on the finish. The best is probably yet to come; it should cellar well. It can take plenty of refrigeration and goes well with oysters.

Quality	♈♈♈♈
Value	★★★¥
Grapes	riesling
Region	Clare Valley, SA
Cellar	🍾 5
Alc./Vol.	12.5%
RRP	$16.30

Wirra Wirra Chardonnay

Proprietor Greg Trott is building his dream home in the bush at McLaren Vale, a stone mansion with an enormous cellar and plenty of room for partying.
CURRENT RELEASE 1996 This is true to the Wirra style, with plenty of evidence of expensive French barrels. Toasted nuts and cedar aromas, just a teensy bit oaky. In the mouth, intense flavour on a medium- to full-bodied frame. The taste is lively and dry with terrific length but also a little oak astringency. May benefit from a little cellar time. Then serve with barbecued chicken.

Quality	♈♈♈♈?
Value	★★★★
Grapes	chardonnay
Region	McLaren Vale, SA
Cellar	➥ 1–5+
Alc./Vol.	14.0%
RRP	$20.50

Wirra Wirra Hand Picked Riesling

Quality	♟♟♟
Value	★★★
Grapes	riesling
Region	McLaren Vale, SA 60%; Clare Valley, SA 40%
Cellar	▮ 4
Alc./Vol.	12.5%
RRP	$15.60

This is the twenty-fifth successive vintage of W2 riesling. It has a dollop of Clare in the blend to give the local stuff a lift.

CURRENT RELEASE 1997   Fine, fragrant and floral, a good riesling, but just a little less sweetness would have been even better. Crisp, clean wine with straw and toast developing on the nose. Soft, broad, almost rich flavour. The grapes were obviously top-quality. Goes well with smoked salmon.

Wirra Wirra Late Picked Riesling

Quality	♟♟♟♟
Value	★★★★
Grapes	riesling
Region	McLaren Vale, SA
Cellar	▮ 5
Alc./Vol.	10.5%
RRP	$15.60 (375 ml)

McLaren Vale is not really top riesling territory, but occasionally a sweetie crops up that tests the theories. Maker Ben Riggs.

CURRENT RELEASE 1997   This is a light, youthful, understated wine in every sense. The colour is pale, the nose sweetly floral and delicate with marked riesling fruit character and just a little botrytis. The taste is medium-sweet but the candy-like flavour is of moderate intensity and could fill out with some age. Go easy on the sweet desserts here; it's best served with fruit salad.

Wirra Wirra Sauvignon Blanc

Quality	♟♟♟
Value	★★★
Grapes	sauvignon blanc
Region	McLaren Vale, SA
Cellar	▮ 1
Alc./Vol.	12.5%
RRP	$17.25

The folk at Wirra Wirra manage to turn out a very fine range of wines across several varieties, some of which are a challenge in McLaren Vale.

CURRENT RELEASE 1997   This is packed with interest and isn't just your bog-average grassy sauvignon. The nose offers cashew, pineapple and lightly herbal aromas. The palate is soft and fruity but finishes nicely dry. There's almost a suspicion of oak although the back label says it's unwooded. Richness with some delicacy. Serve with cold seafood and salads.

Wolf Blass Gold Label Riesling

This wine is unbelievable value. It was selling in some Sydney shops for $10.99 at one point, which is great for drinkers but doesn't do much for riesling's name. Maker Wendy Stuckey.

CURRENT RELEASE 1997   An up-front riesling style which was delightful as soon as it hit the shops. Soft, ripe, floral and stone-fruit aromas. The flavours in the mouth include lime and peach. A stylish, subtle wine with a little firmness on the finish and great length. Drink with snapper quenelles.

Quality	???????
Value	★★★★★
Grapes	riesling
Region	Clare & Eden Valleys, SA
Cellar	▮ 7+
Alc./Vol.	12.5%
RRP	$16.00 Ⓢ

Wolf Blass Semillon Sauvignon Blanc

This is a newie from the Blass stable, catering to the big following that semillon/sauvignon blends have garnered in recent years. Maker Wendy Stuckey.

CURRENT RELEASE 1997   The colour has a nice green tinge indicating freshness – a hallmark of the wine. Straw and hay-like semillon aromas; hints of crushed vine leaves. It's light-bodied in the mouth, tight and tidy, with delicacy and crispness. Not a wine that will fascinate endlessly, but a decent drink at a fair price. Try with caesar salad.

Quality	????
Value	★★★▸
Grapes	semillon; sauvignon blanc
Region	various, SA
Cellar	▮ 1
Alc./Vol.	11.0%
RRP	$13.50

Wyndham Estate TR2 Classic White Reserve

Couldn't they fit any more meaningless, inappropriate buzzwords on the label? Classic and Reserve are words entirely without justification here.

CURRENT RELEASE 1997   The back label reads 'Fresh, lively, aromatic', which translates as 'heavy, coarse, sickly sweet'. This is a cynical exercise in label-writing. The wine has plenty of traminer spice on the nose, and it tastes terrifically sweet, thickly phenolic and oily, and the aftertaste is cloying. They recommend Asian dishes; we recommend you drink beer instead.

Quality	???
Value	★★▸
Grapes	traminer; semillon
Region	not stated
Cellar	▮
Alc./Vol.	11.5%
RRP	$9.00 Ⓢ

Wynns Chardonnay

Quality 🍷🍷🍷🍷
Value ★★★★
Grapes chardonnay
Region Coonawarra, SA
Cellar 3
Alc./Vol. 13.5%
RRP $14.50 (S)

Quite a lot of chardonnay vines have been grafted on to red varieties in Coonawarra recently, which is a sign of what the market wants. Chardonnay does okay there, too.

CURRENT RELEASE 1997 Some milk-powder malolactic aromas here, plus peachy fruit and some cedary oak which could integrate better with a little more time in the cellar. It has plenty of flavour and a medium to full body. Best drinking will be around Christmas 1998. Hard to go past barbecued prawns for a food match.

Wynns Riesling

Quality 🍷🍷🍷🍷🍷
Value ★★★★★
Grapes riesling
Region Coonawarra, SA
Cellar 6+
Alc./Vol. 12.5%
RRP $11.25 (S)

This is one of the best rieslings on the market, and also one of the cheapest! A big win for the consumer. Maker Peter Douglas.

CURRENT RELEASE 1997 A deliciously zingy young riesling that deserves to be everyone's house white. Fresh youthful aromas of flowers and lime. Powerful flavour that verges on austerity, but the dry finish highlights the quality of the fruit. Balance, restraint and length. Will probably be even better after a few years' cellaring. Food: oven-baked scampi.

Xanadu Margaret River Chardonnay

Quality 🍷🍷🍷🍷
Value ★★★½
Grapes chardonnay
Region Margaret River, WA
Cellar 5
Alc./Vol. 13.5%
RRP $29.50

Proprietor Conor Lagan can be a pain in the nether regions, but his opinionated style is never dull.

CURRENT RELEASE 1997 This one has been through the winemaking business. The nose is dominated by oak. There are toast and vanilla aromas and a peach background. The palate has a lees character which adds a chewy texture. There are peach, melon and grapefruit flavours and the oak adds a tinder-dry quality to the finish. Try it with smoked chicken.

Xanadu Margaret River Semillon

This one breaks the mould with the low-alcohol semillon vibes – it has a strength of 14.0%. How it will develop is in the hands of the vinous gods.
CURRENT RELEASE 1997 The nose is a mixture of caramel, vanilla and wintergreen herbs. The palate is round and chewy with some tropical fruit flavour and herbs, and barrel fermentation adds a creamy texture. The finish is dominated by vanillin oak. A big style that doesn't need much chilling. Serve it with veal.

Quality	YYYY
Value	★★★★
Grapes	semillon
Region	Margaret River WA
Cellar	▲ 4
Alc./Vol.	14.0%
RRP	$23.00

Yalumba Barossa Valley Semillon

This line, formerly the Family Reserve, has been re-launched as the 'Growers' series, although the label doesn't say that. The back label lists the grapegrowers.
CURRENT RELEASE 1997 The nose is typical Barossa semillon: herbal and lemony, soft and without evidence of wood-age. It's quite a big wine, ripe, forward, with some richness and a slight grip to the finish. Serve with lemony chicken satay.

Quality	YYYY
Value	★★★★
Grapes	semillon
Region	Barossa Valley, SA
Cellar	▲ 3
Alc./Vol.	12.5%
RRP	$15.25 Ⓢ

Yanmah Ridge Manjimup Chardonnay

This is a substantial new 30-hectare vineyard and the wines are made on contract by John Wade (Howard Park) and Clive Otto (Vasse Felix).
CURRENT RELEASE 1996 Strong, milky malolactic and toasted oak characters are the main elements of this wine, and the fruit is struggling to be visible under it all. Vanilla, smoky and tea-leaf characters abound. There's plenty of flavour but with the subdued fruit, it's just a tad clumsy. An expensive debut. Good with smoked chicken.

Quality	YYYⱳ
Value	★★ⱳ
Grapes	chardonnay
Region	Pemberton, WA
Cellar	▲ 2
Alc./Vol.	12.8%
RRP	$25.40

Yarra Burn Bastard Hill Chardonnay

Quality	♥♥♥♥♥
Value	★★★
Grapes	chardonnay
Region	Yarra Valley, Vic.
Cellar	♦ 2+
Alc./Vol.	13.5%
RRP	$44.50

This comes from BRL Hardy's Hoddles Creek vineyard, which has slopes so steep as to elicit dark oaths from the vineyard workers.

CURRENT RELEASE 1994   A most unusual style: exotic, almost Germanic hints of honey-like botrytis together with vanilla, toast and herbal complexities. It's not particularly chardonnay-like, but a very interesting drop which has retained finesse and tightness with age as it's built heaps of character.

Yarra Burn Chardonnay

Quality	♥♥♥♥
Value	★★★★
Grapes	chardonnay
Region	Yarra Valley, Vic.
Cellar	♦ 2
Alc./Vol.	13.0%
RRP	$21.00 ⑤

German oak was traditionally used for chardonnay at this winery before BRL Hardy took over. Now the wine is made in French barrels. And it's an improvement.

CURRENT RELEASE 1996   The colour is a full yellow, reflecting its age, and there are dusty and resiny characters in the bouquet from oak and bottle-age. It's a full-on style with liberal oak, good fruit concentration, depth and length of flavour. A rich mouthful to serve with chicken galantine.

Yarra Edge Chardonnay

Quality	♥♥♥♥♥
Value	★★★★
Grapes	chardonnay
Region	Yarra Valley, Vic.
Cellar	♦ 4
Alc./Vol.	13.5%
RRP	$27.00

This is made at Yering Station and is a foil for the Yering wine, the malolactic versus the non-malo style. Each to his/her own!

CURRENT RELEASE 1996   Quite a full, rich style with oily texture and malolactic complexity. Good depth, richness and fresh acid enliven the palate and finish. Very long flavour, a smashing wine. Just the shot for a rich lobster main course.

Yarra Ridge Chardonnay

Yarra Ridge is one of the big success stories of the Yarra Valley; the forward momentum of its founder has been carried on in recent years by Mildara Blass.
CURRENT RELEASE 1997 This wasn't expected from a highly touted vintage. The nose is herbal and straw-like, with a high-note of fennel root. The palate is medium to full-bodied, with some oak and alcohol astringency, squashy, herbal characters and a little oak tannin on the finish. Will time reveal more fruit and provide balance? We're not holding our breath.

Quality	♟♟♟♟
Value	★★★
Grapes	chardonnay
Region	Yarra Valley, Vic.
Cellar	♦ 3
Alc./Vol.	13.5%
RRP	$21.20

Yarra Ridge Sauvignon Blanc

The winery and vineyard were commenced by lawyer Louis Bialkower in 1983, but have since passed into Mildara Blass's hands. The wines are not always straight Yarra Valley, which is naughty when Yarra is part of the name. Maker Rob Dolan.
CURRENT RELEASE 1997 Pale yellow colour and pungent pineapple/passionfruit tropical aromas, which also have elements of Granny Smith apple. It tastes very delicate and somewhat flimsy, although there is undoubted sauvignon blanc character. A little more life and intensity on the palate would not go astray. Suits a niçoise salad.

Quality	♟♟♟♟
Value	★★★
Grapes	sauvignon blanc
Region	various Victorian
	regions, including
	Yarra Valley
Cellar	♦ 2
Alc./Vol.	12.5%
RRP	$21.20

Yarra Valley Hills Victoria Chardonnay

These wines draw on three vineyards in various parts of the Yarra Valley, and are vinified by Virgin Hills winemaker Martin Williams.
CURRENT RELEASE 1996 This is about as tropical as wine gets, and has a hint of Golden Circle about it! A pretty wine, very aromatic with hints of pineapple, passionfruit and nectarine. It's fairly light on the palate and trails off towards the finish. Oak has been used sparingly. A fruit bomb. Try it with prawn and mango salad.

Quality	♟♟♟♟
Value	★★★★
Grapes	chardonnay
Region	Yarra Valley, Vic.
Cellar	♦ 2
Alc./Vol.	13.5%
RRP	$20.00

Yering Station Chardonnay

Quality	▼▼▼▼
Value	★★★★
Grapes	chardonnay
Region	Yarra Valley, Vic.
Cellar	🍾 4+
Alc./Vol.	13.0%
RRP	$19.50

Yering Station is part of a remarkable wine complex, with a new winery, vineyard, two excellent restaurants and the region's finest accommodation at Chateau Yering homestead.

CURRENT RELEASE 1997 A fruit-driven style where malolactic plays no part, leaving the grape expressed with great clarity. It's lean and very crisp in the mouth, with good penetrating acidity. The flavours are in the melon–citrus spectrum with a hint of peach, and the finish has real delicacy and freshness. Excellent with prosciutto and melon.

Sparkling Wines

Anderson Pinot Chardonnay Methode Champenoise

Howard Anderson came to the Rutherglen area when Jolimont existed. It flourished briefly in the lovely old-stone Seppelt Clydeside winery.

CURRENT RELEASE 1995 This is a pretty smart bubbly, well-made and stylish, although there's an oaky character that some may find puzzling. The colour is mid-yellow–green, and the mousse is energetic. It smells of flowers, honey and candied fruits, with some oaky spice. It's rich and weighty in the mouth, with a chewy aspect, concentration, texture and length. Try it with smoked herrings.

Quality	♟♟♟♟
Value	★★★★
Grapes	pinot noir; chardonnay
Region	King Valley & Rutherglen, Vic.
Cellar	▮ 2
Alc./Vol.	12.5%
RRP	$19.50 (cellar door)

Andrew Garrett Vintage Brut

This one of the best of many bubbly offerings from the Mildara Blass fizzery. It's composed of the classic grape varieties pinot noir and chardonnay, and the back label says it was given 100% malolactic fermentation 'to soften the wine'.

CURRENT RELEASE 1995 The middling price belies a terrific glass of bubbly. It's a rich, full, satisfying drink. It smells of fresh-baked bread and has an attractive smoky, meaty pinot noir character. It's rich in the mouth and well-balanced with a dry finish. The full price is very reasonable, even more so when widely discounted. Great with anchovy-stuffed green olives.

Quality	♟♟♟♟♟
Value	★★★★★
Grapes	pinot noir, chardonnay
Region	not stated
Cellar	▮ 2
Alc./Vol.	11.5%
RRP	$18.90 Ⓢ

Ashton Hills Blanc de Blancs

Quality	♟♟♟♟♟
Value	★★★★
Grapes	chardonnay
Region	Adelaide Hills, SA
Cellar	🍷 4
Alc./Vol.	13.0%
RRP	$25.00 (cellar door)

Chardonnay tends to take longer than pinot noir to pick up aged character from maturation on lees. This has had five years 'on tirage'. Maker Stephen George.

CURRENT RELEASE 1993   The colour is a remarkably pale yellow for its age. It smells of candied fruits, pear, straw and fresh bread. It has a fluffy mousse and lovely flavour and balance. The finish is dry and savoury with green-apple acidity. Very tasty with almond bread.

Ashton Hills Salmon Brut

Quality	♟♟♟♟♟
Value	★★★★
Grapes	pinot noir
Region	Adelaide Hills, SA
Cellar	🍷 4
Alc./Vol.	13.0%
RRP	$28.70

This is a foil for the same maker's *blanc de blancs*. Quite a different style based on pinot and full of red-grape character.

CURRENT RELEASE 1995   The colour is a full hot pink and the wine has red-grape characters all round. It smells of cherry with a twinge of crushed leaves. The palate is rich and full, with red-grape body and some tannin lending an almost chewy texture. Rich, full, dry and weighty, it would drink nicely with smoked salmon.

Auldstone Sparkling Shiraz

Quality	♟♟♟♟♟
Value	★★★★
Grapes	shiraz
Region	North East Vic.
Cellar	🍷 5+
Alc./Vol.	14.5%
RRP	$21.00

If there's a place that should be able to make ballsy sparkling red, this is it. Its neighbours in the Warby Ranges are Booths and Baileys.

CURRENT RELEASE 1995   A big, rustic, slightly wild style, with many positive attributes. Deep colour, and sweet cherry/berry, anise and cough-lolly aromas, with echoes of spice and mint. Oozes character. Big and unsubtle, quite tannic and drying, with low dosage. Packs a real punch. Try it with barbecued hamburgers.

Barossa Valley Estate Ebenezer Sparkling Pinot Noir

This is a good use for Barossa Valley pinot noir. This white sparkling wine has considerable character.

CURRENT RELEASE *non-vintage*   It has a meaty nose and a full body, with candied overtones and a slight hint of strawberry. The finish is clean and long, with the bubbles giving it a lift. Serve well-chilled with chicken.

Quality	♟♟♟♟
Value	★★★★
Grapes	pinot noir
Region	Barossa Valley, SA
Cellar	▮ 2
Alc./Vol.	13.0%
RRP	$21.00

Bethany Vintage Brut Chardonnay

We don't mean to single out this company, but why do small wineries have to make a complete range of wines from sparkling to fortifieds and all wines in between?

CURRENT RELEASE 1994   This is like a robust sparkling Barossa chardonnay. There's plenty of pressure, so open with caution. The nose is peachy with a background of yeast. The palate is full-bodied with peach and grape flavours. The finish shows soft acid. It should be served well-chilled. Try it with a cold chicken salad.

Quality	♟♟♟♟
Value	★★★☆
Grapes	chardonnay
Region	Barossa Valley, SA
Cellar	▮ 2
Alc./Vol.	12.5%
RRP	$22.00

Brands Sparkling Cabernet Sauvignon

Nice one – the brothers Brand are to be commended for this excellent style.

CURRENT RELEASE 1996   A very attractive wine with the traditional sweetness of the style plus the added bonus of tannin grip. The colour is deep mulberry, and the nose has ripe berry aromas. The palate has a cassis flavour, and the tannin makes for a dry finish. The bubbles are frenzied, so chill well and open with caution.

Quality	♟♟♟♟
Value	★★★★
Grapes	cabernet sauvignon
Region	Coonawarra, SA
Cellar	▮ 4
Alc./Vol.	13.0%
RRP	$19.00

Brown Brothers Pinot Chardonnay Vintage Brut

Quality	♟♟♟♟♟
Value	★★★★
Grapes	pinot noir;
	chardonnay
Region	Whitlands, Vic.
Cellar	♦ 3
Alc./Vol.	12.5%
RRP	$36.50

Cold-climate grapes show their finesse in this wine, which took the show circuit by storm when it was first released. Maker Terry Barnett.

Previous outstanding vintages: '93

CURRENT RELEASE 1994   This is a very dry style with some steely characters. The nose has abundant yeast character and some citrus aromas. The palate continues the citrus theme, and there's a flinty nature to the fruit. The bubbles are very lively, and there's crisp acid on a very long finish. It's cleansing and invigorating. Try it before dinner, and you're bound to be hungry.

Brown Brothers Pinot Noir Chardonnay

Quality	♟♟♟♟
Value	★★★★
Grapes	pinot noir;
	chardonnay
Region	King Valley, Vic.
Cellar	♦
Alc./Vol.	12.0%
RRP	$17.45

This is the economy sparkler from Brown Brothers. It's made to drink now and it shows a lot of class for not much cash.

CURRENT RELEASE *non-vintage*   The nose has a yeast-bun aroma with a hint of stone fruit. The palate is creamy with some attractive citrus characters, and the bubbles offer a fluffy texture. The acid on the finish is crisp. The wine should be served very well-chilled. Try it with an antipasto platter.

Capel Vale Chardonnay Pinot Noir

Quality	♟♟♟♟
Value	★★★
Grapes	chardonnay; pinot
	noir
Region	south-west WA
Cellar	♦ 2
Alc./Vol.	11.5%
RRP	$22.00

Capel Vale's owner and founder is Dr Peter Pratten, a prominent radiologist in the south-west. Winemaker is Rob Bowen, no relation to Doug in Coonawarra.

CURRENT RELEASE 1995   The colour is light yellow with a brassy tint from the 'staining' of the red grapes. It smells dusty and straw-like with little yeast-derived character. There's a peachy fruit flavour and the sweetness in the dosage seems quite high. The finish is clean nonetheless. Try it with chat potatoes and chive cream.

Cassegrain Methode Champenoise

John Cassegrain is a jack of all trades, making very serviceable wines right across the board. The fizz has more than an echo of his French ancestral land.
Previous outstanding vintages: '93
CURRENT RELEASE 1994   Here's a bubbly of character and individual style. The mid-yellow colour has a brassy reflection from the pinot grapes, and it smells of straw, malt and honey. The flavour is quite full in the mouth, nicely rounded, and has some toasted-bread aged character. It finishes with length and balance. Serve with smoked oysters.

Quality	♈♈♈♈
Value	★★★⊦
Grapes	pinot noir; chardonnay
Region	Hastings Valley, NSW
Cellar	♦ 3
Alc./Vol.	12.1%
RRP	$23.60

Croser

We recall Len Evans some years ago accusing Brian Croser of refining his wines too much. 'Croser, you are becoming so refined that one day you are going to disappear altogether!'
Previous outstanding vintages: '90, '92, '93, '94
CURRENT RELEASE 1995   Perhaps it's had insufficient time on lees – or on cork post-disgorgement – but this Croser vintage was very delicate and rather neutral at the time of tasting. The colour is light yellow and it smells herbal, with melon-skin and bracken aromas. The red grapes are not asserting themselves with their usual smoky richness. While the balance is okay and the quality is fine, it doesn't rise above the ruck. Serve with raw oysters.

Quality	♈♈♈♉
Value	★★⊦
Grapes	pinot noir 80%; chardonnay 20%
Region	Adelaide Hills, SA
Cellar	♦ 5
Alc./Vol.	12.5%
RRP	$34.50

Domaine Chandon Late Disgorged Brut

Quality	ΨΨΨΨ
Value	★★★★
Grapes	pinot noir 50%; chardonnay 48%; pinot meunier 2%
Region	various, SA, Tas., Vic.
Cellar	🍷 4
Alc./Vol.	12.5%
RRP	$40.00

It's not that the disgorging gang was late that day – the wine had extra time on yeast lees, which changed the character dramatically. Maker Wayne Donaldson.

CURRENT RELEASE 1992   The extra time on lees means a deeper green–yellow colour, and the nose has a heady cooked-bread, Vegemite and yeast-bun aroma. The palate is substantial with rich nutty flavours, and citrus and meaty characters. It has a lively bead and there's clean acid to tidy up the finish. A good food wine, so trot out the smoked salmon.

Domaine Chandon Vintage Brut

Quality	ΨΨΨΨ
Value	★★★★★
Grapes	pinot noir 51%; chardonnay 48%; pinot meunier 1%
Region	various, SA, Tas., Vic.
Cellar	🍷 2
Alc./Vol.	12.5%
RRP	$30.00

This is the tenth release from this august house, so you'd think they would get it right by now! Only joking, they were right from the start. The wine spent two-and-a-half years on lees.

Previous outstanding vintages: '88, '90, '91, '92, '94

CURRENT RELEASE 1995   Big soda-biscuit and yeast nose that hints at cooked toast. The palate is quite soft and mouthfilling with citrus flavour and a suggestion of honey to the fore. There are plenty of manic bubbles, and the finish has a nutty quality and attractive acid. A good drink any time, particularly before dinner.

Evans & Tate Sparkling Pinot Noir Chardonnay

Quality	ΨΨΨ
Value	★★★
Grapes	pinot noir 60%; chardonnay 40%
Region	Pemberton, WA
Cellar	🍷 4
Alc./Vol.	12.5%
RRP	$30.00

Pemberton is a cool region in the south-west of Western Australia, which should be well-suited to growing grapes for bubbly. Maker Brian Fletcher.

CURRENT RELEASE 1995   The mousse sparkles vigorously and the colour is pale yellow, echoing the youthfulness of the wine. The nose has a hand-cream aroma and is very restrained. The palate is likewise very delicate, a trifle neutral and very soft on the finish. The balance is good. Try it with sashimi.

Galah Wine Sparkling Shiraz

Steve George made this by taking concentrated fruit off old vines, ageing the wine in old wood for five years, champanising it, then liqueuring the result with shiraz vintage ports from 1976 and 1981.

CURRENT RELEASE 1992 Pleasantly rustic in its earthy, herby, dusty aged character. This is a big style with plenty of sweetness on entry which is dried off by some persuasive tannin towards the finish. Generous sweet ripe flavour, but not especially complex for its age. Goes well with duck.

Quality	♥♥♥♥
Value	★★★
Grapes	shiraz
Region	not stated
Cellar	▮ 5
Alc./Vol.	13.0%
RRP	$35.00 (cellar door)

Garden Gully Sparkling Burgundy

This old vineyard, first planted in 1952, is near Great Western and was bought by Warren Randall and Brian Fletcher when they were working at Seppelt's. This wine comes solely from that vineyard.

CURRENT RELEASE 1994 Youthful colour, and fresh cherry plum aromas with hints of licorice. Excellent mousse. It's very youthful, fruity and sweet. There's a jammy note, and high dosage smooths over some firm tannins. Try it with venison.

Quality	♥♥♥♥
Value	★★★★
Grapes	shiraz
Region	Great Western, Vic.
Cellar	▮ 4+
Alc./Vol.	13.0%
RRP	$20.00

Garden Gully Sparkling Pinot Noir

Now that Warren Randall is in McLaren Vale and Brian Fletcher is in WA they run Garden Gully by remote control.

CURRENT RELEASE 1995 This comes from the other side of the country. The colour is palish yellow with a pink shade, and it has the confectionery aroma of pinot noir grapes. It's fruity and youthful with red-grape richness and a long finish. A nice drink, with youth *and* character. Goes well with smoked salmon.

Quality	♥♥♥♥
Value	★★★★
Grapes	pinot noir
Region	Pemberton, WA
Cellar	▮ 3
Alc./Vol.	12.5%
RRP	$20.00

Glenara Adelaide Hills Pinot

Quality	▼▼▼⏉
Value	★★★⏉
Grapes	pinot noir (organic)
Region	Adelaide Hills, SA
Cellar	▮ 4
Alc./Vol.	11.0%
RRP	$19.70 ⓥ

The Verrall family's Glenara was the first new vineyard in the Adelaide Hills in the current wave of modern viticulture. They sure started something. Maker Trevor Jones.

CURRENT RELEASE 1995   Glenara is one of very few organically grown wines in Australia. This is a young bubbly, pale pink in colour, with a straw-hay aroma that's light and undeveloped and has hints of honey and strawberry. Very delicate in the mouth, it has reasonable intensity but could have been more interesting with more time on lees. Try it with oysters.

Grove Hill Marguerite Barrel Fermented Pinot Chardonnay

Quality	▼▼▼⏉
Value	★★★
Grapes	pinot noir; chardonnay
Region	Adelaide Hills, SA
Cellar	▮ 2+
Alc./Vol.	12.0%
RRP	$25.00

The address is Norton Summit, which is a high part of the Adelaide Hills. The base wine was barrel fermented, which is different, to say the least. Maker Roman Bratasiuk.

CURRENT RELEASE 1995   Oak dominates the bouquet with a spicy, honeyed, almost mead-like character. There are hints of candied fruits, caramel and spices (cinnamon and clove). It's fairly full and slightly broad in the mouth, with expansive, weighty, oaky bigness rather than subtlety. A rare and interesting style. Try it with crab cakes.

Hanging Rock Macedon Cuvée V

Quality	▼▼▼▼▼
Value	★★★★
Grapes	pinot noir; chardonnay
Region	Macedon, Vic.
Cellar	▮ 4
Alc./Vol.	12.5%
RRP	$38.00

You'll either love or hate this style. Full marks for having the courage to stand by their convictions. It's intentionally aldehydic to give it extra character.

CURRENT RELEASE non-vintage   The nose is candied with Vegemite and yeast qualities. The palate is chewy with honeyed fruit and lemon flavours. The bubbles work well, giving it a big lift. It's a food-style sparkling wine. Try it with smoked salmon.

Hardys Omni NV

What does the ominous-sounding name mean? Well, it's an omni-variety, omni-regional, non-vintage wine. And it has won four gold medals and a trophy at big city shows in the last year.

CURRENT RELEASE *non-vintage* **This is great value for money but let's not get too carried away with those trophies and things. The colour is pale yellow and it smells of straw, lemon and herby scents, without obvious yeast-autolysis character, while the taste is very soft and palatable. The fruit is somewhat neutral and you could argue the acid is a tad low, but it scores highly for drinkability. Try it with smoked trout pâté.**

Quality	♈♈♈♈
Value	★★★★★
Grapes	not stated
Region	not stated
Cellar	▯ 1
Alc./Vol.	12.5%
RRP	$10.00 Ⓢ

Hardys Sir James Brut de Brut

The Sir James line is a tad confusing; there are two price tiers. This one is at the top of the fighting-brand price bracket.

CURRENT RELEASE *non-vintage* The wine has a smoky, soda-ash nose with hints of yeast. The palate is dry and almost austere. The bubbles have a fine time bestowing a fluffy texture, and there is clean acid on a firm finish. A good pre-dinner style.

Quality	♈♈♈♈
Value	★★★★
Grapes	pinot noir; chardonnay
Region	various, south-east Australia
Cellar	▯
Alc./Vol.	12.0%
RRP	$15.40 Ⓢ

Hardys Sir James Cuvée Brut

This is the one wearing the Everlast head guard and boxing gloves for the BRL Hardy group. It's made for universal appeal and keen pricing.

CURRENT RELEASE *non-vintage* The nose is quite fruity, and there's a marked Vegemite character. The palate has plenty of fruit and citrus tang, and this is balanced by dry acid on a clean finish. The bubbles are quite vigorous. Serve well-chilled at a party.

Quality	♈♈♈♈
Value	★★★★
Grapes	pinot noir; chardonnay
Region	not stated
Cellar	▯
Alc./Vol.	12.0%
RRP	$15.40 Ⓢ

Hardys Sir James Sparkling Shiraz

Quality	♟♟♟♟
Value	★★★★
Grapes	shiraz
Region	not stated
Cellar	▮ 1
Alc./Vol.	13.0%
RRP	$25.00

This wine is a blend of vintages. It leans towards the traditional style with a hint of sweetness and plenty of shiraz character.

CURRENT RELEASE *non-vintage* The nose has beetroot and rhubarb aromas. The palate is chewy with rich plum and berry flavours, and the bubbles add a lift to the finish. It drinks well with a solid chill. Try it with tuna steak.

Hardys Sir James Vintage Brut

Quality	♟♟♟♟♟
Value	★★★★ⱦ
Grapes	pinot noir; chardonnay
Region	not stated
Cellar	▮ 2
Alc./Vol.	12.5%
RRP	$25.00

This is the top of the line in the BRL sparkling list. It's a well-made and complex wine.

CURRENT RELEASE 1993 It comes with a bready nose. The palate has a nutty quality with a faint hint of strawberry, thanks to the presence of pinot noir. The overall effect is soft and mouthfilling, and the finish is clean and dry. It makes a good pre-dinner drink.

Quality	♟♟♟♟♟
Value	★★★★ⱦ
Grapes	chardonnay; pinot noir; pinot meunier
Region	Yarra Valley, Vic.; Tas.
Cellar	▮ 2
Alc./Vol.	12.5%
RRP	$25.00

CURRENT RELEASE 1994 A very delicate but complex wine. The nose has a slight hint of cooked bread and cracked yeast characters. The palate is crisp with chardonnay and citrus flavours. The bubbles work like mad and there is crisp acid on a lingering finish. The wine should be served well-chilled. A good pre-dinner, make-you-ravenous style.

Katnook Estate Chardonnay Brut

Chardonnay doesn't tend to benefit a lot from extended age on lees, hence this spends just 14 months on yeast and is a fruit-driven style. Maker Wayne Stehbens.

CURRENT RELEASE 1994 True to the variety, this has a pale yellow colour and the aroma is delicate with light toast and straw-like fruit aromas. A fresh, youthful style with dryness, delicacy and beautiful balance. Excellent aperitif style. Drink with oysters.

Quality	🍷🍷🍷🍷
Value	★★★★
Grapes	chardonnay
Region	Coonawarra, SA
Cellar	4
Alc./Vol.	12.5%
RRP	$24.60

Killawarra Premier Brut

This is a brand without a home: it's always been a brand, not a winery. The wines are made in various Southcorp wineries and turned into fizz at Great Western.

CURRENT RELEASE 1995 This is top value for money: a wine that's full of character and doesn't stint on flavour. The dominant notes are meaty pinot noir characters and breadiness from ageing on yeast lees. Soft peach flavours fill out the palate and there's some vanilla/caramel development. Serve it with smoked trout mousse.

Quality	🍷🍷🍷🍷
Value	★★★★½
Grapes	pinot noir; chardonnay
Region	various
Cellar	1
Alc./Vol.	11.0%
RRP	$13.55% ($)

McLarens On The Lake Brut Cuvée

This is described as Brut but we guess they must have had Brut 33 in mind. It's a heavily perfumed wine that would be better described as a spumante or moscato style.

CURRENT RELEASE *non-vintage* Intense muscat (fronti or traminer?) aromatics bounce out of the glass, and the taste is really quite sweet. It's very young and fruity, and shows no real age or 'champagne' character. A well-made, pleasant, grapey style that most resembles Asti spumante. Drink with a fresh peach after an alfresco summer lunch.

Quality	🍷🍷🍷
Value	★★★
Grapes	not stated
Region	not stated
Cellar	1
Alc./Vol.	11.5%
RRP	$12.80

Meadowbank Mardi Brut

Quality	♟♟
Value	★★
Grapes	pinot noir; chardonnay
Region	Derwent Valley, Tas.
Cellar	▮ 3
Alc./Vol.	11.5%
RRP	$29.00

The first sparkling wine from this vineyard. BRL Hardy has financed the planting of a major new vineyard at Meadowbank, but as far as we know they don't have anything to do with the winemaking.
CURRENT RELEASE 1996 This is a very young wine whose fierce acidity points to its cold-climate provenance. It smells appley and has some unusual lees-derived characters, and more than a suspicion of oxidation. The finish is dry and the acid makes it somewhat unbalanced. Needs food: try Tassie abalone.

Milburn Park Pinot Chardonnay

Quality	♟♟♟
Value	★★★
Grapes	pinot noir; chardonnay
Region	Murray Valley, Vic.
Cellar	▮
Alc./Vol.	12.0%
RRP	$16.40 Ⓢ

Growing fizz base-wine in the Riverland is a real challenge. Normally one would look towards cooler climes.
CURRENT RELEASE 1995 This is an unusual wine: it has reasonable flavour intensity and finishes dry with a slight grip, but the overall impression is of a fairly frail wine. The most unusual aspect is the bouquet. It has a cosmetic pinot-ish character and a high note that reminds one of methylated spirit. Mix it with fruit juice to make a party punch.

Miranda Brut Blanc de Blancs

Quality	♟♟♟
Value	★★★★
Grapes	not stated
Region	Riverina, NSW
Cellar	▮
Alc./Vol.	11.0%
RRP	$5.00

Miranda is the king of passion pop, Golden Gate spumante and other delights. This cheapie falls into a similar category.
CURRENT RELEASE *non-vintage* The colour is a marked buttercup yellow and the aroma is of non-champagne grapes, probably a muscat variety or even riesling. Whatever, it's a floral fruit-driven style, which is simple, uncomplicated and easy to drink. Hard to complain about the price.

Miranda Shiraz Cabernets Brut

Is there a market for $5 red fizz? If it's called Lambrusco, sure, but otherwise . . .

CURRENT RELEASE *non-vintage* The colour is very light and the aromas are of dusty, earthy and cherry notes with grassy herbal underripe inflexions. It's very light in the mouth, with a dilute and rather green herbal taste. The balance is good, but maybe it would be better sweeter. Whip it down with a hamburger.

Quality	🍷🍷
Value	★★★
Grapes	shiraz; cabernets
Region	Riverina, NSW
Cellar	🍾
Alc./Vol.	11.5%
RRP	$5.00

Peter Rumball Pinot Noir Chardonnay

PR is back in business after a spell of self-imposed exile. Like the winemaker, this is a very lively style, so open with caution.

CURRENT RELEASE 1995 The colour is a bright lemon–yellow, and the nose has distinct autolysed yeast characters. The palate is very fresh, showing no hint of bottle-age. It has a strong citrus flavour and the bubbles work well. The acid on the finish completes the wine, giving it an assertive finish. Serve very well-chilled before dinner.

Quality	🍷🍷🍷🍷
Value	★★★★
Grapes	chardonnay; pinot noir
Region	not stated
Cellar	🍾 3
Alc./Vol.	13.0%
RRP	$20.00

Peter Rumball Sparkling Shiraz

This is the right (or should that be red?) stuff.

CURRENT RELEASE *non-vintage* The nose is a wonderful mixture of spices, plums and crushed berries. The palate is substantial, with sweet fruit flavours, slabs of cherry, plum and some enlivening spices. It's a very complex mixture of flavours that has the support of substantial tannins and persistent grip. It can be served well-chilled with turkey.

Quality	🍷🍷🍷🍷🍷
Value	★★★★★
Grapes	shiraz
Region	Coonawarra, SA
Cellar	🍾 3
Alc./Vol.	12.5%
RRP	$20.00

Peter Rumball The Pink

Quality	▼▼▼▼
Value	★★★★
Grapes	chardonnay; pinot noir; cabernet sauvignon
Region	not stated
Cellar	▮ 1
Alc./Vol.	12.5%
RRP	$20.00

Pink makes the boys wink, or so the theory goes. In some cases that isn't a desirable side effect!
CURRENT RELEASE *non-vintage*   The wine has an electric pink colour – very vibrant indeed! It's made from chardonnay, pinot noir and a dash of cabernet sauvignon. The nose is quite fruity, and the palate also shows some fruit characters as well as a suggestion of attractive sweetness. The flavour is charming and the bubbles entertain. There's plenty of acid on the finish. Serve it very well-chilled. This is a party-style sparkling wine.

Scarpantoni Black Tempest

Quality	▼▼▼▼▼
Value	★★★★
Grapes	shiraz; cabernet sauvignon
Region	McLaren Vale, SA
Cellar	▮ 5+
Alc./Vol.	14.0%
RRP	$30.00

The neck-tag tells us this wine got its name by being big, rich and wild. It's a blend of vintages and varieties. Makers Filippo and Michael Scarpantoni.
CURRENT RELEASE *non-vintage*   Lives up to its name! Deep colour introduces a big, powerful wine with massive, sweet, ripe fruit flavours that conclude with a terrific tannin kick. As splurgundies go, it's a monster. Plum, licorice, echoes of port and plenty of sweetness to balance the other elements. Those who love the big style will find this has plenty of grunt. Try it with BBQ pork spare ribs and plum sauce.

Seaview Edwards & Chaffey Pinot Noir Chardonnay

Quality	▼▼▼▼▼
Value	★★★★★
Grapes	pinot noir 72%; chardonnay 28%
Region	Adelaide Hills, SA; Yarra Valley, Vic.
Cellar	▮ 3
Alc./Vol.	12.0%
RRP	$24.00

Edwards and Chaffey were the chaps who gave the Seaview property its name and made it a household word. Today it's a Southcorp brand.
CURRENT RELEASE 1993   This is all about smoky, toasty developed character, and there's a nice touch of Champagne-like honeysuckle in the palate. Biscuity aromas too, and the flavour is very much built on bottle-age. Rich, full-bodied, long palate with appley acidity enlivening it. Try it with grissini dipped in truffle pâté.

Seaview Pinot Noir Chardonnay Vintage Reserve Brut

Marketeers love cramming words onto fizz labels. It's hard to know how to identify a wine like this. It's the superior Seaview, the one in the broad-bottomed bottle.

CURRENT RELEASE 1994 This is a generous, big-flavoured bubbly with lots of cracked-yeast character, in keeping with the house style. Peach and mango scents also power through on the bouquet. It's a fairly 'in-ya-face' style (that is, unsubtle) and represents very good value for money. Food: devils on horseback.

Quality	🍷🍷🍷🍷
Value	★★★★
Grapes	pinot noir; chardonnay
Region	various
Cellar	🍾 2
Alc./Vol.	11.5%
RRP	$17.80 (S)

Seppelt Drumborg Show Sparkling Reserve

This extended lees-aged beauty has won a couple of trophies and several gold medals. It comes from one of the coldest fizz vineyards on the mainland. Maker Ian McKenzie and team.

CURRENT RELEASE 1990 Age has conferred great character on this one. It has a medium-yellow colour and a slightly burnt-toast, bready aged bouquet with plenty of yeast-autolysis character. The mousse is very fine and persistent, and it's rich and full in the mouth with vanilla and a parade of other aged characters. The finish is dry and long, and it would go well with oysters sprinkled with caviar.

Quality	🍷🍷🍷🍷🍷
Value	★★★★★
Grapes	pinot noir; chardonnay; pinot meunier
Region	Drumborg, Vic.
Cellar	🍾 2
Alc./Vol.	12.0%
RRP	$26.25

Seppelt Fleur de Lys Vintage

Funny how sparkling wines are often associated with things French. Do we have *fleur de lys* growing wild in Oz paddocks? Maker Ian McKenzie and team.

CURRENT RELEASE 1992 There's more chardonnay than pinot here, and it shows. Sweet honeydew melon aroma, some citrus and candied fruit notes, but light on cracked-yeast character. It's soft and fruity in the mouth, with good acid, but smooth and easy on the gums. Goes well with sushi.

Quality	🍷🍷🍷🍷
Value	★★★★
Grapes	chardonnay; pinot noir
Region	Adelaide Hills, SA; Snowy Mountains, NSW; Strathbogie Ranges, Yarra Valley & Mornington Peninsula, Vic.
Cellar	🍾 2
Alc./Vol.	11.5%
RRP	$17.20 (S)

Seppelt Harpers Range

Quality	♟♟♟♟
Value	★★★★
Grapes	chardonnay; pinot noir; pinot meunier
Region	Adelaide Hills, SA; Strathbogie Ranges, Mount Beauty, Yarra Valley, Vic.; Tooma, NSW
Cellar	▮ 2
Alc./Vol.	11.5%
RRP	$18.40 ⑤

Yet another in the ample ranks of Southcorp bubblies. This is scarcely different in price from the Fleur de Lys. CURRENT RELEASE 1992 A fine, fruit-driven style with chardonnay the main event in the blend. Peach and nectarine fruit aromas, some candied-fruit on the palate, together with fresh acid. Not terribly complex but very good drinking. Goes well with smoked eel pâté.

Seppelt Original Sparkling Shiraz

Quality	♟♟♟♟♟
Value	★★★★★
Grapes	shiraz
Region	Padthaway, Coonawarra & Barossa Valley, SA
Cellar	▮ 5+
Alc./Vol.	13.5%
RRP	$17.60 ⑤

These people are the splurgundy experts, and even their low-rent version is a stunner. Maker Ian McKenzie and the Great Western team.
Previous outstanding vintages: '91, '92
CURRENT RELEASE 1993 A big, rich, cuddly mouthful of sparkling red, chockablock with sweet berry plummy flavour and a hint of oak, starting to build gamy aged complexities. Rich and lingering with nicely balanced smooth tannin. Great with Peking duck.

Seppelt Show Sparkling Shiraz

Quality	♟♟♟♟♟
Value	★★★¢
Grapes	shiraz
Region	Great Western, Vic.
Cellar	▮ 2+
Alc./Vol.	13.0%
RRP	$52.50

The show record of 18 gold medals and two trophies attests to the benchmark status of this style. For the tech heads, it spent 16 months in large oak, and more than eight years on lees in the bottle. Maker Ian McKenzie.
Previous outstanding vintages: '54, '64, '67, '84, '85
CURRENT RELEASE 1986 The mid-ruby colour has developed a brick-red edge, and positive bottle-aged characters run throughout this superb wine. The bouquet is of Ribena/cassis in the same mould as the famous '85, a sweet jammy-berry scent that's quite alluring in a wine such as this. Soft, sweet, mellow aged complexities flood the palate. It has a very long, smooth finish which ends clean and dry. Serve with roast turkey.

Seppelt Sunday Creek Pinot Noir Chardonnay

Evocative name, you have to admit. It conjures up a lazy Sunday afternoon, a picnic hamper spread out beside willows and a babbling brook, a loaf o' bread, a jug o' wine, and thou . . . The rest is censored.

CURRENT RELEASE *non-vintage* The pinot makes its presence felt here, with a faintly bronze-tinted colour, rich vanilla and caramel aromas, some weight and developed flavours. The finish is smooth and dry. It goes well with oysters and babbling brooks.

Quality	🍷🍷🍷
Value	★★★½
Grapes	pinot noir; chardonnay
Region	Drumborg, Great Western, Vic; Coonawarra, Padthaway, SA; Barooga, NSW
Cellar	🍾
Alc./Vol.	12.0%
RRP	$11.20 (S)

St Francis Sparkling Shiraz

There are many ways to be in the wine business, and this is one. No vineyards, no winery; everything's made by other companies and sold inexpensively at a lively cellar door outlet to a steady stream of tourists.

CURRENT RELEASE *non-vintage* This is a decent wine which trades on rather green fruit character and a very sweet palate. It's soft with low tannin and plum-skin fruit aromas. The palate is jazzed up by a combination of sugar and acid. Serve with Cantonese pork and black bean sauce.

Quality	🍷🍷🍷
Value	★★★
Grapes	shiraz
Region	not stated
Cellar	🍾 2
Alc./Vol.	11.0%
RRP	$13.50

St Huberts Pinot Noir Chardonnay

This is a newie, and the price suggests this shoots straight to the centre of the Mildara bubble pond, ahead of all the Yellowglens.

CURRENT RELEASE 1994 This involves some barrel fermentation and maturation plus 100-per-cent malolactic fermentation, but none of it dominates. An intriguing wine, full of candied-fruit, small-flower and restrained yeast characters. In the mouth it's dry, delicate and lingering, with a trace of austerity. A welcome addition. Try it with green olives stuffed with anchovy.

Quality	🍷🍷🍷🍷½
Value	★★★½
Grapes	pinot noir 56%, chardonnay 39%, pinot meunier 5%
Region	various
Cellar	🍾 3
Alc./Vol.	11.5%
RRP	$35.00

St Matthias Tasmanian Brut

Quality	♥♥♡
Value	★★★
Grapes	pinot noir 100%
Region	Tamar Valley, Tas.
Cellar	▲ 4
Alc./Vol.	12.0%
RRP	$15.00

This is the second label of Moorilla Estate, named after a vineyard on the West Tamar that Moorilla bought several years ago.
CURRENT RELEASE 1995   A very light, delicate wine that has no faults but lacks depth of flavour, suggesting it might have benefited from more time on its yeast lees. The colour is pale yellow and it has the faintest whiff of cracked yeast. The mousse is very vigorous and the taste is rather straightforward, with a suitably dry finish. Serve with raw Tasmanian oysters.

Taltarni Cuvée Brut

Quality	♥♥♥
Value	★★★
Grapes	pinot noir; chardonnay; pinot meunier
Region	Pyrenees, Vic.
Cellar	▲ 1
Alc./Vol.	12.0%
RRP	$17.50

This is a blend of the classics: pinot noir, chardonnay and pinot meunier grown in the Pyrenees district near Avoca.
CURRENT RELEASE *non-vintage*   The nose is slightly funky with some feral characters as well as yeast and cooked bread. The palate is dominated by citrus flavours, and the bubbles do their job. There's soft acid on the finish. It needs a big chill. Serve it before dinner.

Tatachilla Bluestone Brut

Quality	♥♥♥♡
Value	★★★↟
Grapes	pinot noir; chardonnay
Region	Barossa Valley, McLaren Vale & Padthaway, SA
Cellar	▲ 1
Alc./Vol.	11.5%
RRP	$16.50

This wasn't made in Pentridge Prison. The wine is made in bluestone cellars from fruit sourced from the Barossa, McLaren Vale and Padthaway.
CURRENT RELEASE *non-vintage*   It has a soft fruity nose with a hint of yeast. The palate has crispness and steely fruit flavours centred on citrus. There's plenty of acid on the finish, and with a big chill it's very refreshing.

Tatachilla Sparkling Malbec

The grapes were grown at Padthaway, and the result is a very pleasant, if rather immature, sparkling red wine in the traditional mould.

CURRENT RELEASE *non-vintage*   The colour is rich ruby and the bubbles are lively. There's a sweet malbec aroma on the nose. The palate has a hint of sugar, and there are slight earthy overtones on the palate. The finish is clean and dry. It should be served very well-chilled. Try it with tuna.

Quality	♈♈♈♈
Value	★★★★
Grapes	malbec
Region	Padthaway, SA
Cellar	▮ 1
Alc./Vol.	12.5%
RRP	$19.70

Tulloch Brut Methode Champenoise

There's nothing classic about this style, but thank God for that. This Hunter wine has character and flavour. It's a blend of semillon and pinot noir with the benefit of bottle-age.

CURRENT RELEASE 1994   The wine has a distinctive toasty, candied nose. The palate is full-flavoured and quite complex, with rich semillon characters and a hint of developed fruit. There's also a honeyed, candied character, and the bubbles add life to the wine. The finish is dry and clean. Serve extra cold.

Quality	♈♈♈♈
Value	★★★★
Grapes	semillon; pinot noir
Region	Hunter Valley, NSW
Cellar	▮ 2
Alc./Vol.	11.0%
RRP	$13.50

Willow Creek Methode Champenoise

This spent 18 months maturing on its yeast lees and probably would have benefited from more time. Maker Peter Harris.

CURRENT RELEASE 1995   This is delicate in every regard. The colour is pale brass and it smells very restrained with just a little maturity. It's likewise fairly attenuated to taste with fairly neutral straw, melon and slightly nutty flavours, winding out to a dry finish. No faults, just lacks depth of character. Try it with oysters.

Quality	♈♈♈
Value	★★
Grapes	pinot noir; chardonnay
Region	Mornington Peninsula, Vic.
Cellar	▮ 3+
Alc./Vol.	12.1%
RRP	$24.00

Wolf Blass Vintage Brut

Quality	▼▼▼⁷
Value	★★★
Grapes	pinot noir; chardonnay
Region	not stated
Cellar	▮ 2
Alc./Vol.	11.5%
RRP	$18.40 Ⓢ

There is a veritable battery of bubblies from the Mildara stable these days, under the Yellowglen, Garrett, Blass and St Huberts brands, and many of them taste very similar. This one's right down the middle of the house style.

CURRENT RELEASE 1995   It won't offend, but neither will it titillate. It has a light straw colour and smells of melon-like fruit, straw and a faint hint of yeast. It tastes delicate and refined, if a tad straightforward. Technically A1, with delicacy and balance. You can drink more than one glass. Try it with almond bread.

Yalumba Angas Brut

Quality	▼▼▼
Value	★★★★
Grapes	various
Region	various, SA
Cellar	▮ 1
Alc./Vol.	11.5%
RRP	$8.50 Ⓢ

This marque maintains its style and quality while some of the other popular, mass-produced fizzes in its price-league are letting their standards slip. Maker Louisa Rose and team.

CURRENT RELEASE non-vintage   There are some malty, vanilla developed characters along with candied fruit, and it tastes as though there's some riesling in the blend. In the mouth it's soft, lightly floral with some aged characters that take it out of the 'simple-fruit' category. It won't disgrace you at a party.

Yalumba Angas Brut Rosé

Quality	▼▼▼⁷
Value	★★★★★
Grapes	various
Region	various, SA
Cellar	▮ 1
Alc./Vol.	11.5%
RRP	$8.50 Ⓢ

George Fife Angas was a Barossa pioneer. He gave his name to the town of Angaston, and to this very slurpable people's fizz.

CURRENT RELEASE non-vintage   Outstanding value for money: we could drink this by the bucket (and frequently do). The colour is a fresh light pink, the bouquet has stewed cherry and plum-like red fruit aromas and is young – with no yeastiness. There's a hint of sweetness and the flavour is youthful, fresh and clean. Chill well and serve with smoked salmon blinis.

Yalumba 'D'

This has been the flagship sparkling at Yalumba, but now that they've bought the Jansz brand, the hierarchy could be about to change. Maker Louisa Rose.
CURRENT RELEASE 1995   A very neat, clean, trim sparkler that exemplifies the prevailing Aussie style. It's well made, but there's an inescapable suspicion that another year on the lees would have invested it with more character. Light yellow hue; delicate nose of small flowers and white fruits, with little cracked-yeast character. The balance is good and it has finesse. Serve with almond bread.

Quality	▼▼▼▼
Value	★★★
Grapes	pinot noir; chardonnay; pinot meunier
Region	various
Cellar	▮ 4
Alc./Vol.	12.0%
RRP	$29.50 Ⓢ

Yarra Burn Chardonnay Pinot Noir

Hoddles Creek is an Upper Yarra vineyard that Hardys bought before swallowing Yarra Burn. It's a chilly, moist vineyard which often has a botrytis attack.
CURRENT RELEASE 1993   Somewhat bizarre in its fruit style, this has a pungently tropical aroma with pineapples predominating. It's very up-front and some may find that it comes on a bit strong. It's soft and fruity in the mouth, but a trifle plain, and the honeyed/malty exotic nuances suggest botrytis influence. Try it with prawn and mango salad.

Quality	▼▼▼▮
Value	★★▮
Grapes	chardonnay; pinot noir
Region	Yarra Valley, Vic.
Cellar	▮ 2
Alc./Vol.	12.5%
RRP	$21.65 Ⓢ

Yellowglen Cuvée Victoria

This is no longer made exclusively from Victorian grapes, which is a bit naughty. But there is no doubting the fine quality.
CURRENT RELEASE 1995   Typical Yellowglen style: fine, youthful and fruit-driven. It smells of fresh green apples and honeydew melon, with a slight nuttiness. It's very intense in the mouth, with fresh zippy fruit and great persistence. Tastes like a chardonnay-dominant blend, but the label suggests otherwise. Good with almond bread.

Quality	▼▼▼▼▼
Value	★★★★▮
Grapes	'mainly cool-climate pinot noir'
Region	not stated
Cellar	▮ 4
Alc./Vol.	11.5%
RRP	$30.60 Ⓢ

Yellowglen Pinot Noir Chardonnay

Quality	♟♟♟
Value	★★⊦
Grapes	pinot noir;
	chardonnay
Region	various
Cellar	╽ 2
Alc./Vol.	11.5%
RRP	$17.60 Ⓢ

Yellowglen was the name of a goldmine that occupied the site of the vineyard during the Ballarat gold rush, over a century ago.

CURRENT RELEASE *non-vintage*   A very basic, inoffensive sparkler that just lacks intensity and character. The colour is pale yellow, and it smells of white grapes: white peach, nectarine, melon-skin. The mousse is nicely vigorous, and the wine is light and almost flimsy in the mouth with no faults, but few frills either. It ain't cheap no longer, neither! Serve it with pistachios.

Yellowglen Vintage Brut

Quality	♟♟♟♟
Value	★★★
Grapes	pinot noir 70%;
	chardonnay 24%;
	pinot meunier 6%
Region	not stated
Cellar	╽ 4
Alc./Vol.	11.5%
RRP	$21.60 Ⓢ

This comes in a bottle that would be useful on a yacht. The beamy base would stop it falling over in nasty weather.

CURRENT RELEASE 1995   Its 18 months on lees haven't given it a great deal of aged character. The colour is light yellow and there are straw, melon and fig-like fruit aromas. The palate starts with a major impact and tails off somewhat. It's a good, if straightforward, bubbly that goes well with chat potatoes and chive cream.

Yellowglen Yellow

Quality	♟♟
Value	★★⊦
Grapes	not stated
Region	not stated
Cellar	╽
Alc./Vol.	11.5%
RRP	$13.20 Ⓢ

Groovy packaging – the word Yellow is baked onto the glass, and there's very little else by way of identification. We guess it's pitched at the young and reckless.

CURRENT RELEASE *non-vintage*   This should be a success: there's not much aroma or flavour to cause offence! The colour is pale brass and there's a faintly grapey scent. It's very light and neutral in the mouth and just lacks flavour and character. A good carrier for orange juice (Buck's Fizz).

Yellowglen 'Y' Premium

This comes in a snappy package, with a capital Y baked directly onto the bottle. It's not original: California's Jordan 'J' was the first we can recall.

CURRENT RELEASE *non-vintage*   A delicate style, this is light in every regard: colour, aroma and taste. It's not too demanding and it slips down easily. There are melon, straw and bracken aromas, and yeastiness is not greatly in evidence. Technically good, it has some palate length and would team well with salty sautéed almonds.

Quality	♀♀♀⟨
Value	★★★
Grapes	chardonnay; pinot noir
Region	not stated
Cellar	▮ 3
Alc./Vol.	11.6%
RRP	$21.60 Ⓢ

Yellowglen 'Y' Premium Sparkling Burgundy

Yellowglen and Andrew Garrett are still making hay while they're allowed, with the old and rather passé name of sparkling burgundy. This is a fine example of the style.

CURRENT RELEASE *non-vintage*   Here's a splurgundy with some grunt. The colour is a deepish, youthful purple–red and it smells of plum and coconut. There's plenty of ripe fruit flavour, and it has good depth and concentration. A muscular style that ends with some grip and avoids excessive sweetness. Try it with roast turkey.

Quality	♀♀♀♀⟨
Value	★★★★
Grapes	not stated
Region	not stated
Cellar	▮ 5+
Alc./Vol.	13.5%
RRP	$21.60 Ⓢ

Fortified Wines

All Saints Classic Release Muscat

Quality	♛♛♛♛♛
Value	★★★★
Grapes	red frontignac
Region	Rutherglen, Vic.
Cellar	▮
Alc./Vol.	18.0%
RRP	$19.50

When you're in the Rutherglen area, make sure you drop in to All Saints at lunchtime: they have a great alfresco restaurant called The Terrace.
CURRENT RELEASE *non-vintage* The colour is a deepish tawny brown/red and the nose is a complex amalgam of dusty, oak-aged rancio characters and developed raisiny fruit. It's not especially muscatty to sniff but it's a wine of great depth and serious complexity. One to nurse while pondering the eternal verities.

All Saints Classic Release Tokay

Quality	♛♛♛♛♛
Value	★★★★
Grapes	muscadelle
Region	Rutherglen, Vic.
Cellar	▮
Alc./Vol.	17.0%
RRP	$19.50

This won a Penguin award for best bargain fortified two years ago, and the wine is still the goods.
CURRENT RELEASE *non-vintage* Delicious stuff! It has a classic bouquet all right: tea-leafy, vanilla, and malty with evidence of considerable wood age. It's complex and luscious, with some younger fruitier blending material showing, and some spirit warmth on the finish. Great with coffee and caramels after dinner.

All Saints Show Reserve Old Liqueur Muscat

Quality	♛♛♛♛♛
Value	★★★★
Grapes	red frontignac
Region	Rutherglen, Vic.
Cellar	▮
Alc./Vol.	18.5%
RRP	$59.50

The Hall of Fame is All Saints' tribute to the 20-odd winemakers of the district, and a very generous gesture it is. Stop by for a visit if you're in the region.
CURRENT RELEASE *non-vintage* An extraordinary old muscat which explodes with flavour in the mouth. Layers of rancio, dried fruit and vanilla flavours and seemingly endless palate length. It's more a matter of aged complexity than primary muscat fruit, and is pretty close to the pinnacle of the style. Try it with stilton cheese.

Angove's Anchorage Old Tawny Port

This is one of the few Aussie fortifieds represented in the liquor stores of Canada. We can only assume they enjoy the link with the capital of Alaska. However, it's probably inspired by the riverboats of the Murray.

CURRENT RELEASE *non-vintage* The colour is a rather faded tawny brown and the nose has mellow, slightly cooked, mature vanilla and raisin characters. The palate is fairly light and sweet, without a huge aftertaste, but it's adequate at the price and will keep most sippers safely anchored to their armchairs. Try fresh nuts.

Quality	🍷🍷🍷½
Value	★★★½
Grapes	not stated
Region	Riverland, SA
Cellar	🍾
Alc./Vol.	17.4%
RRP	$9.85 (S)

Angove's Dry Flor Fino Sherry

There's no better winter aperitif than a dry fino sherry; it beats sparkling wine hands down. This is one of the most affordable sherries around.

CURRENT RELEASE *non-vintage* A straightforward soft, fuller style of fino with a slightly cheesy yeastiness. There are nutty, salty/sea-breezy characteristics and the finish is soft and dry. It stimulates the appetite and gets those tastebuds ready for a feed. Try it with tapas, such as black olives and cured meats.

Quality	🍷🍷🍷
Value	★★★½
Grapes	not stated
Region	Riverland, SA
Cellar	🍾
Alc./Vol.	17.4%
RRP	$13.00 (S)

Auldstone Boweya Muscat

This is one of about four wineries in the Taminick area near Glenrowan. It's located near Booth's and was formerly Hercenyia Vineyard. Maker Michael Reid.

CURRENT RELEASE *non-vintage* This is a young, straightforward muscat with a reddish-amber colour and a sweet fruity nose recalling Turkish delight and candy. It hasn't had time to acquire complexity but it's a serviceable muscat and suits drizzling over ice-cream.

Quality	🍷🍷🍷
Value	★★★
Grapes	red frontignac
Region	North East Vic.
Cellar	🍾
Alc./Vol.	18.0%
RRP	$15.00 (cellar door)

Baileys Founder Liqueur Muscat

Quality	♥♥♥♥
Value	★★★★
Grapes	red frontignac
Region	North East Vic.
Cellar	▮
Alc./Vol.	18%
RRP	$18.00

The Founder series is at the affordable end of the fortified spectrum, therefore it's much younger and fresher that its esteemed top-shelf cousins.

CURRENT RELEASE *non-vintage* The colour is deep brown with an orange tinge. The nose is fresh with ripe muscat aromas. The palate is a middleweight with sweet raisin fruit flavours and berry characters. Some warming spirit and clean acid offset these. It's good over vanilla ice-cream.

Baileys Founder Liqueur Tokay

Quality	♥♥♥♥
Value	★★★★
Grapes	muscadelle
Region	North East Vic.
Cellar	▮
Alc./Vol.	18%
RRP	$18.00

Young, fresh and frisky and at the right price. This is a good introduction to the world of wood-aged fortified white wines.

CURRENT RELEASE *non-vintage* An interesting drab olive colour and the nose is dominated by spirit and a hint of cold black tea. The palate is middleweight with sweet fruit and raisin characters. Some lively spirit lifts the finish. This is another one for the homemade vanilla ice-cream.

Baileys Winemakers Selection Old Muscat

Quality	♥♥♥♥♥
Value	★★★★
Grapes	red frontignac
Region	North East Vic.
Cellar	▮
Alc./Vol.	18.0%
RRP	$55.00

Baileys winery must feel like a ping-pong ball; it keeps bouncing from management to management. Now it's part of the Mildara Blass group.

CURRENT RELEASE *non-vintage* This is the goods, in a quintessential Australian style. It's a deep-brown colour and has a complex nose with demerara sugar, nuts and raisins. The palate is mouthfilling and intense with malty rancio, dried fruit and peel flavours. There is cleansing acid on the finish. It goes well with soft blue cheese.

Brown Brothers Liqueur Muscat

This liqueur muscat is bottled only as required from a solera. The baumé for this batch was 12.1 degrees, which gives an idea of the level of residual sugar.
CURRENT RELEASE *non-vintage* The colour is an indication of the age; this is a dusky brown. The nose has strong raisin and malt extract characters. The palate is rich with sweet concentrated muscat flavours; these are enhanced by some high-toned spirit and lively acid. There is also a strong wood influence that leaves the mouth with a dry sensation. Sip it after dinner with nuts and coffee.

Quality	♥♥♥♥
Value	★★★ǀ
Grapes	red frontignac
Region	North East Vic.
Cellar	▮
Alc./Vol.	18.0%
RRP	$30.80

Brown Brothers Reserve Muscat

This is the cooking muscat (sorry about that, BB). It was made for everyday drinking and to sell at a reasonable price.
CURRENT RELEASE *non-vintage* The wine has a slight lactic or cheesy aroma and some distinct raisin characters. The medium-bodied palate has sweet dried fruit and plum-pudding flavours. There is a strong wood presence on the finish and the spirit is warming. It's a sipping style with Anzac biscuits.

Quality	♥♥♥ǀ
Value	★★★ǀ
Grapes	red frontignac
Region	North East Vic.
Cellar	▮
Alc./Vol.	18.0%
RRP	$16.30

Brown Brothers Reserve Port

It would be unkind to call this a cooking port, so let's settle on fighting commercial brand.
CURRENT RELEASE *non-vintage* A mere slip of a port, youthful and simple with vanilla and plum aromas. The palate is sweet and fruity and there is a balance of spirit on a warming finish. Try it chilled on the rocks as a pre-dinner drink.

Quality	♥♥ǀ
Value	★★★
Grapes	shiraz; grenache; mataro; carignan; cabernet sauvignon
Region	North East Vic.
Cellar	▮
Alc./Vol.	18.0%
RRP	$13.15

Brown Brothers Very Old Port

Quality	�♛♛♛?
Value	★★★★★
Grapes	shiraz
Region	North East Vic.
Cellar	▲
Alc./Vol.	18.5%
RRP	$25.60

Hands up all those who can remember when this style used to be marketed in a clear Baitz liqueur bottle with a foil capsule. It means you are a very seasoned drinker or started your port career as an under-age drinker.

CURRENT RELEASE *non-vintage* Nice work. The wine is an exercise in careful blending. The colour is a deep russet and the bouquet has strong rancio character, citrus peel, vanilla and dark chocolate. The palate floods the mouth with flavour. It's sweet and mellow with some true tawny flavours. The finish shows some fresh material and clean acid. A seductive drop that's great with coffee and halva.

Brown Brothers Very Old Tokay

Quality	♛♛♛♛♛
Value	★★★★★
Grapes	muscadelle
Region	North East Vic.
Cellar	▲
Alc./Vol.	18.5%
RRP	$30.80

This wine was the best fortified wine in last year's *Guide*. It was gratifying to see other critics also laud this style. Modesty forbids us to mention we saw it first. The wine remains outstanding value.

CURRENT RELEASE *non-vintage* Complexity and depth are extraordinary. The nose has tea-leaf, cedar, yeast, malt and rancio characters. The palate is powerful with concentrated dried fruit flavours that dazzle the taste-buds. These are offset by some lingering acid, for perfect balance. Sip slowly with consenting adults.

Brown Brothers Vintage Port

Quality	♛♛♛♛?
Value	★★★★⋆
Grapes	shiraz
Region	North East Vic.
Cellar	▲ 8
Alc./Vol.	18.0%
RRP	$20.35

Blessed be the Brothers Brown for they are one of the few companies to keep the vintage-port style alive. They are committed even if the market no longer understands or buys these wines.

CURRENT RELEASE 1992 This is a very convincing wine with style and impeccable balance. The nose is spicy with ripe shiraz and spirit aromas. The palate is medium-bodied with attractive blackberry, licorice and chocolate flavours. Then comes the best bit: the persistent finish is tinder-dry and long. It really hangs on, making the wine perfect for a soft blue cheese like Milawa blue.

Campbells Liquid Gold Tokay

The swanky clear-glass bottle, which shows off the golden colour a treat, was minted to mark the company's 125th anniversary.
CURRENT RELEASE *non-vintage* A delicious, almost addictive wine that relies on the charm of its tokay fruit to seduce, rather than great wood-age or rancio character. The colour is medium gold/amber and it smells of honey, tea-leaf, toffee and vanilla. In the mouth, it's smooth and unctuous with terrific fruit intensity and luscious sweetness. Goes with creamy blue-mould cheeses, such as Meredith sheep's blue.

Quality	☆☆☆☆☆
Value	★★★★
Grapes	muscadelle
Region	Rutherglen, Vic.
Cellar	🍾
Alc./Vol.	17.5%
RRP	$40.00 (500 ml)

Campbells Merchant Prince Muscat

The Merchant Prince was a ship that brought the first Rutherglen Campbell to Australia. This wine has an average age of 25 years and the oldest material is over 60. Maker Colin Campbell.
CURRENT RELEASE *non-vintage* The Campbell style is slightly lighter and fresher than some of the greats of the district. It's no less a wine, however, and together with its partner Isabella Tokay, Merchant Prince is at the very pinnacle of the style. Superb raisin, toffee and vanilla aromas, hints of spice and fruit-cake, tremendous intensity and length on palate. Great muscat! Serve with gorgonzola cheese.

Quality	☆☆☆☆☆
Value	★★★
Grapes	red frontignac
Region	Rutherglen, Vic.
Cellar	🍾
Alc./Vol.	18.5%
RRP	$95.00

Cassegrain Cassaé

Quality	🍷🍷🍷🍷
Value	★★★★
Grapes	not stated
Region	Hastings Valley, NSW
Cellar	🍷
Alc./Vol.	18.0%
RRP	$17.75 (350 ml)

The Cassegrains are from the land of *le coq sportif*, and this is based on the Pineau des Charentes style from Cognac: a wood-aged, fortified grape-juice. Maker John Cassegrain.

CURRENT RELEASE *non-vintage*   A very unusual, sweet fortified aperitif. The orange–amber colour has a brown tint, reflecting wood-age, and there are citrus peel, cedarwood and vanilla aromas, together with some rancio complexity. The flavour has quite a lot of oak and warm alcohol, and it lingers for ages on the tongue. Can be chilled as an aperitif or served after dinner with fruit and cheese.

Chateau Reynella Vintage Port

Quality	🍷🍷🍷🍷🍷
Value	★★★★★
Grapes	shiraz
Region	McLaren Vale, SA
Cellar	➥ 2–20+
Alc./Vol.	20.5%
RRP	$21.65 Ⓢ 🍷

You can also buy this classic in a half-bottle (for $12.40), which makes a lot of sense in the age of the health club and random breath testing.

Previous outstanding vintages: innumerable

CURRENT RELEASE 1994   A Prozac style: it's milder-mannered and calmer than some of its aggro competitors. The colour is very deep purple–red and stains the glass. It has a powerful aroma of blackberry fruit with brandy spirit and touches of licorice. The flavour is intense and beautifully balanced, with nothing out of place. The tannins are smooth and harmonious. A great wine of poise and focus, terrific fruit/tannin/spirit balance and an endless finish. Great with stilton.

Clocktower Tawny Port

Quality	🍷🍷🍷
Value	★★★★
Grapes	not stated
Region	Barossa Valley, SA
Cellar	🍷
Alc./Vol.	17.5%
RRP	$10.00 Ⓢ

This used to wear the Yalumba name, but it slipped off the label when Mildara bought the Yalumba fortified brands. The clocktower refers to the one on the winery.

CURRENT RELEASE *non-vintage*   Not very tawny, but it's a decent, if fairly spirity, ruby style. The dominant flavour note is licorice rising above plum and raisin, and there's plenty of fruit on the mid-palate. A port for drinkin', not thinkin'. Serve with panforte.

Coolangatta Estate Anniversary Vintage Port

This was released to celebrate three milestones: 50 years of the Bishop family at this estate; 200 years since George Bass found the Shoalhaven River, and 175 years since white settlement in the area. Maker Tyrrell's.
CURRENT RELEASE 1997   A chambourcin vintage port? Well, why not. The only problem is this grape always seems to lack structure, and vintage port needs structure. The wine is medium–deep, vivid purple–red, and the nose has peppery, licorice and dark-cherry aromas. It tastes rather raw and somewhat bitter, but it's difficult to judge a wine so immature. It should not be opened for at least three years, preferably five, when it will be a lighter, fruitier, softer style of VP. Then serve with aged cheddar.

Quality	♥♥♥♡
Value	★★★
Grapes	chambourcin
Region	South Coast, NSW
Cellar	➙ 3–6+
Alc./Vol.	18.7%
RRP	$15.00 (375 ml)

d'Arenberg Nostalgia Very Old Port

Sipping this port while sitting on d'Arry's verandah, which is a very swish restaurant serving very fine fare and d'Arenberg wines, is a much recommended pastime.
CURRENT RELEASE *non-vintage*   Very sweet stuff that is attenuated by obvious wood character. The colour is a ruddy tawny, and the nose has spirit, rancio and dried fruit aromas. The palate shows concentrated sweetness and this is balanced by high acid on a lingering finish. A good post-dinner drink.

Quality	♥♥♥♥
Value	★★★⊁
Grapes	grenache; shiraz
Region	McLaren Vale, SA
Cellar	∎
Alc./Vol.	18.5%
RRP	$21.00

d'Arenberg Vintage Fortified Shiraz

The name is a bit of a handle, a consequence of trying to deal with the European Union, which bans the use of generic names such as port. It's a vintage port by any other name.
CURRENT RELEASE 1995   This is one for the long haul. The colour is a bright ruby with purple tinges. The nose is spicy with obvious spirit and shiraz aromas. The palate is gutsy and heavily pressed. The tannin on the astringent finish tends to be on the bitter side and there is plenty of grip. Drink it with stilton.

Quality	♥♥♥♡
Value	★★★⊁
Grapes	shiraz
Region	McLaren Vale, SA
Cellar	➙ 8–15+
Alc./Vol.	17.5%
RRP	$21.00

De Bortoli 8-Year-Old Tawny

Quality	☆☆☆☆
Value	★★★★★
Grapes	not stated
Region	Riverina, NSW
Cellar	▮
Alc./Vol.	18.5%
RRP	$14.20

Wink, wink, nudge, nudge, know what I mean. This is a steal. One day they'll wake up at De Bortoli, so drink up before that happens.
CURRENT RELEASE *non-vintage*   Very Aussie style going cheap. A mid-tawny colour, and there are savoury rancio and fruit aromas on the nose. The palate shows aged material and a concentration of flavour. A lively finish. It needs some soft blue cheese.

De Bortoli Show Liqueur Muscat

Quality	☆☆☆☆☆
Value	★★★★★
Grapes	red frontignac
Region	Riverina, NSW;
	Rutherglen, Vic.
Cellar	▮
Alc./Vol.	18.4%
RRP	$14.50

This wine won our bargain fortified in last year's guide. We received a lot of feedback and all of it was positive. Keep those cards and letters coming folks, and keep on drinking.
CURRENT RELEASE *non-vintage*   Great value and very delicious. It smells of raisins, caramel and plum pudding. A younger component adds solid muscat flavours. There is lusciousness in the mouth and the balance is near enough to perfection. Serve with brandied figs and mascarpone.

Director's Special Tawny Port

Quality	☆☆☆
Value	★★★
Grapes	not stated
Region	Barossa Valley, SA
Cellar	▮
Alc./Vol.	17.5%
RRP	$13.00 Ⓢ

This is a port for company directors on tight expense accounts. The wine is still made by Yalumba in the Barossa Valley, but the profits tumble into the pocket of Mildara Blass.
CURRENT RELEASE *non-vintage*   A respectable budget tawny, it has the right sort of tawny-red colour and a dusty, slightly fish-oily bouquet which also features sweet plum, prune and vanilla characters. The oak contribution is mild and there is some aged character, together with a sweet but balanced finish. Goes well with cheddar.

Galway Pipe Fine Old Tawny Port

A pipe is the traditional Portuguese barrel used for maturing port. What has this to do with the Barossa? Duzzen madder. Just drink it.

CURRENT RELEASE *non-vintage*   Addictive stuff, and the quality has been maintained since Mildara Blass purchased the Yalumba fortified wine business from the Hill Smiths. It's a classic tawny port that's rich, smooth and mellow, the flavour flooding the mouth with prune, raisin and toffee nuances that reverberate around your mouth for a long time. Age confers a pleasing dryness to the finish. Pair it with coffee and a cigar.

Quality	♥♥♥♥♥
Value	★★★★✦
Grapes	not stated
Region	Barossa Valley, SA
Cellar	▮
Alc./Vol.	18.7%
RRP	$31.00 $

Hardys Liqueur Sauvignon Blanc

Seek and ye shall find – it's well worth the effort because it's oddballs like this wine that make life interesting. Trivia buffs note that the cuttings for these vines were from Chateau d'Yquem, and were planted in 1860.

CURRENT RELEASE *non-vintage*   Amazing wine; the colour is a remarkable greenish-brown with golden highlights. The nose has some rich treacle aromas and a waft of spirit. The palate is thick and rich with some unique flavours and rancio character. The finish has been freshened and is clean and lingering. It's a wine to take to a masked tasting if you're crass. If you're sophisticated you will sip it slowly and keep the secret. It will never be made again.

Quality	♥♥♥♥♥
Value	★★★★★
Grapes	sauvignon blanc
Region	McLaren Vale, SA
Cellar	▮
Alc./Vol.	19.0%
RRP	$44.00

Hardys Show Port

Quality	♥♥♥♥♥
Value	★★★★★
Grapes	shiraz; grenache
Region	McLaren Vale, SA
Cellar	▮
Alc./Vol.	19.5%
RRP	$40.00

Languishing in the twilight of sales is this famous wine of great distinction. Fortified wines now account for 8% of national wine sales and there is a spurious rumour they only appeal to old drinkers.

CURRENT RELEASE *non-vintage* This is a fine style and the price makes it a great buy. The colour is a mid-tawny and the nose has distinct rancio characters on the complex nose. You'll smell nuts, peel, vanilla and malt extract. The palate is equally complex with a mellow mixture of flavours. These are heightened by some fresh acid which adds to the balance of the wine. The finish leaves the mouth tingling fresh. Sip it with a Romeo y Julieta corona.

Hardys Tall Ships Tawny Port

Quality	♥♥♥♥
Value	★★★★⊦
Grapes	not stated
Region	McLaren Vale, SA
Cellar	▮
Alc./Vol.	17.0%
RRP	$10.50

With Sir Jim's love of nautical pursuits there is undeniable logic in this Hardys label. We are likely to see the tall ships return for the Olympics.

CURRENT RELEASE *non-vintage* This is a bargain, and one that shows plenty of character. There are raisins with a hint of rancio and the palate is sweet with a fruit-cake flavour that is balanced by some soft acid on a fresh finish. It's a good sipping style.

Hardys Vintage Port

Quality	♥♥♥♥♥
Value	★★★★★
Grapes	shiraz
Region	McLaren Vale, SA
Cellar	▮ 4
Alc./Vol.	20.5%
RRP	$24.00

Can you keep a secret? I don't suppose you can. This is a fabulous wine and one of the best-kept secrets. It's great to see a wine company keeping this old flame alight.

Previous outstanding vintages: '45, '51, '54, '56, '71, '73, '75, '81

CURRENT RELEASE 1983 As soon as the cork is pulled you'll smell something special. There are licorice, aniseed, berries and funky spirit. The palate is complex and rich. There are strong blackberry flavours and loads of spices. Dry grippy tannin makes for a lively finish and gives the impression further development is possible. Serve with soft blue cheese.

Hardys Whiskers Blake Tawny Port

Whiskers Blake was an old codger who was deaf as a post and therefore ideal for the role of bird control with a 12-gauge shotgun. He worked for the company for many years.

CURRENT RELEASE *non-vintage* This wine could find its way into the sweet white class. That about sums it up. Light, simple and sweet, the nose has spirit and raisin aromas. The palate has concentrates of dried fruit and sugar, and the finish is soft. It a chug-a-lug style.

Quality	♟♟♟
Value	★★★
Grapes	not stated
Region	McLaren Vale, Riverland, Barossa Valley, SA
Cellar	▮
Alc./Vol.	18.0%
RRP	$12.95

Kay Brothers Tawny Port

Kay's Amery is one of the veteran wineries of McLaren Vale, founded in 1890. Winemaker today is Colin Kay, a direct descendant of the founders.

CURRENT RELEASE *non-vintage* This won't break any records, but neither will it fracture the bank. It's a fair exchange for your money, although the price has gone up from last year's $15. It has a little aged character blended with the dominant element of youthful, fruity material. It smells nutty, and has smooth, sweet flavour and decent balance. Goes well with lightly fortified fruit-cake.

Quality	♟♟♟
Value	★★★
Grapes	not stated
Region	McLaren Vale, SA
Cellar	▮
Alc./Vol.	18.0%
RRP	$17.70

Lauriston Show Port

They've run riot in the packaging department yet again. The wine now comes in clear 500 ml bottles with transparent labels that are difficult to read. Never mind, we decided to shut up and drink.

CURRENT RELEASE *non-vintage* The wine is a classic with lots of complexity. The colour is a mid-tawny brown and the nose has lifted spirit, prunes and raisin aromas. The palate has rancio character and complex dried-fruit flavours. There is a freshness on the finish that gives the wine a zesty lift. Great with coffee and fruit-cake.

Quality	♟♟♟♟♟
Value	★★★★
Grapes	not stated
Region	not stated
Cellar	▮
Alc./Vol.	19.5%
RRP	$27.00

Lindemans Macquarie Port

Quality	♟♟♟♟
Value	★★★★
Grapes	grenache; shiraz
Region	Barossa Valley, SA
Cellar	▮
Alc./Vol.	18.0%
RRP	$18.00 Ⓢ

This wine is almost as historic as its namesake, Governor Macquarie. It was a stepping stone to the once-glorious but now hardly ever promoted Lindemans Show Series. CURRENT RELEASE *non-vintage* The colour is light amber and the nose has strong raisin aromas. The medium-bodied palate is not overly sweet but there are some strong fruit flavours. Some attractive acid on the finish matches these. It's a good after-dinner style.

Maglieri FJL Vintage Shiraz

Quality	♟♟♟♟♟
Value	★★★★
Grapes	shiraz
Region	McLaren Vale, SA
Cellar	▮ 5+
Alc./Vol.	18.0%
RRP	$29.50 (500 ml) ▮

Here's an erstwhile vintage port with a thoroughly PC name. FJL is the winemaker, John Loxton. CURRENT RELEASE 1988 A typically rich, ultra-ripe, blackberry-ish McLaren Vale VP style with lovely mellow spirit and 'black olive' aged character. A complex wine starting to hit its peak, with rich mellow fruit, smoky/earthy nuances, and a lush silky texture with supple tannins. Yum! Drink with stilton cheese.

Marienberg 12-Year-Old Tawny Port

Quality	♟♟♟♟
Value	★★★⊁
Grapes	shiraz; grenache; mataro
Region	McLaren Vale, SA
Cellar	▮
Alc./Vol.	19.0%
RRP	$18.00

Marienberg was originally run by Ursula Pridham, one of the first (possibly *the* first) women winemakers in Australia. It's now part of Terry Hill's Hill International group. CURRENT RELEASE *non-vintage* This mellow blend has all the sunny warmth of McLaren Vale. The nose breathes to show sweet rich toffee, caramel aromas and it's a decent mouthful of flavour, with some mellowness from age and a lot of sweetness. A goodly dollop of richness on the palate, too. Try it with dried figs and nuts.

McWilliams Family Reserve Muscat

McWilliams seems to be one of the few wine companies actually creating more fortified wine brands, rather than closing them down. This is one.

CURRENT RELEASE *non-vintage* A youngish fruity style with an amber–brown colour and excellent muscat aromatics. It has a bit more aged complexity than others in its price range, and the finish goes on and on. A newie and a real find. Food: mild blue cheeses.

Quality	♥♥♥♥
Value	★★★★
Grapes	red frontignac
Region	Riverina, NSW
Cellar	▮
Alc./Vol.	18.0%
RRP	$12.30 Ⓢ

McWilliams Family Reserve Old Tawny Port

The notes say this has spent at least five years in 'small wood', which means small barrels – barriques, hogsheads or puncheons.

CURRENT RELEASE *non-vintage* This is more ruby in style than tawny. It has a full, rich red colour, a sweet grapey nose without obvious oak or aged character, and is slightly jammy with a suggestion of muscat. In the mouth it's light, sweet and fruity, with firm youthful flavour and structure. Clean as a whistle and balanced a little towards sweetness. Try dates and dried figs with it.

Quality	♥♥♥
Value	★★★⊦
Grapes	not stated
Region	Riverina, NSW
Cellar	▮
Alc./Vol.	18.0%
RRP	$12.30 Ⓢ

McWilliams Hanwood 10-Year-Old Port

The wine is named after the village of Hanwood, just outside Griffith, where the winery is located. Indeed, it's almost part of Griffith these days.

CURRENT RELEASE *non-vintage* There's plenty of mellow aged character in this well-known brand. The colour is a lightish brick-red tawny shade, and the bouquet is of old leather armchairs, raisins and prunes. The palate has length and is quite sweet, finishing with a little astringency. Food: Tarago River blue cheese.

Quality	♥♥♥♥
Value	★★★⊦
Grapes	shiraz
Region	Riverina, NSW
Cellar	▮
Alc./Vol.	18.0%
RRP	$18.00 Ⓢ

McWilliams Show Reserve Amontillado

Quality	�
Value	★★★⯪
Grapes	palomino; pedro ximinez
Region	Riverina, NSW
Cellar	▮
Alc./Vol.	18.5%
RRP	$32.80

Wine show results for fortifieds are sometimes mysterious. The blurb says this wine won nine gold medals at shows between 1981 and 1987. Is the wine in the bottle really the same wine that won the medals? Didn't it change over the six years? And hasn't it changed in the 11 years since?

CURRENT RELEASE *non-vintage*   Very slick packaging: a smart get-up for a smart wine. This has a mid-amber colour and a mellow nose with some oak plus mixed citrus peel and a little rancio complexity. There's a trace of sweetness and the palate has very good flavour with a slight hotness from spirit on the finish. Goes well with consommé.

McWilliams Show Reserve Liqueur Muscat

Quality	YYYYY
Value	★★★★
Grapes	red frontignac
Region	Riverina, NSW
Cellar	▮
Alc./Vol.	18.5%
RRP	$59.00

This is the former McW11 muscat, and has more medals than Idi Amin. Like, 52 gold medals, six trophies and a championship.

CURRENT RELEASE *non-vintage*   Very dark old colour; fabulous wood-aged complexity to sniff, stacks of rancio. It's a mellow rather than fruity bouquet. Superb aged palate, full of character, very sweet but with a drier finish balanced up by drying wood and acid. Outstanding wine, perhaps the best Australian muscat outside North East Victoria. Try it with brandied figs.

McWilliams Show Reserve Oloroso

Quality	YYYY
Value	★★★⯪
Grapes	palomino; pedro ximinez
Region	Riverina, NSW
Cellar	▮
Alc./Vol.	18.5%
RRP	$32.80

Funny how the squat, dumpy fortified wine bottles of yesteryear are gradually being replaced by long, slender anorexic ones. Fat is out, slim is in.

CURRENT RELEASE *non-vintage*   This is quite a tasty oloroso and we can forgive the hint of 'vinegar fly' in the bouquet. There is also rancio and plenty of character, and the wine is intense on both nose and palate. The sweetness is in good balance and the finish is nice and long. Serve with French onion soup.

Morris Black Label Old Tawny Port

Everything's bigger in North East Victoria, and their tawnies are no exception. They're at the richer, firmer and darker end of the spectrum.

CURRENT RELEASE *non-vintage* This is a good service-able commercial tawny port, but it ain't all that old. Raisin-like, grapey aromas, a gentle kiss of wood-age, and attractive sweet flavour. Try it with chocolate biscuits.

Quality	♟♟♟
Value	★★★
Grapes	not stated
Region	Rutherglen, Vic.
Cellar	🍶
Alc./Vol.	17.5%
RRP	$11.30 ⑤

Morris Liqueur Muscat Canister

If you buy a dozen of these, as one of the authors had occasion to, you get 12 expensive-looking canisters to throw away. It's a waste of packaging. But the wine is special by itself.

CURRENT RELEASE *non-vintage* **Scrumptious stuff – lovely fresh fruity muscat aromas, sweet and toffee-like and spicy, just burstin' with grapiness. The taste is sweet and toffee-like with raisin and malt nuances. Great length and balance (it's even won a gold medal in Canberra). This very affordable wine shows just what Rutherglen muscat is all about. Serve with Tim Tams and strong brewed coffee.**

Quality	♟♟♟♟♟
Value	★★★★★
Grapes	red frontignac
Region	Rutherglen, Vic.
Cellar	🍶
Alc./Vol.	18.0%
RRP	$15.00 ⑤

PENGUIN BEST BARGAIN FORTIFIED

Morris Old Premium Liqueur Muscat

A benchmark for Rutherglen muscat, and a seriously great wine in anybody's language. Mick Morris's son David is now the carrier of the flame. This has finally succumbed to the popular fad for fangled packaging. It's now in 500 ml bottles with a new label.

CURRENT RELEASE *non-vintage* This even looks excit-ing as it reposes in the glass! It's dark tawny with a blackish green edge, showing great age. The nose is as powerful as muscat gets, wonderfully deep and complex with muscat fruit shining through great aged characters. The unctuous palate is rich and luscious without exces-sive or cloying sweetness, but tremendous power and balance. Goes beautifully with hazelnut soufflé and a light chocolate sauce.

Quality	♟♟♟♟♟
Value	★★★★★
Grapes	red frontignac
Region	Rutherglen, Vic.
Cellar	🍶
Alc./Vol.	18.5%
RRP	$44.00 (500 ml)

Orlando Liqueur Port

Quality	▼▼▼?
Value	★★★⯪
Grapes	not stated
Region	not stated
Cellar	▮
Alc./Vol.	17.5%
RRP	$14.75 $

What exactly is a liqueur port? It's one of those words the wine industry shies away from defining. Originally it meant a deeper, redder coloured port with high sweetness and less 'tawny' character. There we go again: wanna definition of tawny? See Seppelt DP 90.

CURRENT RELEASE *non-vintage* Rich fruit, lots of sweetness, a hint of muscat grapes which lifts the aroma, and quite modest oak-aged characters make for a pleasant, medium-priced port that's not too challenging. It has acceptable balance and length, and works well with dried fruit and nuts.

Penfolds Club Port

Quality	▼▼▼
Value	★★★
Grapes	shiraz; grenache; mataro
Region	various, SA
Cellar	▮
Alc./Vol.	18.0%
RRP	$10.00 $

Long gone are the business lunches where a bottle of Club would hit the restaurant table at 3.30 p.m. Then it was back to the desk for a snooze. These days it's a bowl of pasta and a glass of house white. Tough times indeed.

CURRENT RELEASE *non-vintage* It's young and fresh, and although complexity takes a holiday, there are no vices. The nose has sweet fruit aromas. The palate is centred around sugary raisins and there is a warmth of spirit on the finish. Drink it with coffee at playlunch.

Penfolds Grandfather Port

Quality	▼▼▼▼▼
Value	★★★★
Grapes	shiraz; mataro
Region	Barossa Valley, SA
Cellar	▮
Alc./Vol.	19.0%
RRP	$90.00

The blend was started back in the days of Jeff Penfold Hyland and each year a little is drawn off for bottling and the casks are refreshed with younger material.

CURRENT RELEASE *non-vintage* The age is readily apparent from the dark colour and the complex nose shows concentrated fruit, oak and rancio characters. The palate is intense with sweet raisin flavours and the finish has a wonderful persistence. It's a style to savour with reverence.

Penfolds Great Grandfather Port

MS wonders about the popularity of motor magazines featuring exotic cars like Lamborghini, Ferrari and Porsche that are beyond the realms of the average driver. Automotive voyeurism, he guesses. This is the vinous equivalent.

CURRENT RELEASE *non-vintage* There is evidence of great cask ageing. The style is nutty with pronounced rancio characters as well as coffee grounds, caramel, toffee and wood. The poised palate is mouthfilling with dried fruit, peel, marzipan and coffee. The finish has great mellowness and this is one you won't gulp or serve to the in-laws.

Quality	▼▼▼▼▼
Value	n/a
Grapes	not stated
Region	Barossa Valley, SA
Cellar	▮
Alc./Vol.	19.0%
RRP	price on application

Penfolds Reserve Club Port

This is a relatively recent development. We guess this stuff is targeted at the wood-panelled gentlepersons' clubs that would have people like us for members.

CURRENT RELEASE *non-vintage* You get more bang for the extra bucks; there is more intensity and complexity here than in some others of similar price range. The nose has a hint of rancio and there is some fruit-cake aroma. The palate relies on sweetness, and there is clean acid and spirit on the finish. It would go well with brandy snaps and coffee.

Quality	▼▼▼▼
Value	★★★★
Grapes	shiraz; grenache; mataro
Region	various, SA
Cellar	▮
Alc./Vol.	18.0%
RRP	$14.00 Ⓢ

Peter Lehmann Bin AD 2015

The optimum date for drinking appears on the label, so when you put it away you should be fit or come from a family with longevity genes.

Previous outstanding vintages: every label released

CURRENT RELEASE 1994 A good wine with loads of character; it's already chewy and highly entertaining. The nose has some funky spirit and strong blackberry smells. The full-bodied palate has blackberry, chocolate and licorice flavours. There is bold tannin and full-on spirit on the finish. It can be drunk now but the best is surely yet to come.

Quality	▼▼▼▼▼
Value	★★★★★
Grapes	shiraz
Region	Barossa Valley, SA
Cellar	➡ 3–10+
Alc./Vol.	20.0%
RRP	$20.00 ▮

Peter Lehmann Reserve Fino

Quality 🍷🍷🍷🍷
Value ★★★★★
Grapes palomino
Region Barossa Valley, SA
Cellar 🍾
Alc./Vol. 18.0%
RRP $10.00 (Cellar door)

This is Peter and Margaret Lehmann's diet drink. The drink you have when you're not having a gin and tonic. It's also available through the cellar door.

CURRENT RELEASE *non-vintage* This is a fresh and lively bone-dry sherry. The colour is pale yellow and the nose has a milky, nutty fino character. The palate is quite smooth with a creamy texture and muted grape flavours. This is matched by a very crisp and dry finish. Just the thing to make you hungry.

R L Buller & Son Liqueur Muscat

Quality 🍷🍷🍷🍷
Value ★★★★
Grapes red frontignac
Region North East Vic.
Cellar 🍾
Alc./Vol. 18%
RRP $22.00

Liqueur muscat is still the apple of the Rutherglen eye. It's a unique style produced from red frontignac grapes. Evaporation plays a large part in concentrating the flavours.

CURRENT RELEASE *non-vintage* This is a benchmark style with a strong nose. It invades the room the moment the bottle is opened. The aroma is of crushed berries and wood. The palate is sweet with concentrated dried-fruit characters. There is also evidence of fresh, younger material that adds life to the finish. Sip it with coffee.

R L Buller & Son Victoria Madeira

Quality 🍷🍷🍷🍷
Value ★★★★
Grapes pedro ximinez
Region North East Vic.
Cellar 🍾
Alc./Vol. 17.8%
RRP $15.00

For 'madeira' read medium-dry sherry. This is a light, fresh style that is easy to drink.

CURRENT RELEASE *non-vintage* The colour is pale tawny brown with orange highlights. The nose offers sweet fruit and delicate wood aromas. There's an attractive toffee character and also a hint of caraway seed on the palate. The finish is clean and fresh and the wine could be served chilled for a reflective autumnal drink.

Seppelt DP 38 Show Oloroso

The Australia–Europe wine labelling agreement has decreed that we stop using words like sherry on our wines, and so we should. No need anyway: oloroso says it all.

CURRENT RELEASE *non-vintage* This is a medium-sweet wine which has an interesting blend of amontillado-like flor yeast aromas plus wood-aged rancio. Many years in the wood have darkened the colour and imparted a multi-faceted nutty, glacé fruit character with hints of fruit-cake and vanilla. There's considerable sweetness on the mid-palate which dries out beautifully on the finish. Great with clear soups.

Quality	♟♟♟♟♟
Value	★★★★★
Grapes	palomino
Region	Barossa Valley, SA
Cellar	▮
Alc./Vol.	22.0%
RRP	$19.70 (375 ml)

Seppelt DP 57 Rutherglen Show Tokay

In days of yore, when customs and excise inspectors darkened the doorsteps of wineries like Seppeltsfield, the code DP was used to signify any batch of wine on which the duty had been paid. Anything else was under bond. **CURRENT RELEASE** *non-vintage* The tradition continues although Seppelt no longer has a winery at Rutherglen. This is a top-notch tokay: luscious fruit and sweetness, smooth and mellow with oak-aged character, and a charming bouquet of toffee, malt and tea leaves. Each sip lingers on the tongue for several minutes. It's great with caramels.

Quality	♟♟♟♟♟
Value	★★★★★
Grapes	muscadelle
Region	Rutherglen, Vic.
Cellar	▮
Alc./Vol.	19.0%
RRP	$25.40 (375 ml)

Seppelt DP 63 Rutherglen Show Muscat

When Seppelt changed the presentation of its Rutherglen sweeties to half-bottles, sales went through the roof. It's a trend that's gathering pace: why did it take 'em so long? Maker James Godfrey and team.

CURRENT RELEASE *non-vintage* Terrifically complex stuff: you could throw the thesaurus at it and no-one would challenge the descriptions. It's very ancient but the fine perfume of muscat grapes can still be sniffed in its ultra-complex bouquet. Very raisiny, toffee-like and lusciously sweet, with a never-ending finish. It goes perfectly with Gippsland's Tarago River blue cheese.

Quality	♟♟♟♟♟
Value	★★★★★
Grapes	red frontignac
Region	Rutherglen, Vic.
Cellar	▮
Alc./Vol.	18.0%
RRP	$25.40 (375 ml)

Seppelt DP 90 Show Tawny

Quality	♟♟♟♟♟
Value	★★★★ŕ
Grapes	shiraz; grenache; mourvèdre; and others
Region	Barossa Valley, SA
Cellar	∎
Alc./Vol.	21.5%
RRP	$75.00 (500 ml)

This is probably the definitive Australian tawny. Tawny-port style is characterised by a tawny-brown colour with flashes of red (like the authors' eyes the morning after), and very mellow as opposed to fruity aromas that result from a long time's ageing in small oak barrels.

CURRENT RELEASE *non-vintage*   Mellow's the word. The bouquet and flavour reveal rancio, aged fruit and wood aromas of great complexity which are in such perfect harmony that no single feature stands out. Concentration due to great age gives tremendous intensity in the mouth. Although it's not a big wine, the aftertaste lingers long after it's gone down the hatch. Magnificent. Serve with fine coffee and a Havana cigar.

Seppelt DP 117 Show Fino

Quality	♟♟♟♟♟
Value	★★★★★
Grapes	palomino
Region	Barossa Valley, SA
Cellar	∎
Alc./Vol.	15.5%
RRP	$19.70 (375 ml)

This wine has benefited from a change in the law which allows James Godfrey to bottle fino with just 15.5% alcohol instead of 17.0%. For complex technical reasons, this means the wine is younger, fresher and more vibrant. Result? It's winning more trophies than ever – and the hearts and minds of drinkers.

CURRENT RELEASE *non-vintage*   **We've always liked DP117 but now it's better than ever. Frisky freshness and sea-breezy flor yeast character come bounding out of the glass. In the mouth it's very fresh and tangy, with intense flavour, but also the sort of appley lightness that makes you want to quaff another and another. Drink it fresh and note the packing date on the label. Great with tapas – black olives, anchovies, BBQ octopus, frittata . . .**

Stanton & Killeen Vintage Port

The subtitle is 'Jack's Block Vineyard', which refers to an old block planted by Jack Stanton, co-founder of the firm. Present winemaker Chris Killeen is one of the most passionate vintage-port advocates in Australia.

CURRENT RELEASE 1986   This trophy-winner is S & K at full steam ahead. Marvellously complex and gloriously mature, it has a medium brick-red colour and smells of leather, blackberry and chocolate. The flavour is very intense and the balance and completeness of the wine leave little wanting. Power, richness and impressive length. Serve with stilton cheese.

Quality	♆♆♆♆♆
Value	★★★★★
Grapes	shiraz 95%; durif 5%
Region	Rutherglen, Vic.
Cellar	▮ 5
Alc./Vol.	18.5%
RRP	$24.00 (375 ml) ▮

St Peters Reserve Rutherglen/Hanwood Tawny Port

This brand is owned by Steve Chatterton and comes from the Wilton Estate winery at Yenda. It's fortified with brandy from the winery's cognac still – the only Charentais still in Australia.

CURRENT RELEASE *non-vintage*   Not really a tawny, more like a mild vintage port with lots of character and spirit on the nose. Heaps of grapey flavour. The colour is rich deep tawny red, the nose is youthful with a fruity and peppery, taily spirit which also adds fire to the palate. There's some astringency and the palate has serious intensity and length, finishing quite dry. Try it with rich fruit-cake. Interesting stuff.

Quality	♆♆♆♆♆
Value	★★★★
Grapes	not stated
Region	Rutherglen, Vic; Riverina, NSW
Cellar	▮ 5+
Alc./Vol.	20.0%
RRP	$16.95 (375 ml)

Westfield Liqueur Muscat

Quality	♟♟♟♟
Value	★★★★
Grapes	red frontignac
Region	Swan Valley, WA
Cellar	🍶
Alc./Vol.	18%
RRP	$20.00

This is a very unusual style that has distinct Malaga qualities. It's easy to see the temperatures attained in the Swan Valley. Maker John Kosovich.

CURRENT RELEASE *non-vintage*   The wine has a consistency and appearance of diff oil (and that is not being sarcastic). The nose has a strong rancio aroma and malt extract and sweet muscat smells. The palate is mouth-filling with an explosion of concentrated malty muscat flavour and a filling, melting sweetness. There is freshness on the finish that restores the balance somewhat. It's a slow sipping style that goes well with Turkish coffee.

Wolf Blass Reserve Tawny Port

Quality	♟♟♟♟♟
Value	★★★★★
Grapes	not stated
Region	Barossa Valley, SA
Cellar	🍶
Alc./Vol.	19.5%
RRP	$13.50 Ⓢ

This comes in a very snappy bottle, not the sort of shape hitherto associated with port. The bean-counters must have slipped with their calculator fingers: it's worth a lot more than the asking price.

CURRENT RELEASE *non-vintage*   This is a marvellous port, though Blass is not well-known for ports. The colour is medium–light amber/tawny, and the bouquet has a generous quota of rancio born of ample maturity. There are nutty, vanilla and caramel characters, and they come into their own on the palate. Profound flavour, depth and richness, complexity, tremendous length and a pleasingly dry aftertaste. Delicious! Sip it with a Churchill cigar.

Food/Wine Combinations – Reds

Antipasto

Chain of Ponds Novello Rosso
Charles Melton Rose of Virginia
Grant Burge Rubycind

Beef

(air-cured; braised; carpaccio; hamburgers; kebabs; meatballs; pan-fried; pot-roast; rissoles; roast; steak; steak and kidney pie)

Balgownie Estate Shiraz
Best's Great Western Shiraz
Bowen Estate Shiraz
Brokenwood Shiraz Rayner Vineyard
Brown Brothers Family Reserve Cabernet Sauvignon
Cape Mentelle Trinders Cabernet Merlot
Crofters Cabernet Merlot
De Bortoli Yarra Valley Cabernet Sauvignon
Elderton Merlot
Greenock Creek Cabernet Sauvignon
Grosset Gaia
Hanging Rock Victoria Shiraz
Hardys Tintara Shiraz
Henschke Mount Edelstone
Ingoldby Cabernet Sauvignon
Jamiesons Run
Katnook Estate Odyssey Cabernet Sauvignon
Knappstein Cabernet Merlot
Knappstein Enterprise Shiraz

Leasingham Bin 56 Cabernet Malbec
Leasingham Bin 61 Shiraz
Maglieri Steve Maglieri Shiraz
Majella Cabernet
Martinborough Vineyard Pinot Noir
Mount Horrocks Shiraz
Oakridge Estate Reserve Cabernet Sauvignon
Parker Estate First Growth
Penfolds Old Vine Shiraz Mourvèdre Grenache
Reynella Shiraz
Ribbon Vale Estate Cabernet Sauvignon
R L Buller & Son Cabernet Sauvignon
R L Buller & Son Calliope Shiraz
Rosemount Shiraz
St Leonards Wahgunyah Shiraz
Tait Wines Shiraz
Wandin Valley WVE Reserve Cabernet Sauvignon
Warrenmang Estate Shiraz
Wendouree Shiraz
Yarra Edge Cabernets

Casseroles
(beef; cassoulet; goulash; Irish stew; kid; lamb; mince; osso bucco;
savoury shepherd's pie; veal)

Barossa Valley Estate Ebenezer Sauvignon Merlot
Chapel Hill Shiraz
Charles Melton Nine Popes
Grant Burge Meshach Shiraz
Greenock Creek Seven Acre Shiraz
Hardys Hunter Ridge Shiraz
Hardys Padthaway Cabernet Sauvignon
Henschke Keyneton Estate
Kangaroo Island Vines Florance Cabernet Merlot
Katnook Estate Cabernet Sauvignon
Lowe Orange Red
Luigi Riserva

Mitchell Cabernet Sauvignon
Penfolds Bin 407 Cabernet Sauvignon
Peter Lehmann Shiraz
Reynella Cabernet Sauvignon
Ribbon Vale Estate Cabernet Sauvignon Merlot
Rufus Stone Shiraz
Saltram Mamre Brook Cabernet Sauvignon
Sandalford Shiraz
Tarchalice Magna Carta Shiraz
Tim Gramp Shiraz
Waterwheel Cabernet Sauvignon
Wynns Shiraz

Cheese

Arrowfield Show Reserve Cabernet Sauvignon
Canobolas-Smith Alchemy
Evans & Tate Cabernet Sauvignon
Evans & Tate Margaret River Shiraz
Henschke Hill of Grace
Leasingham Classic Clare Cabernet Sauvignon
Majella The Mallea
Montrose Sangiovese
Moondah Brook Cabernet Sauvignon
Pikes Reserve Shiraz
Saltram No. 1 Shiraz
Seppelt Drumborg Cabernet Sauvignon
St Hallett Faith Shiraz
Stonyfell Metala Original Plantings Shiraz

Chicken

Ashwood Grove Murphy's Block Mourvèdre Shiraz

Curry

Seppelt Harpers Range Cabernet Sauvignon
Yarra Ridge Cabernet Sauvignon

Duck
(confit; Peking; roast; sausages; tea-smoked; warm salad; wild)

Annie's Lane Cabernet Merlot
Arrowfield Shiraz
Brown Brothers Everton
Cloudy Bay Pinot Noir
d'Arenberg The High Trellis Cabernet Sauvignon
Giesen Canterbury Reserve Pinot Noir
Monichino Merlot
Oakridge Reserve Merlot
Redgate Cabernet Sauvignon
Waimarama Estate Cabernet Merlot
The Wilson Vineyard Zinfandel
Yarra Ridge Reserve Pinot Noir

Fish
(fish balls; salmon; soup; tuna)

Ashton Hills Pinot Noir
Lindemans Padthaway Vineyard Pinot Noir
Portree Damask
Rowan Pinot Noir
Yering Station Pinot Noir Rosé ED

Game
(buffalo; hare; rabbit; venison)

Arlewood Cabernet Sauvignon
Batista Pinot Noir
Campbells The Barkly Durif
Charles Melton Shiraz
Cowra Estate Classic Bat Pinot Noir
Elderton Cabernet Sauvignon
Elderton Shiraz
Happs Merlot
Hardys Eileen Hardy Shiraz

Hardys Thomas Hardy Cabernet Sauvignon
Kingston Estate Reserve Petit Verdot
Maglieri Shiraz
Merrivale Tapestry Shiraz
Mitchelton Reserve Cabernet Sauvignon
Pikes Shiraz
Saddlers Creek Equus Shiraz
Scarpantoni Cabernet Sauvignon
Stephen John Shiraz
Wirra Wirra Original Blend Grenache Shiraz
Wirra Wirra RSW Shiraz
Yalumba Reserve Shiraz
Yarra Burn Pinot Noir

Game Birds
(goose; guineafowl; mutton-bird; pheasant; pigeon; quail; squab)

Bannockburn Pinot Noir
Bannockburn Serré Pinot Noir
Bass Phillip Reserve Pinot Noir
Coldstream Hills Reserve Pinot Noir
Fire Gully Pinot Noir
Grosset Reserve Pinot Noir
Houghton Jack Mann
Montrose Barbera
Mount William Pinot Noir
Notley Gorge Vineyard Pinot Noir
Redgate Shiraz
Shottesbrooke Merlot
Zema Estate Cluny

Kangaroo
(chargrilled; pan-fried; stewed)

Jeanneret Shiraz
Majella Shiraz
Skillogalee Shiraz

Tim Adams Cabernet
Warrenmang Grand Pyrenees
Waterwheel Shiraz

Lamb
(BBQ; chops; kebabs; Middle Eastern; mutton; pan-fried fillets; satays;
shanks; smoked; spicy; tandoori)

Angove's Mondiale Shiraz Cabernet
Baileys 1920s Block Shiraz
Brokenwood Graveyard Shiraz
Eyton Cabernets
Eyton Pinot Noir
Goundrey Reserve Cabernet Sauvignon
Goundrey Reserve Shiraz
Grant Burge Shadrach Cabernet Sauvignon
Happs Cabernet Merlot
Hardys Nottage Hill Cabernet Shiraz
Henschke Cyril Henschke Cabernet Sauvignon
Houghton Cabernet Sauvignon
Lindemans Padthaway Vineyard Cabernet Merlot
McWilliams Barwang Cabernet Sauvignon
Mildara Coonawarra Cabernet Sauvignon
Mount Mary Cabernets Quintet
Penley Estate Shiraz Cabernet
Petaluma Coonawarra
Redman Coonawarra Cabernet Sauvignon
R L Buller & Son Victoria Classic
Robertson's Well Cabernet Sauvignon
Rosemount Coonawarra Cabernet Sauvignon
Saltram Mamre Brook Shiraz
Seppelt Terrain Series Cabernet Sauvignon
Seville Estate Cabernet Sauvignon
Stanley Brothers Black Sheep
St Huberts Cabernet Merlot
Tisdall Shiraz Cabernet
Wynns Cabernet Sauvignon

Wynns Cabernet Shiraz Merlot
Yering Station Cabernet Sauvignon Merlot

Mixed Grill

Garden Gully Shiraz
Wirra Wirra Church Block

Offal
(kidneys; liver; oxtail; pâté; sweetbreads; tripe)

Cape Mentelle Shiraz
Cape Mentelle Zinfandel
Henschke Abbotts Prayer
Kangarilla Road Cabernet Sauvignon
Knappstein Enterprise Cabernet Sauvignon
Mitchell The Growers Grenache
Redgate Cabernet Franc
Seaview Grenache
Seppelt Great Western Vineyard Shiraz

Pasta
(meat sauce; tomato sauce)

Bethany Cabernet Merlot
Brown Brothers Barbera
Brown Brothers King Valley Cabernet Sauvignon
Evans & Tate Gnangara Shiraz
Geographe Red One Shiraz
Kingston Estate Merlot
Lowe Merlot
Milburn Park Reserve Cabernet Sauvignon
Mildara Blass Stellar Shiraz
Moorebank Merlot
Moss Brothers Cabernet Merlot
Redman Coonawarra Shiraz
Seppelt Terrain Series Shiraz

Woolshed Cabernet Shiraz Merlot
Yalumba Oxford Landing Merlot

Pizza and Takeaway Food

Elderton Command Shiraz
Goundrey Cabernet Merlot
McWilliams Hanwood Cabernet Sauvignon
Peter Lehmann Grenache
Yalumba Oxford Landing Cabernet Shiraz

Pork

Brown Brothers Merlot
Chapel Hill Cabernet Sauvignon
Glaetzer Shiraz
Miranda Rovalley Ridge Grey Series Shiraz
Paringa Estate Pinot Noir
Seaview Shiraz
St Hallett Old Block Shiraz

Quiche

Mountadam Pinot Noir

Risotto

De Bortoli Melba Barrel Select
De Bortoli Yarra Valley Pinot Noir
Mount Pleasant Philip
Rotherhythe Pinot Noir

Salad

Brown Brothers Tarrango

Sausages

Black Rock Cabernet Sauvignon
Boston Bay Merlot
Cobaw Ridge Shiraz
Deakin Estate Shiraz
Evans & Tate Margaret River Merlot
Geoff Merrill Shiraz
Gramps Cabernet Merlot
Grant Burge Cameron Vale Cabernet Sauvignon
Grant Burge Filsell Shiraz
Hardys Insignia Cabernet Sauvignon Shiraz
Innisfail Pinot Noir
McWilliams John James McWilliam Shiraz
Montrose Black Shiraz
Moss Brothers Moses Rock Red
Sharefarmers Red
Yalumba Oxford Landing Merlot

Veal

Capel Vale Merlot
Cassegrain Cabernet Merlot
Coldstream Hills Briarston
Geoff Merrill Cabernet Merlot
Katnook Estate Merlot
Leasingham Classic Clare Shiraz
Montana Reserve Merlot
Old Station Watervale Shiraz Grenache
Salisbury Cabernet Merlot
Tuck's Ridge Pinot Noir
Wantirna Estate Cabernet Merlot

Food/Wine Combinations – Whites

Antipasto

Brown Brothers Pinot Noir Chardonnay
St Huberts Roussanne

Asian Food
(lightly spicy)

De Bortoli Yarra Valley Chardonnay

Asparagus

Grosset Watervale Riesling
Knappstein Sauvignon Blanc Semillon
Main Ridge Estate Chardonnay
Vavasour Single Vineyard Sauvignon Blanc

Calamari

Houghton Semillon Sauvignon Blanc
Leasingham Classic Clare Rhine Riesling
Ryecroft Unoaked Chardonnay

Cheese
(including soufflé)

Shaw & Smith Reserve Chardonnay
d'Arenberg White Ochre

Chicken

Arlewood Sauvignon Blanc Semillon
Arrowfield Show Reserve Semillon
Bethany Vintage Brut Chardonnay
Brokenwood Graveyard Chardonnay
Brown Brothers Semillon
Campbells Chardonnay
Chain of Ponds Chardonnay
Chain of Ponds Semillon
Cullen Sauvignon Blanc Semillon
Deakin Estate Alfred Chardonnay
Eyton Chardonnay
Goundrey Reserve Chardonnay
Hardys Hunter Ridge Chardonnay
Hardys Siegersdorf Chardonnay
Henschke Croft Chardonnay
Kumeu River Mate's Vineyard Chardonnay
Lindemans Bin 65 Chardonnay
Lindemans Padthaway Vineyard Chardonnay
McWilliams Mount Pleasant Chardonnay
Mitchelton Reserve Marsanne
Monichino Chardonnay
Mount Helen Chardonnay
Penfolds Old Vine Semillon
Sarantos Soft Press Chardonnay
Tarrawarra Chardonnay
Tisdall Chardonnay Semillon
Tuck's Ridge Chardonnay
Wirra Wirra Chardonnay
Yarra Burn Chardonnay

Crustaceans
(crab; crayfish; prawns; yabbies)

Alkoomi Frankland River Riesling
Amberley Estate Semillon Sauvignon Blanc

Bannockburn Chardonnay
Brown Brothers King Valley Riesling
Canobolas-Smith Chardonnay
Chapel Hill Unwooded Chardonnay
Chapel Hill Verdelho
Cranswick Estate Vignette Unoaked Chardonnay
Evans & Tate Margaret River Chardonnay
Evans & Tate Two Vineyards Chardonnay
Hardys Hunter Ridge Semillon
Henschke Julius Riesling
Kumeu River Chardonnay
Massoni Red Hill Chardonnay
McWilliams Mount Pleasant Elizabeth
Mitchelton Marsanne
Morton Estate Hawkes Bay Chardonnay
Mountadam Chardonnay
Mount Mary Chardonnay
Murrindindi Chardonnay
Orlando St Helga Riesling
Petaluma Chardonnay
Saltram Mamre Brook Chardonnay
Stonier's Reserve Chardonnay
Waterwheel Bendigo Chardonnay
Wynns Chardonnay
Yarra Edge Chardonnay

Desserts
(crème brûlée; fruit tarts; summer pudding)

Brown Brothers Noble Riesling
Hardys Padthaway Noble Riesling
Miranda Golden Botrytis
Westend 3 Bridges Golden Mist

Dim Sum/Sashimi/Sushi/Wontons

Campbells Trebbiano
Capel Vale CV Sauvignon Blanc Chardonnay

Celtic Farm Riesling
Craneford Riesling
Knappstein Dry Style Gewürztraminer
Orlando St Hilary Chardonnay
Quelltaler Carlsfield Vineyard Riesling
Scribbly Gum Semillon
Shaw & Smith Sauvignon Blanc

Duck

Cloudy Bay Chardonnay
Penfolds Yattarna Chardonnay

Fish
(battered; cakes; deep-fried; grilled; raw; smoked – all varieties)

All Saints Riesling
Andrew Garrett Riesling
Angoves Mondiale
Annie's Lane Riesling
Ashwood Grove Chardonnay
Banrock Station Semillon Chardonnay
Brown Brothers Family Reserve King Valley Riesling
Cassegrain Semillon
Castle Crossing Colombard Chardonnay
Chateau Tahbilk Chardonnay
Crabtree Watervale Riesling
d'Arenberg White Ochre
Glenguin Semillon
Goundrey Reserve Riesling
Greenstone Chardonnay
Grosset Polish Hill Riesling
Hamilton Chardonnay
Hanging Rock Victoria Riesling
Hardys Padthaway Unwooded Chardonnay
Houghton White Burgundy
Jamiesons Run Chardonnay

Krondorf Rhine Riesling
Mitchell Watervale Riesling
Orlando Russet Ridge Chardonnay
Orlando Steingarten Riesling
Peter Lehmann Chardonnay
Pewsey Vale Riesling
Pierro Semillon Sauvignon Blanc LTC
Pikes Reserve Riesling
Rosemount Roxburgh Chardonnay
Salisbury Chardonnay Semillon
T'Gallant Chardonnay
Wolf Blass Gold Label Riesling

Fruit
(including prosciutto melone)

Edenhope Chardonnay
Geoff Merrill Chardonnay
Moorebank Late Harvest Gewürztraminer
Wirra Wirra Late Picked Riesling
Yering Station Chardonnay

Game

Basedow Chardonnay
Bridgewater Mill Chardonnay
Grove Mill Chardonnay

Octopus/Calamari

Sharefarmers Chardonnay Sauvignon Blanc

Offal

Le Grys Sauvignon Blanc
Moondah Brook Chardonnay
T'Gallant Tribute

Pasta

Miranda Christy's Land Semillon Sauvignon Blanc
Mitchell The Growers Semillon
Mount Horrocks Semillon
T'Gallant Pinot Grigio

Pizza and Takeaway Food

Hardys Nottage Hill Chardonnay
Milburn Park Reserve Chardonnay
Mildara Blass Half Mile Creek Chardonnay

Quiche

de Gyffarde Sauvignon Blanc
Henschke Joseph Hill Gewürztraminer
Knappstein Hand Picked Riesling
Seppelt Drumborg Riesling

Risotto/Paella

Brown Brothers King Valley Verdelho
Coolangatta Estate Alexander Berry Chardonnay
Mount Horrocks Chardonnay
Seppelt Corella Ridge Chardonnay

Salad

Arrowfield Chardonnay
Ashton Hills Riesling
Capel Vale Reserve Whispering Hill Riesling
Cape Mentelle Semillon Sauvignon Blanc
Moondah Brook Chenin Blanc
Moondah Brook Maritime WA Dry White
Oakland Semillon Sauvignon Blanc
Prentice Chenin Blanc

Redgate OFS Semillon
Ribbon Vale Estate Semillon Sauvignon Blanc
Seresin Sauvignon Blanc
Wolf Blass Semillon Sauvignon Blanc
Yarra Ridge Sauvignon Blanc

Shellfish
(mussels; oysters; pipis; scallops)

Austin's Barrabool Chardonnay
Babich Sauvignon Blanc
Brown Brothers King Valley Sauvignon Blanc
Castle Rock Riesling
Cockfighter's Ghost Semillon
Evans & Tate Mount Barker Riesling
Grant Burge Thorn Riesling
Grove Mill Sauvignon Blanc
Hardys Sir James Chardonnay
Henschke Green's Hill Riesling
Howard Park Riesling
Kim Crawford Marlborough Dry Riesling
Kingston Estate Reserve Chardonnay
Leasingham Bin 7 Rhine Riesling
Leasingham Bin 37 Chardonnay
Mitchelton Blackwood Park Riesling
Moorilla Estate Chardonnay
Mount Mary Triolet
Penfolds Adelaide Hills Trial Bin Chardonnay
Redgate Reserve Sauvignon Blanc
Ribbon Vale Estate Sauvignon Blanc
Skillogalee Riesling
St Matthias Chardonnay
T'Gallant Celias White Pinot
Tyrrell's Moon Mountain Chardonnay

Soup

Brown Brothers King Valley Gewürztraminer
Ingleburne Unwooded Semillon
McWilliams Hanwood Chardonnay

Vegetables

Glenguin Chardonnay
Gramps Chardonnay
Kingston Estate Chardonnay
Kingston Estate Semillon Sauvignon Blanc
Orlando Jacob's Creek Riesling
Somerton Semillon Chardonnay
Stanley Brothers Chardonnay Pristine

Wine Terms

The following are commonly used winemaking terms.

ACID There are many acids that occur naturally in grapes and it's in the winemaker's interest to retain the favourable ones because these promote freshness and longevity.

AGRAFE A metal clip used to secure champagne corks during secondary bottle fermentation.

ALCOHOL Ethyl alcohol (C_2H_5OH) is a by-product of fermentation of sugars. It's the stuff that makes people happy and it adds warmth and texture to wine.

ALCOHOL BY VOLUME (A/V) The measurement of the amount of alcohol in a wine. It's expressed as a percentage, e.g. 13.0% A/V means there is 13.0% pure alcohol as a percentage of the total volume.

ALDEHYDE An unwanted and unpleasant organic compound formed between acid and alcohol by oxidation. It's removed by sulfur dioxide.

ALLIER A type of oak harvested in the French forest of the same name.

APERITIF A wine that stimulates the appetite.

AROMATIC A family of grape varieties that have a high terpene content. Riesling and gewürztraminer are examples, and terpenes produce their floral qualities.

AUTOLYSIS A Vegemite or fresh-baked bread taste and smell imparted by spent yeast cells in sparkling wines.

BACK BLEND To add unfermented grape juice to wine or to add young wine to old wine in fortifieds.

BARREL FERMENTATION The process of fermenting a red or white wine in a small barrel, thereby adding a creamy texture and toasty or nutty characters, and better integrating the wood and fruit flavours.

BARRIQUE A 225-litre barrel.

BAUMÉ   The measure of sugar in grape juice used to estimate potential alcohol content. It's usually expressed as a degree, e.g. 12 degrees baumé juice will produce approximately 12.0% A/V if it's fermented to dryness. The alternative brix scale is approximately double baumé and must be divided by 1.8 to estimate potential alcohol.

BENTONITE   A fine clay (drillers mud) used as a clarifying (fining) agent.

BLEND   A combination of two or more grape varieties and/or vintages. *See also* Cuvée

BOTRYTIS CINEREA   A fungus that thrives on grapevines in humid conditions and sucks out the water of the grapes thereby concentrating the flavour. Good in white wine but not so good in red. (There is also a loss in quantity.)

BREATHING   Uncorking a wine and allowing it to stand for a couple of hours before serving. This introduces oxygen and dissipates bottle odours. Decanting aids breathing.

BRIX   *see* Baumé

BRUT   The second lowest level of sweetness in sparkling wine; it does not mean there is no added sugar.

BUSH VINE   Although pruned the vine is self-supporting in a low-to-the-ground bush. (Still common in the Barossa Valley.)

CARBONIC MACERATION   Fermentation in whole (uncrushed) bunches. This is a popular technique in Beaujolais. It produces bright colour and softer tannins.

CHARMAT PROCESS   A process for making sparkling wine where the wine is fermented in a tank rather than in a bottle.

CLONE (CLONAL)   A recognisable subspecies of vine within a varietal family, e.g. there are numerous clones of pinot noir and these all have subtle character differences.

COLD FERMENTATION   (Also Controlled Temperature Fermentation) Usually applied to white wines where the ferment is kept at a low temperature (10–12 degrees Centigrade).

CORDON   The arms of the trained grapevine that bear the fruit.

CORDON CUT   A technique of cutting the fruit-bearing arms and allowing the berries to dehydrate to concentrate the flavour.

CRUSH   Crushing the berries to liberate the free-run juice (*q.v.*). Also used as an expression of a wine company's output: 'This winery has a 1000-tonne crush'.

CUVÉE   A Champagne term meaning a selected blend or batch.

DISGORGE   The process of removing the yeast lees from a sparkling wine. It involves freezing the neck of the bottle and firing out a plug of ice and yeast. The bottle is then topped up and recorked.

DOWNY MILDEW   A disease that attacks vine leaves and fruit. It's associated with humidity and lack of air circulation.

DRIP IRRIGATION   An accurate way of watering a vineyard. Each vine has its own dripper and a controlled amount of water is applied.

DRYLAND VINEYARD   A vineyard that has no irrigation.

ESTERS   Volatile compounds that can occur during fermentation or maturation. They impart a distinctive chemical taste.

FERMENTATION   The process by which yeast converts sugar to alcohol with a by-product of carbon dioxide.

FINING   The process of removing solids from wine to make it clear. There are several methods used.

FORTIFY   The addition of spirit to increase the amount of alcohol in a wine.

FREE-RUN JUICE   The first juice to come out of the press or drainer (as opposed to pressings).

GENERIC   Wines labelled after their district of origin rather than their grape variety, e.g. Burgundy, Chablis, Champagne etc. These terms can no longer legally be used on Australian labels. *Cf.* Varietal.

GRAFT   Changing the nature/variety of a vine by grafting a different variety on to a root stock.

IMPERIAL   A 6-litre bottle (contains eight 750-ml bottles).

JEROBOAM   A 4.5-litre champagne bottle.

LACCASE   A milky condition on the surface of red wine caused by noble rot. The wine is usually pasteurised.

LACTIC ACID   One of the acids found in grape juice; as the name suggests, it's milky and soft.

LACTOBACILLUS   A micro-organism that ferments carbohydrates (glucose) or malic acid to produce lactic acid.

LEES   The sediment left after fermentation. It consists mainly of dead yeast cells.

MALIC ACID   One of the acids found in grape juice. It has a hard/sharp taste like a Granny Smith apple.

MALOLACTIC FERMENTATION   A secondary fermentation process that converts malic acid into lactic acid. It's encouraged in red wines when they are in barrel. If it occurs after bottling, the wine will be fizzy and cloudy.

MERCAPTAN Ethyl mercaptan is a sulfur compound with a smell like garlic, burnt rubber or asparagus water.

MÉTHODE CHAMPENOISE The French method for producing effervescence in the bottle; a secondary fermentation process where the carbon dioxide produced is dissolved into the wine.

METHOXYPYRAZINES Substances that give sauvignon blanc and cabernet sauvignon that added herbaceousness when the grapes aren't fully ripe.

MOUSSE The froth or head on sparkling wine.

MUST *see* Free-run juice

NOBLE ROT *see* Botrytis cinerea

NON-VINTAGE A wine that is a blend of two or more years.

OAK The least porous wood, genus *Quercus*, and used for wine storage containers.

OENOLOGY The science of winemaking.

ORGANIC VITICULTURE Growing grapes without the use of pesticides, fungicides or chemical fertilisers. Certain chemicals, e.g. copper sulfate, are permitted.

ORGANIC WINES Wines made from organically grown fruit without the addition of chemicals.

OXIDATION Browning caused by excessive exposure to air.

pH The measure of the strength of acidity. The higher the pH the higher the alkalinity and the lower the acidity. Wines with high pH values should not be cellared.

PHENOLICS A group of chemical compounds which includes the tannins and colour pigments of grapes. A white wine described as 'phenolic' has an excess of tannin, making it taste coarse.

PHYLLOXERA A louse that attacks the roots of a vine, eventually killing the plant.

PIGEAGE To foot-press the grapes.

PRESSINGS The juice extracted by applying pressure to the skins after the free-run juice has been drained.

PRICKED A wine that is spoilt and smells of vinegar, due to excessive volatile acidity. *Cf.* Volatile.

PUNCHEON A 500-litre barrel.

RACKING   Draining off wine from the lees or other sediment to clarify it.

SAIGNÉE   French for bleeding: the winemaker has run off part of the juice of a red fermentation to concentrate what's left.

SKIN CONTACT   Allowing the free-run juice to remain in contact with the skins; in the case of white wines, usually for a very short time.

SOLERO SYSTEM   Usually a stack of barrels used for blending maturing wines. The oldest material is at the bottom and is topped up with younger material from the top barrels.

SOLIDS   Minute particles suspended in a wine.

SULFUR DIOXIDE (SO₂)   (Code 220) A chemical added to a wine as a preservative and a bactericide.

SUR LIE   Wine that has been kept on lees and not racked or filtered before bottling.

TACHÉ   A French term that means to stain, usually by the addition of a small amount of red wine to sparkling wine to turn it pink.

TANNIN   A complex substance derived from skins, pips and stalks of grapes as well as the oak casks. It has a preservative function and imparts dryness and grip to the finish.

TERROIR   Arcane French expression that describes the complete growing environment of the vine, including climate, aspect, soil, etc., and the direct effect this has on the character of its wine.

VARIETAL   An industry-coined term used to refer to a wine by its grape variety, e.g. 'a shiraz'. *Cf.* Generic.

VÉRAISON   The moment when the grapes change colour and gain sugar.

VERTICAL TASTING   A tasting of consecutive vintages of one wine.

VIGNERON   A grapegrower or vineyard worker.

VINEGAR   Acetic acid produced from fruit.

VINIFY   The process of turning grapes into wine.

VINTAGE   The year of harvest, and the produce of a particular year.

VOLATILE   Excessive volatile acids in a wine.

YEAST   The micro-organism that converts sugar into alcohol.

Tasting Terms

The following terms refer to the sensory evaluation of wine.

AFTERTASTE The taste (sensation) after the wine has been swallowed. It's usually called the finish.

ASTRINGENT (ASTRINGENCY) Applies to the finish of a wine. Astringency is caused by tannins that produce a mouth-puckering sensation and coat the teeth with dryness.

BALANCE 'The state of . . .'; the harmony between components of a wine.

BILGY An unfortunate taste like the bilge of a ship. Usually caused by mouldy old oak.

BITTERNESS A sensation detected at the back of the tongue. It's not correct in wine but is desirable in beer.

BOUQUET The aroma of a finished or mature wine.

BROAD A wine that lacks fruit definition; usually qualified as soft or coarse.

CASSIS A blackcurrant flavour common in cabernet sauvignon. It refers to a liqueur produced in France.

CHALKY An extremely dry sensation on the finish.

CHEESY A dairy character sometimes found in wine, particularly sherries.

CIGAR BOX A smell of tobacco and wood found in cabernet sauvignon.

CLOUDINESS A fault in wine that is caused by suspended solids that make it look dull.

CLOYING Excessive sweetness that clogs the palate.

CORKED Spoiled wine that has reacted with a tainted cork, and smells like wet cardboard. (The taint is caused by trichloroanisole.)

CREAMY The feeling of cream in the mouth, a texture.

CRISP   Clean acid on the finish of a white wine.

DEPTH   The amount of fruit on the palate.

DRY   A wine that does not register sugar in the mouth.

DULL   Pertaining to colour; the wine is not bright or shining.

DUMB   Lacking nose or flavour on the palate.

DUSTY   Applies to a very dry tannic finish; a sensation.

EARTHY   Not as bad as it sounds, this is a loamy/mineral character that can add interest to the palate.

FINESSE   The state of a wine. It refers to balance and style.

FINISH   *see* Aftertaste

FIRM   Wine with strong, unyielding tannins.

FLABBY   Wine with insufficient acid to balance ripe fruit flavours.

FLESHY   Wines of substance with plenty of fruit.

FLINTY   A character on the finish that is akin to sucking dry creek pebbles.

GARLIC   *see* Mercaptan (in Wine Terms)

GRASSY   A cut-grass odour, usually found in semillon and sauvignon blancs.

GRIP   The effect on the mouth of tannin on the finish; a puckering sensation.

HARD   More tannin or acid than fruit flavour.

HERBACEOUS   Herbal smells or flavour in wine.

HOLLOW   A wine with a lack of flavour in the middle palate.

HOT   Wines high in alcohol that give a feeling of warmth and a slippery texture.

IMPLICIT SWEETNESS   A just detectable sweetness from the presence of glycerin (rather than residual sugar).

INKY   Tannate of iron present in a wine which imparts a metallic taste.

INTEGRATED (WELL)   The component parts of a wine fit together without gaps or disorders.

JAMMY   Ripe fruit that takes on the character of stewed jam.

LEATHERY   A smell like old leather, not necessarily bad if it's in balance.

LENGTH (LONG)   The measure of the registration of flavour in the mouth. (The longer the better.)

LIFTED   The wine is given a lift by the presence of either volatile acid or wood tannins, e.g. vanillan oak lift.

LIMPID A colour term usually applied to star-bright white wine.

MADEIRISED Wine that has aged to the point where it tastes like a madeira.

MOULDY Smells like bathroom mould; dank.

MOUTH-FEEL The sensation the wine causes in the mouth; a textural term.

MUSTY Stale, flat, out-of-condition wine.

PEPPER A component in either the nose or the palate that smells or tastes like cracked pepper.

PUNGENT Wine with a strong nose.

RANCIO A nutty character found in aged fortifieds that is imparted by time on wood.

RESIDUAL SUGAR The presence of unfermented grape sugar on the palate; common in sweet wines.

ROUGH Unpleasant, aggressive wine.

ROUND A full-bodied wine with plenty of mouth-feel (*q.v.*).

SAPPY A herbaceous character that resembles sap.

SHORT A wine lacking in taste and structure. *See also* Length

SPICY A wine with a high aromatic content; spicy character can also be imparted by wood.

STALKY Exposure to stalks, e.g. during fermentation. Leaves a bitter character in the wine.

TART A lively wine with a lot of fresh acid.

TOASTY A smell of cooked bread.

VANILLAN The smell and taste of vanilla beans; usually imparted by oak ageing.

VARIETAL Refers to the distinguishing qualities of the grape variety used in the wine.

Directory of Wineries

AFFLECK VINEYARD
RMB 244
Millynn Rd (off Gundaroo
 Rd)
Bungendore NSW 2651
(06) 236 9276

ALAMBIE WINES
Campbell Ave
Irymple Vic. 3498
(03) 5024 6800
fax (03) 5024 6605

ALKOOMI
Wingeballup Rd
Frankland WA 6396
(08) 9855 2229
fax (08) 9855 2284

ALLANDALE
Lovedale Rd
Pokolbin NSW 2320
(02) 4990 4526
fax (02) 4990 1714

ALLANMERE
Lovedale Rd
Pokolbin NSW 2320
(02) 4930 7387

ALL SAINTS ESTATE
All Saints Rd
Wahgunyah Vic. 3687
(03) 6033 1922
fax (03) 6033 3515

AMBERLEY ESTATE
Wildwood & Thornton
 Rds
Yallingup WA 6282
(08) 9755 2288
fax (08) 9755 2171

ANDERSON WINERY
Lot 13 Chiltern Rd
Rutherglen Vic. 3685
(03) 6032 8111

ANDREW GARRETT
Kangarilla Rd
McLaren Vale SA 5171
(08) 8323 8853
fax (08) 8323 8550

ANGOVES
Bookmark Ave
Renmark SA 5341
(08) 8595 1311
fax (08) 8595 1583

ANTCLIFFE'S CHASE
RMB 4510
Caveat
via Seymour Vic. 3660
(03) 5790 4333

ARROWFIELD
Denman Rd
Jerry's Plains NSW 2330
(02) 6576 4041
fax (02) 6576 4144

ASHTON HILLS
Tregarthen Rd
Ashton SA 5137
(08) 8390 1243
fax (08) 8390 1243

ASHWOOD GROVE
(not open to public)
(03) 5030 5291

AVALON
RMB 9556
Whitfield Rd
Wangaratta Vic. 3677
(03) 5729 3629

BABICH WINES
Babich Rd
Henderson NZ
(09) 833 8909

BAILEYS
Taminick Gap Rd
Glenrowan Vic. 3675
(03) 5766 2392
fax (03) 5766 2596

BALDIVIS ESTATE
Lot 165 River Rd
Baldivis WA 6171
(09) 525 2066
fax (09) 525 2411

BALGOWNIE
Hermitage Rd
Maiden Gully Vic. 3551
(03) 5449 6222
fax (03) 5449 6506

BANNOCKBURN
Midland Hwy
Bannockburn Vic. 3331
(03) 5281 1363
fax (03) 5281 1349

BANROCK STATION
(*see* Hardys)

BAROSSA SETTLERS
Trial Hill Rd
Lyndoch SA 5351
(08) 8524 4017

BAROSSA VALLEY ESTATE
Heaslip Rd
Angle Vale SA 5117
(08) 8284 7000
fax (08) 8284 7219

BARRATT
(not open to public)
PO Box 204
Summertown SA 5141
(08) 8390 1788
fax (08) 8390 1788

BARWANG
(*see* McWilliam's)

BASS PHILLIP
Tosch's Rd
Leongatha South Vic. 3953
(03) 5664 3341

BERRI ESTATES
Sturt Hwy
Glossop SA 5344
(08) 8582 0300
fax (08) 8583 2224

BESTS GREAT WESTERN
Western Hwy
Great Western Vic. 3377
(03) 5356 2250
fax (03) 5356 2430

BETHANY
Bethany Rd
Bethany
via Tanunda SA 5352
(08) 8563 2086
fax (08) 8563 2086

BIANCHET
187 Victoria Rd
Lilydale Vic. 3140
(03) 9739 1779
fax (03) 9739 1277

BINDI
(not open to public)
145 Melton Rd
Gisborne Vic. 3437
(03) 5428 2564
fax (03) 5428 2564

BIRDWOOD ESTATE
PO Box 194
Birdwood SA 5234
(08) 8263 0986

BLACKJACK VINEYARD
Calder Hwy
Harcourt Vic. 3452
(03) 5474 2528
fax (03) 5475 2102

BLEASDALE
Wellington Rd
Langhorne Creek SA 5255
(08) 8537 3001

BLEWITT SPRINGS
Recreational Rd
McLaren Vale SA 5171
(08) 8323 8689

BLOODWOOD ESTATE
4 Griffin Rd
via Orange NSW 2800
(02) 6362 5631

BLUE PYRENEES ESTATE
Vinoca Rd
Avoca Vic. 3467
(03) 5465 3202
fax (03) 5465 3529

BOSTON BAY
Lincoln Hwy
Port Lincoln SA 5605
(08) 8684 3600

BOTOBOLAR
Botobolar La.
PO Box 212
Mudgee NSW 2850
(02) 6373 3840
fax (02) 6373 3789

BOWEN ESTATE
Penola–Naracoorte Rd
Coonawarra SA 5263
(08) 8737 2229
fax (08) 8737 2173

BOYNTONS OF BRIGHT
Ovens Valley Hwy
Porepunkah Vic. 3740
(03) 5756 2356

BRANDS LAIRA
Naracoorte Hwy
Coonawarra SA 5263
(08) 8736 3260
fax (08) 8736 3208

BREMERTON LODGE
Strathalbyn Rd
Langhorne Creek SA 5255
(08) 8537 3093
fax (08) 8537 3109

BRIAGOLONG ESTATE
118 Boisdale St
Maffra Vic. 3860
(03) 5147 2322
fax (03) 5147 2400

BRIAR RIDGE
Mount View
Mt View NSW 2321
(02) 4990 3670
fax (02) 4998 7802

BRIDGEWATER MILL
Mount Barker Rd
Bridgewater SA 5155
(08) 8339 3422
fax (08) 8339 5253

BRINDABELLA HILLS
Woodgrove Cl.
via Hall ACT 2618
(06) 230 2583

BROKENWOOD
McDonalds Rd
Pokolbin NSW 2321
(02) 4998 7559
fax (02) 4998 7893

BROOK EDEN
Adams Rd
Lebrina Tas. 7254
(03) 6395 6244

BROOKLAND VALLEY
Caves Rd
Willyabrup WA 6284
(08) 9755 6250
fax (08) 9755 6214

BROWN BROTHERS
Meadow Crk Rd (off the
 Snow Rd)
Milawa Vic. 3678
(03) 5720 5500
fax (03) 5720 5511

BROWNS OF PADTHAWAY
PMB 196
Naracoorte SA 5271
(08) 8765 6063
fax (08) 8765 6083

BULLER & SONS, R L
Calliope
Three Chain Rd
Rutherglen Vic. 3685
(03) 5037 6305

BULLER (RL) & SON
Murray Valley Hwy
Beverford Vic. 3590
(03) 5037 6305
fax (03) 5037 6803
fax (03) 6032 8005

**BURGE FAMILY
WINEMAKERS**
Barossa Hwy
Lyndoch SA 5351
(08) 8524 4644
fax (08) 8524 4444

BURNBRAE
Hargraves Rd
Erudgere
Mudgee NSW 2850
(02) 6373 3504
fax (02) 6373 3601

CALAIS ESTATE
Palmers La.
Pokolbin NSW 2321
(02) 4998 7654
fax (02) 4998 7813

CALLATOOTA ESTATE
Wybong Rd
Wybong NSW 2333
(02) 6547 8149

CAMBEWARRA ESTATE
520 Illaroo Rd
Cambewarra NSW 2541
(02) 4446 0170
fax (02) 4446 0170

CAMPBELLS
Murray Valley Hwy
Rutherglen Vic. 3685
(02) 6032 9458
fax (02) 6032 9870

CANOBOLAS–SMITH
Cargo Rd
Orange NSW 2800
(02) 6365 6113

CAPE CLAIRAULT
via Caves Rd
or Bussell Hwy
CMB Carbunup River
   WA 6280
(08) 9755 6225
fax (08) 9755 6229

CAPELVALE
Lot 5
Capel North West Rd
Capel WA 6271
(08) 9727 2439
fax (08) 9727 2164

CAPE MENTELLE
Wallcliffe Rd
Margaret River WA 6285
(08) 9757 3266
fax (08) 9757 3233

CAPERCAILLIE
Londons Rd
Lovedale NSW 2325
(02) 4990 2904
fax (02) 4991 1886

CASSEGRAIN
Fern Bank Ck Rd
Port Macquarie NSW 2444
(02) 6583 7777
fax (02) 6584 0353

CASTLE ROCK ESTATE
Porongurup Rd
Porongurup WA 6324
(08) 9853 1035
fax (08) 9853 1010

CHAIN OF PONDS
Gumeracha Cellars
PO Box 365
Main Rd
Gumeracha SA 5233
(08) 8389 1415
fax (08) 8336 2462

CHAMBERS ROSEWOOD
Corowa–Rutherglen Rd
Rutherglen Vic. 3685
(03) 6032 8641
fax (03) 6032 8101

CHAPEL HILL
Chapel Hill Rd
McLaren Vale SA 5171
(08) 8323 8429
fax (08) 8323 9245

CHARLES CIMICKY
Gomersal Rd
Lyndoch SA 5351
(08) 8524 4025
fax (08) 8524 4772

CHARLES MELTON
Krondorf Rd
Tanunda SA 5352
(08) 8563 3606
fax (08) 8563 3422

**CHARLES STURT
UNIVERSITY**
Boorooma St
North Wagga Wagga
   NSW 2678
(02) 6933 2435
fax (02) 6933 2107

CHATEAU REYNELLA
Reynella Rd
Reynella SA 5161
(08) 8392 2222
fax (08) 8392 2202

CHATEAU TAHBILK
Tabilk Vic. 3607
via Nagambie
(03) 5794 2555
fax (03) 5794 2360

CHATEAU YALDARA
Gomersal Rd
Lyndoch SA 5351
(08) 8524 4200
fax (08) 8524 4678

CHATSFIELD
O'Neill Rd
Mount Barker WA 6324
(08) 9851 1704
fax (08) 9841 6811

CLARENDON HILLS
(not open to public)
(08) 8364 1484

CLEVELAND
Shannons Rd
Lancefield Vic. 3435
(03) 5429 1449
fax (03) 5429 2017

CLONAKILLA
Crisps La.
Murrumbateman
  NSW 2582
(06) 251 1938 (A.H.)

CLOUDY BAY
(*see* Cape Mentelle)

CLOVER HILL
(*see* Taltarni)

COBAW RIDGE
Perc Boyer's La.
East Pastoria
via Kyneton Vic. 3444
(03) 5423 5227

COLDSTREAM HILLS
31 Maddens La.
Coldstream Vic. 3770
(03) 5964 9388
fax (03) 5964 9389

CONSTABLE HERSHON
1 Gillards Road
Pokolbin NSW 2320
(02) 4998 7887
fax (02) 4998 7887

COOLANGATTA ESTATE
Coolangatta Resort
via Berry NSW 2535
(02) 4448 7131
fax (02) 4448 7997

COOMBEND
Swansea Tas. 7190
(03) 6257 8256
fax (03) 6257 8484

COOPERS CREEK WINERY
Highway 16
Haupai
Auckland NZ
(09) 412 8560

COPE WILLIAMS WINERY
Glenfern Rd
Romsey Vic. 3434
(03) 5429 5428
fax (03) 5429 2655

CORIOLE
Chaffeys Rd
McLaren Vale SA 5171
(08) 8323 8305
fax (08) 8323 9136

COWRA ESTATE
Boorowa Rd
Cowra NSW 2794
(02) 6342 3650

CRABTREE WATERVALE CELLARS
North Tce
Watervale SA 5452
(08) 8843 0069
fax (08) 8843 0144

CRAIG AVON
Craig Avon La.
Merricks North Vic. 3926
(03) 5989 7465

CRAIGIE KNOWE
Cranbrook Tas. 7190
(03) 6223 5620

CRAIGLEE
Sunbury Rd
Sunbury Vic. 3429
(03) 9744 1160

CRAIGMOOR
Craigmoor Rd
Mudgee NSW 2850
(02) 6372 2208

CRAIGOW
Richmond Rd
Cambridge Tas. 7170
(03) 6248 5482

CRANEFORD
Main St
Springton SA 5235
(08) 8568 2220
fax (08) 8568 2538

CRAWFORD RIVER
Condah Vic. 3303
(03) 5578 2267

CULLENS
Caves Rd
Willyabrup
via Cowaramup WA 6284
(08) 9755 5277

CURRENCY CREEK
Winery Rd
Currency Creek SA 5214
(08) 8555 4069

DALFARRAS
(*see* Chateau Tahbilk)

DALRYMPLE
Pipers Brook Rd
Pipers Brook Tas. 7254
(03) 6382 7222

DALRY ROAD
(*see* Eyton on Yarra)

DALWHINNIE
Taltarni Rd
Moonambel Vic. 3478
(03) 5467 2388

d'ARENBERG
Osborn Rd
McLaren Vale SA 5171
(08) 8323 8206

DARLING ESTATE
(by appointment only)
Whitfield Rd
Cheshunt Vic. 3678
(03) 5729 8396
fax (03) 5729 8396

DARLING PARK
Lot 1 Browne La.
Red Hill 3937
(03) 5989 2732
fax (03) 5989 2254

DAVID TRAEGER
399 High St
Nagambie Vic. 3608
(03) 5794 2514

DAVID WYNN
(*see* Mountadam)

DEAKIN ESTATE
(*see* Katnook)

De BORTOLI
De Bortoli Rd
Bibul NSW 2680
(02) 6964 9444
fax (02) 6964 9400

De BORTOLI
Pinnacle La.
Dixons Creek Vic. 3775
(03) 5965 2271

DELAMERE
4238 Bridport Rd
Pipers Brook Tas. 7254
(03) 6382 7190

DELATITE
Stoney's Rd
Mansfield Vic. 3722
(03) 5775 2922
fax (03) 5775 2911

DEMONDRILLE
RMB 97 Prunevale Rd
Prunevale
via Harden NSW 2587
(02) 6384 4272
fax (02) 6384 4292

DENNIS'S OF McLAREN VALE
Kangarilla Rd
McLaren Vale SA 5171
(08) 8323 8665
fax (08) 8323 9121

DEVIL'S LAIR
(not open to public)
PO Box 212
Margaret River WA 6285
(08) 9757 7573
fax (08) 9757 7533

DIAMOND VALLEY VINEYARDS
Kinglake Rd
St Andrews Vic. 3761
(03) 9710 1484
fax (03) 9739 1110

DOMAINE CHANDON
Maroondah Hwy
Coldstream Vic. 3770
(03) 9739 1110
fax (03) 9739 1095

DOONKUNA ESTATE
Barton Hwy
Murrumbateman
    NSW 2582
(02) 6227 5811
fax (02) 6227 5085

DRAYTON'S BELLEVUE
Oakey Creek Rd
Pokolbin NSW 2320
(02) 4998 7513
fax (02) 4998 7743

DROMANA ESTATE
Bittern–Dromana Rd
Dromana Vic. 3936
(03) 5987 3275
fax (03) 5981 0714

DUNCAN ESTATE
Spring Gully Rd
Clare SA 5453
(08) 8843 4335

EDEN RIDGE
(see Mountadam)

ELAN VINEYARD
17 Turners Rd
Bittern Vic. 3918
(03) 5983 1858

ELDERTON
3 Tanunda Rd
Nuriootpa SA 5355
(08) 8862 1058 or
1800 88 8500
fax (08) 8862 2844

ELGEE PARK
(no cellar door)
Junction Rd
Merricks Nth
PO Box 211
Red Hill South Vic. 3926
(03) 5989 7338
fax (03) 5989 7553

EPPALOCK RIDGE
Metcalfe Pool Rd
Redesdale Vic. 3444
(03) 5425 3135

EVANS & TATE
38 Swan St
Henley Brook WA 6055
(09) 296 4666

EVANS FAMILY
Palmers La.
Pokolbin NSW 2320
(02) 4998 7333

EYTON ON YARRA
Cnr Maroondah Hwy
    & Hill Rd
Coldstream Vic. 3770
(03) 5962 2119
fax (03) 5962 5319

FERGUSSON'S
Wills Rd
Yarra Glen Vic. 3775
(03) 5965 2237

FERMOY ESTATE
Metricup Rd
Willyabrup WA 6284
(08) 9755 6285
fax (08) 9755 6251

FERN HILL ESTATE
Ingoldby Rd
McLaren Flat SA 5171
(08) 8383 0167
fax (08) 8383 0107

FIDDLER'S CREEK
(see Blue Pyrenees Estate)

FIRE GULLY
(see Pierro)

FORREST ESTATE
Blicks Rd
Renwick
Blenheim NZ
(03) 572 9084
fax (03) 572 9084

FOX CREEK
Malpas Rd
Willunga SA 5172
(08) 8556 2403
fax (08) 8556 2104

FRANKLAND ESTATE
Frankland Rd
Frankland WA 6396
(08) 9855 1555
fax (08) 9855 1549

FREYCINET VINEYARD
Tasman Hwy
Bicheno Tas. 7215
(03) 6257 8587

GALAFREY
114 York St
Albany WA 6330
(08) 9841 6533

GALAH WINES
Box 231
Ashton SA 5137
(08) 8390 1243

GARDEN GULLY
Western Hwy
Great Western Vic. 3377
(03) 5356 2400

GEOFF MERRILL
(*see* Mount Hurtle)

GEOFF WEAVER
(not open to public)
2 Gilpin La.
Mitcham SA 5062
(08) 8272 2105
fax (08) 8271 0177

GIACONDA
(not open to public)
(03) 5727 0246

GILBERT'S
Albany Hwy
Kendenup WA 6323
(08) 9851 4028
(08) 9851 4021

GLENARA
126 Range Rd Nth
Upper Hermitage SA 5131
(08) 8380 5056
fax (08) 8380 5056

GLENGUIN
Lot 8 Milbrodale Rd
Broke NSW 2330
(02) 6579 1011
fax (02) 6579 1009

GOONA WARRA
Sunbury Rd
Sunbury Vic. 3429
(03) 9744 7211
fax (03) 9744 7648

GOUNDREY
Muir Hwy
Mount Barker WA 6324
(08) 9851 1777
fax (08) 9848 1018

GRAMP'S
(*see* Orlando)

GRAND CRU ESTATE
Ross Dewell's Rd
Springton SA 5235
(08) 8568 2378

GRANT BURGE
Jacobs Creek
Barossa Valley Hwy
Tanunda SA 5352
(08) 8563 3666

GREENOCK CREEK
Radford Rd
Seppeltsfield SA 5360
(08) 8562 8103
fax (08) 8562 8259

GREEN POINT
(*see* Domaine Chandon)

GROSSET
King St
Auburn SA 5451
(08) 8849 2175

HAINAULT
255 Walnut Road
Bickley WA 6076
(08) 9293 8339
fax (08) 9293 8339

HANGING ROCK
Jim Rd
Newham Vic. 3442
(03) 5427 0542
fax (03) 5427 0310

HANSON WINES
'Oolorong'
49 Cleveland Ave
Lower Plenty Vic. 3093
(03) 9439 7425

HAPP'S
Commonage Rd
Dunsborough WA 6281
(08) 9755 3300
fax (08) 9755 3846

**HARCOURT VALLEY
VINEYARD**
Calder Hwy
Harcourt Vic. 3453
(03) 5474 2223

HARDYS
(*see* Chateau Reynella)

HASELGROVE WINES
Foggo Rd
McLaren Vale SA 5171
(08) 8323 8706
fax (08) 8323 8049

HAY SHED HILL
Harmans Mill Rd
Willyabrup WA 6285
(08) 9755 6234
fax (08) 9755 6305

HEATHCOTE WINERY
183 High St
Heathcote Vic. 3523
(03) 5433 2595
fax (03) 5433 3081

HEEMSKERK
Pipers Brook Tas. 7254
(03) 6382 7133
fax (03) 6382 7242

HEGGIES
(*see* Yalumba)

HELM'S
Yass River Rd
Murrumbateman
  NSW 2582
(02) 6227 5536 (A.H.)
(02) 6227 5953

HENSCHKE
Moculta Rd
Keyneton SA 5353
(08) 8564 8223
fax (08) 8564 8294

HERITAGE WINES
Seppeltsfield Rd
Marananga
via Tununda SA 5352
(08) 8562 2880

HICKINBOTHAM
(not open to public)
(03) 9397 1872
fax (03) 9397 2629

HIGHBANK
Main Naracoorte–Penola
  Rd
Coonawarra SA 5263
(08) 8737 2020

HIGHFIELD
Brookby Rd
RD 2 Blenheim NZ
(03) 572 8592
fax (03) 572 9257

HILL SMITH ESTATE
(*see* Yalumba)

HILLSTOWE WINES
104 Main Rd
Hahndorf SA 5245
(08) 8388 1400
fax (08) 8388 1411

HOLLICK
Racecourse Rd
Coonawarra SA 5263
(08) 8737 2318
fax (08) 8737 2952

HORSESHOE VINEYARD
Horseshoe Road
Horses Valley
Denman NSW 2328
(02) 6547 3528

HOTHAM VALLEY
(by appointment only)
South Wandering Rd
Wandering WA 6308
(08) 9884 1525
fax (08) 9884 1079

HOUGHTON
Dale Rd
Middle Swan WA 6056
(09) 274 5100

HOWARD PARK
(not open to public)
PO Box 544
Denmark WA 6333
(08) 9848 2345
fax (08) 9848 2064

HUGH HAMILTON WINES
PO Box 615
McLaren Vale SA 5171
(08) 8323 8689
fax (08) 8323 9488

HUGO
Elliott Rd
McLaren Flat SA 5171
(08) 8383 0098
fax (08) 8383 0446

HUNGERFORD HILL
(*see* Tulloch or Lindemans)

HUNTER'S WINES
Rapaura Rd
Blenheim NZ
(03) 572 8489
fax (03) 572 8457

HUNTINGTON ESTATE
Cassilis Rd
Mudgee NSW 2850
(06) 373 3825
fax (06) 373 3730

IAN LEAMON
Calder Hwy
Bendigo Vic. 3550
(03) 5447 7995

IDYLL
Ballan Rd
Moorabool Vic. 3221
(03) 5276 1280
fax (03) 5276 1537

INGLEWOOD
18 Craig Street
Artarmon NSW 2064
(02) 9436 3022
fax (02) 9439 7930

INGOLDBY
Kangarilla Rd
McLaren Vale SA 5171
(08) 8383 0005

INNISFAIL
(not open to public)
(03) 5276 1258

JAMES IRVINE
Roeslers Rd
Eden Valley SA 5235
PO Box 308
Angaston SA 5353
(08) 8564 1046
fax (08) 8564 1046

JASPER HILL
Drummonds La
Heathcote Vic. 3523
(03) 5433 2528

JEIR CREEK WINES
Gooda Creek Rd
Murrumbateman
   NSW 2582
(06) 227 5999

JENKE VINEYARDS
Jenke Rd
Rowland Flat SA 5352
(08) 8524 4154
fax (08) 8524 4154

JIM BARRY
Main North Rd
Clare SA 5453
(08) 8842 2261

JINDALEE
(not open to public)
13 Shepherd Court
North Geelong Vic. 3251

JINGALLA
Bolganup Dam Rd
Porongurup WA 6324
(08) 9853 1023
fax (08) 9853 1023

JOHN GEHRIG
Oxley Vic. 3678
(03) 5727 3395

JOSEPH
(*see* Primo Estate)

KARINA VINEYARDS
RMB 4055
Harrisons Rd
Dromana Vic. 3936
(03) 5981 0137

KARRIVALE
Woodlands Rd
Porongurup WA 6324
(08) 9853 1009
fax (08) 9853 1129

KARRIVIEW
RMB 913
Roberts Rd
Denmark WA 6333
(08) 9840 9381

KATNOOK ESTATE
Riddoch Hwy
Coonawarra SA 5263
(08) 8737 2394
fax (08) 8737 2397

KAYS
Kays Rd
McLaren Vale SA 5171
(08) 8323 8211
fax (08) 8323 9199

KIES ESTATE
Hoffnungsthal Rd
Lyndoch SA 5351
(08) 8524 4511

KILLAWARRA
(*see* Kaiser Stuhl)

KILLERBY
Minnimup Rd
Gelorup WA 6230
(08) 9795 7222
fax (08) 9795 7835

KINGS CREEK
(not open to public)
(03) 5983 2102

KNAPPSTEIN WINES
2 Pioneer Ave
Clare SA 5453
(08) 8842 2600
fax (08) 8842 3831

KNIGHTS
Burke and Wills Track
Baynton
via Kyneton Vic. 3444
(03) 5423 7264
mobile 015 843 676
fax (03) 5423 7288

KOPPAMURRA
(no cellar door)
PO Box 110
Blackwood SA 5051
(08) 8271 4127
fax (08) 8271 0726

KRONDORF
Krondorf Rd
Tanunda SA 5352
(08) 8563 2145
fax (08) 8562 3055

KYEEMA
(not open to public)
PO Box 282
Belconnen ACT 2616
(02) 6254 7557

LAANECOORIE
(cellar door by
   arrangement)
RMB 1330
Dunolly Vic. 3472
(03) 5468 7260
mobile 018 518 887

LAKE'S FOLLY
Broke Rd
Pokolbin NSW 2320
(02) 4998 7507
fax (02) 4998 7322

LALLA GULLY
(not open to public)
(03) 6331 2325
fax (03) 6331 7948

LAMONT'S
Bisdee Rd
Millendon WA 6056
(08) 9296 4485
fax (08) 9296 1663

LANCEFIELD WINERY
Woodend Rd
Lancefield Vic. 3435
(03) 5433 5292

LARK HILL
RMB 281
Gundaroo Rd
Bungendore NSW 2621
(02) 6238 1393

LAUREL BANK
(by appointment only)
130 Black Snake La.
Granton Tas. 7030
(03) 6263 5977
fax (03) 6263 3117

LAURISTON
(*see* Hardys)

LEASINGHAM
7 Dominic St
Clare SA 5453
(08) 8842 2555
fax (08) 8842 3293

LECONFIELD
Narracoorte–Penola Rd
Coonawarra SA 5263
(08) 8737 2326
fax (08) 8737 2285

LEEUWIN ESTATE
Stevens Rd
Margaret River WA 6285
(08) 9757 6253
fax (08) 9757 6364

LELAND ESTATE
PO Lenswood SA 5240
(08) 8389 6928

LENGS & COOTER
24 Lindsay Tce
Belair SA 5052
(08) 8278 3998

LENSWOOD VINEYARDS
3 Cyril John Crt
Athelstone SA 5076
(08) 8365 3766
fax (08) 8365 3766

LENTON BRAE
Caves Rd
Willyabrup WA 6280
(08) 9755 6255
fax (08) 9755 6268

LEO BURING
Stuart Hwy
Tanunda SA 5352
(08) 8563 2184
fax (08) 8563 2804

LEYDENS VALE
(*see* Blue Pyrenees Estate)

LILLYDALE VINEYARDS
Davross Crt
Seville Vic. 3139
(03) 5964 2016

LILLYPILLY ESTATE
Farm 16
Lilly Pilly Rd
Leeton NSW 2705
(02) 6953 4069
fax (02) 6953 4980

LINDEMANS
McDonalds Rd
Pokolbin NSW 2320
(02) 4998 7501
fax (02) 4998 7682

LONG GULLY
Long Gully Rd
Healesville Vic. 3777
(03) 5962 3663
fax (03) 59807 2213

LONGLEAT
Old Weir Rd
Murchison Vic. 3610
(03) 5826 2294
fax (03) 5826 2510

LOVEGROVE OF COTTLES BRIDGE
Heidelberg Kinglake Road
Cottlesbridge Vic. 3099
(03) 9718 1569
fax (03) 9718 1028

MADEW
(by appointment only)
Westering Vineyard
Federal Hwy
Lake George NSW 2581
(02) 4848 0026
fax (02) 4848 0026

MADFISH BAY
(*see* Howard Park)

MAGLIERI
Douglas Gully Rd
McLaren Flat SA 5171
(08) 8323 8648

MAIN RIDGE
Lot 48 Williams Rd
Red Hill Vic. 3937
(03) 5989 2686

MALCOLM CREEK
(not open to public)
(08) 8264 2255

MARIENBERG
2 Chalk Hill Rd
McClaren Vale SA 5171
(08) 8323 9666
fax (08) 8323 9600

MASSONI HOME PTY LTD
(by appointment only)
Mornington–Flinders Rd
Red Hill Vic. 3937
(03) 5989 2352

MASTERSON
(*see* Peter Lehmann)

MAXWELL
Cnr Olivers & Chalkhill
  Rds
McLaren Vale SA 5171
(08) 8323 8200

McALISTER
(not open to public)
(03) 5149 7229

McGUIGAN BROTHERS
Cnr Broke & McDonalds
  Rds
Pokolbin NSW 2320
(02) 4998 7400
fax (02) 4998 7401

McWILLIAM'S
Hanwood NSW 2680
(02) 6963 0001
fax (02) 6963 0002

MEADOWBANK
Glenora Tas. 7140
(03) 6286 1234
fax (03) 6286 1133

MERRICKS ESTATE
Cnr Thompsons La.
  & Frankston–Flinders Rd
Merricks Vic. 3916
(03) 5989 8416
fax (03) 9629 4035

MIDDLETON ESTATE
Flagstaff Hill Rd
Middleton SA 5213
(08) 8555 4136
fax (08) 8555 4108

MILBURN PARK
(*see* Salisbury Estate)

MILDARA
(various locations)
(03) 9690 9966
(head office)

MILDURA VINEYARDS
Campbell Ave
Irymple Vic. 3498

MINTARO CELLARS
Leasingham Rd
Mintaro SA 5415
(08) 8843 9046

MIRAMAR
Henry Lawson Dr.
Mudgee NSW 2850
(02) 6373 3874

MIRANDA WINES
57 Jordaryan Ave
Griffith NSW 2680
(02) 6962 4033
fax (02) 6962 6944

MIRROOL CREEK
(*see* Miranda)

MITCHELL
Hughes Park Rd
Sevenhill via Clare
  SA 5453
(08) 8843 4258

MITCHELTON WINES
Mitcheltstown
Nagambie 3608
(03) 5794 2710
fax (03) 5794 2615

MONTANA
PO Box 18-293
Glen Innis
Auckland NZ
(09) 570 5549

MONTARA
Chalambar Rd
Ararat Vic. 3377
(03) 5352 3868
fax (03) 5352 4968

MONTROSE
Henry Lawson Dr.
Mudgee NSW 2850
(02) 6373 3853

MOONDAH BROOK
(*see* Houghton)

MOORILLA ESTATE
655 Main Rd
Berridale Tas. 7011
(03) 6249 2949

MOOROODUC ESTATE
Derril Rd
Moorooduc Vic. 3933
(03) 5978 8585

MORNING CLOUD
(cellar door by
  appointment)
15 Ocean View Ave
Red Hill South Vic. 3937
(03) 5989 2762
fax (03) 5989 2700

**MORNINGTON
VINEYARDS**
(by appointment only)
Moorooduc Rd
Mornington Vic. 3931
(03) 5974 2097

MORRIS
off Murray Valley Hwy
Mia Mia Vineyards
Rutherglen Vic. 3685
(02) 6026 7303
fax (02) 6026 7445

MOSS BROTHERS
Caves Rd
Willyabrup WA 6280
(08) 9755 6270
fax (08) 9755 6298

MOSS WOOD
Metricup Rd
Willyabrup WA 6280
(08) 9755 6266
fax (08) 9755 6303

MOUNTADAM
High Eden Ridge
Eden Valley SA 5235
(08) 8564 1101

MOUNT AVOCA
Moates La.
Avoca Vic. 3467
(03) 5465 3282

MOUNT HORROCKS
PO Box 72
Watervale SA 5452
(08) 8849 2243
fax (08) 8849 2243

MOUNT HURTLE
291 Pimpala Rd
Woodcroft SA 5162
(08) 8381 6877
fax (08) 8322 2244

MOUNT LANGI GHIRAN
Warrak Rd
Buangor Vic. 3375
(03) 5354 3207
fax (03) 5354 3277

MOUNT MARY
(not open to public)
(03) 9739 1761
fax (03) 9739 0137

MOUNT PRIOR VINEYARD
Cnr River Rd & Popes La.
Rutherglen Vic. 3685
(02) 6026 5591
fax (02) 6026 5590

MT PLEASANT
Marrowbone Rd
Pokolbin NSW 2321
(02) 4998 7505

MT WILLIAM WINERY
Mount William Rd
Tantaraboo Vic. 3764
(03) 5429 1595
fax (03) 5429 1998

MURRINDINDI
(not open to public)
(03) 5797 8217

NATTIER
(*see* Mitchelton)

NAUTILUS
(*see* Yalumba)

NEPENTHE VINEYARDS
(not open to public)
(08) 8389 8218

NGATARAWA
Ngatarawa Rd
Bridge Pa
Hastings NZ
(070) 79 7603

NICHOLSON RIVER
Liddells Rd
Nicholson Vic. 3882
(03) 5156 8241

NORMANS
Grants Gully Rd
Clarendon SA 5157
(08) 8383 6138
fax (08) 8383 6089

NOTLEY GORGE
(vineyard only)
Loop Road
Glengarry Tas. 7275
(03) 6396 1166
fax (03) 6396 1200

NUTFIELD
(*see* Hickinbotham)

OAKRIDGE ESTATE
864 Maroondah Hwy
Coldstream Vic. 3770
(03) 5964 3379
fax (03) 5964 2061

OAKVALE WINERY
Broke Rd
Pokolbin NSW 2320
(02) 4998 7520

OLD KENT RIVER
Turpin Rd
Rocky Gully WA 6397
(08) 9855 1589
fax (08) 9855 1589

ORLANDO
Barossa Valley Way
Rowland Flat SA 5352
(08) 8521 3111
fax (08) 8521 3102

PALMER WINES
Caves Rd
Willyabrup WA 6280
(08) 9797 1881
fax (08) 9797 0534

PANKHURST WINES
Woodgrove Rd
Hall ACT 2618
(06) 230 2592

PARADISE ENOUGH
(weekends & holidays only)
Stewarts Rd
Kongwak Vic. 3951
(03) 5657 4241

PARINGA ESTATE
44 Paringa Rd
Red Hill South Vic. 3937
(03) 5989 2669

**PARKER COONAWARRA
ESTATE**
Penola Rd
Coonawarra SA 5263
(Contact Leconfield)
(08) 8737 2946
fax (08) 8737 2945

PASSING CLOUDS
Powlett Rd
via Inglewood
Kingower Vic. 3517
(03) 5438 8257

PATTERSONS
St Werburghs Rd
Mount Barker WA 6324
(08) 9851 2063
fax (08) 9851 2063

PAULETT'S
Polish Hill River Rd
Sevenhill SA 5453
(08) 8843 4328
fax (08) 8843 4202

PEEL ESTATE
Fletcher Rd
Baldivis WA 6210
(08) 9524 1221

PEGASUS BAY
Stockgrove Rd
Waipara
Amberley RD 2
North Canterbury NZ
(03) 314 6869
fax (03) 355 5937

PENDARVES ESTATE
Lot 12 Old North Rd
Belford NSW 2335
(02) 6574 7222

PENFOLDS
(*see* Southcorp Wines)

PENLEY ESTATE
McLean's Rd
Coonawarra 5263
(08) 8736 3211
fax (08) 8736 3211

PEPPERS CREEK
Cnr Ekerts & Broke Rds
Pokolbin NSW 2321
(02) 4998 7532

PEPPER TREE WINES
Halls Rd
Pokolbin NSW 2320
(02) 4998 7539
fax (02) 4998 7746

PETALUMA
(not open to public)
(08) 8339 4122
fax (08) 8339 5253

PETER LEHMANN
Para Rd
Tanunda SA 5352
(08) 8563 2500
fax (08) 8563 3402

PETERSONS
PO Box 182
Mount View Rd
Mount View NSW 2325
(02) 4990 1704

PFEIFFER
Distillery Rd
Wahgunyah Vic. 3687
(02) 6033 3889

PHILLIP ISLAND WINES
Lot 1 Berrys Beach Rd
Phillip Island Vic. 3922
(03) 5956 8465

PIBBIN FARM
Greenhill Rd
Balhannah SA 5242
(08) 8388 4794

PICARDY
(not open to public)
(08) 9776 0036
fax (08) 9776 0036

PICCADILLY FIELDS
(not open to public)
(08) 8390 1997

PIERRO
Caves Rd
Willyabrup WA 6280
(08) 9755 6220
fax (08) 9755 6308

PIKES POLISH HILL ESTATE
Polish Hill River Rd
Seven Hill SA 5453
(08) 8843 4370
fax (08) 8843 4353

PIPERS BROOK
3959 Bridport Hwy
Pipers Brook Tas. 7254
(03) 6382 7197
fax (03) 6382 7226

PIRRAMIMMA
Johnston Rd
McLaren Vale SA 5171
(08) 8323 8205
fax (08) 8323 9224

PLANTAGENET
Albany Hwy
Mount Barker WA 6324
(08) 9851 2150
fax (08) 9851 1839

PLUNKETT'S
Cnr Lambing Gully Rd &
  Hume Fwy
Avenel Vic. 3664
(03) 5796 2150
fax (03) 5796 2147

POOLE'S ROCK
(not open to public)
Lot 41 Wollombi Road
Broke NSW 2330
(02) 6579 1251
fax (02) 6579 1277

PORT PHILLIP ESTATE
261 Red Hill Rd
Red Hill Vic. 3937
(03) 5989 2708
fax (03) 5989 2891

PORTREE VINEYARD
RMB 700
Lancefield Vic. 3435
(03) 5429 1422
fax (03) 5429 2205

PREECE
(*see* Mitchelton)

PRIMO ESTATE
Cnr Old Port Wakefield
  & Angle Vale Rds
Virginia SA 5120
(08) 8380 9442

PRINCE ALBERT
Lemins Rd
Waurn Ponds Vic. 3221
(03) 5243 5091
fax (03) 5241 8091

QUEEN ADELAIDE
(*see* Seppelt)

QUELLTALER ESTATE
Main North Rd
Watervale SA 5452
(08) 8843 0003
fax (08) 8843 0096

REDBANK
Sunraysia Hwy
Redbank Vic. 3478
(03) 5467 7255

RED HILL ESTATE
53 Red Hill–Shoreham Rd
Red Hill South Vic. 3937
(03) 5989 2838

REDMAN
Riddoch Hwy
Coonawarra SA 5263
(08) 8736 3331
fax (08) 8736 3013

RENMANO
Renmark Ave
Renmark SA 5341
(08) 8586 6771
fax (08) 8586 5939

REYNOLDS YARRAMAN
Yarraman Rd
Wybong NSW 2333
(02) 6547 8127
fax (02) 6547 8013

RIBBON VALE ESTATE
Lot 5 Caves Rd
via Cowaramup
Willyabrup WA 6284
(08) 9755 6272

RICHARD HAMILTON
Willunga Vineyards
Main South Rd
Willunga SA 5172
(08) 8556 2288
fax (08) 8556 2868

RICHMOND GROVE
(*see* Orlando)

RIDDOCH
(*see* Katnook)

ROBERT THUMM
(*see* Chateau Yaldara)

ROBINVALE WINES
Sealake Rd
Robinvale Vic. 3549
(03) 5026 3955
fax (03) 5026 1123

ROCHECOMBE
(*see* Heemskerk)

ROCHFORD
Romsey Park
via Woodend Rd
Rochford Vic. 3442
(03) 5429 1428

ROCKFORD
Krondorf Rd
Tanunda SA 5352
(03) 8563 2720

ROMSEY PARK
(*see* Rochford)

ROMSEY VINEYARDS
(*see* Cope Williams)

ROSABROOK ESTATE
Rosa Brook Rd
Margaret River WA 6285
(08) 9757 2286
fax (08) 9757 3634

ROSEMOUNT
Rosemount Rd
Denman NSW 2328
(02) 6547 2467
fax (02) 6547 2742

ROTHBURY ESTATE
Broke Rd
Pokolbin NSW 2321
(02) 4998 7555
fax (02) 4998 7553

ROUGE HOMME
(*see* Lindemans)

ROWAN
(*see* St Huberts)

RUFUS STONE
(*see* Tyrrell's)

RYECROFT
Ingoldby Rd
McLaren Flat SA 5171
(08) 8383 0001

RYMILL COONAWARRA WINES
The Riddoch Run
    Vineyards (off Main Rd)
Coonawarra SA 5263
(08) 8736 5001
fax (08) 8736 5040

SADDLERS CREEK WINERY
Marrowbone Rd
Pokolbin NSW 2321
(02) 4991 1770
fax (02) 4991 1778

SALISBURY ESTATE
(*see* Alambie)

SALITAGE
Vasse Hwy
Pemberton WA 6260
(08) 9776 1599
fax (08) 9776 1504

SALTRAM
Angaston Rd
Angaston SA 5353
(08) 8563 8200

SANDALFORD
West Swan Rd
Caversham WA 6055
(09) 274 5922
fax (09) 274 2154

SANDSTONE VINEYARD
(cellar door by
    appointment)
Caves & Johnson Rds
Willyabrup WA 6280
(08) 9755 6271
fax (08) 9755 6292

SCARBOROUGH WINES
Gillards Rd
Pokolbin NSW 2321
(02) 4998 7563

SCARPANTONI
Kangarilla Rd
McLaren Flat SA 5171
(08) 8383 0186
fax (08) 8383 0490

SCHINUS
(*see* Dromana Estate)

SCOTCHMAN'S HILL
Scotchmans Rd
Drysdale Vic. 3222
(03) 5251 3176
fax (03) 5253 1743

SEAVIEW
Chaffeys Rd
McLaren Vale SA 5171
(08) 8323 8250

SEPPELT
Seppeltsfield
via Tanunda SA 5352
(08) 8562 8028
fax (08) 8562 8333

SEVENHILL
College Rd
Sevenhill
via Clare SA 5453
(08) 8843 4222
fax (08) 8843 4382

SEVILLE ESTATE
Linwood Rd
Seville Vic. 3139
(03) 5964 4556
fax (03) 5943 4222

SHANTELL
Melba Hwy
Dixons Creek Vic. 3775
(03) 5965 2264
fax (03) 9819 5311

SHAREFARMERS
(*see* Petaluma)

SHAW & SMITH
(not open to public)
(08) 8370 9725

SHOTTESBROOKE
(*see* Ryecroft)

SIMON HACKET
(not open to public)
(08) 8331 7348

SIMON WHITLAM
(*see* Arrowfield)

SKILLOGALEE
Skillogalee Rd
via Sevenhill SA 5453
(08) 8843 4311
fax (08) 8843 4343

SMITHBROOK
(not open to public)
(08) 9772 3557
fax (08) 9772 3579

SOUTHCORP WINES
Tanunda Rd
Nuriootpa SA 5355
(08) 8560 9389
fax (08) 8560 9669

STANTON & KILLEEN
Murray Valley Hwy
Rutherglen Vic. 3685
(02) 6032 9457

STEPHEN JOHN WINES
Government Rd
Watervale SA 5452
(08) 8843 0105
fax (08) 8843 0105

STEVENS CAMBRAI
Hamiltons Rd
McLaren Flat SA 5171
(08) 8323 0251

ST FRANCIS
Bridge St
Old Reynella SA 5161
(08) 8381 1925
fax (08) 8322 0921

ST HALLETT'S
St Halletts Rd
Tanunda SA 5352
(08) 8563 2319
fax (08) 8563 2901

ST HUBERTS
Maroondah Hwy
Coldstream Vic. 3770
(03) 9739 1118
fax (03) 9739 1015

ST LEONARDS
St Leonard Rd
Wahgunyah Vic. 3687
(02) 6033 1004
fax (02) 6033 3636

ST MARY'S VINEYARD
V and A La.
via Coonawarra SA 5263
(08) 8736 6070
fax (08) 8736 6045

STONELEIGH
Corbans Wines
Great Northern Rd
Henderson NZ
(09) 836 6189

STONEY VINEYARD/ DOMAINE A
Teatree Rd
Campania Tas. 7026
(03) 6260 4174
fax (03) 6260 4390

STONIER'S WINERY
362 Frankston–Flinders Rd
Merricks Vic. 3916
(03) 5989 8300
fax (03) 5989 8709

SUMMERFIELD
Main Rd
Moonambel Vic. 3478
(03) 5467 2264
fax (03) 5467 2380

SUTHERLAND
Deasey's Rd
Pokolbin NSW 2321
(02) 4998 7650

TALTARNI VINEYARDS
off Moonambel–Stawell Rd
Moonambel Vic. 3478
(03) 5467 2218
fax (03) 5467 2306

TAMBURLAINE WINES
McDonalds Rd
Pokolbin NSW 2321
(02) 4998 7570
fax (02) 4998 7763

TANGLEWOOD DOWNS
Bulldog Creek Rd
Merricks North
(03) 5974 3325

TAPESTRY
Merrivale Wines
Olivers Rd
McLaren Vale SA 5171
(08) 8323 9196
fax (08) 8323 9746

TARRAWARRA
Healesville Rd
Yarra Glen Vic. 3775
(03) 5962 3311
fax (03) 5962 3311

TATACHILLA WINERY
151 Main Rd
McLaren Vale SA 5171
(08) 8323 8656
fax (08) 8323 9096

TAYLORS
Mintaro Rd
Auburn SA 5451
(08) 8849 2008

TEMPLE BRUER
Angas River Delta
via Strathalbyn SA 5255
(08) 8537 0203
fax (08) 8537 0131

T'GALLANT
Lot 2 Mornington–Flinders
   Rd
Main Ridge Vic. 3937
(03) 5989 6565
fax (03) 5989 6577

THALGARA ESTATE
De Beyers Rd
Pokolbin NSW 2321
(02) 4998 7717

TIM ADAMS
Wendouree Rd
Clare SA 5453
(08) 8842 2429
fax (08) 8842 2429

TIM GRAMP
PO Box 810
Unley SA 5061
(08) 8379 3658
fax (08) 8338 2160

TISDALL
Cornelia Creek Rd
Echuca Vic. 3564
(03) 5482 1911
fax (03) 5482 2516

TOLLANA
(*see* Penfolds)

TORRESAN ESTATE
Manning Rd
Flagstaff Hill SA 5159
(08) 8270 2500

TRENTHAM ESTATE
Sturt Hwy
Trentham Cliffs
via Gol Gol NSW 2738
(03) 5024 8888
fax (03) 5024 8800

TULLOCH
De Beyers Rd
Pokolbin NSW 2321
(02) 4998 7503
fax (02) 4998 7682

TUNNEL HILL
(*see* Tarrawarra)

TURKEY FLAT
James Rd
Tanunda SA 5352
(08) 8563 2851
fax (08) 8563 3610

TYRRELL'S
Broke Rd
Pokolbin NSW 2321
(02) 4998 7509
fax (02) 4998 7723

VASSE FELIX
Cnr Caves & Harmans Rds
Cowaramup WA 6284
(08) 9755 5242
fax (08) 9755 5425

VERITAS
94 Langmeil Rd
Tanunda SA 5352
(08) 8563 2330

VIRGIN HILLS
(not open to public)
(03) 5423 9169

VOYAGER ESTATE
Stevens Rd
Margaret River WA 6285
(08) 9757 6358
fax (08) 9757 6405

WANDIN VALLEY ESTATE
Wilderness Rd
Rothbury NSW 2321
(02) 4930 7317
fax (02) 4930 7814

WANINGA
Hughes Park Rd
Sevenhill
via Clare SA 5453
(08) 8843 4395
fax (08) 8843 4395

WANTIRNA ESTATE
(not open to public)
(03) 9801 2367

**WARDS GATEWAY
CELLARS**
Barossa Valley Hwy
Lyndoch SA 5351
(08) 8524 4138

WARRAMATE
27 Maddens La.
Gruyere Vic. 3770
(03) 5964 9219

WARRENMANG
Mountain Ck Rd
Moonambel Vic. 3478
(03) 5467 2233
fax (03) 5467 2309

**WATERWHEEL
VINEYARDS**
Lyndhurst St
Bridgewater-on-Loddon
Bridgewater Vic. 3516
(03) 5437 3060
fax (03) 5437 3082

WELLINGTON WINES
34 Cornwall St
Rose Bay Tas. 7015
(03) 6248 5844

WENDOUREE
Wendouree Rd
Clare SA 5453
(08) 8842 2896

WESTFIELD
Memorial Ave
Baskerville WA 6056
(09) 296 4356

WIGNALLS KING RIVER
Chester Pass Rd
Albany WA 6330
(08) 9841 2848

WILD DUCK CREEK
Springflat Rd
Heathcote Vic. 3523
(03) 5433 3133

WILDWOOD
St Johns La.
via Wildwood Vic. 3428
(03) 9307 1118

WILLESPIE
Harmans Mill Rd
Willyabrup WA 6280
(08) 9755 6248
fax (08) 9755 6210

WILLOWS VINEYARD, THE
Light Pass Rd
Barossa Valley SA 5355
(08) 8562 1080

WILSON VINEYARD, THE
Polish Hill River
via Clare SA 5453
(08) 8843 4310

WILTON ESTATE
Whitton Stock Route
Yenda NSW 2681
(02) 6968 1303
fax (02) 6968 1328

WINCHELSEA ESTATE
C/- Nicks
  Wine Merchants
(03) 9639 0696

WING FIELDS
(*see* Water Wheel)

WIRILDA CREEK
Lot 32 McMurtrie Rd
McLaren Vale SA 5171
(08) 8323 9688

WIRRA WIRRA
McMurtrie Rd
McLaren Vale SA 5171
(08) 8323 8414
fax (08) 8323 8596

WOLF BLASS
Sturt Hwy
Nuriootpa SA 5355
(08) 8562 1955
fax (08) 8562 2156

WOODSTOCK
Douglas Gully Rd
McLaren Flat SA 5171
(08) 8383 0156
fax (08) 8383 0437

WOODY NOOK
Metricup Rd
Metricup WA 6280
(08) 9755 7547
fax (08) 9755 7547

WYANGAN ESTATE
(*see* Miranda)

WYANGA PARK
Baades Rd
Lakes Entrance Vic. 3909
(03) 5155 1508
fax (03) 5155 1443

WYNDHAM ESTATE
Dalwood Rd
Dalwood NSW 2321
(02) 4938 3444
fax (02) 4938 3422

WYNNS
Memorial Dr.
Coonawarra SA 5263
(08) 8736 3266

XANADU
Terry Rd (off
  Railway Tce)
Margaret River WA 6285
(08) 9757 2581
fax (08) 9757 3389

YALUMBA
Eden Valley Rd
Angaston SA 5353
(08) 8561 3200
fax (08) 8561 3392

YARRA BURN
Settlement Rd
Yarra Junction Vic. 3797
(03) 5967 1428
fax (03) 5967 1146

YARRA RIDGE
Glenview Rd
Yarra Glen Vic. 3775
(03) 9730 1022
fax (03) 9730 1131

YARRA VALLEY HILLS
Old Don Rd
Healesville Vic. 3777
(03) 5962 4173
fax (03) 5762 4059

YARRA YERING
Briarty Rd
Gruyere Vic. 3770
(03) 5964 9267

YELLOWGLEN
White's Rd
Smythesdale Vic. 3351
(03) 5342 8617

YERINGBERG
(not open to public)
(03) 9739 1453
fax (03) 9739 0048

YERING STATION
Melba Hwy
Yering Vic. 3775
(03) 9730 1107
fax (03) 9739 0135

ZEMA ESTATE
Narracoorte–Penola Rd
Coonawarra SA 5263
(08) 8736 3219
fax (08) 8736 3280